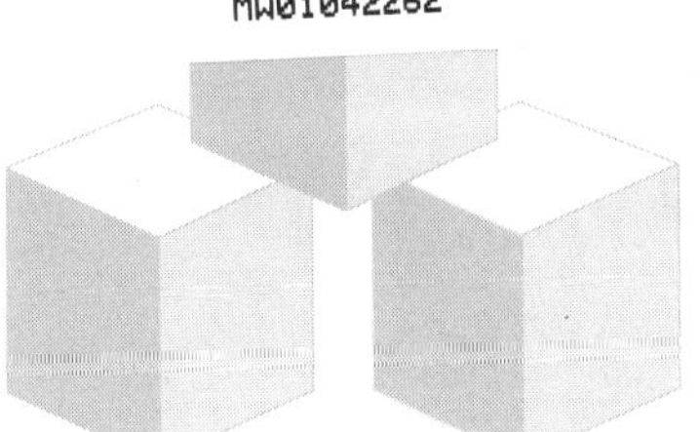

Hands On VB6 for Web Development

Send Us Your Comments:

To comment on this book or any other PRIMA TECH title, visit Prima's reader response page on the Web at **www.primapublishing.com/comments.**

How to Order:

For information on quantity discounts, contact the publisher: Prima Publishing, P.O. Box 1260BK, Rocklin, CA 95677-1260; (916) 632-4400. On your letterhead, include information concerning the intended use of the books and the number of books you wish to purchase. For individual orders, turn to the back of this book for more information, or visit Prima's Web site at **www.prima-tech.com.**

Hands On VB6 for Web Development

Rod Paddock

with

Richard Campbell

John V. Petersen

A Division of Prima Publishing

A Division of Prima Publishing

Prima Publishing and colophon are registered trademarks of Prima Communications, Inc., Rocklin, California 95677.

Publisher: Matthew H. Carleson
Managing Editor: Dan J. Foster
Senior Acquisitions Editor: Deborah F. Abshier
Project Editor: Chris Haidri
Technical Reviewer: John V. Petersen
Interior Layout: Marian Hartsough
Indexer: Katherine Stimson
Cover Designer: Prima Design Team

Important: If you have problems running Visual Basic, check Microsoft's Web site at **www.microsoft.com** for support and technical information, or check the online Help for technical support information. Prima Publishing cannot provide software support.

Prima Publishing and the authors have attempted throughout this book to distinguish proprietary trademarks from descriptive terms by following the capitalization style used by the manufacturers.

ISBN: 0-7615-1647-6
Library of Congress Catalog Card Number: 98-66119
Printed in the United States of America

00 01 02 DD 10 9 8 7 6 5 4 3 2

This book is dedicated to my loving wife, Maria.
Great things are possible because of you.

Acknowledgments

First, I would like to thank my wife, Maria. Maria puts up with the long nights and technobabble dreams that go into the production of one of these.

Next, I would like to thank Chris Haidri, the project manager for this book. His eye for detail was a real godsend in creating a quality book. Thanks for all your hard work.

Next, I would like to thank Debbie Abshier. I have worked with Debbie for quite a while and she has made my life in the publishing business great.

Also on the list I would like to thank my writing partners on this book, John Petersen and Richard Campbell. Thanks also to Bill Orvis for the material he contributed. I am happy to have some of the best authors in the industry on my team.

Next, I would like to thank people in the development community who have helped me get where I am today. Thanks go out to Paul Litwin, Ken Getz, Erik Ruthruff, Ron Talmage, Jeff Winchell, and a host of other great people.

Finally, no book would be a complete object without some inspiring music, places, and people. I would like to thank The Ivy at The Shore, The Comedy Store, 3G, LucasFilm, AC/DC (Back in Black, of course), the folks at The Tom Leykis Show, Dr. Drew and Adam Corolis, and finally the group from Banned at the Ranch.

—RJP

About the Authors

Rod Paddock is President and Founder of Dash Point Software, Inc. DPSI, based in Seattle, Washington, specializes in developing applications and training software developers. DPSI develops with Visual InterDev, VFP, VB, and SQL Server. DPSI's clients include ADTC, SBT Accounting, the U.S. Coast Guard, the U.S. Navy, Pinnacle Publishing, Intel, and Azalea Software. Dash Point Software, Inc. was a finalist in the 1998 Visual FoxPro Excellence Awards. Rod has been a featured speaker at the 1996/1997 German Fox Pro DevCons, the 1995 and 1998 FoxPro Developers Conferences, and the 1995-1997 FoxTeach conferences. Rod writes for several database publications including Data Based Advisor, Foxtalk and Dbase Advisor. Rod's other books include Visual FoxPro Enterprise Development from Prima Publishing. DPSI can be found at `www.dashpoint.com`.

John V. Petersen is Vice President of Software Development and R&D for IDT Marketing Systems and Services, Inc., a Philadelphia-based marketing database consulting firm. In addition to providing database design and modeling-consulting services, John's firm specializes in the creation of data marts, data-hygiene and query tools, and marketing-based Internet applications using such tools as Visual FoxPro, Visual InterDev, Visual Basic, and SQL Server.

John has been a columnist for FoxTalk (Pinnacle Publishing's high-end technical journal for FoxPro) during the past three years. A two-time recipient of Microsoft's MVP Award, John is also co-author of Hands on Visual Basic 5 for Web Development, from Prima Publishing. He has spoken at numerous conferences including DevCon 1997/1998, FoxTeach, Southwest Visual FoxPro Conference, Tech-Ed Europe 1997, Tech-Ed 1998 and Developer Days 1995, 1997, and 1998. John can be reached by e-mail at `johnpetersen@mail.com`.

Richard Campbell is a consultant, writer, trainer, and analyst for the Client/Server and Internet development communities. In recent years he has worked with a variety of companies, including MCI, the U.S. Air Force, Barnes & Noble, and Reuters. He is a Technical Editor for Access/Office/VB Advisor, Contributing Editor to E-Business Advisor, and co-author of the "Ask Advisor" column.

Contents at a Glance

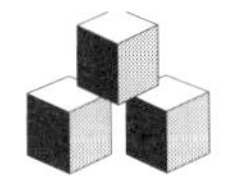

Contents

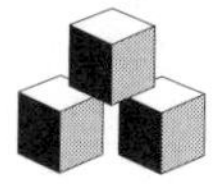

Introduction

Welcome to *Hands On VB6 for Web Development*! This book is dedicated to helping you make the most of Microsoft Corporation's premier application development tool, Visual Basic 6. The ultimate purpose of this book is to introduce you to the concepts of integrating Visual Basic 6 into your Internet or intranet applications. As such, this book is targeted at the Visual Basic developer who has a good understanding of Visual Basic but needs to "get up" on the Net with little or no hassle. At a minimum, you should be experienced with basic Visual Basic development techniques such as coding and using the VB IDE. Also, you should be familiar with how to use a Web browser such as Internet Explorer or Netscape Communicator.

This book is meant to be a hands-on guide to integrating VB and the Internet. One of the areas that many books miss is just the simple how-to, because those books immediately launch into very esoteric or complicated subject matter, without giving the basics. This book covers its topics, including those basics, in a thorough and organized manner.

This book begins with an Internet primer. Chapter 1 introduces you to important Internet basics—particularly terminology—that you need to know. Chapter 2 gives you an understanding of how to create Web pages with HTML, and covers the most common HTML tags you need. Finally, you move on to VBScript in Chapter 3, where you learn to use VB code directly in your Web pages.

After you've looked at the Internet primer, you can move into the projects. This book has four projects:

- The first project, in Chapters 4 through 7, takes you through the process of creating a Visual Basic front end, using tools found in VB and third-party sources.
- The second project, in Chapters 8 through 11, introduces you to Active Server Pages, one of the newest and most promising Web

technologies. This project shows you how to create dynamic and intelligent Web pages. You learn how to access data from your Web pages in a dynamic fashion by creating this project.

- The third project, in Chapters 12 through 15, takes what you learned in the earlier projects and expands that knowledge even further. You explore querying data and you learn how to save and update data from Web pages.
- The final project, in Chapters 16 through 19, demonstrates using some of the newest and most advanced Internet features found in Visual Basic. You learn about creating and deploying ActiveX controls, Dynamic HTML, and ADO features in your applications.

How This Book Is Organized

This book was written in six distinct parts:

- **Visual Basic/Internet Primer.** This part of the book provides a solid foundation in using VB to work with the Internet and World Wide Web, including a thorough-but-quick introduction to Internet terminology and HTML coding.
- **Hands On Project 1—The VBBrowser.** In this project, you build a browser-style application with VB, using controls from Visual Basic and from third-party companies to create a powerful front end to the World Wide Web.
- **Hands On Project 2—The VBResearcher.** This project integrates VB and Active Server Pages into a database publishing system. This project introduces you to Active Server Pages (ASP), one of the newest technologies that allows developers to embed code into their Web pages. The VBResearcher uses this capability to access code developed in Visual Basic.
- **Hands On Project 3—The CustomerTracker.** Integrating VB and ASP into a Web-based database system is the thrust of the third project. You take what you've learned in earlier projects and apply it to a fully developed Web site. This site allows users to query and add data to the databases that it manages.
- **Hands On Project 4—The Real Estate Companion.** Integrating ActiveX controls, Dynamic HTML, and ActiveX Data Objects (ADO) into a Web-based database system is the thrust of the final project. You

explore the implications of creating ActiveX controls, using ADO, and deploying Dynamic HTML pages. This application demonstrates techniques for using what you already know about VB and extending that knowledge to the Web.

- **Appendixes.** To be able to write Internet code that works as you want it to, you need at least a passing familiarity with HTML and VB. These appendixes augment the information in your head with a handy reference you can use to look up HTML tags (in both alphabetical and functional order) and VBScript language elements. The glossary that completes this part contains brief definitions of common terms mentioned in this book and others on Internet topics.

Hardware and Software Requirements

To use the code from this book, you need the following hardware and software:

- A Web browser (Internet Explorer, Netscape Communicator, etc.)
- A text editor (Visual Notepad, Visual Edlin, MS Write, etc.)
- An Internet server (Personal Web Server or Internet Information Server 3.0 or 4.0—available from Microsoft for free at `www.microsoft.com`)
- The Active Server Pages Extensions (ASP comes with IIS version 3.0 on NT Service Pack 3, or with IIS version 4.0)
- Visual Basic version 5 or 6

What's on the CD?

The CD that accompanies this book contains the following files:

- All code samples from the text
- WinZip
- WS FTP
- Chili!ASP

Conventions Used in This Book

To make it easier for you to use this book, Prima uses some conventions for consistently presenting different kinds of information. You should review these conventions before moving on in the book:

- **Menu names, commands, and dialog box options.** In virtually all Windows programs, each menu name, command name, and dialog box option name contains an underlined letter called a hot key. The hot key is used to make that particular selection via the keyboard, usually in conjunction with the Ctrl or Alt key. In this book, hot keys are indicated as underlined letters, as in the File menu. If a menu command and option combination is used, a comma separates the parts of the command: File, Exit.
- **Code, items that appear onscreen, and Internet/Web addresses.** A special `monospace` typeface is used in this book to make the following items easier to distinguish: VB or HTML code, error messages, command syntax, file names, directory names, and Internet or Web addresses. If a command line or syntax line includes placeholder or variable information that you should replace with an actual name or value, it appears in *`italic monospace`*.
- **Text you type.** When you need to type some text to complete a procedure, or when we provide an example of text that you can enter, the text you need to type appears in **`bold monospace`**, as in the following instruction: Specify **`frmBrowser`** as your startup object.
- **Long code lines.** The code-continuation character is used when one line of code is too long to fit on one line of the book. Here's an example:

  ```
  strMsg = strMsg + Chr(10) + Chr(13)+"The error was caused by: " &
  ➥Err.Source & "."
  ```

  When typing these lines, you would type them as one long line without the code-continuation character.

Special Elements

Margin notes are used to provide definitions of new terms.

At times, you'll be provided with information that supplements the discussion at hand. This special information is set off in easy-to-identify sidebars, so you can review or skip these extras as you see fit. You'll find the following types of special elements in this book:

Tips provide shortcuts to make your job easier, or better ways to accomplish certain tasks.

Notes provide supplemental information that probably will be of interest to you, but isn't essential to performing the task at hand.

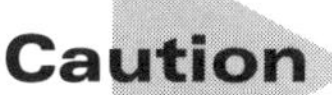

Cautions alert you to potential pitfalls, or warn you when a particular operation is risky and might cause you to lose data or some of your work.

EXERCISE

Exercises give you a chance to practice using a particular skill just introduced in the regular text. Each exercise is identified by a special bar next to all the instructions.

ANALYSIS

After certain code examples, an Analysis section walks you through the code line-by-line and explains particular statements in greater detail. After reading the analysis, you'll have an understanding of the specific logic of that code example and you'll know the exact purpose of all the keywords and expressions used in the code.

This icon informs you that it is time to save your work before continuing.

This icon indicates that a paragraph of text includes an Internet or World Wide Web address where you can find more information, applicable programs, and so on.

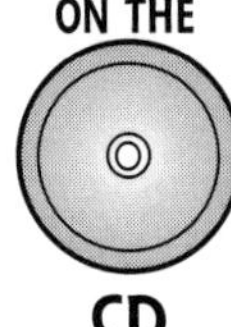

This icon is used to refer you to items found on the CD that accompanies this book. All of the sample code in the book is included on the CD; therefore, this icon is used sparingly, to indicate sections of code that you might want to copy from the CD rather than enter by hand.

Chapter 1

An Introduction to the Internet

This book is devoted to one thing—developing Visual Basic-based applications for the Internet. To reinforce the material, a set of exercises is included in the book that outlines how to create a set of VB applications for use with the World Wide Web. The specifics of what comprises the projects and the applications are discussed a bit later in this chapter.

Before diving into the core material and writing code, it's a good idea to take a few moments to review just what the Internet is today. Even if you work on the World Wide Web on a daily basis, you may not be familiar with the history of the Internet and how the WWW has evolved. Like every other area of the computer world, topics dealing with the Internet are chock-full of new jargon to learn. If you have never connected to the Internet before, you may have questions on what's involved in getting connected. The goal of this chapter is to address all of these questions.

What Is the Internet?

The Internet itself is not a single network. Rather, it can be considered a conduit that links many networks. This conduit is what allows individuals all over the world to communicate with each other. The original foundations of today's Internet were laid almost 40 years ago. Could the people who performed the earliest work on the Internet ever have imagined what it has grown into? The following paragraphs give a brief history of the Internet and outline some of the significant events that have transpired. But first, take a glimpse at the applications you'll create in this book for use on the WWW.

Introducing the Sample Applications

An integral part of this book entails working on a set of exercises that culminates in the creation of four useful Internet-based applications:

- The **VBBrowser** provides a coherent client-side front-end application that can be used to access useful functions found on the Internet and encapsulate them into a simple, useful interface. (This project is in Chapters 4 through 7.)
- The **VBResearcher** is a Visual Basic server-based Internet application that provides access to information stored in databases. It focuses on providing information about a company's products, and can generate Web pages dynamically from product databases and provide mechanisms for finding product information simply. (This project is in Chapters 8 through 11.)
- The **CustomerTracker** is an automated solution in which customers fill out a form that's stored directly in a database. The form covers not only the customer's personal contact information, but a list of products as well. The customer can select which products he'd like to be notified about when new information is available in your database. (This project is in Chapters 12 through 15.)
- The **Real Estate Companion** is a set of components representing information that will be tracked by a real estate company. This project has a number of components, including a page for customers to request information, a page for listing entries, and an ActiveX mortgage calculator. (This project is in Chapters 16 through 19.)

Each project guides you through the process of creating every component required to implement the application. The final chapter of the book provides a look at the future of the Internet and Internet-based business.

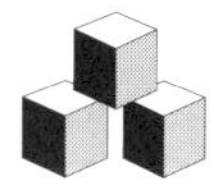

Before you can start working with Internet-based applications, of course, you need some grounding in how the Internet and World Wide Web function. This first part of the book provides the basics required to create Web pages and integrate VBScript into those pages.

A Brief History of the Internet

The Internet was started in 1957. Back then, it was known as ARPAnet (Advanced Research Projects Agency network). ARPA was part of the Department of Defense (DOD). The fundamental purpose of the ARPAnet was to exchange information between the DOD and its vendors and researchers. ARPA was formed in the shadows of the USSR launching Sputnik into outer space. ARPA's mission was to regain the United States' lead in military applications of science and technology.

By 1969, educational institutions such as UCLA, Stanford University, the University of California at Santa Barbara, and the University of Utah were connected to the ARPAnet. This was spawned by a DOD initiative to do research into networking.

In 1973, the file transfer protocol (FTP) specification was created. This protocol is one of the primary means by which files are exchanged over the Internet.

In 1974, the first writings on the transmission control protocol (TCP) were presented by Vint Cerf and Bob Kahn. As will be discussed shortly, TCP/IP is the primary protocol of the Internet.

In 1977, the first e-mail specifications were introduced.

In 1982, ARPA formally adopted TCP and the Internet protocol (IP)—collectively known as TCP/IP—as the protocol standard of the Internet. The word *internet* was formally defined as a "set of connected networks using TCP/IP." The word *Internet* (with a capital I) was defined as "a set of connected internets."

In 1984, the domain name system (DNS) was established. The DNS established five top-level domain names: `.gov`, `.com`, `.net`, `.edu`, and `.org`. These top-level domains correspond to government institutions, commercial entities, network providers, educational institutions, and organizations, respectively. Today, the InterNIC is responsible for assigning second-level domain names for each of these top-level domains. This topic is discussed later in this chapter.

In 1986, the NSFNET (National Science Foundation network) was created. NSFNET is the backbone of the Internet. The initial speed of this backbone was 56Kbps. The NSF established several supercomputing centers at Princeton

University, the University of Pittsburgh, the University of California at San Diego, the University of Illinois at Champaign-Urbana, and Cornell University. These centers facilitated a large number of educational institutions going online. Also, the network news transfer protocol (NNTP) was developed. NNTP is the protocol of the many newsgroups that exist on the Internet today.

In 1988, the NSFNET backbone was upgraded to T1 (1.544Mbps). In addition to the U.S., the following countries connected to NSFNET: Canada, Denmark, Finland, France, Iceland, Norway, and Sweden.

In 1989, the number of hosts on the Internet exceeded 100,000. The following countries/territories joined NSFNET: Australia, Germany, Israel, Italy, Japan, Mexico, the Netherlands, New Zealand, Puerto Rico, and the United Kingdom.

In 1990, ARPAnet officially ceased to exist. The world's first Internet service provider (ISP) was established (`world.std.com`). The following countries joined NSFNET: Argentina, Austria, Belgium, Brazil, Chile, Greece, India, Ireland, South Korea, Spain, and Switzerland.

In 1991, the NSF lifted restrictions for conducting commerce on the Internet. The NSFNET backbone was upgraded to T3 (44.736Mbps). The World Wide Web was introduced at Conseil European pour la Recherche Nucleaire (CERN). The following countries connected to NSFNET: Croatia, Czech Republic, Hong Kong, Hungary, Poland, Portugal, Singapore, South Africa, Taiwan, and Tunisia.

In 1992, the number of hosts on the Internet exceeded 1,000,000. The Internet Society (ISOC) was formed. The following countries connected to the NSFNET: Cameroon, Cyprus, Ecuador, Estonia, Kuwait, Latvia, Luxembourg, Malaysia, Slovakia, Slovenia, Thailand, and Venezuela.

In 1993, the InterNIC was formed by the NSF. Among many services, the InterNIC is responsible for the registration of domain names. The White House went online with the following e-mail addresses: `president@whitehouse.gov` and `vice-president@whitehouse.gov`. The Mosaic Web browser became commercially available. The HTML 1.0 specification was drafted by Tim Berners Lee and Daniel Connolly, and presented to the Internet Engineering Task Force (IETF). The following countries connected to NSFNET: Bulgaria, Costa Rica, Egypt, Fiji, Ghana, Guam, Indonesia, Kazakhstan, Kenya, Liechtenstein, Peru, Romania, Russian Federation, Turkey, Ukraine, United Arab Emirates, and Virgin Islands.

In 1994, the first shopping malls arrived on the Internet. Several radio stations began broadcasting directly over the Internet. Mosaic Communications, later to become Netscape Communications, was formed. The HTML 2.0 specifi-

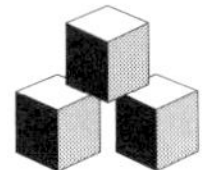

cation was drafted. The first meeting of the World Wide Web consortium (W3C) was held at MIT. The W3C is a standards body consisting of members from corporations, educational institutions, and government agencies. The U.S. Senate went online. The following countries connected to NSFNET: Algeria, Armenia, Bermuda, Burkina Faso, China, Columbia, French Polynesia, Jamaica, Lebanon, Lithuania, Macau, Morocco, New Caledonia, Nicaragua, Niger, Panama, Philippines, Senegal, Sri Lanka, Swaziland, Uruguay, and Uzbekistan.

In 1995, NSFNET was replaced by a group of network providers to carry U.S. network traffic. The WWW surpassed FTP as the service with the largest amount of traffic on NSFNET. Several online service providers, such as CompuServe, Prodigy, and AOL, began providing Internet access. Netscape became a public company. The Vatican and the Canadian government went online.

In 1996, Microsoft became a major software vendor in the Internet world. The Internet Phone was introduced. The HTML 3.2 specification was drafted and approved.

In 1997, the HTML 4.0 specification was released. Microsoft released Internet Explorer 4.0 with Dynamic HTML capabilities. Java continued making ground as a "write once, run anywhere" standard and the industry continued innovating Internet development.

In 1998, the XML standard was approved by the W3C. Netscape released the source code to its Communicator product and there is surely more to come . . .

If you factor in every event, as much (or even more) has occurred with the Internet in the last three years as in all of the previous years combined. There are no signs that this trend is going to slow down. You can't read a trade newspaper such as *PC Week* or *InfoWorld* without seeing many pages devoted to new and emerging technologies dealing with the Internet in one way or another. Today, the greatest strides in technology appear to be centered on integrating the Internet with desktop applications. The Microsoft Office and Visual Studio suites fully embrace the Internet to the extent that the Internet can be accessed through developed applications, and the applications themselves can be deployed across the Internet.

Internet Terminology

Every aspect of the computer world has its own terminology and jargon. The Internet is no exception. The following list defines many of the terms that you may encounter.

Applet

A small program that works only inside of another program. It can't start up on its own because it needs another program's operating system and files. For example, to run a Java applet (such as clickable buttons or moving words), you need a Java-aware Web browser.

Backbone

A high-speed line or series of connections that forms a major pathway within a network.

Bandwidth

Specifies how much data can be transmitted through a connection. Usually measured in bits per second (bps).

Baud

In common usage, the *baud rate* of a modem is how many bits it can send or receive per second. Technically, *baud* is the number of times per second that the carrier signal shifts value—for example, a 1200bps modem actually runs at 300 baud, but it moves 4 bits per baud (4 × 300 = 1200 bits per second).

cgi-bin

The most common name of a directory on a Web server in which CGI programs are stored.

Client

A software program used to contact and obtain data from a server software program on another computer, often across a great distance. Each client program is designed to work with one or more specific kinds of server programs, and each server requires a specific kind of client (for example, a Web browser).

Common Gateway Interface (CGI)

A set of rules that describe how a Web server communicates with another piece of software on the same machine, and how the other piece of software (the *CGI program*) talks to the Web server. Any piece of software can be a CGI program if it handles input and output according to the CGI standard.

Usually a CGI program is a small program that takes data from a Web server and does something with it, such as putting the content of a form into an e-mail message, or turning the data into a database query.

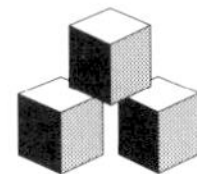

Cookie

The most common meaning of *cookie* on the Internet refers to a piece of information sent by a Web server to a Web browser, which the browser software is expected to save and send back to the server whenever the browser makes additional requests from the server.

Depending on the type of cookie used and the browser's settings, the browser may either accept or not accept the cookie, and may save the cookie for either a short time or a long time.

Cookies might contain information such as login or registration information, online "shopping cart" information, user preferences, and so on.

When a server receives a request from a browser that includes a cookie, the server is able to use the information stored in the cookie. For example, the server might customize what is sent back to users, or keep a log of particular users' requests.

Cookies are usually set to expire after a predetermined amount of time and are usually saved in memory until the browser software is closed down, at which time they may be saved to disk if their "expire time" has not been reached.

Domain Name

The unique name that identifies an Internet site. Domain names always have two or more parts, separated by dots (periods). The part on the left is the most specific, and the part on the right is the most general.

Dynamic HTML (DHTML)

A version of HTML that allows developers to alter the contents of a Web page after it has been rendered in a Web browser.

Electronic Mail (E-mail)

Messages, usually text, sent from one person to another via computer.

Fiber Distributed Data Interface (FDDI)

A standard for transmitting data on optical fiber cables at a rate of around 100,000,000 bps (ten times as fast as Ethernet, about twice as fast as T3).

File Transfer Protocol (FTP)

A very common method of moving files between two Internet sites. FTP is a special way to log into another Internet site for the purpose of retrieving and/or sending files. Many Internet sites have established publicly-accessible repositories of material that can be obtained using FTP, by logging in using the account name `anonymous`; these sites are called *anonymous FTP servers.*

To make things even easier, FTP sites can be accessed directly through a Web browser. Figure 1.1 shows how to do this.

Finger

An Internet software tool for locating people on other Internet sites. Finger is also sometimes used to give access to non-personal information, but the most common use is to see whether a person has an account at a particular Internet site.

Firewall

A combination of hardware and software that separates a LAN into two or more parts for security purposes. One common application of a firewall is to protect a LAN from access via the Internet.

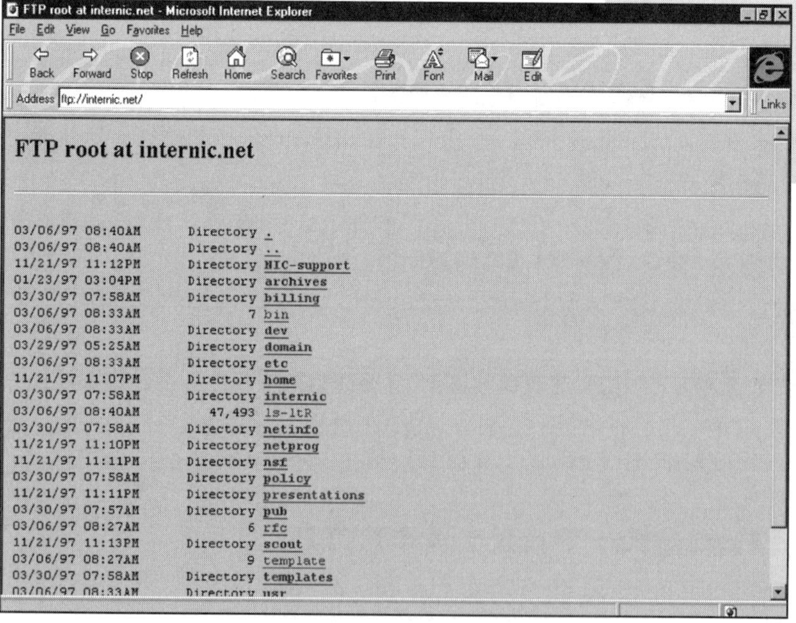

Figure 1.1
A Web browser can provide a graphical interface for an FTP site.

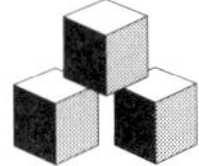

Gopher

A widely successful method of making menus of material available over the Internet. Gopher is a client/server-style program, which requires that the user have a Gopher client program. Although Gopher spread rapidly across the globe in only a couple of years, it now has been largely supplanted by *hypertext*, also known as the WWW (World Wide Web). There are still thousands of Gopher servers on the Internet, however, and they're likely to remain for a while.

Figure 1.2 shows a Gopher server still in use today.

Graphical Interchange Format (GIF)

GIF files are a type of graphic file displayed on Web pages.

Home Page

The main page of a Web site. When a Web site is accessed, the home page is the first page displayed.

Host

Any computer on a network that is a repository for services available to other computers on the network.

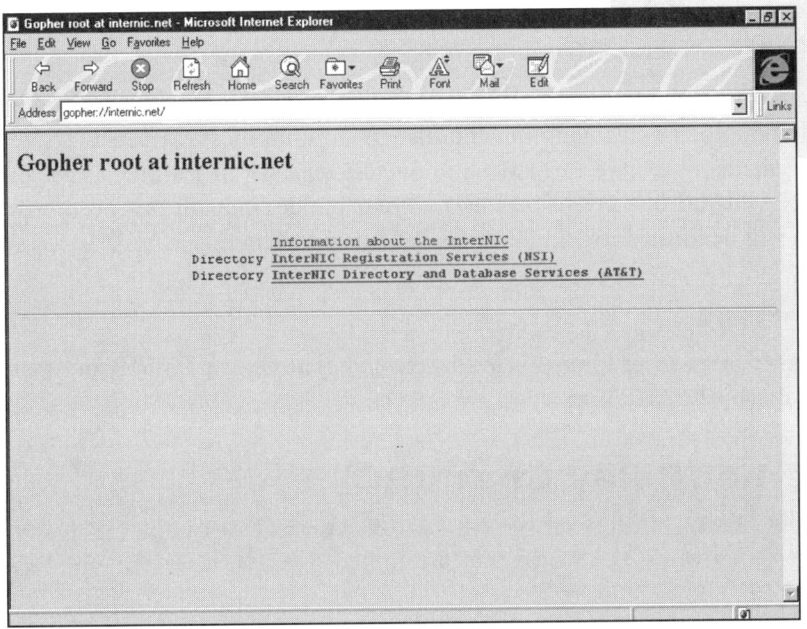

Figure 1.2 This Gopher server can be found at `internic.net`.

Hypertext

Generally, any document that contains links to other documents.

Hyperlink

A text or graphical link embedded in a document. When selected, this link will automatically transfer the reader to the linked document.

Hypertext Markup Language (HTML)

The coding language used to create hypertext documents for use on the World Wide Web. HTML looks a lot like old-fashioned typesetting code, where you surround a block of text with codes that indicate how it should appear; additionally, in HTML you can specify that a word, block of text, or graphic be linked to another file on the Internet. HTML files are viewed with a Web browser.

Hypertext Transport Protocol (HTTP)

The protocol for moving hypertext files across the Internet. Requires an HTTP client program on one end and an HTTP server program on the other end. HTTP is the most important protocol used on the World Wide Web (WWW).

Integrated Services Digital Network (ISDN)

Basically a way to move more data over existing regular phone lines. ISDN is rapidly becoming available to much of the U.S. and in most markets is priced very comparably to standard analog phone circuits. It can provide speeds of roughly 128,000 bits per second over regular phone lines. In practice, most people will be limited to 56,000 or 64,000 bits per second.

Internet

The vast collection of interconnected networks that all use TCP/IP and that evolved from the ARPAnet.

Internet Relay Chat (IRC)

Basically a huge multiuser live-chat facility. There are a number of major IRC servers around the world that are linked to each other. Anyone can

create a channel and anything that anyone types in a given channel is seen by all others in the channel. Private channels can be created for multi-person conference calls.

Internet Service Provider (ISP)

An organization through which an individual or a business establishes a dial up networking connection to gain access to the Internet. ISPs usually provide e-mail services as well as Internet access services.

Intranet

A private network inside a company or organization—intranets provide the same kinds of software that you find on the public Internet, but for internal use only.

IP Address

A unique number consisting of four parts. An example of an IP address is `120.110.201.1`. Every machine on the Internet has its own IP address.

Joint Photographic Experts Group (JPEG)

Like GIF files, JPEG files are a popular graphical format for displaying images on Web pages.

Listserv

The most common kind of mail list.

Mail List

A system (usually automated) that allows people to send e-mail to one address, whereupon their message is copied and sent to a number of other subscribers who belong to that mail list. In this way, people who have many different kinds of e-mail access can participate in discussions together.

Moving Pictures Expert Group (MPEG)

MPEG is a multimedia file format deployed across the Internet.

Multipurpose Internet Mail Extensions (MIME)

The standard for attaching non-text files to Internet mail messages.

Network News Transport Protocol (NNTP)

The protocol used by many newsgroups on the Internet.

Newsgroup

Discussion groups on Usenet.

Ping

A method of checking to see whether a particular system is online.

Point-to-Point Protocol (PPP)

PPP is the protocol that allows a computer to use a regular telephone line and modem to make TCP/IP connections and thus gain access to the Internet.

Post Office Protocol (POP)

A POP server receives and stores e-mail text files. When checking e-mail for new messages received, an e-mail client (e-mail program) logs onto the POP server and asks to see the messages in a particular mailbox.

Protocol

A standard that permits two computers to exchange data.

Router

Special-purpose hardware or software that handles the connections between two or more networks. Routers spend all their time looking at the destination addresses of the packets passing through them and deciding which route to send the packets.

Secure Sockets Layer (SSL)

A protocol designed by Netscape Communications to enable encrypted, authenticated communications across the Internet.

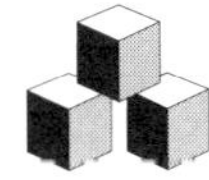

Security Certificate

A chunk of information (often stored as a text file) that is used by the SSL protocol to establish a secure connection.

Each security certificate contains information about who it belongs to, who it was issued by, a unique serial number or other unique identification, valid dates, and an encrypted "fingerprint" that can be used to verify the contents of the certificate. For an SSL connection to be created, both sides must have a valid security certificate.

Serial Line Internet Protocol (SLIP)

A standard for using a regular telephone line (a serial line) and a modem to connect a computer as a real Internet site. SLIP is gradually being replaced by PPP.

Server

Hardware or software that provides a specific kind of service to client software running on other computers.

Simple Mail Transport Protocol (SMTP)

The SMTP server sends e-mail text files. When sending e-mail, an e-mail client (e-mail program) contacts the SMTP server, which then moves the e-mail to a POP server for storage.

T1

A leased-line connection capable of carrying data at 1,544,000 bits per second.

T3

A leased-line connection capable of carrying data at 44,736,000 bits per second.

Transmission Control Protocol/ Internet Protocol (TCP/IP)

The suite of protocols that defines the Internet.

Uniform Resource Locator (URL)

The standard way to give the address of any resource on the Internet that's part of the WWW. An example URL is `http://www.microsoft.com/vbasic`. The URL usually consists of three parts. The first is the service. In this example, `http` is the service used to gain access to the resource. Other services include FTP, news, and Gopher. The second part consists of the host. In this example, the host is `microsoft.com`. The third part is the resource path. In this example, the resource is the Visual Basic Web site, which in turn is hosted by `microsoft.com`.

Usenet

A worldwide system of discussion groups allowing people to post messages, graphics, and other files for others to view or comment upon.

Web Browser

The client software used for accessing the resources found on the WWW. The two dominant Web browsers today are Microsoft's Internet Explorer and Netscape Communications' Navigator.

Web Page

A single HTML document contained within a Web site.

Web Site

A page or collection of pages on the WWW, accessible to anyone with Internet access and Web browser software. Web sites can be either personal or commercial. Figure 1.3 shows a Web browser pointed to the InterNIC Web site.

World Wide Web (WWW)

There are two basic definitions. First, the collection of resources that can be accessed using Gopher, FTP, HTTP, Telnet, Usenet, WAIS, and some other tools. Second, the universe of hypertext servers (HTTP servers) that allow text, graphics, sound files, and so on to be mixed together.

XML (Extensible Markup Language)

A new standard that allows developers to extend HTML by creating their own tags and interpreters for those tags.

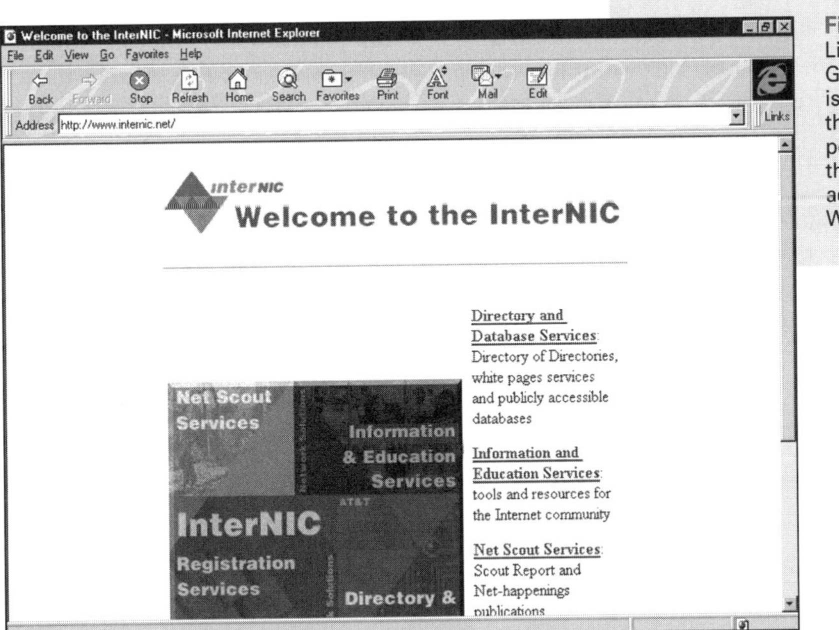

Figure 1.3 Like FTP and Gopher, HTTP is another (and the most popular) service that can be accessed with a Web browser.

Connecting to the Web

Putting all of the history and terminology aside, how does one connect to the Web? It's actually quite easy. The following list outlines the essential elements you need to get connected:

- **Web browser.** To gain access to Web sites and to view HTML documents, you need a Web browser. Microsoft's Internet Explorer is available for the right price—free.
- **Modem.** Unless you have dedicated access, you need a modem. This is one area where you don't want to shortchange yourself, because speed really counts. Today, the fastest modem on the market is 56Kbps. New to many areas is residential ISDN service, which roughly doubles the speed of the fastest modems available. ISDN isn't cheap, and requires a special modem card that can handle the increased speeds; therefore, make sure to do your homework before making this big purchase.
- **ISP.** Again, unless you have dedicated access to the Internet, you'll need to find an ISP. There are thousands of them today, and the current magic price for monthly unlimited access seems to be $19.95.

However, you can achieve substantial savings by pre-purchasing anywhere from one to three years of Internet access. Rates can go as low as $7.00 per month with a three-year plan. Make sure that you deal with a stable provider—one that has robust equipment. Typically, you'll want a provider that has T3 access to the Internet. Otherwise, you may have to deal with system slowdowns and bottlenecks because the ISP can't handle the bandwidth. Many ISPs can get you connected within minutes if you have access to the Web and fill out an online application.

Once you have a browser, modem, and provider, you're ready to get connected. Many ISPs allow you to gain access from a dial-up networking connection. Creating a dial-up connection in Windows 95 is very simple:

1. Make sure that you have the Dial-Up Adapter installed as a network adapter. This can be verified by checking the Network icon in the Windows Control Panel.
2. Make sure that the TCP/IP protocol is installed. This too can be verified by checking the Network icon in the Control Panel.
3. Double-click the My Computer icon on the desktop.
4. Double-click the Dial-Up Networking folder.
5. Double-click the Make New Connection icon.
6. Follow the steps in the New Connection Wizard.

Summary

To say that there's an explosion of new information regarding the Internet would be an understatement. The Internet has a rich and interesting history and most certainly a promising future. It's continually evolving and growing. The newest area of growth deals with Internet-based applications. Most new software released today supports and embraces the Internet—Microsoft Office and Microsoft Visual Studio are two examples—but the projects in this book focus your attention on creating customized, powerful, Internet-based applications so that you can take full advantage of the world of information and features on the Internet for yourself and your clients.

Now that the history and terminology of the Internet have been discussed, the next chapter discusses how to create basic Web pages. Chapter 3 concludes this section with a discussion of how VBScript can be incorporated into Web pages. Mastering the material in the first section is required for completing the projects in this book.

Chapter 2

An Introduction to HTML

Before undertaking the task of developing Web applications, you must have—at the very least—a basic understanding of HTML. HTML is the language of the Web, as it's the basis of every Web page you will encounter.

Web pages *are sometimes referred to as* **HTML documents.** *When appropriate, this chapter will use either term.*

HTML stands for *hypertext markup language*. Hypertext is a means of linking information together. Go to any page on the World Wide Web (WWW) and you'll see how hyperlinks are implemented. Just about every Web page you encounter includes hyperlinks that, when clicked with the mouse, immediately point the Web browser to a different page, thus displaying different information. An example of implementing hyperlinks is illustrated in the following section.

Until a very short time ago, it was necessary to understand the actual code that makes up the HTML specification. Today, however, many tools are available that facilitate building Web pages in a graphical environment. Among the most popular of the Web page authoring tools is Microsoft FrontPage. While it's not necessary to learn the actual code to create effective Web pages, it's important to understand some of the basic components found in most Web pages today. In some cases, you might find it easier to "go behind the scenes" and edit the code manually, instead of relying solely on the graphical interface of the editor.

The beginning of this chapter illustrates how to create a very basic Web page using the world's simplest and least-expensive Web page authoring tool—the Windows Notepad program! In fact, all of the examples are created with Notepad. It should be stressed that this chapter isn't intended to be an exhaustive study of every nuance of HTML. There are many fine books in print today dedicated solely to HTML. Rather, this chapter is intended to equip you with an understanding of the basics and essentials of HTML. In particular, this chapter is designed to provide you with a basic understanding of HTML that will allow you to design the Web pages associated with the applications you will create in the projects in this book. This chapter also focuses on Web tables; user-input components, including text boxes, check boxes, list boxes, etc.; frames; and image map files. Although these latter examples are a bit more complicated, they too were created with Notepad.

Creating Basic Web Pages

If this is your first experience writing HTML code, think in terms of learning both a new programming language and a new word-processing application at the same time. Like any spoken language or programming language, HTML has a syntax. Unlike other computer languages, HTML is not compiled. Rather, it's interpreted line by line by your browser. Also unlike many other computer languages, HTML is very easy and fun to learn. Like a word-processing application, HTML has the power of formatting text in a variety of styles. Enough of the theory—let's dive in and create a Web page!

The Anatomy of a Web Page

There are two basic sections of a Web page:

- **Head.** As the name suggests, the head section appears at the beginning of the HTML document. Elements such as the title and one or more headings appear in this section.
- **Body.** The body section of the HTML document contains the main content of the page. Think of the body section as everything that isn't in the head section of the Web page.

To begin the first example, open Notepad and copy the following code:

```
<HTML>
<HEAD>
<TITLE>This is my first Web page!</TITLE>
</HEAD>
</HTML>
```

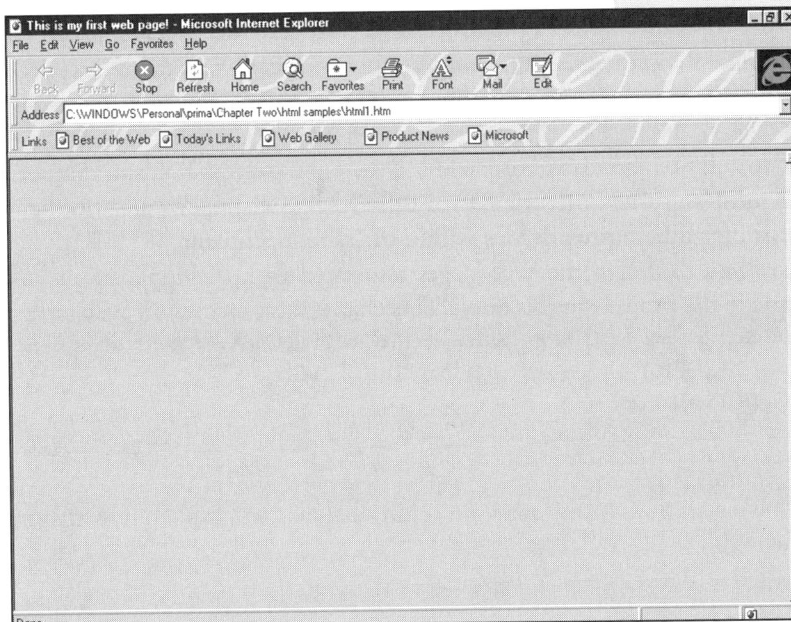

Figure 2.1
A Web browser such as Internet Explorer can open HTML documents that reside on your local hard drive.

ANALYSIS

Once you have written the code, save the document as `HTML1.HTM`. After the document has been saved, you can use your Web browser to open the document. This is typically accomplished by choosing File, Open and directing the Open dialog to your new document. Figure 2.1 shows the HTML code in Internet Explorer.

Let's break down the code of our first Web page to see what each element does. The following table describes each tag:

Tag	Description
<HTML>	Specifies that the document is an HTML document.
<HEAD>	Specifies the beginning of the head section of the document.
<TITLE>	Specifies that the following text is to be displayed in the title bar of the Web browser.
</TITLE>	Specifies the end of the title text—all ending tags are preceded by a slash (/).
</HEAD>	Specifies the end of the head section.
</HTML>	Specifies the end of the HTML document.

Before going further, it's important to understand the concept of *tags*. Tags can be interpreted as directives to the browser to treat text in a specified manner. Tags almost always come in pairs. For example, to specify text that's to appear in the title bar, the text is preceded by the `<TITLE>` tag. After the title bar text appears, the `</TITLE>` tag tells the browser where the title text ends. If you're familiar with RTF (Rich Text Format) files, the same concept holds in that formatting must be turned on and turned off. Otherwise, there would not be a mechanism for different text styles within the same document.

There are a few tags that work alone and do not require an ending tag—for example, the horizontal rule (<HR>) and break (<BR>) tags.

The following sections introduce some additional tags and explain how they're implemented.

Heading Tags

Another set of useful tags is the heading tags. In HTML, you can specify up to six levels of heading text. The syntax is very simple. For example, to specify a first-level heading, issue the tag <H1>. And, in keeping with the concept of tag pairs, to turn off the first-level heading tag attributes, issue the command </H1>. The following code expands on the earlier example. Copy the code from the first HTML example, create a file called HTML2.HTM, and issue the following code:

```
<HTML>
<HEAD>
<TITLE>This is a Web page with multiple headings!</TITLE>
<H1>This is a first level heading</H1>
<H2>This is a second level heading</H2>
<H3>This is a third level heading</H3>
<H4>This is a fourth level heading</H4>
<H5>This is a fifth level heading</H5>
<H6>This is a sixth level heading</H6>
</HEAD>
</HTML>
```

Figure 2.2 illustrates how this code is translated in the Web browser.

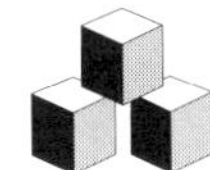

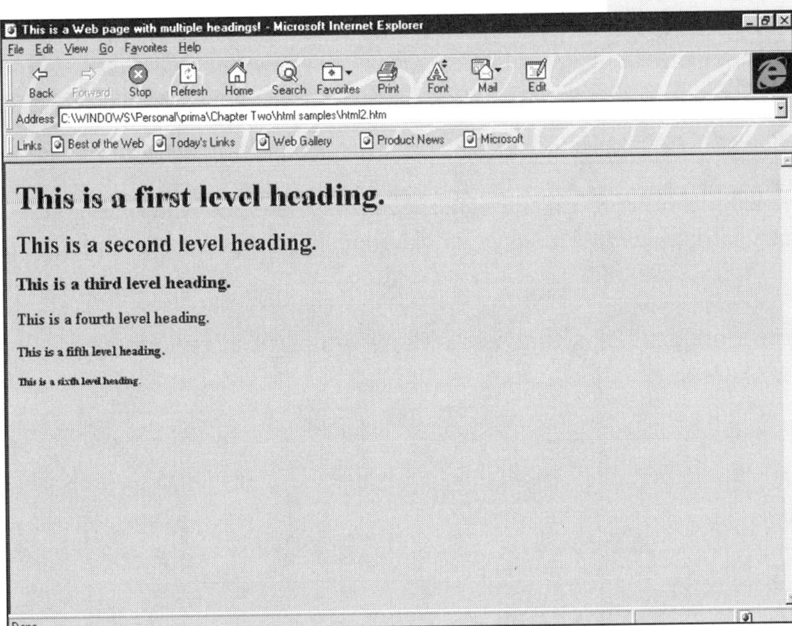

Figure 2.2 Dramatic effects can be achieved with the use of multi-level headings in HTML documents.

BODY TAG

Up to this point in the chapter, the Web pages you've created haven't used the <BODY> tag. As previously stated, this tag specifies the beginning of the body section of the page. The following example illustrates how the body section is positioned in the document relative to the head section:

```
<HTML>
<HEAD>
<TITLE>This Web page is starting to take shape!</TITLE>
<H1>Welcome to my first Web page.</H1>
<H4>With the fourth level heading, we may opt to place an introductory
paragraph.</H4>
</HEAD>
<BODY>
<H3>We can also use heading tags in the body of the document.</H3>
<H4>We can also use heading tags in the body of the document.</H4>
<H5>We can also use heading tags in the body of the document.</H5>

In addition, we can enter plain text as well.
</BODY>
</HTML>
```

Figure 2.3 illustrates how this code is displayed in the browser.

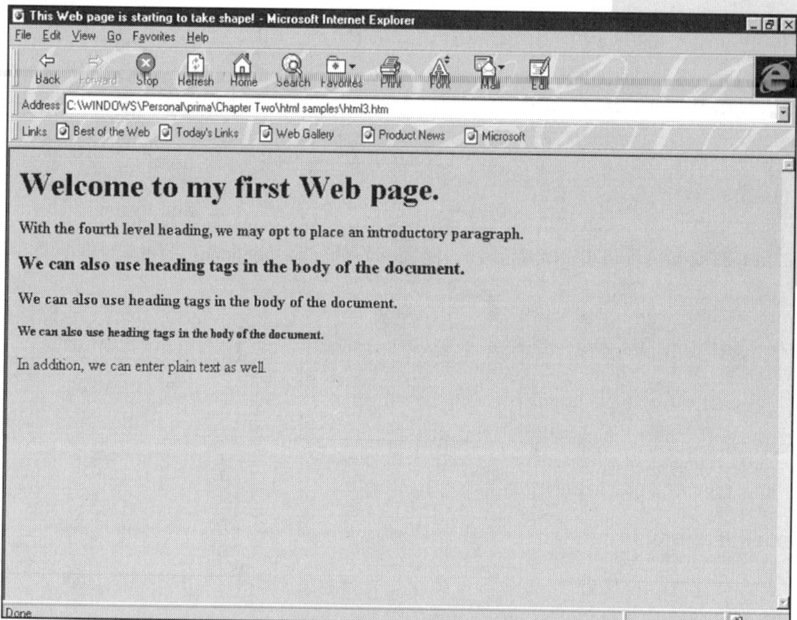

Figure 2.3 Even though this Web document has a body section, there's no distinction between the body and head sections.

Okay, take a moment to see what you've accomplished. While it has some important elements, in reality Figure 2.3 looks like a confused mess! There are some critical elements missing. For one thing, there's no clear distinction between the head and body sections of the document. Also, it would be nice to be able to separate text by more than one line. Finally, it also would be nice if text other than heading text could be formatted.

Fortunately, all of this is possible. With the use of more HTML tags, it's very easy.

Horizontal Rule, Bold/Italic, and Line Break Tags

The tags discussed in this section include the *horizontal rule* (<HR>), *line break* (<BR>), *bold* (<B>), and *italic* (<I>) tags. With strategic placement of these tags, the quality of the page illustrated in Figure 2.3 can be improved dramatically. Here's the code:

```
<HTML>
<HEAD>
```

```
<TITLE>This Web page is starting to take shape!</TITLE>
<H1>Welcome to my first Web page.</H1>
<H4>With the fourth level heading, we may opt to place an introductory
paragraph.</H4>
<HR>
</HEAD>
<BODY>
<H3>We can also use heading tags in the body of the document.</H3>
<H4>We can also use heading tags in the body of the document.</H4>
<H5>We can also use heading tags in the body of the document.</H5>
<BR>
<BR>
<B><I>In addition, we can enter plain text as well.</B></I>
</BODY>
</HTML>
```

Figure 2.4 illustrates how these tags alter the appearance of the Web page in Figure 2.3.

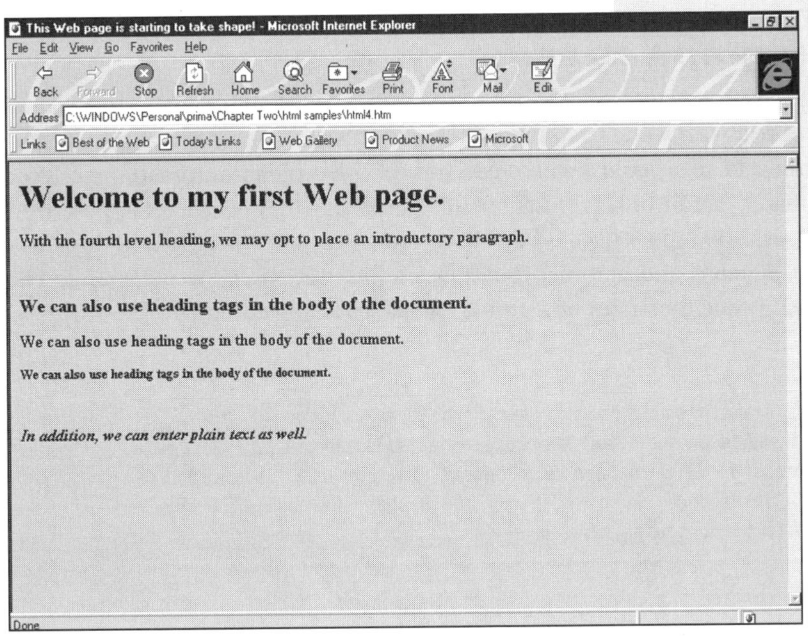

Figure 2.4
By adding a horizontal rule, line breaks, and text attributes, you can make the Web page more readable.

Comments

With more features comes added complexity. At the beginning of this chapter, an assertion was made that learning to write HTML documents was akin to learning a programming language. Just as all programs should have at least one comment, so too should HTML documents. Comments can be embedded anywhere in an HTML document, except inside preformatted text. Preformatted text will be discussed a bit later in this chapter.

To specify text as a comment, the text needs to be wrapped with the tags <!- and ->. For example, the code in the preceding example could have the following comments at the beginning of the document:

```
<!-This example shows how several tags such as horizontal rules
and line breaks can be used to make an HTML document more readable.->
```

If the comments are wrapped with the appropriate tags, the text won't be visible in the Web browser. Remember the tags used for commenting, because these tags will be used in Chapter 3 to embed VBScript into HTML documents.

Paragraph Breaks

In all of the previous examples, the text consisted of single lines. To separate lines of text with a line feed, the <BR> tag was used. Wouldn't it be nice if multiple lines of text could be entered, and followed by an automatic line feed? Fortunately, a pair of tags exists for this purpose—they're called the *paragraph break tags* (<P> and </P>). They allow you to organize multiple lines of text into paragraphs and automatically place a line feed after the paragraph. The following code illustrates how to use the paragraph break tags:

```
<HTML>
<HEAD>
<!-This example shows how the paragraph break tag works.->
<TITLE> Hands On VB 6 for Web Development</TITLE>
<H1> Hands On VB 6 for Web Development</H1>
<I>By: Rod Paddock, John Petersen, and Richard Campbell</I>
<H2>Table of Contents</H2>
<HR>
</HEAD>
<BODY>
<H3>Section 1: VB/Internet Primer</H3>
<H4>Chapter One: Introduction to the Internet</H4>
<P>This chapter discusses what the Internet is, Internet terminology,
and the basics of how to connect to the World Wide Web.</P>
<H4>Chapter Two: An HTML Primer</H4>
```

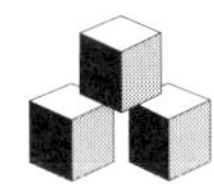


```
<P>This chapter demonstrates how to create basic Web pages.
In addition, advanced Web page elements such as tables, user input controls,
frames and image maps are discussed.</P>
<H4>Chapter Three: A VBScript Primer</H4>
<P>This chapter introduces the reader to the Visual Basic Scripting Edition
Language (VBScript). In addition, the reader is introduced to techniques that
validate user input with VBScript.</P>
</BODY>
</HTML>
```

Figure 2.5 shows how this code appears in the Web browser.

Preformatted Text

Often, you may need to preserve the formatting of text. This is particularly true with data that needs to be presented in a tabular format. Unless you specifically direct the viewer that displays the HTML document, special formatting such as embedded tabs will be lost. To specify a block of text as preformatted, wrap it with the `<PRE>` and `</PRE>` tags. The following code and Figure 2.6 illustrate how the preformatted text tag works:

```
<HTML>
<HEAD>
```

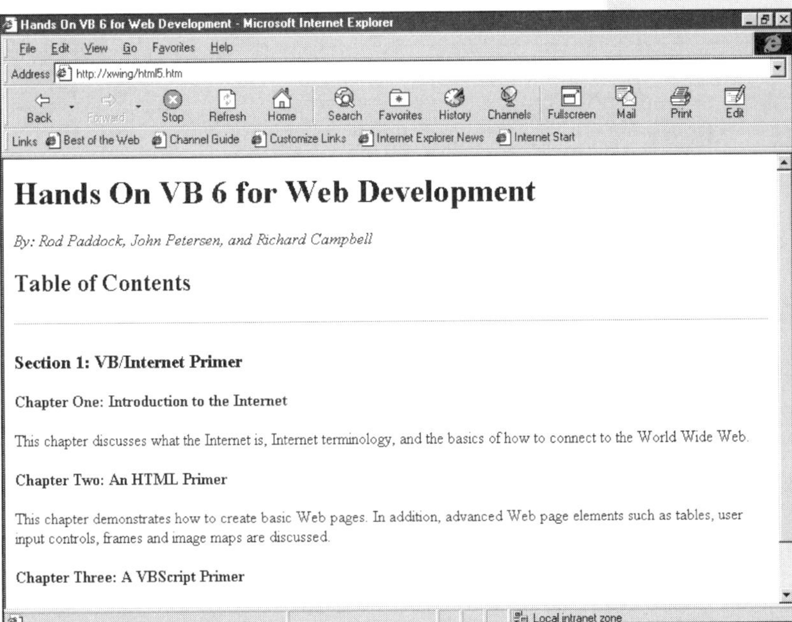

Figure 2.5 Paragraph break tags allow for the easy organization of text within an HTML document.

```
<!-This example shows how to embed preformatted text into a Web page.->
<TITLE>Preformatted text example</TITLE>
<H1>Preformatted text can be entered with the PRE Tag.</H1>
<HR>
</HEAD>
<BODY>
<H2>1996 Sales by Region</H2>
<H3>(in thousands $)</H3>
<BR>
<PRE>
       North   East    South   West
Q1     100     150       0     200
Q2     150     100     100     300
Q3     200       0     300     100
Q4       0     200     200     100
       ---     ---     ---     ---
       450     450     500     700
       ===     ===     ===     ===
</PRE>
</BODY>
</HTML>
```

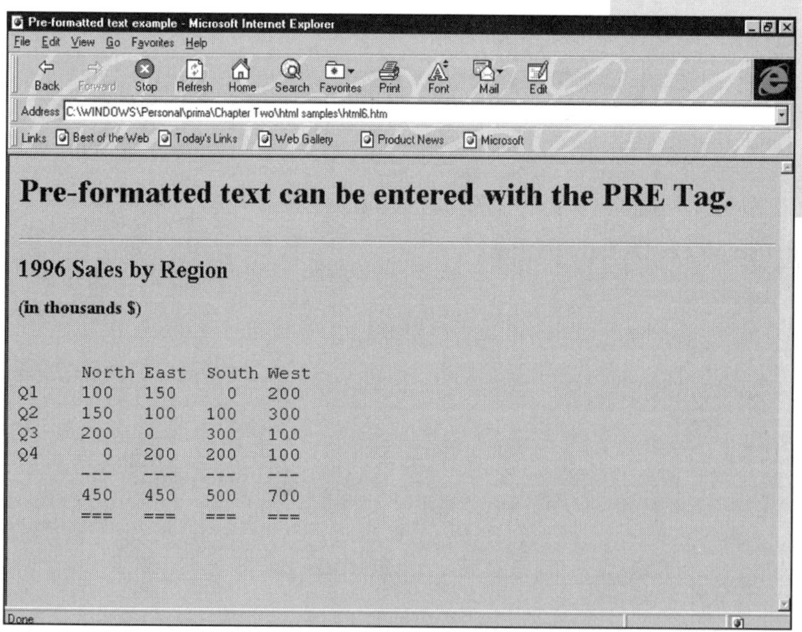

Figure 2.6 The preformatted text tag makes it very easy to enter tabular data.

Hyperlinks and Lists

Up to this point, the sample Web pages created have been passive to the extent that their sole function has been to display text. None of the examples has illustrated the use of hyperlinks, the mechanism that links different Web pages together. Embedding hyperlinks into a page is very simple. In order to create links, a few new HTML tags need to be introduced. The following code illustrates how to embed hyperlinks into an HTML document:

```
<HTML>
<HEAD>
<TITLE>Page Link Example</TITLE>
<H1>This page contains some valuable Web links.</H1>
<HR>
</HEAD>
<BODY>
<UL>
<LI><A HREF="http://www.primapublishing.com">Prima Publishing</A>
<LI><A HREF="http://www.microsoft.com/vbasic">Visual Basic</A>
</UL>
</BODY>
</HTML>
```

This code block introduces a few new tags, as described in the following table:

Tag	Description
<UL>	Begins an unordered bulleted list.
<LI>	Denotes a list item.
</UL>	Ends an unordered bulleted list.
<A>	An anchor tag that designates the destination of the link.
</A>	Ends an anchor.

While not required, presenting Web links in the context of a list helps with readability. Figure 2.7 shows the preceding code viewed with Internet Explorer.

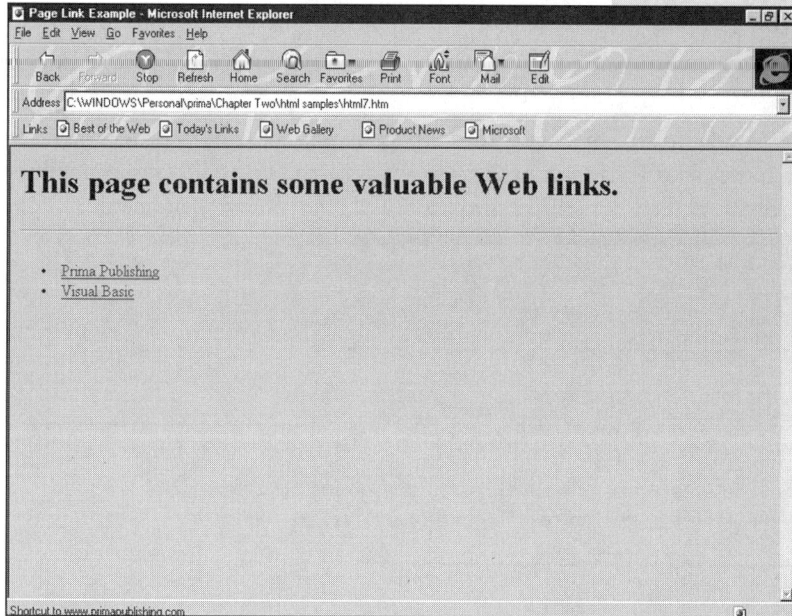

Figure 2.7 Hyperlinks stand apart from other text by having a different color and by being underlined. This helps hyperlinks to be easily identifiable.

E-mail Links

Have you noticed in some Web pages a hyperlink that, when clicked, sends e-mail to a specified recipient? Usually, such a link is present to facilitate the sending of comments. These e-mail links are just like links to other Web pages—with one notable exception. Instead of `http://` in the reference portion of the link, `mailto:` is used. The following code and Figure 2.8 illustrate how to embed e-mail links into a Web page:

```
<HTML>
<HEAD>
<TITLE>E-mail Link Example</TITLE>
<H1>This page contains some valuable E-mail links.</H1>
<HR>
</HEAD>
<BODY>
<UL>
<LI><A HREF="mailto:debbie@primapublishing.com">Debbie at Prima</A>
<LI><A HREF="mailto:billg@microsoft.com">Big Bill at Microsoft</A>
</UL>
</BODY>
</HTML>
```

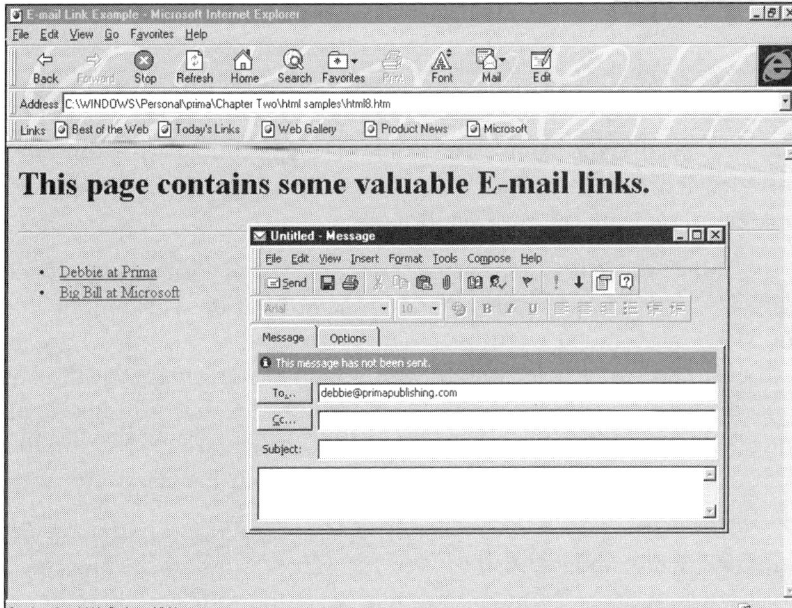

Figure 2.8
When an e-mail link is clicked, the e-mail program specified by the Web browser as the default is launched automatically.

Images

This section of the chapter concludes with a discussion on embedding image files into a Web page. Certainly the more aesthetically pleasing Web sites you've visited are those with fancy graphics. Just as links can be attached to text, they also can be attached to graphic images. To attach an image to an HTML document, you use the `<IMG>` tag. The following code sample modifies the example illustrated in Figure 2.7:

```
<HTML>
<HEAD>
<TITLE>Page Link Example</TITLE>
<H1>This page contains some valuable Web links.</H1>
<H3>Instead of text hyperlinks, graphic images can be used.</H3>
<HR>
</HEAD>
<BODY>
<P>
<A HREF="http://www.microsoft.com/vbasic"><IMG SRC="VB.GIF" ALT="Link to
Visual Basic Site"></A>
</P>
<P>
```

```
<A HREF="http://www.primapublishing.com"><IMG SRC="PRIMA.GIF" ALT="Link to
Prima Site"></A>
</P>
</BODY>
</HTML>
```

The `<IMG>` tag specifies the name of the graphic element to display. In this case, two GIF files are included: `VB.GIF` and `PRIMA.GIF`. Figure 2.9 shows how these images are presented in the Web browser.

Notice the ToolTip text that appears over the link to the Visual Basic site at Microsoft. This feature was enabled by using the `ALT` attribute in conjunction with the `<IMG>` tag. The `ALT` attribute actually serves two purposes. First, it enables ToolTip text to be displayed. Second, it provides an alternative display option in case the image file is unavailable or the Web browser is incapable of displaying Web images. To illustrate this capability, the `VB.GIF` reference in the HTML source was modified to `V.GIF`. Because no such file exists, the Web browser reverts to the alternative display (see Figure 2.10).

While images are nice and add flair to Web pages, they can slow the process of users accessing your pages. Not every machine accessing your site is a Pentium

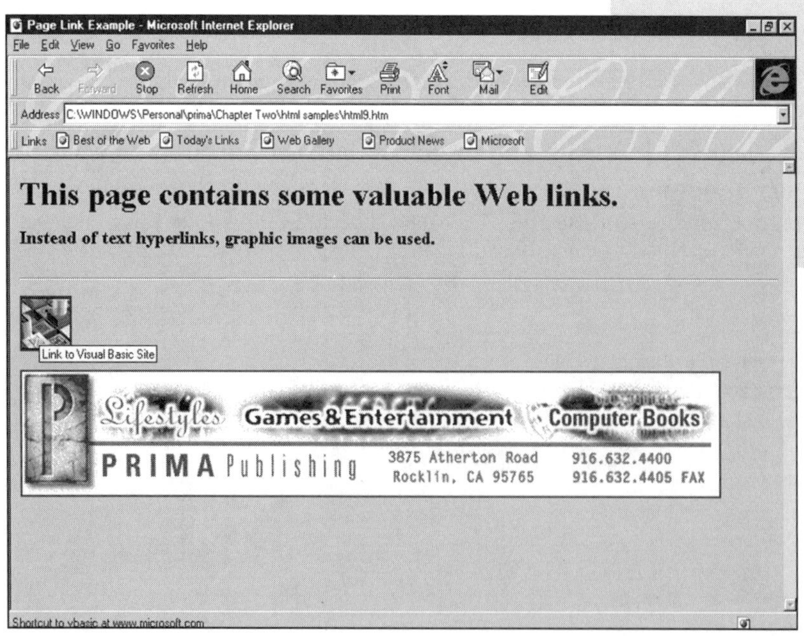

Figure 2.9 Displaying images in a Web page can make for a much more aesthetically pleasing document.

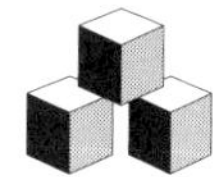

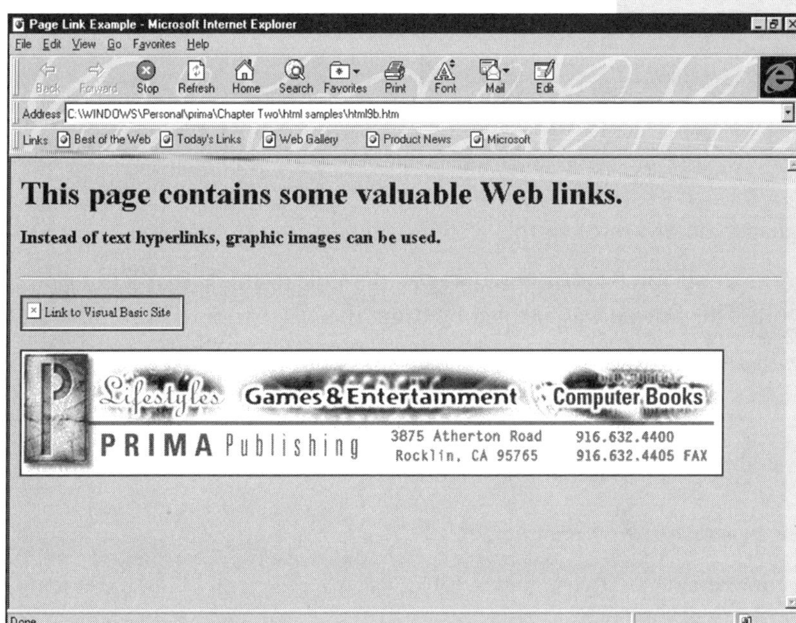

Figure 2.10 The ALT attribute provides for an alternative display in case the image is unavailable or the Web browser is incapable of displaying images.

II 400MHz-based PC with 80MB of RAM! Strike a balance when possible. Use enough images to make your site interesting without your user having to wait while downloading image after image. Remember, your site needs to convey information. The process can be frustrating for your visitors if it takes five minutes to download all the images for a page.

Image Map Files

The hyperlinks in an image map are also referred to as **hot spots.**

Another type of HTML image is known as an *image map*. An image map consists of a graphic that's divided into separate regions. These regions are hyperlinks just like the hyperlinks created earlier in this chapter. Unlike the previous examples where one image corresponded to one hyperlink, however, image maps contain several hyperlinks.

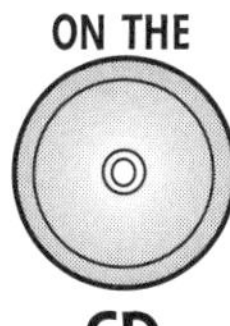

The most difficult task in defining an image map is specifying the boundaries of each hot spot. Unless you use a graphical editor such as MapEdit, the task can prove very difficult. An evaluation version of MapEdit is included on the CD that accompanies this book.

The following code illustrates how an image map works:

```
<HTML>
<HEAD>
<H2>A hot spot exists for each of the three book categories listed.</H2>
By moving the mouse over each hot spot, the URL associated with each hot
spot is displayed in the lower-left portion of the Web browser.
<HR>
</HEAD>
<BODY>
<P><A HREF="prima.map"><IMG SRC="prima.gif" ISMAP usemap="#prima"></A>
<MAP NAME="prima">
<AREA SHAPE="rect" COORDS="76,5,216,64" HREF="lifestyles.htm">
<AREA SHAPE="rect" COORDS="222,7,510,66" HREF="games_ent.htm">
<AREA SHAPE="rect" COORDS="516,8,703,65" HREF="computer.htm">
</MAP>
</BODY>
</HTML>
```

Figure 2.11 shows the image map.

The key to creating an image map involves the use of several HTML elements, as described in the following table:

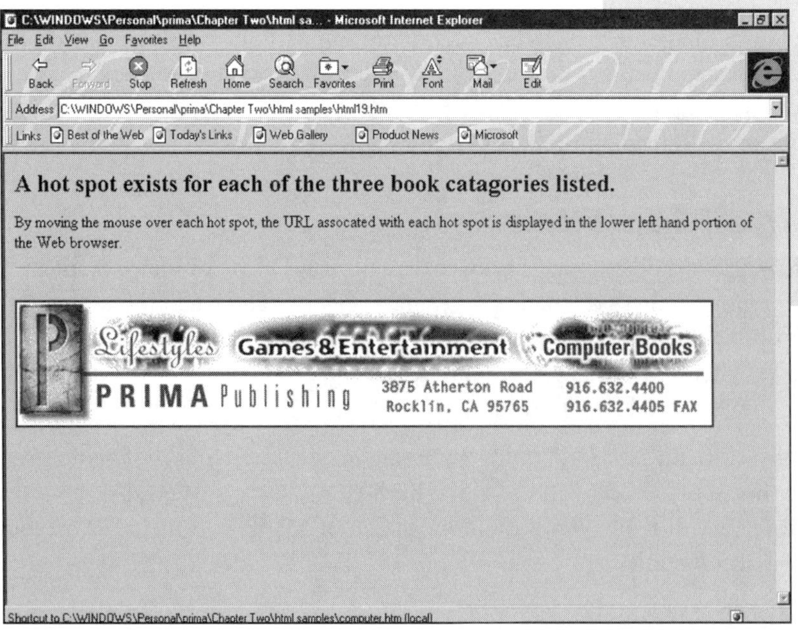

Figure 2.11 When the mouse pointer is positioned over a hot spot, the URL linked to that hot spot is displayed in the lower-left corner of the browser.

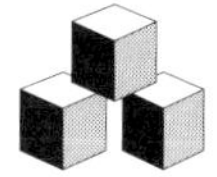

Tag	Description
ISMAP	This attribute of the <IMG> tag designates that the associated graphic file uses an image map. In this example, the image map is named prima.
<MAP NAME>	This tag defines an image map. Everything between this tag and the </MAP> tag specifies the boundaries of all hot spots in the image map.
<AREA>	This tag defines the boundary for a specific hot spot in an image map. This example uses the rectangle shape. Other available shapes include polygons and circles. The COORDS attribute of the <AREA> tag specifies X and Y coordinates of the hot spot. The X coordinate represents the upper-left corner and the Y coordinate represents the lower-right corner.

A Final Word on Basic Pages

This section of the chapter has provided you with a no-nonsense, bare-bones introduction to some fundamental elements of creating basic Web pages. At this point, you should have a good understanding of the sections that make up an HTML document and the most common elements found in typical Web pages. In addition, you should have enough of an understanding to go forward with learning the more advanced topics presented in the remainder of this chapter. There are many more elements to the HTML specification and many good books devoted to that subject. For a complete introduction to HTML, I suggest consulting one of those books.

The remainder of this chapter builds on the basics discussed thus far. The upcoming topics include Web tables, user input, and frames.

Web Tables

Like the preformatted text tag discussed earlier, Web tables offer another way to organize text. Like other features in HTML, using Web tables involves learning how to use new HTML tags. The following table describes tags used in the creation of Web tables:

Tag	Description
<CAPTION> and </CAPTION>	Specifies the caption for the table.
<TR> and </TR>	Specifies a new row for the table.
<TH> and </TH>	Specifies table headings.
<TD> and </TD>	Specifies table data.

Figure 2.6 illustrated how to use the `<PRE>` tag by displaying financial data. The following code uses the same data, but displays it in a Web table:

```
<HTML>
<HEAD>
<TITLE>Web Table Example</TITLE>
<H2>Web Tables Can Really Jazz Up Output!!</H2>
<HR>
</HEAD>
<BODY>
<TABLE BORDER>
<CAPTION>1996 Sales by Region (000's)</CAPTION>
<TR><TH> Quarter   <TH> North    <TH> East     <TH> South     <TH> West    </TR>
<TR><TH> Q1         TD> 100      TD> 150     <TD>   0      <TD> 200    </TR>
<TR><TH> Q2        <TD> 150     <TD> 100     <TD> 100      <TD> 300    </TR>
<TR><TH> Q3        <TD> 200     <TD>   0     <TD> 200      <TD> 100    </TR>
<TR><TH> Q4        <TD>   0     <TD> 200     <TD> 200      <TD> 100    </TR>
<TR><TH> Total     <TH> 450     <TH> 450     <TH> 500      <TH> 700    </TR>
</BODY>
</HTML>
```

Figure 2.12 shows the modified display.

In this example, all elements of the Web table fit nicely into each cell. But sometimes this won't be the case. Often, text in a Web table may need to span

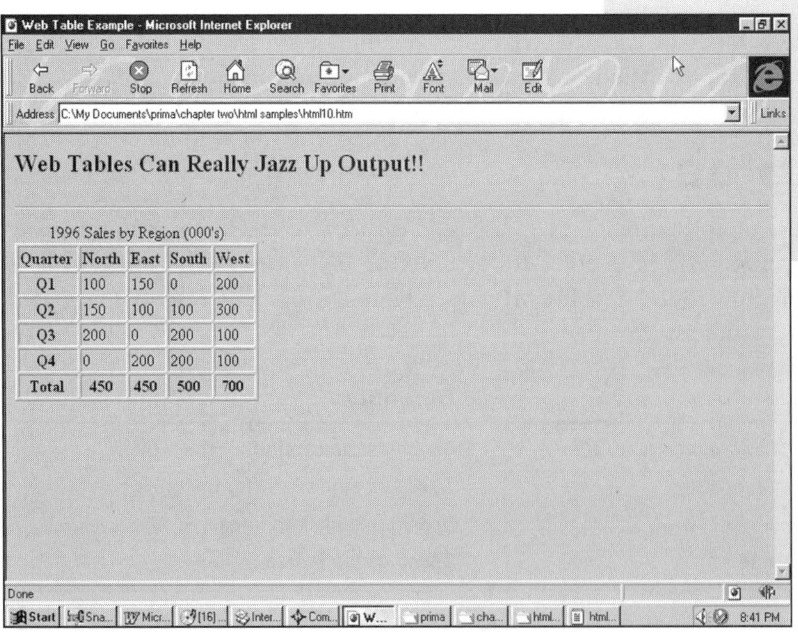

Figure 2.12 Web tables, like the preformatted text tag, make presenting formatted data a very easy task.

multiple columns and rows. To accomplish this, you can augment the <TH> with one of two attributes, as shown in the following table:

Attribute	Example
COLSPAN	<TH COLSPAN=3 This heading will span three table columns </TH>
ROWSPAN	<TH ROWSPAN=2 This heading will span two table rows </TH>

The following code slightly modifies the example illustrated in Figure 2.12:

```
<HTML>
<HEAD>
<TITLE>Web Table Example</TITLE>
<H2>Web Tables Can Really Jazz Up Output!!</H2>
<H3>Text can span more than one column or row with the
use of COLSPAN/ROWSPAN elements.</H3>
<CENTER>
<H4>Text and tables can also be centered using the CENTER tag!</H4>
</CENTER>
<HR>
</HEAD>
<BODY>
<CENTER>
<TABLE BORDER>
<TH COLSPAN=5>1996 Sales by Region (000's)</TH>
<TR><TH> Quarter  <TH> North    <TH> East     <TH> South     <TH> Wes t </TR>
<TR><TH> Q1        TD> 100       TD> 150     <TD>   0      <TD> 200   </TR>
<TR><TH> Q2       <TD> 150      <TD> 100     <TD> 100      <TD> 300   </TR>
<TR><TH> Q3       <TD> 200      <TD>   0     <TD> 200      <TD> 100   </TR>
<TR><TH> Q4       <TD>   0      <TD> 200     <TD> 200      <TD> 100   </TR>
<TR><TH> Total    <TH> 450      <TH> 450     <TH> 500      <TH> 700   </TR>
</BODY>
</HTML>
```

Figure 2.13 shows the new version.

In addition to containing text, Web tables can contain images. The following code illustrates how the ROWSPAN attribute can be used to display a graph of the financial data along with the raw numbers:

```
<HTML>
<HEAD>
<TITLE>Web Table Example</TITLE>
<H2>Web Tables Can Really Jazz Up Output!!</H2>
<H3>Text and images can span more than one column or row with the
use of COLSPAN/ROWSPAN elements.</H3>
```

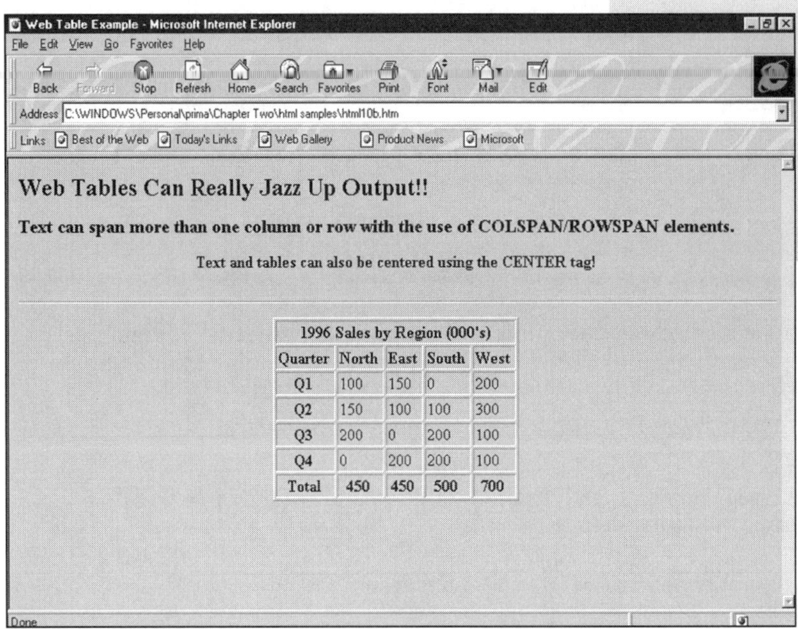

Figure 2.13 In addition to spanning rows and columns, contents of a Web page can be centered using the <CENTER> tag.

```
<CENTER>
<H4>Text and tables can also be centered using the CENTER tag!</H4>
</CENTER>
<HR>
</HEAD>
<BODY>
<CENTER>
<TABLE BORDER>
<TH COLSPAN=7>1996 Sales by Region (000's)</TH>
<TR><TH ROWSPAN=6><IMG SRC="1996.GIF"></TH>
<TR><TH> Quarter    <TH> North    <TH> East    <TH> South    <TH> West
</TR>
<TR><TH> Quarter   <TH> North    <TH> East    <TH> South    <TH> West   </TR>
<TR><TH> Q1         TD> 100       TD> 150     <TD>   0      <TD> 200    </TR>
<TR><TH> Q2        <TD> 150      <TD> 100     <TD> 100      <TD> 300    </TR>
<TR><TH> Q3        <TD> 200      <TD>   0     <TD> 200      <TD> 100    </TR>
<TR><TH> Q4        <TD>   0      <TD> 200     <TD> 200      <TD> 100    </TR>
<TR><TH> Total     <TH> 450      <TH> 450     <TH> 500      <TH> 700    </TR>
</BODY>
</HTML>
```

Figure 2.14 shows the result.

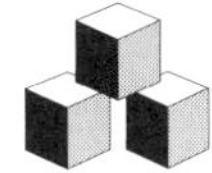

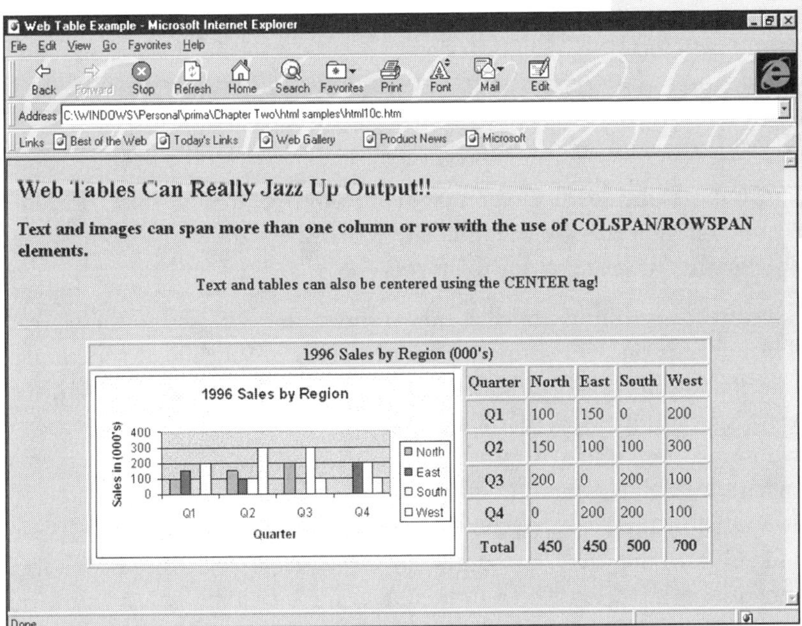

Figure 2.14 Combining graphics with numeric data in Web tables can make for a powerful presentation

HTML has no native capabilities for exact placement of text and graphics. The most common solution to this problem is the use of tables (without borders) as an alignment tool.

User Input

Your only interaction with the Web pages produced thus far has been limited to clicking a hyperlink that points the Web browser to another Web page. Not long ago, this functionality represented the scope of what Web pages did. Today, however, Web sites and their associated pages provide sophisticated data-entry facilities that were once limited to PC/LAN-based applications. Just like everything else in HTML, a new set of tags must be learned to facilitate user input in Web pages. The following sections outline the different types of user-input controls that can be displayed in a Web page. Before getting into the specifics of controls, however, I need to discuss the concept of forms.

Forms

Just as forms can be created in products like Visual Basic and Visual FoxPro to capture data input, forms also can be created in Web pages. The area that designates the boundaries of a form in a Web page is indicated by the <FORM> HTML tag. Like many other HTML tags, <FORM> has an ending tag, </FORM>.

Forms are typically made up of a group of controls dedicated to some common purpose. Web page forms are no different. When specifying a form, you specify both a method and action for the form:

- The `method` attribute describes how information is passed to the server. There can be one of two methods: `POST` or `GET`. With the `GET` method, information is passed to the server via the browser's URL line. With the `POST` method, the data that has been entered into the page is grouped with other data into a "package" that is then passed to the Web server for processing. The method of choice is normally the `POST` method, for two reasons: first, it keeps the mechanisms for manipulating data hidden from the user; second, the URL line has string-length limitations. One item you'll notice about these two mechanisms for sending data is that `GET` implies retrieval of data and `POST` implies sending data. Why the inconsistency? The answer lies in the sidebar titled "`GET` and `POST`: The mystery solved."
- The `ACTION` attribute specifies the URL to the program that accepts the data from the form.

Following is an example of how to define a form:

```
<FORM method="POST" ACTION="myprogram.exe">
```

A little later in this section, you'll see how to place a submit button on the Web page. When the submit button is pressed, the program specified in the `ACTION` portion of the <FORM> tag is invoked.

Note

It should be stressed that the focus of this chapter is to present the basics of creating Web pages. It's beyond the scope of this chapter to explain in detail how Web pages interact with server-side programs. Although the following examples use the <FORM> tag, the tag won't be active.

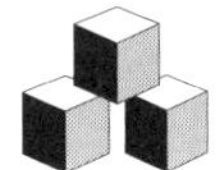

GET and POST: The mystery solved

During my Internet development classes the question always comes up: Why are the **METHOD** parameters of the **<FORM>** tag called **POST** and **GET** when they both send data to the Web server? At first I could not come up with an answer for this inconsistency. After some research I finally found the answer. The inconsistency has to do with the history of the HTTP protocol. The original version of HTTP (0.9) had one command, **GET**. The original intent of the HTTP protocol was to simply retrieve documents, images, and other binary data from Web servers. Well, the Internet would be a pretty boring place if all you could do was retrieve documents.

To work around the problem of the HTTP protocol only supporting the **GET** command, Web developers began loading up their document requests with extra information. This extra information then was parsed out and stored on a server, but there were some limitations. Browsers were limited in the amount of data they could send in a **GET** command. Hence, the HTTP protocol was further updated with some new commands. The following table shows some of the commands available for each version of the HTTP protocol:

HTTP Version	Commands Supported
HTTP .09	GET
HTTP 1.0	GET, POST, PUT, HEAD, DELETE, LINK, UNLINK
HTTP 1.1	GET, POST, PUT, HEAD, DELETE, OPTIONS, TRACE

Text Box Control

The most common data entry control is the text box. There are two types of text box entry controls available. The first type accepts plain text input. The second is specially designed to accept password entry. Password entry is typically masked with the asterisk (*) or another character so that the input can't be discovered by other individuals. The following code illustrates how to place a text box on a Web page:

```
<HTML>
<HEAD>
<TITLE>User Input Examples</TITLE>
<H2>Web pages can also capture user input.</H2>
<HR>
</HEAD>
<BODY>
<CENTER>
<FORM method="" ACTION="">
Customer ID: <INPUT NAME="CUSTID" SIZE="5" MAXLENGTH="5" VALUE="99999">
</FORM>
</CENTER>
</BODY>
</HTML>
```

Figure 2.15 shows the text box created by this code.

The line that defines the text box actually does quite a bit of work. The `SIZE` directive specifies how large the text box should be. The `MAXLENGTH` directive specifies how many characters can be entered into the text box. The `VALUE` directive specifies the default value that is contained in the text box.

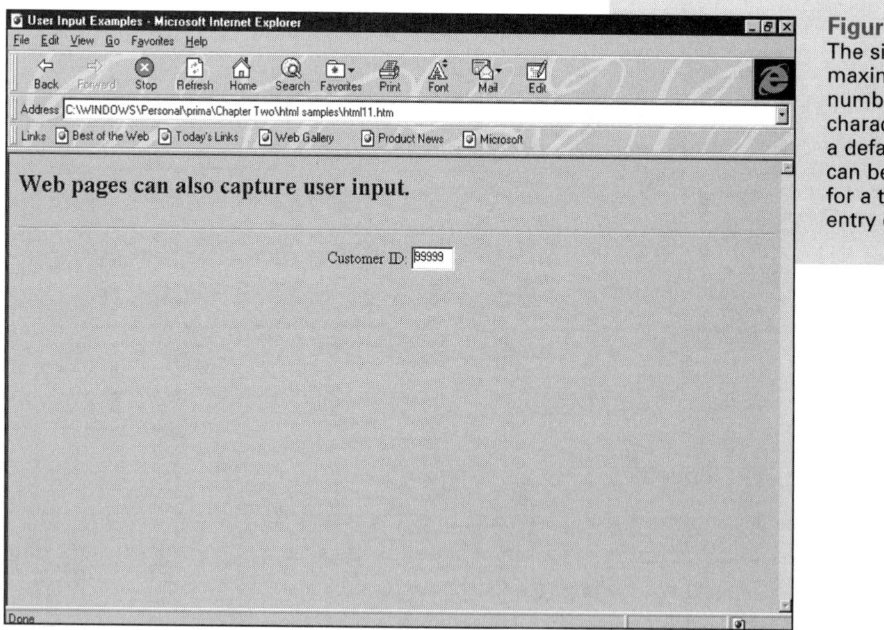

Figure 2.15 The size, maximum number of characters, and a default value can be specified for a text box entry control.

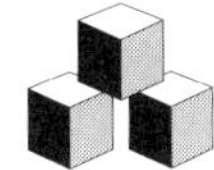

The following code adds a password-entry text box:

```
<HTML>
<HEAD>
<TITLE>User Input Examples</TITLE>
<H2>Web Site Logon</H2>
<H3>Please Specify User ID and Password</H3>
<HR>
</HEAD>
<BODY>
<CENTER>
<FORM method="" ACTION="">
<PRE>
User ID:  <INPUT NAME="USERID" SIZE="5" MAXLENGTH="5" VALUE="99999" >
Password: <INPUT TYPE="password" NAME="PASSWORD" SIZE="5"
MAXLENGTH="5" VALUE="">
<HR>
</PRE>
</FORM>
</CENTER>
</BODY>
</HTML>
```

Figure 2.16 shows the resulting control.

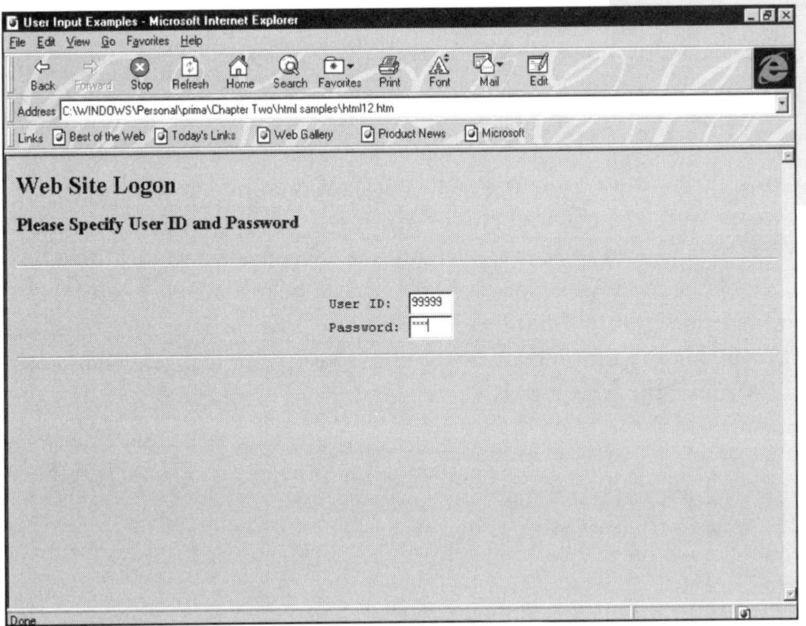

Figure 2.16 Facilitate secured entry with the use of the password text box control.

Command Button Control

There are two types of command button controls:

- **Reset button.** Resets the controls on a form to their default values.
- **Submit button.** Sends data to the server. The program invoked on the server is specified by the `ACTION` attribute in the `<FORM>` tag.

The following code illustrates how to create both submit and reset command buttons:

```
<HTML>
<HEAD>
<TITLE>User Input Examples</TITLE>
<H2>Customer Search Form</H2>
<HR>
</HEAD>
<BODY>
<H3>Please Enter a Customer ID</H3>
<FORM method="" ACTION="">
<PRE>
Customer ID:  <INPUT NAME="USERID" SIZE="5" MAXLENGTH="5" VALUE="">
<INPUT TYPE="submit" VALUE="Search Customer Database"><INPUT TYPE="reset"
VALUE="Reset">
</PRE>
</FORM>
</BODY>
</HTML>
```

Figure 2.17 shows the command buttons in the Web page.

Drop-Down Lists and List Box Controls

Drop-down lists and list boxes provide a handy way to present a list of predefined choices for the user. The choice of which one to use depends on whether multiple selections need to be made. If multiple selections are valid, the list box control should be used. When only one choice can be made, either control can be used, depending on the number of choices. If many choices are possible, you may opt for the drop-down list to conserve space. The following code shows how to use the list controls:

```
<HTML>
<HEAD>
<TITLE>User Input Examples</TITLE>
<H2>Sales Report for 1996</H2>
<HR>
</HEAD>
<BODY>
```

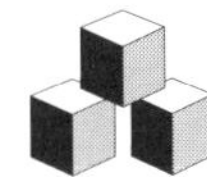

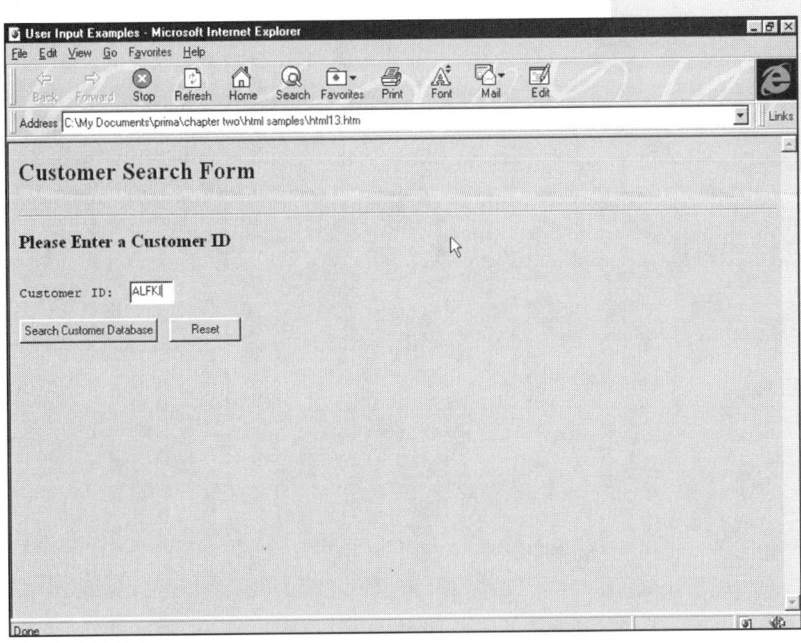

Figure 2.17 Clicking the submit button, which has a caption of `Search Customer Database`, sends data to the server. Clicking the reset button makes all controls on the form revert to their default values.

```
<H4>Select a region from the drop-down list and then press the
Run Selected Reports Button to review data.</H4>
<FORM method="" ACTION="">
<PRE>
Region:       <SELECT NAME="REGION">
              <OPTION>North
              <OPTION>South
              <OPTION>East
              <OPTION>West
</SELECT>

Report Type:  <SELECT Name = "Report Type" Multiple Size="5">
              <OPTION>Sales by Month
              <OPTION>Sales by Quarter
              <OPTION>Sales by Month By Salesman
              <OPTION>Sales by Quarter By Salesman
</SELECT>

<INPUT TYPE="submit" VALUE="Run Selected Reports">
</PRE>
</FORM>
</BODY>
</HTML>
```

Figure 2.18 shows the resulting lists.

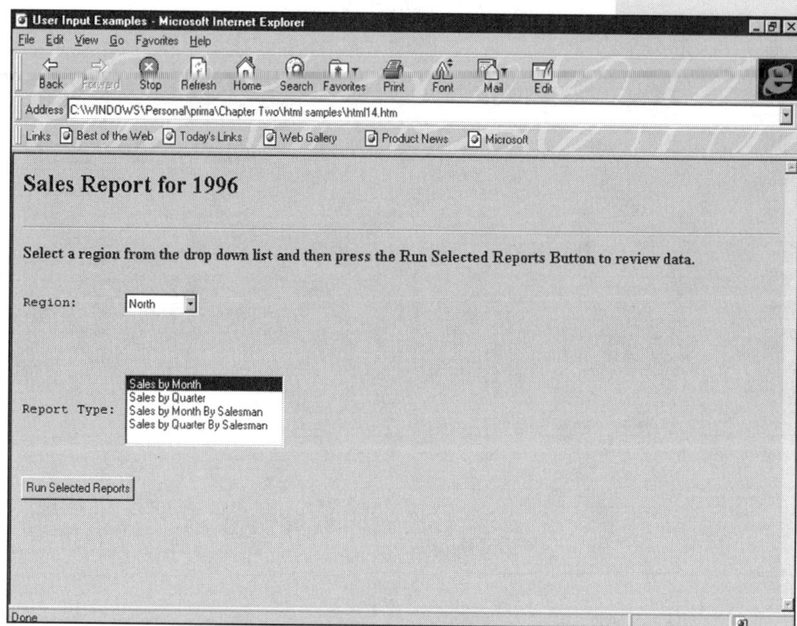

Figure 2.18 Lists and drop-down lists make for an effective way to control user input by presenting only valid choices.

The list box in Figure 2.18 supports multiple selected items. The following code line provides this capability:

```
<SELECT Name = "Report Type" Multiple Size="5">
```

If only one item should be selected, the `Multiple` attribute would be removed, as follows:

```
<SELECT Name = "Report Type" Size="5">
```

The `Size` attribute specifies the number of items that are visible at a time.

Option Button Control

Like drop-down lists and list box controls, the *option button control* provides a list of predefined choices, of which only one can be chosen at a time. When a choice is made in an option button group, whatever was previously selected immediately becomes deselected in favor of the new choice. The following code slightly modifies the example illustrated in Figure 2.18:

```
<HTML>
<HEAD>
<TITLE>User Input Examples</TITLE>
```

```
<H2>Sales Report for 1996</H2>
<HR>
</HEAD>
<BODY>
<H4>Select a region from the drop-down list and then press the
Run Selected Report Button to review data.</H4>
<FORM method="" ACTION="">
<PRE>
Region:  <SELECT NAME="REGION">
         <OPTION>North
         <OPTION>South
         <OPTION>East
         <OPTION>West
         </SELECT>

Report Selection: <INPUT TYPE="radio" NAME="reports"
Value ="Sales by Month" CHECKED>Sales by Month
             <INPUT TYPE="radio" NAME="reports"
Value = "Sales by Quarter">Sales by Quarter
             <INPUT TYPE="radio" NAME="reports"
Value = "Sales by Month By Salesman">Sales by Month By Salesman
             <INPUT TYPE="radio" NAME="reports"
Value = "Sales by Quarter By Salesman">Sales by Quarter By Salesman

<INPUT TYPE="submit" VALUE="Run Selected Report">
</PRE>
</FORM>
</BODY>
</HTML>
```

Figure 2.19 shows the modified page.

Memo Editor Control

There are times when freeform text needs to be captured. The tool for this job is the *memo editor control.* The memo editor control can often be found in guestbook Web pages. Many sites have a page dedicated for visitors to leave comments so the site can be improved. The following code creates a sample guestbook page that uses the memo editor control:

```
<HTML>
<HEAD>
<TITLE>User Input Examples</TITLE>
<H2>Guest Book</H2>
<H4>What do you think of our Web site? Please provide your comments.</H4>
<HR>
</HEAD>
<BODY>
```

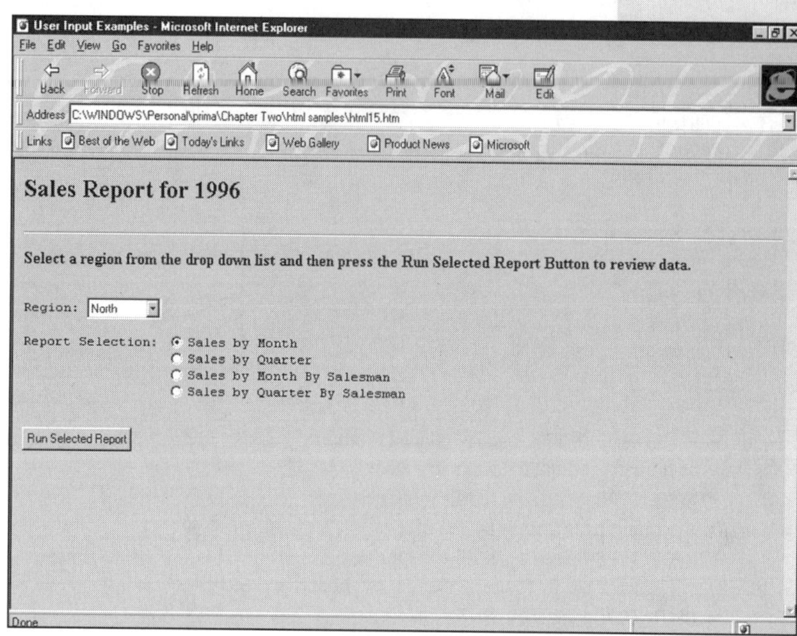

Figure 2.19 By including the CHECKED attribute, a default choice is specified. In this example, the Sales by Month report is the default.

```
<FORM method="" ACTION="">
<PRE>
E-mail Address: <INPUT NAME="email" SIZE=40 MAXLENGTH=40 VALUE = "">

Rating:  <INPUT TYPE="radio" NAME="rating" VALUE=5 CHECKED> Excellent
         <INPUT TYPE="radio" NAME="rating" VALUE=4 > Very Good
         <INPUT TYPE="radio" NAME="rating" VALUE=3 > Good
         <INPUT TYPE="radio" NAME="rating" VALUE=2 > Fair
         <INPUT TYPE="radio" NAME="rating" VALUE=1 > Poor

General Comments

<TEXTAREA NAME="comments" ROWS="5" COLS="80"></TEXTAREA>

<INPUT TYPE="submit" VALUE="Submit Comments"> <INPUT TYPE="reset"
VALUE="Reset">
</PRE>
</FORM>
</BODY>
</HTML>
```

Figure 2.20 shows the memo editor control in the Web page.

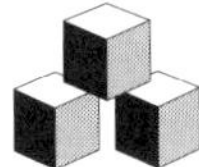

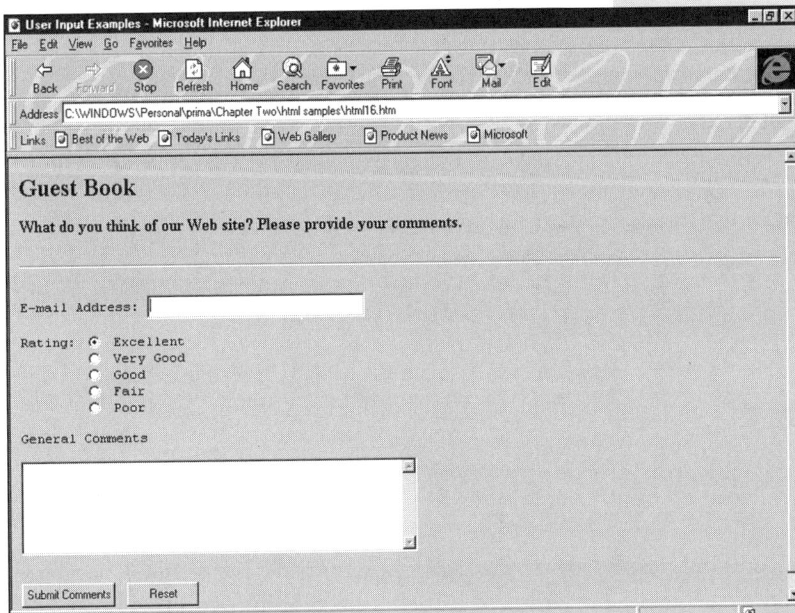

Figure 2.20
By using the ROWS and COLS attributes, the dimensions of the memo editor control can be specified.

Check Box Control

The final user-input control that will be discussed is the *check box control.* This control is used to capture one of two values—Yes or No. The following code extends the guestbook example to include a check box control:

```
<HTML>
<HEAD>
<TITLE>User Input Examples</TITLE>
<H2>Guest Book</H2>
<H4>What do you think of our Web site? Please provide your comments.</H4>
<HR>
</HEAD>
<BODY>
<FORM method="" ACTION="">
<PRE>
E-mail Address: <INPUT NAME="email" SIZE=40 MAXLENGTH=40 VALUE = "">
```

```
Rating:  <INPUT TYPE="radio" NAME="rating" VALUE=5 CHECKED> Excellent
         <INPUT TYPE="radio" NAME="rating" VALUE=4 > Very Good
         <INPUT TYPE="radio" NAME="rating" VALUE=3 > Good
         <INPUT TYPE="radio" NAME="rating" VALUE=2 > Fair
         <INPUT TYPE="radio" NAME="rating" VALUE=1 > Poor

General Comments

<TEXTAREA NAME="comments" ROWS="4" COLS="80"></TEXTAREA>

<INPUT TYPE="checkbox" NAME="update" VALUE="receive_updates" CHECKED>
Do you wish to receive notification when site is updated?

<INPUT TYPE="submit" VALUE="Submit Comments"> <INPUT TYPE="reset"
VALUE="Reset">
</PRE>
</FORM>
</BODY>
</HTML>
```

Like the option button control, the check box control has a CHECKED attribute. This allows the check box initially to be checked automatically. Figure 2.21 shows the modified guestbook example.

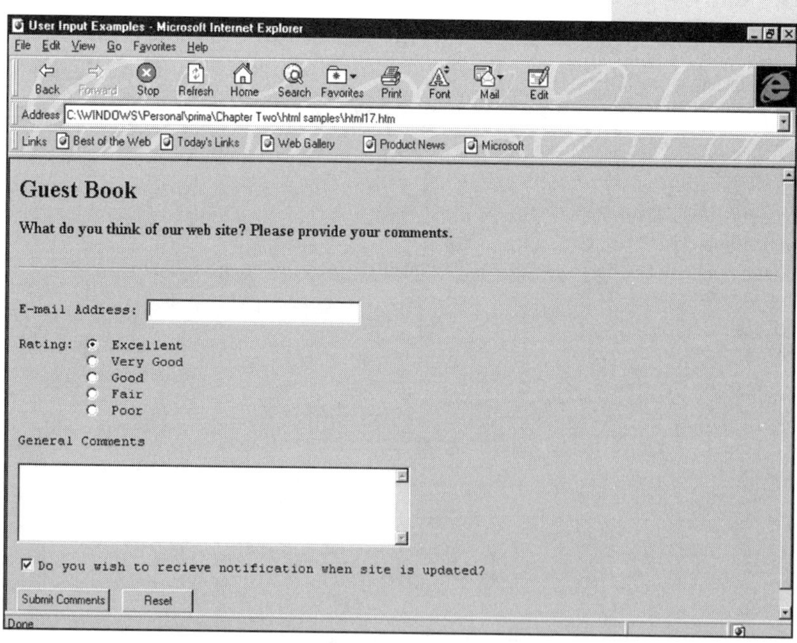

Figure 2.21 Check box controls can be prechecked with the use of the CHECKED attribute.

A Final Word on User-Input Controls

Like anything in the world of programming, there's always more than one way to accomplish the same task in HTML. You may be faced with the question, "Do I use the drop-down list, the list box, or the option group control?" The answer is, "It depends!" All the controls might do an equally adequate job. Whatever your choice, be sure to use the controls in a consistent manner. One of the most irritating things is an inconsistent interface, which often leads to frustrated and unhappy users. In other words, you may not get nice comments in your guestbook!

Frames

One of the most popular features found in Web pages today is the use of *frames*. Frames are nothing more than a means of splitting up the viewing area of the browser into sections. Frames can actually be thought of as a Web page within a Web page. Up to this point, all the samples have used the entire viewing area of the browser. Now, however, the viewing area will be partitioned to make better use of the space.

The typical application of frames involves one frame that acts as a table of contents for the site. Clicking a hyperlink in the table of contents frame causes another frame in the browser to point to the URL referenced in the hyperlink. When this happens, the table of contents frame remains undisturbed while the other frame's content changes. This makes the process of navigating within a site much easier.

Figure 2.22 demonstrates how the Visual Basic Web Site at Microsoft uses frames to make navigation as easy as possible.

Frame-based pages consist of two basic parts:

- **Master page.** This is the page that specifies how the frames are to be displayed in the Web browser. This page makes use of the HTML tags required to display frames. The following paragraphs discuss these tags in detail.
- **Source pages.** As previously discussed, frames are like Web pages within a Web page. As such, frames display HTML content—just like a Web page does. The content of a frame is stored in a separate document. It's the master page that defines how the different pages are displayed.

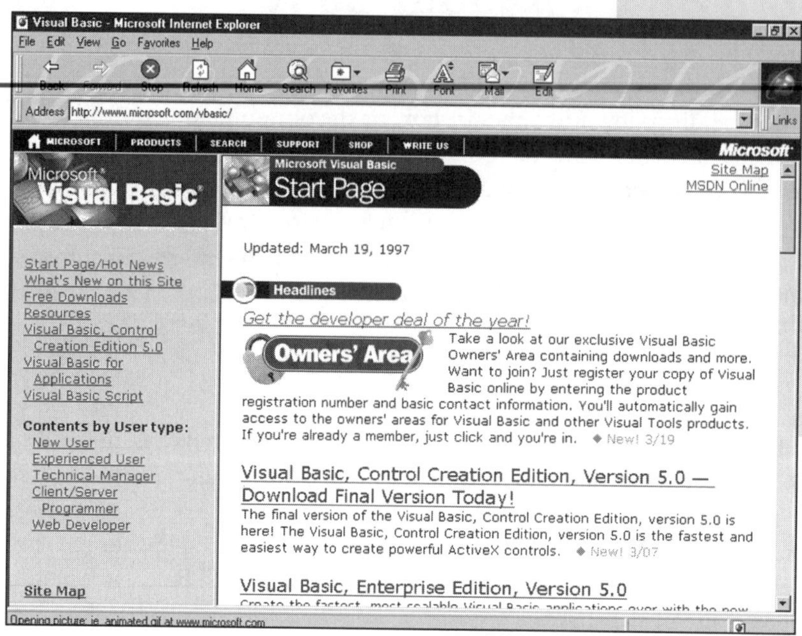

Figure 2.22 The Visual Basic Web site uses two frames. The left frame acts as a table of contents and site map. The right frame holds the contents of the URL specified by the selected hyperlink in the left frame.

Just like everything else in the HTML language, the ability to use frames is predicated on the use of specific HTML tags. The following table describes the relevant tags:

Tag	Description
<FRAMESET>	Specifies how the master page is to be split into its frame components.
<FRAME>	Defines the source document for a specific frame.
<NOFRAMES>	Specifies content that will be used for browsers that don't support the use of frames.
<BASE TARGET>	Specifies the frame that is to change based on the selected URL. For example, selecting a hyperlink in the table of contents frame causes the frame specified by the <BASE TARGET> tag to jump to the URL that the hyperlink references.

The following code sets up a master page:

```
<HTML>
<HEAD>
```

```
<TITLE>Master Frame Page</TITLE>
</HEAD>
<FRAMESET ROWS="15%,85%">
<FRAME SRC="banner.htm" NAME="banner" MARGINWIDTH="1" MARGINHEIGHT="1">
<FRAMESET COLS="35%,65%">
<FRAME SRC="sitemap.htm" NAME="sitemap" MARGINWIDTH="1" MARGINHEIGHT="1">
<FRAME SRC="main.htm" NAME="main" MARGINWIDTH="1" MARGINHEIGHT="1">
</FRAMESET>
<NOFRAMES>
<HEAD>
<TITLE>No frames version of the master page</TITLE>
<H2>This is the No Frames Version of the Master Page.</H2>
<HR>
</HEAD>
<BODY>
<H3>Table of Contents</H3>
<P><A HREF="company.htm">Company History</A></P>
<P><A HREF="product.htm">Product Line</A></P>
<P><A HREF="contact.htm">Company Contact Information</A></P>
</BODY>
</NOFRAMES>
</FRAMESET>
</HTML>
```

Figure 2.23 shows the Web page.

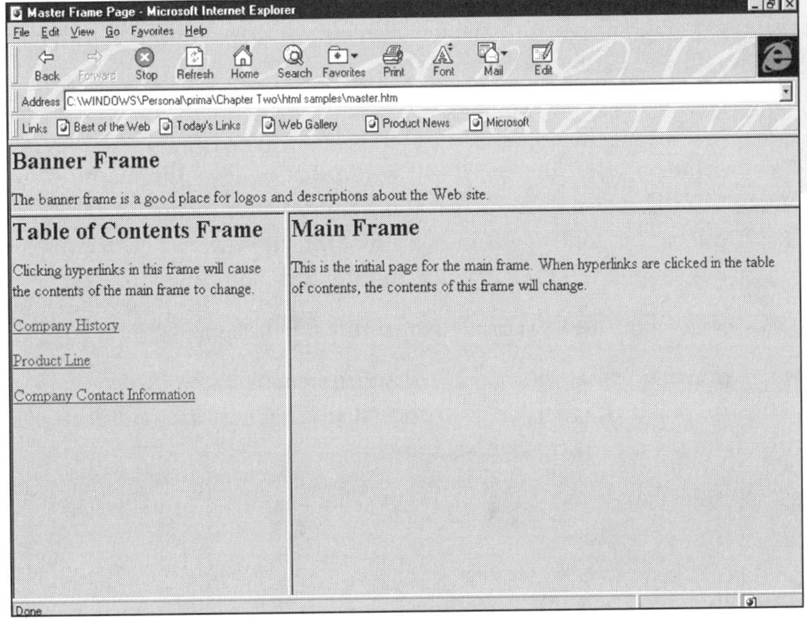

Figure 2.23 With the use of a few HTML tags, frame-based pages are very simple to put together.

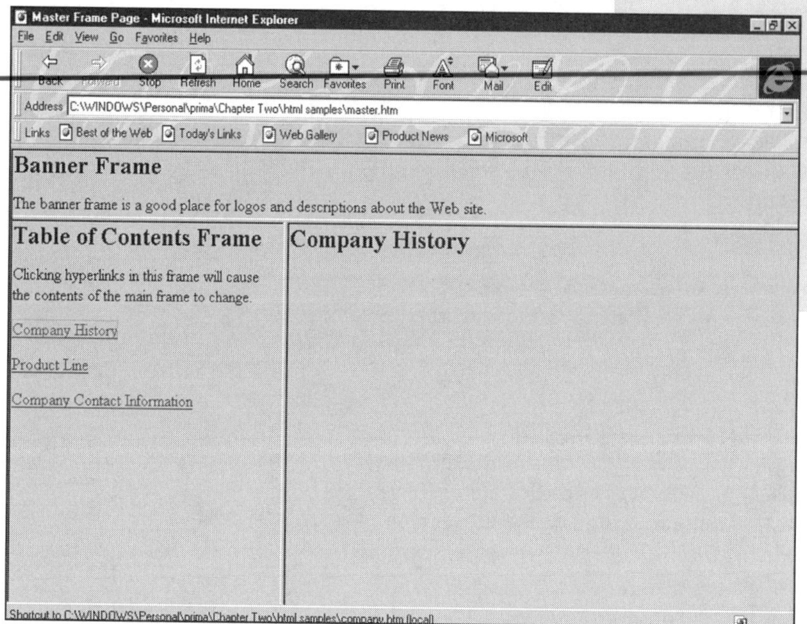

Figure 2.24 When making selections in the table of contents frame, the contents of the main frame will change to reflect the URL of the selected hyperlink.

ANALYSIS

Upon initial display, the main frame has an assigned page of `main.htm`. When the company history hyperlink is selected, the contents of the main frame will display the contents of `company.htm`. Figure 2.24 illustrates the new look.

The following paragraphs outline the key portions of this example. Each code line is followed by a description.

```
<FRAMESET ROWS="15%,85%">
```

The `ROWS` attribute in this line specifies the number of rows the master page will contain and the percentage of the available area that each row will consume. Here, the banner frame consumes 15% of the viewing area. The remaining row space is assigned to the table of contents and main frames.

```
<FRAME SRC="banner.htm" NAME="banner" MARGINWIDTH="1" MARGINHEGHT="1">
```

The `SRC` attribute specifies which HTML document is to be displayed in a frame. Because this is the first block of code that references a frame, it relates to the first frame, which is the banner frame.

```
<FRAMESET COLS="35%,65%">
```

Just as row proportions can be assigned, so can column proportions. In this example, the table of contents consumes 35% of the column area underneath the banner and the main frame consumes the remaining 65%.

```
<FRAME SRC="sitemap.htm" NAME="sitemap" MARGINWIDTH="1" MARGINHEIGHT="1">
<FRAME SRC="main.htm" NAME="main" MARGINWIDTH="1" MARGINHEIGHT="1">
```

Just as the banner is assigned a source page, so are the table of contents and main frames.

```
<NOFRAMES>
```

What appears between the `<NOFRAMES>` and `</NOFRAMES>` tags designates what is presented in the Web browser if the browser does not support frames. It's important to have code to account for such instances, as you can never count on a visitor to your site having a browser with specific features. In addition, some browsers can turn off frame support at will; this is another reason why having a no-frames option is important. Figure 2.25 illustrates what the page would look like if a browser didn't support frames.

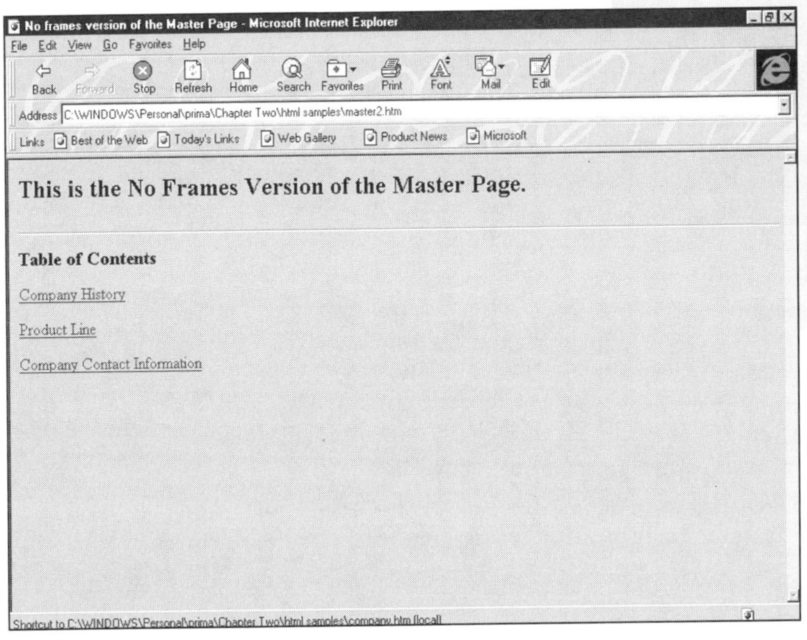

Figure 2.25 While this version of the master Web page doesn't look as nice as the frames version, it has all of the functionality of the frames version.

The fundamental question at this point is, "How does the browser know to direct the output to the main frame?" The following code block, which is the source of the table of contents frame, should answer the question:

```
<HTML>
<HEAD>
<TITLE>Table of Contents Page</TITLE>
<BASE TARGET = "main">
</HEAD>
<H2>Table of Contents Frame</H2>
Clicking hyperlinks in this frame will cause the contents of the main frame
to change.
<P><A HREF="company.htm">Company History</A></P>
<P><A HREF="product.htm">Product Line</A></P>
<P><A HREF="contact.htm">Company Contact Information</A></P>
</BODY>
</HTML>
```

The `SITEMAP.HTM` file uses the `<BASE TARGET>` tag, which was defined earlier. Its functionality is simple: Any hyperlinks selected in this page are to be directed to the main frame. The source code for the remaining source HTML documents is as follows:

BANNER.HTM

```
<HTML>
<HEAD>
<TITLE>Banner Page</title>
</HEAD>
<H2>Banner Frame</H2>
The banner frame is a good place for logos and descriptions about
the Web site.
</BODY>
</HTML>
```

MAIN.HTM

```
<HTML>
<HEAD>
<TITLE>Initial Page for Main Frame</TITLE>
</HEAD>
<H2>Main Frame</H2>
This is the initial page for the main frame. When hyperlinks are clicked
in the table of contents, the contents of this frame will change.
</HTML>
```

COMPANY.HTM

```
<HTML>
<HEAD>
<TITLE>Company History Page</TITLE>
```

```
</HEAD>
<H2>Company History</H2>
</BODY>
</HTML>
```

PRODUCT.HTM

```
<HTML>
<HEAD>
<TITLE>Product Line Page</title>
</HEAD>
<H2>Product Line</H2>
</BODY>
</HTML>
```

CONTACT.HTM

```
<HTML>
<HEAD>
<TITLE>Company Contacts Page</TITLE>
</head>
<H2>Company Contacts</H2>
</BODY>
</HTML>
```

Summary

The goal of this chapter has been to provide you with an overview of the basic elements of HTML. As this chapter has illustrated, HTML is a bona fide programming language that's both powerful and rich in features. While much can be accomplished with a simple editor like Notepad, you'll find that the use of graphic editors such as Microsoft FrontPage 98 will make the task of creating HTML documents very simple. Even word processing programs such as Microsoft Word have the ability to produce HTML code. The main advantage to these graphical editors is that people don't need to remember all the individual codes discussed in this chapter. Although the graphical editors are nice, it's still a good idea to have an understanding of the code that the editors produce.

In the next chapter, you learn how to combine HTML with VBScript to validate user input.

A VBScript Primer

Chapter 2 introduced you to the hypertext markup language (HTML). In that chapter, your HTML documents consisted of static text and graphic files. You also learned how to place common form controls such as text boxes, command buttons, and check boxes in your documents. Just as these controls are housed in data-entry forms in Visual Basic, these controls can be housed in form definitions embedded in an HTML document. Also, just as input is validated in a data-entry form, input can be validated in an HTML form.

The ability to validate user input is facilitated by embedding scripts into HTML documents. While text is simply displayed in the Web browser, scripts are lines of code that are compiled and executed on-the-fly. The two most common Web scripting languages today are VBScript and JavaScript. Adding scripting to HTML documents adds powerful capabilities, along with a new set of issues. This chapter is dedicated to providing you with the information you need to implement scripting successfully in your HTML documents.

Although HTML coding doesn't require a background in programming, scripting languages such as VBScript are bona fide programming languages, complete with facilities for variable declaration, parameter passing, if-then and looping constructs, as well as function calls. This chapter assumes that you have programmed in at least one language and are familiar with these concepts.

This chapter focuses on the following areas:

- What scripting is
- How scripting is integrated into HTML documents
- Validating input with VBScript
- Client-side versus server-side scripting

Before continuing, it's important to note that this chapter isn't meant to be an exhaustive study or a complete tutorial on the VBScript language. There are many fine books devoted to the subject of VBScript. Two such books are *VBScript Master's Handbook* by Christopher J. Goddard and Mark White (Prima Publishing, ISBN 0-7615-0769-8) and *VBScript Web Page Interactivity* by William J. Orvis (Prima Publishing, ISBN 0-7615-0684-5). In addition, a variety of resources can be freely downloaded from the Microsoft Web site. The URL for these downloadable documents is mentioned a bit later in this chapter.

Instead, this chapter provides the basics of embedding scripts into your Web pages. Some experience in Visual Basic or Visual Basic for Applications is assumed; not every line of programming code will be explained.

What Is Scripting? An Introduction to VBScript

Scripting is simply the act of embedding code into an HTML document that will eventually be compiled and executed by either the client or the server. When the Web browser does the work of compiling and executing, *client-side scripting* is occurring. When the Web server does the job of compiling and executing, this is known as *server-side scripting*. Microsoft's implementation of server-side scripting uses a product called *Active Server Pages (ASP)*. The specifics of server-side scripting are discussed toward the end of the chapter. This introduction to scripting and VBScript is in the context of the client.

VBScript is the newest member of the Visual Basic family of programming products from Microsoft. Like Visual Basic for Applications (VBA), VBScript is also a subset of the Visual Basic (VB) programming language. In fact, if you're familiar with either VB or VBA, you already know the VBScript syntax. The only thing standing between you and programming with VBScript is understanding how VBScript is embedded into an HTML document.

It's important to understand how VBScript and HTML documents work together because some of the exercises later in this book make use of VBScript. This chapter equips you with a basic understanding of VBScript that will

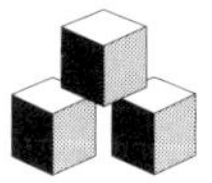

enable you to build the Web pages that serve as the user interface for the CustomerTracker application, for example.

How Scripting Is Integrated into HTML Documents

Like everything else associated with HTML, the first step in understanding how something is implemented lies in learning new HTML tags. Embedding scripts into an HTML document is no exception. Consider the following HTML code:

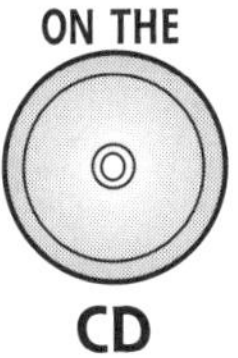


```
<HTML>
<HEAD>
<TITLE>A sample script</TITLE>
<SCRIPT LANGUAGE="VBScript">
<!-
Sub Button1_OnClick
    MsgBox "This VBScript made a call to MsgBox.",48
End Sub
->
</SCRIPT>
</HEAD>
<BODY>
<H3>A sample script</H3>
<FORM><INPUT NAME="Button1" TYPE="button" VALUE="Execute VBScript">
</FORM>
</BODY>
</HTML>
```

Chapter 2 introduced you to many HTML tags. This code listing contains just one new tag: `<SCRIPT>` both identifies the scripting language that will be used and wraps the various blocks of script procedures. By default, Internet Explorer (IE) assumes that the scripting language is JavaScript. For IE to recognize VBScript, the script language must be explicitly identified as VBScript (or just VBS). The line could appear this way:

```
<SCRIPT LANGUAGE="VBS">
```

Like other tags, the `<SCRIPT>` tag has an ending tag: `</SCRIPT>`. In addition to the `<SCRIPT>` tag, the comment tags `<!-` and `->` introduced in Chapter 2 are also used in this example. For those browsers that don't support scripting, script code would be displayed in the browser window if the comment tags weren't used.

Figure 3.1 illustrates how the HTML document looks in the Web browser.

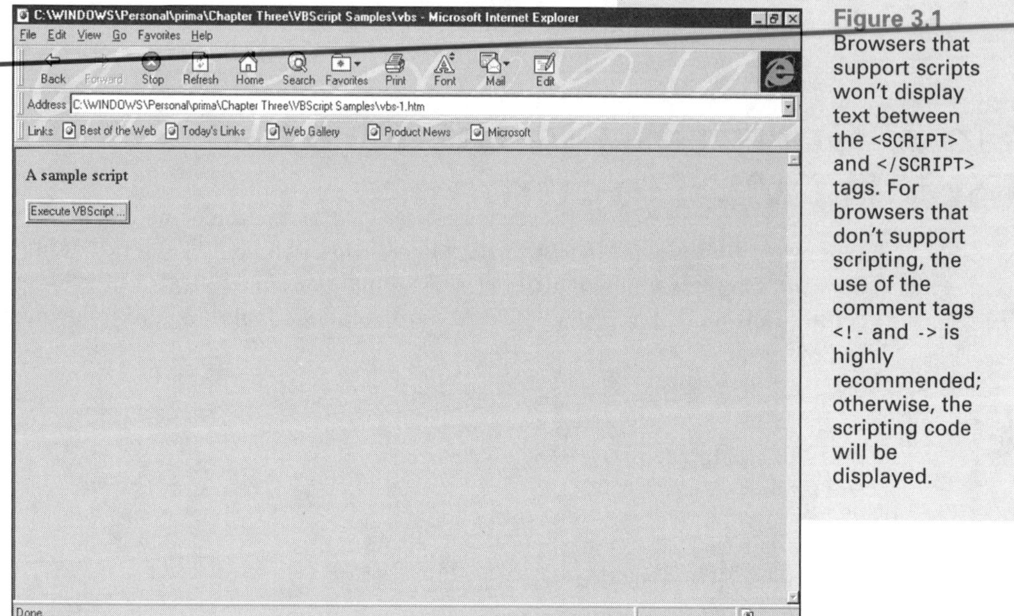

Figure 3.1
Browsers that support scripts won't display text between the `<SCRIPT>` and `</SCRIPT>` tags. For browsers that don't support scripting, the use of the comment tags `<!-` and `->` is highly recommended; otherwise, the scripting code will be displayed.

When the button is pressed, the standard Windows `messagebox` function is called. Figure 3.2 shows the new script code in action.

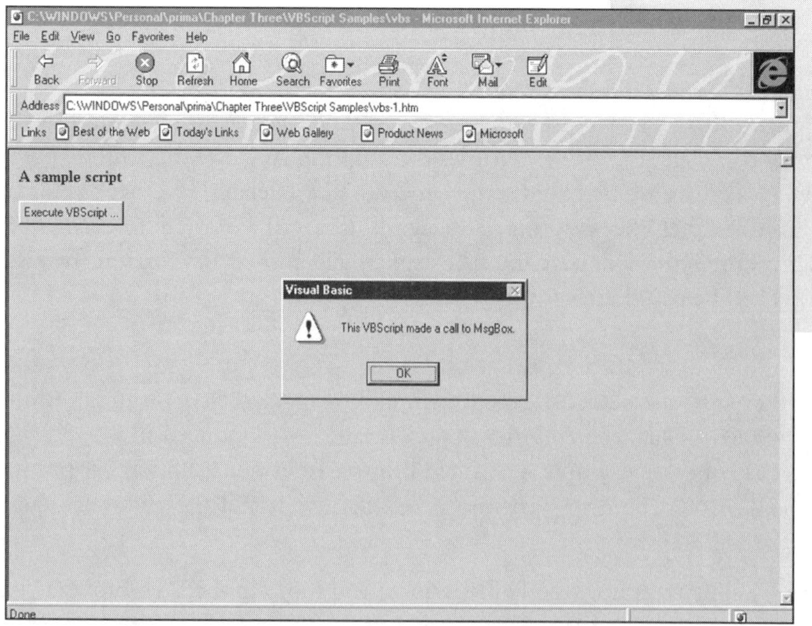

Figure 3.2
The standard Windows `messagebox` function can be called in an HTML document in the same manner as in a Visual Basic application.

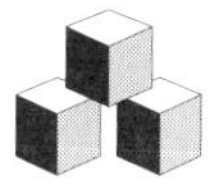

How Scripts and Objects Are Linked—Part I

When the command button in the preceding example is clicked, the standard Windows message box dialog appears. The question is, how are the script and the command button object linked? The key lies in knowing the object's name. In the first example, the name of the command button is `Button1`. The name of the script procedure is `Button1_OnClick()`. Because the name of the procedure begins with the name of the object, they're linked. Thus, when the `Button1` command button's `OnClick()` event fires, the `OnClick()` method code associated with `Button1` will execute. If the procedure is renamed to just `cmd_OnClick()`, nothing will happen when `Button1` is clicked. Why? Because no procedure named `Button1_OnClick()` exists. Thus, while the `OnClick()` event will fire, there is no method code to execute.

The Role of Forms in Scripting

As mentioned in the preceding section, the key to linking objects and scripts lies in knowing the names of objects. The name of an object can be thought of as a handle or an address to the object. Once this handle is known, various properties and methods of the object become available.

Another key to accessing objects embedded on a Web page through scripting lies in understanding the object hierarchy. Chapter 2 introduced the concept of HTML forms, which are created in HTML through the use of the `<FORM>` tag. Forms as they exist in HTML are basically the same as forms in Visual Basic. Each has the ability to contain one or more objects with which a user will interact.

A typical Visual Basic application is composed of several forms. Each form is devoted to a specific task. Instead of creating one big monolithic form that would be cluttered and confusing, several forms are created to make for a more user-friendly and intuitive application. The same concept holds true for HTML documents. A single HTML document may contain several form definitions, each serving a specific purpose.

While forms aid in a more user-friendly interface, they also facilitate the communication with objects. For example, assume in the first example that after the user pressed the command button and the message box was displayed, you wanted the button to have its caption reworded to read `You just clicked me!!`. The revised HTML code illustrates how to achieve this behavior:

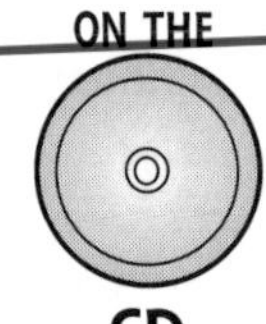

```
<HTML>
<HEAD>
<TITLE>A sample script</TITLE>
<SCRIPT LANGUAGE="VBScript">
<!-
Sub cmdTest_OnClick
    MsgBox "This VBScript made a call to MsgBox.",48
    frmSample.cmdTest.Value = "You just clicked me!!"
End Sub
->
</SCRIPT>
</HEAD>
<BODY>
<H3>A sample script</H3>
<FORM NAME="frmSample">
<INPUT NAME="cmdTest" TYPE="button" VALUE="Execute VBScript ...">
</FORM>
</BODY>
</HTML>
```

Notice that the form has been named `frmSample`. In the `OnClick()` method, the button's `Value` property is accessed by first referencing the form. You must traverse the object hierarchy properly to gain the ability to access the properties and methods of an object. In the case of VBScript, you must know the name of the form in which the object resides. Because names are so important, it's a good idea to adopt a naming convention when naming your objects. This topic is discussed in detail a bit further on in this chapter.

How Much Alike Are VBScript, VBA, and VB?

Consider Figure 3.3, which illustrates a simple Visual Basic form and an Excel worksheet that mimics the HTML document in Figure 3.1. This is the code attached to the `Click()` event of the command button in the VB form:

```
Private Sub Command1_Click()
    MsgBox "This VB Code made a call to MsgBox.", 48
End Sub
```

This is the VBA code attached to the command button in the Excel worksheet:

```
Sub Button1_Click()
    MsgBox "This VBA Code made a call to MsgBox.", 48
End Sub
```

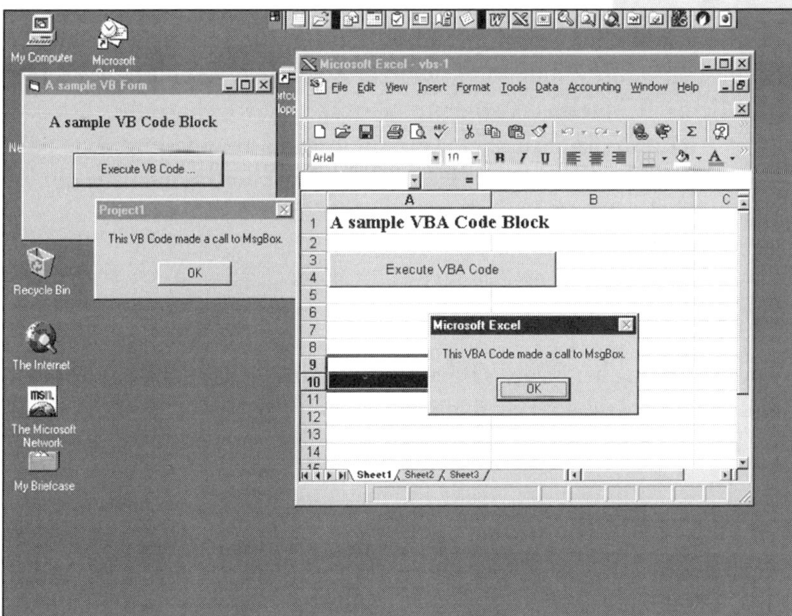

Figure 3.3
With a few exceptions, VBScript is almost identical to VB and VBA.

While not used in the VBScript version of the `Sub` declaration, VBScript subroutines can be declared public or private, just as they can be declared in VBA or VB. The one notable difference is in the name of the event. In VB and VBA, the event fired when a command button is pressed is called `Click()`. In VBScript, the event is called `OnClick()`. In all cases, the name of the object prefaces the call. In VB, the name of the sub is `Button1_Click()`. In VBScript, the name of the sub is `Button1_OnClick()`. In addition, the `LostFocus()` event in VB and VBA is called `OnBlur()` in VBScript. Finally, while different datatypes can be declared in VB and VBA, only one datatype exists in VBScript—`Variant`.

For the most part, VBScript is very much like VB and VBA. The language structure, in terms of procedure and variable declaration, looping constructs, and syntax, is essentially identical. The biggest difference lies in the names of various elements. There are elements found in VBA that don't exist in VBScript, and conversely, there are elements in VBScript that aren't found in VBA. Complete documentation of VBScript and a useful tutorial can be found at the following URL:

`http://www.microsoft.com/VBScript/us/download/vbsdoc.exe`

A Word about Netscape Navigator

For all of the power that scripting with VBScript offers, there's one major drawback in that there's only one Web browser that supports VBScript natively—Microsoft Internet Explorer. Netscape Navigator only supports JavaScript as a scripting language. However, a third-party plug-in can be purchased from Ncompass that gives the Netscape Navigator browser the ability to make use of both VBScript and ActiveX controls.

Programming Guidelines

Like any programming language, VBScript has a published set of guidelines for coding and naming variables. These guidelines are basically the same as those for both VB and VBA.

Script Placement

Regarding script placement, scripts can reside anywhere in the HTML document. However, following this practice would make for a very disorganized document. A common practice is to place all required scripts in the head section of the document. Just as variables are declared at the beginning of a program, it's a good idea to declare all procedures at the beginning of an HTML document. By grouping the procedures together at the top of the document, a developer can immediately see at a glance all of the associated procedures.

Comments

Additionally, it's recommended that comments be used liberally. Consider the following HTML document (found in the file `comroutine.htm` on the CD):

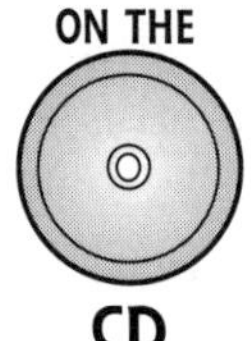


```
<HTML>
<HEAD>
<TITLE>Implementing common routines</TITLE>
<SCRIPT LANGUAGE="VBScript">
<!-

Option Explicit

Sub MyMsgBox(tcMsg,tcType,tcButtons)
     ' This is a custom message box function
     ' that is called by other subs in this document
     ' Parameters: tcMsg - This is the message string
     ' that will be displayed in the msgbox
     ' tcType - Depending on whether the user passes
     ' an exclamation mark or a question mark, the appropriate icon
```

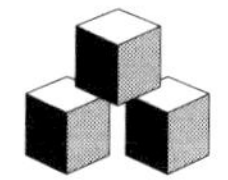


```
    ' will be displayed.
    ' tcButtons - Depending on what is passed, different buttons
    ' will appear in the msgbox dialog. For example
    ' passing "ARI" will make the Abort, Retry, Ignore buttons appear

    Dim lnType,lnButtons
    lnType = 0
    lnButtons = 0
    Select Case tcType
        Case "?"
            lnType = 32
        Case "!"
            lnType = 48
        Case Else
            lnType = 16
    End Select

    Select Case tcButtons
        Case "OC"
            lnButtons = 1
        Case "ARI"
            lnButtons = 2
        Case "RC"
            lnButtons = 5
        Case "YN"
            lnButtons = 4
        Case "YNC"
            lnButtons = 3
        Case Else
            lnButtons = 0
    End Select

    MsgBox tcMsg,lnType+lnButtons
End Sub

Sub Button1_OnClick
    MyMsgBox "This VBScript made a call to MsgBox.","?","ARI"
End Sub
->
</SCRIPT>

</HEAD>
<BODY>
<H3>A sample script</H3>
<FORM>
<INPUT NAME="Button1" TYPE="button" VALUE="Execute VBScript ...">
</FORM>
</BODY>
</HTML>
```

In this HTML document, a common routine has been created called MyMsgBox. Its intent is to relieve the programmer from having to remember all of the bit settings for the MsgBox function. Implementing reusable, common routines helps to streamline code. The less code is duplicated, the easier it is to maintain. By adding comments such as those shown at the beginning of the MyMsgBox function, a programmer immediately knows some important facts, such as what purpose the routine serves and the types of arguments the procedure accepts. Figure 3.4 shows how the results of executing the script have changed.

Variable and Object Naming

Of course, a discussion on good programming practice can't ignore the subject of naming conventions. The VB language already has a published naming convention for objects and variables; the same convention can be used with VBScript. Regardless of the convention you use, the key is to be consistent. The consistent use of a standard naming convention will greatly improve the readability of your code. Typically, the name of a variable or an object will have a standard prefix followed by a description of the variable's or object's contents. Tables 3-1 and 3-2 document a suggested standard to follow.

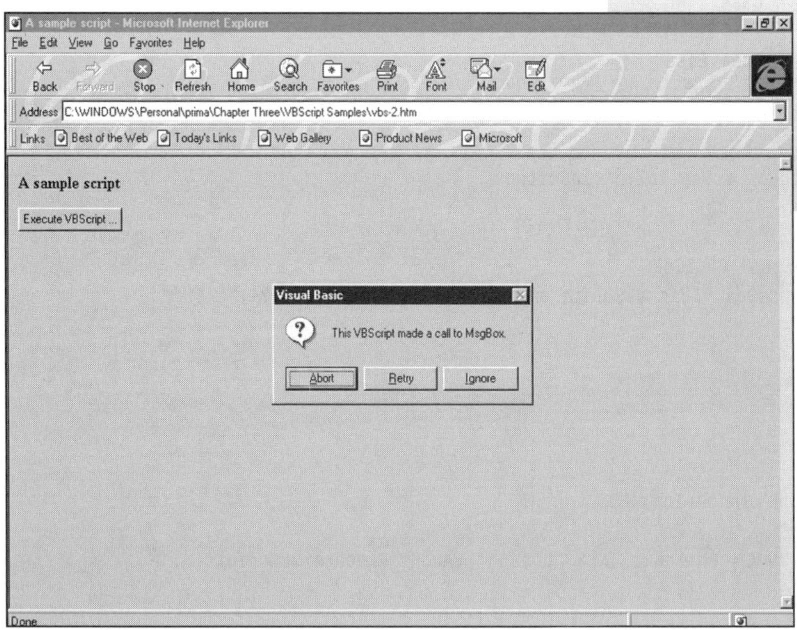

Figure 3.4 By implementing common routines, script code can be greatly streamlined.

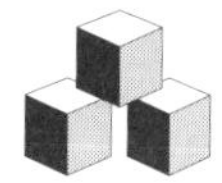

Table 3-1 Naming Convention Guideline for Variables

Data Type	Prefix
Boolean	bln
Byte	byt
Integer	int
Long	lng
Single	sng
Double	dbl
Date	dtm
String	str
Object	obj
Error	err

Table 3-2 Naming Convention Guideline for Objects

Object Type	Prefix
Form	frm
Command button	cmd
Check box	chk
Combo box	cbo
Option button	opt
Text box	txt
Text area	txa

The Option Explicit Statement

Among its many rich features, VB has one useful feature particularly—the `Option Explicit` statement. In the full VB programming language, this feature is set at the project level. With VBScript, this setting is made at the beginning of your script. When the `Option Explicit` statement is used, all variables must be explicitly declared with the `Dim` statement. If this statement isn't used, variables can be declared on-the-fly—which can lead to very unstructured code. Figure 3.5 illustrates the error message presented to the user when the

`Option Explicit` statement is used and a variable hasn't been declared properly before it has been used. Of course, you'll never want your users to be presented with an error message like this. Rather, you'll want to develop an error handler to deal with errors. The subject of error handling is covered in the next section.

Error Trapping

When working with any programming language to develop applications, errors are bound to occur. Whether the error occurs because of syntax, a variable not defined, or a missing file, one thing is constant—it must be handled. Programming with VBScript is no exception. Although the applications developed are different from those traditionally developed in other tools, such as VB, the same type of errors can occur. Fortunately, just like VBA and VB, VBScript has the capacity to trap errors and deal with them appropriately.

Like some other languages, VBScript has a default error handler. The default error handler for VBScript was shown in the preceding section (refer to Figure 3.5). As mentioned earlier, this error occurred because a variable was not defined before referencing the variable in a line of code. Because the `Option Explicit` statement was used, the error was generated. The default dialog displays information such as the line number and the line of code on which the

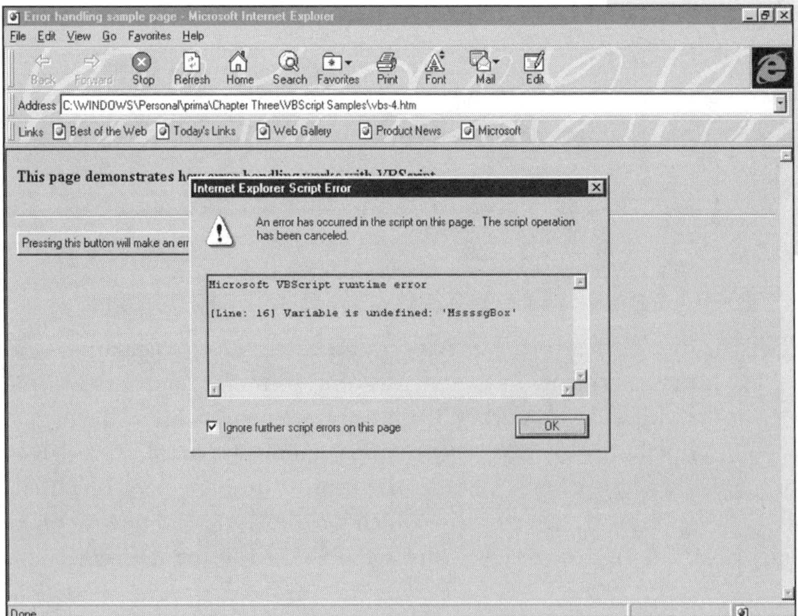

Figure 3.5 This figure illustrates the default VBScript error handler reporting an error to the user.

EXERCISE

error occurred. While this information may be helpful to the programmer who developed the page, it can be confusing for a user who is attempting to view and interact with the page in his or her Web browser. The user needs to know what went wrong so that the error can be reported, but the information needs to be presented in a better manner. What's needed is some mechanism for trapping the error and either attempting to recover from the error or presenting a dialog to the user that explains that an error has occurred and whom to contact to get the code repaired.

There are three basic steps in trapping and dealing with errors in VBScript. First, VBScript must be told not to invoke its default handler when an error occurs. This is accomplished by issuing the following line of code:

```
On Error Resume Next
```

This code causes the next line of code to execute when an error is encountered, bypassing the default error dialog produced by VBScript. This code should be placed at the beginning of each subroutine in which you want to use inline error trapping. This type of error trapping is called *inline* because the error trapping occurs in the lines of program code. This method is the converse of a *global error handler*, which is established once, and any subroutine can invoke the error handler specified by the global handler.

The next step involves checking the `Number` property of the `Err` object to determine whether an error occurs. The `Err` object is a global object that has several properties that are updated when an error occurs. Typically, code is identified in which an error can occur and an `If...End If` code block is placed directly after a line of code that may cause an error. Here's an example:

```
If Err.Number <> 0 Then

   'Invoke some code to inform the user what has happened.

   Exit Sub
End If
```

VBScript doesn't have global error-handling capability. All error trapping must be done on an inline basis.

In this case, if the `Number` property of the `Err` object is not equal to zero, an error of some sort has occurred. When this scenario occurs, a choice must be made. As the developer, you have the choice of writing error-handling code in

the same block of code that was used to test for the existence of an error, or creating a common error-handling routine that will be called in various locations to deal with errors as they occur. The latter of these two choices is a far better design, because your code will be more streamlined and more maintainable. This leads to the third step in dealing with errors—creating your common error-handling routine. The following code block illustrates a sample error-handling routine:

```
Sub Error_Handler

Dim strMsg
strMsg = "The following error has occurred: " & Err.Description & "."
strMsg = strMsg + Chr(10) + Chr(13)+"The error was caused by: "
    & Err.Source & "."
strMsg = strMsg + Chr(10) + Chr(13) +
    "Please call the systems support at 555-1212 to "
strMsg = strMsg + "report this error."
MsgBox strMsg,16,"An error has occurred"

Err.Clear
End Sub
```

This error-handling routine simply displays the standard Windows `MsgBox` dialog with information about the error and a point of contact for reporting the error. The information about the error is obtained by referring to two other properties of the `Err` object, `Description` and `Source`. The `Description` property contains the description of the error that occurred. The `Source` property specifies the name of the object or application that generated the error.

Having completed the specifics of trapping errors and a discussion of what the `Err` object is, it's time to put it all together. The following HTML code (found in the file `vbs-4a.htm` on the CD) illustrates how error handling is incorporated into a script:

```
<HTML>
<HEAD>
<TITLE>Error handling sample page</TITLE>
<SCRIPT LANGUAGE="VBScript">
<!-
' Force all variables to be defined with Dim Statement

Option Explicit

Sub cmdError_OnClick
        'Here, we will set up our error handler
    On Error Resume Next
```

```
        'This misspelled call to MsgBox will cause an error to occur

    MssssgBox "Test",16

        'At this point, we will check the Number Property of the Error
        'object to see if an error has occurred.

    If Err.Number <> 0 Then

            ' To streamline code, we have created a common error handler
            ' that will build the dialog that is presented to the user.
            Error_Handler

            ' Because an error occurred, we are going to bail out of the
            ' subroutine with the Exit Sub Statement
            Exit Sub
    End If
End Sub

Sub Error_Handler

' The error handler routine is responsible for obtaining properties
' of the error object and building the dialog which will be
' presented to the user.

Dim strMsg
strMsg = "The following error has occurred: " & Err.Description & "."
strMsg = strMsg + Chr(10) + Chr(13) + "The error was caused by: "
strMsg = strMsg + Err.Source & "."
strMsg = strMsg + Chr(10) + Chr(13) + "Please call the systems support "
strMsg = strMsg + "at 555-1212 to report this error."
MsgBox strMsg,16,"An error has occurred"

' Once the user has been presented with the information about
' the error, we will explicitly clear the property settings
' of the Error object.
Err.Clear

End Sub

->
</SCRIPT>

</HEAD>
<BODY>
<H3>This page demonstrates how error handling works with VBScript</H3>
<HR>
<FORM>
```

```
<INPUT NAME="cmdError" TYPE="button"
  VALUE="Pressing this button will make an error occur. ">
</FORM>
</BODY>
</HTML>
```

Figure 3.6 shows the result of this code.

Not All Errors Are the Same

To conclude this discussion on error handling, it's important to recognize that all errors are not the same. In the previous example, regardless of the type of error that occurs, the subroutine is exited immediately. This may or may not be appropriate. When developing your error-handling routine, you may want to design it with the ability to return a value that will determine whether the subroutine should be exited. In other words, some errors are fatal and some are nonfatal. Fatal errors cause subroutines to be exited; nonfatal errors result in a dialog to the user, but allow processing to continue. With this scenario, the test for an error may change to resemble the following:

```
If Err.Number <> 0 Then
    error_handler
```

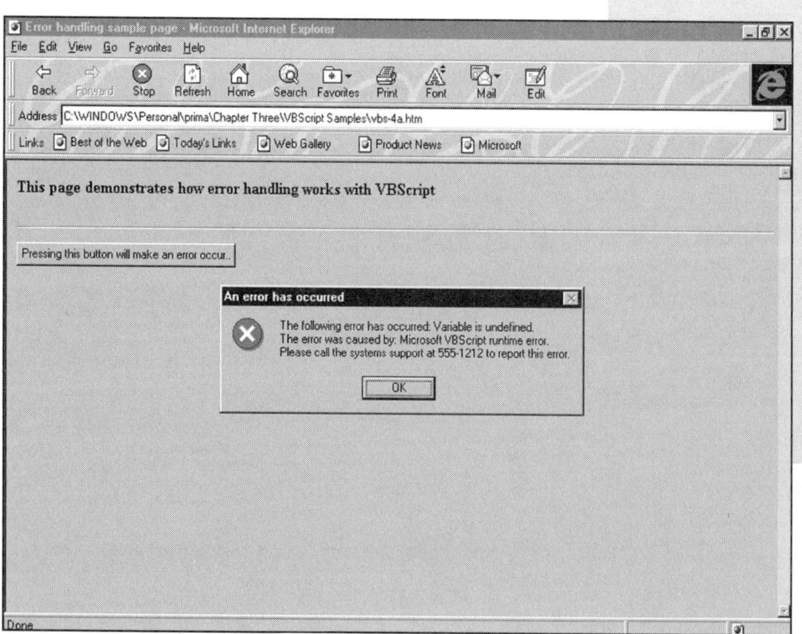

Figure 3.6 Creating your own error-handling routine can enhance the usability of your Web pages by both creating the ability to deal with errors and presenting users with intuitive dialogs about errors that occur.

```
    If Err.Description = "FATAL"
        Exit Sub
    End If
End If
```

Finally, the error handler routine may resemble something like this:

```
Sub Error_Handler

' This version of the error handler routine
' updates the description property of the error
' object if the error is fatal. A case statement is
' used to determine if the error is fatal.
' Whether an error is fatal or not is left
' solely to the determination of the developer.

Dim strMsg,lnErr
lnErr = Err.Number
strMsg = "The following error has occurred: " & Err.Description & "."
strMsg = strMsg + Chr(10) + Chr(13)+"The error was caused by: "
strMsg = strMsg + Err.Source & "."
strMsg = strMsg + Chr(10) + Chr(13) +
    "Please call the systems support at 555-1212 to "
strMsg = strMsg + "report this error."
MsgBox strMsg,16,"An error has occurred"

Err.Clear

Select Case lnErr
    Case 500
        Err.Description = "FATAL"
    Case Else
End Select

If Err.Description= "FATAL" Then
    MsgBox "The currently running procedure will be immediately
➥terminated",16
End if
End Sub
```

Note

The job of the error handler is not to handle errors. Rather, its job is to report that an error has occurred, and, if necessary, report a fatal error to terminate processing of the currently running procedure. The vast majority of errors are not recoverable; therefore, you'll most likely choose to immediately terminate processing of the current procedure.

How Scripts and Objects Are Linked—Part II

The script illustrated in Figure 3.4, while streamlined, isn't very flexible. For one thing, the call to the `MsgBox` function is hard-coded. A better solution would be to accept input from the user and have the `MsgBox` call driven by what the user entered. The following code (on the CD in the file `vbs-3.htm`), which can be viewed in Figure 3.7, shows how to obtain and use input from the user with text box and radio button controls:

```
<HTML>
<HEAD>
<TITLE>Message Box Dialog Builder Page</TITLE>
<SCRIPT LANGUAGE="VBScript">
<!-

' Force all variables to be defined with Dim Statement
Option Explicit

Sub cmdMsgBox_OnClick
    Dim count,lnIcn,lnBtn,lnChoice,lcText,lnBitSetting
    lnIcn = 0
    lnBtn = 0
    lnBitSetting = 0
    ' In order to find out which option has been checked, we need
    ' to loop through both sets of radio buttons. Because each button
    ' represents a separate element in the form, each button has a
    ' different element number. The textbox is element 0. The first
    ' option group contains elements 1 through 6. The second
    ' group contains elements 7 through 10.

    For count = 1 TO 6
        If Document.frmMsgDemo.Elements(count).Checked Then
            lnBtn = Document.frmMsgDemo.Elements(count).Value
            Exit For
        End if
    Next

    For count = 7 To 10
        If Document.frmMsgDemo.Elements(count).Checked Then
            lnIcn = Document.frmMsgDemo.Elements(count).Value
        Exit For
        End if
    Next

    lnBitSetting = cint(lnBtn)+cint(lnIcn)
    ' Here, we are capturing which button has been pressed
```

```
    lnChoice = MsgBox(frmMsgDemo.txtMsgBox.Value,lnBitSetting)

    ' Finally, we will populate the last textbox in
       the form with an indication of which
    ' button was pressed.

    lcText = "You chose the "
    Select Case lnChoice
        Case 1
            lcText = lcText + "OK"
        Case 2
            lcText = lcText + "Cancel"
        Case 3
            lcText = lcText + "Abort"
        Case 4
            lcText = lcText + "Retry"
        Case 5
            lcText = lcText + "Ignore"
        Case 6
            lcText = lcText + "Yes"
        Case 7
        lcText = lcText + "No"
    End Select
    lcText = lcText + " Button"
    frmMsgDemo.txtChoice.Value = lcText
End Sub

->
</SCRIPT>

</HEAD>
<BODY>
<H3>Message Box Builder Page</H3>
<HR>
<FORM NAME="frmMsgDemo">
Message Box Text: <INPUT NAME="txtMsgBox" TYPE="textbox" >
<BR><BR>
Message Box Buttons:

<INPUT NAME="optBtn" TYPE="radio" VALUE="0" CHECKED>OK
<INPUT NAME="optBtn" TYPE="radio" VALUE="1">OK/Cancel
<INPUT NAME="optBtn" TYPE="radio" VALUE="2">Abort/Retry/Ignore
<INPUT NAME="optBtn" TYPE="radio" VALUE="5">Retry/Cancel
<INPUT NAME="optBtn" TYPE="radio" VALUE="4">Yes/No
<INPUT NAME="optBtn" TYPE="radio" VALUE="3">Yes/No/Cancel
<BR><BR>
Message Box Icons:
```

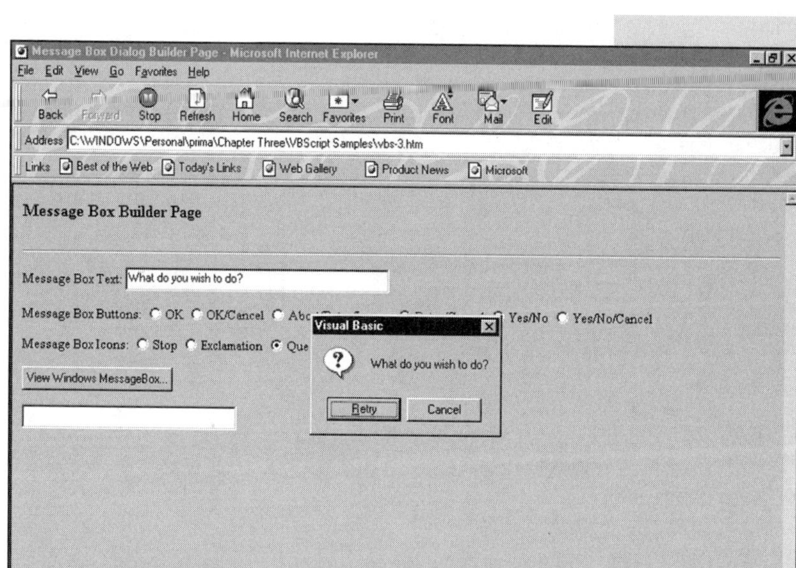

Figure 3.7 Once you know the names and locations of objects in an HTML document, incorporating user input and VBScript is very simple.

```
<INPUT NAME="optIcn" TYPE="radio" VALUE="16" CHECKED>Stop
<INPUT NAME="optIcn" TYPE="radio" VALUE="48">Exclamation
<INPUT NAME="optIcn" TYPE="radio" VALUE="32">Question
<INPUT NAME="optIcn" TYPE="radio" VALUE="64">FYI
<BR><BR>

<INPUT NAME="cmdMsgBox" TYPE="button" VALUE="View Windows MessageBox...">

<BR><BR>

<INPUT NAME="txtChoice" TYPE="textbox" SIZE=40>

</FORM>

</BODY>
</HTML>
```

Validating Input with VBScript

The process of validating user input consists of nothing more than checking the status of properties of form objects and comparing those property values to established business rules to determine whether processing should continue.

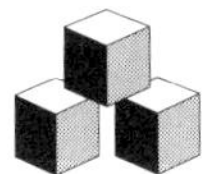

Validating user input on a Web page is essentially the same as validating input in a traditional application.

Consider the guestbook HTML form created in Chapter 2. Figure 3.8 illustrates how the document appears in the Web browser.

While on the surface the guestbook form in this chapter and the one in Chapter 2 look the same, beneath the surface is a big difference. In this chapter's version, VBScript has been implemented to validate user input before data is sent to the Web server. The following HTML code (found in the `vbs-5.htm` file on the CD) contains the VBScript that handles the user-input validation:

```
<HTML>
<HEAD>
<SCRIPT LANGUAGE="VBSCRIPT">
<!-
Option Explicit
Sub cmdSubmit_OnClick
Dim lcemail,lcComments,lcMsg,lnCount,lcRating
lcemail = frmGuestBook.txtemail.Value
lcComments =  frmGuestBook.txacomments.Value
If Trim(lcemail) = "" Then
        MsgBox "You must provide an E-mail address.",16
    Else If Trim(lcComments) = "" Then
```

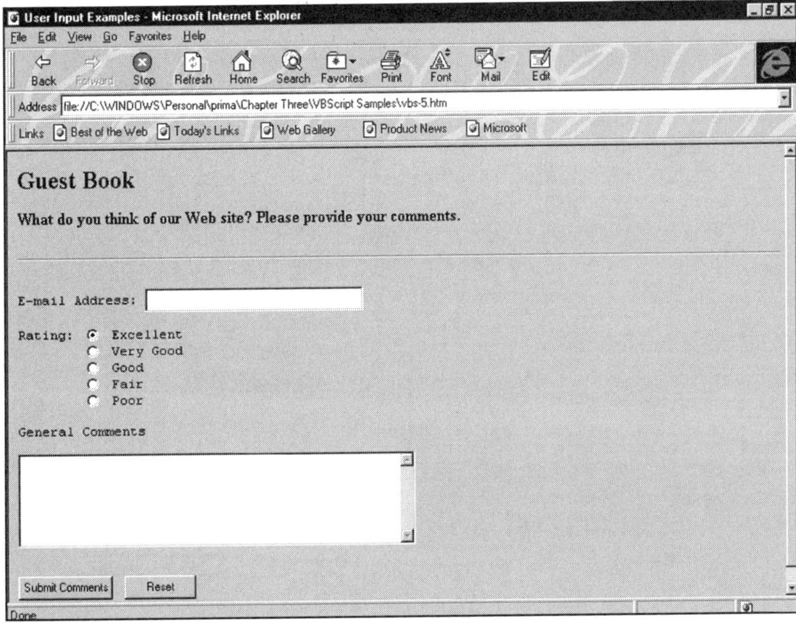

Figure 3.8 This guestbook form was originally created in Chapter 2.

```
            MsgBox "You must provide a comment.",16
        Else
            For lncount = 1 TO 6
                If Document.frmguestBook.Elements(lncount).Checked Then
                    lcRating = Document.frmguestbook.Elements
➥(lncount).Value
                    Exit For
                End if
                    Next
                lcMsg = "You rated our Web site as: " & lcRating & "." &
➥Chr(10) & Chr(13)
                lcMsg = lcMsg & "Your E-mail address is " &
➥frmGuestBook.txtemail.Value
            MsgBox lcMsg,48
            MsgBox "Your comments have been submitted.",48
        End if
    End if
End Sub
->
</SCRIPT>

<TITLE>User Input Examples</TITLE>
<H2>Guest Book</H2>
<H4>What do you think of our Web site? Please provide your comments.</H4>
<HR>
</HEAD>
<BODY>
<FORM NAME="frmGuestBook">
<PRE>
E-mail Address: <INPUT NAME="txtemail" SIZE=40 MAXLENGTH=40 VALUE = "">

Rating: <INPUT TYPE="radio" NAME="rating" VALUE="Excellent"
➥CHECKED> Excellent
            <INPUT TYPE="radio" NAME="rating" VALUE="Very Good" > Very Good
            <INPUT TYPE="radio" NAME="rating" VALUE="Good" > Good
            <INPUT TYPE="radio" NAME="rating" VALUE="Fair" > Fair
            <INPUT TYPE="radio" NAME="rating" VALUE="Poor" > Poor

General Comments

<TEXTAREA NAME="txacomments" ROWS="5" COLS="80"></TEXTAREA>


<INPUT TYPE="button" NAME="cmdSubmit" VALUE="Submit Comments">
<INPUT TYPE="reset" VALUE="Reset">
</PRE>
</FORM>
</BODY>
</HTML>
```

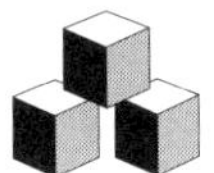

In this case, if the user leaves either the e-mail text box or the comments text area region empty, a message box dialog informs the user that he or she must provide some missing information. If both pieces of data are provided, the data is allowed to be sent back to the Web server. (In this page, no real processing is occurring between the page and a server.) Figure 3.9 illustrates what will happen if data is omitted when the user selects to submit data to the Web server.

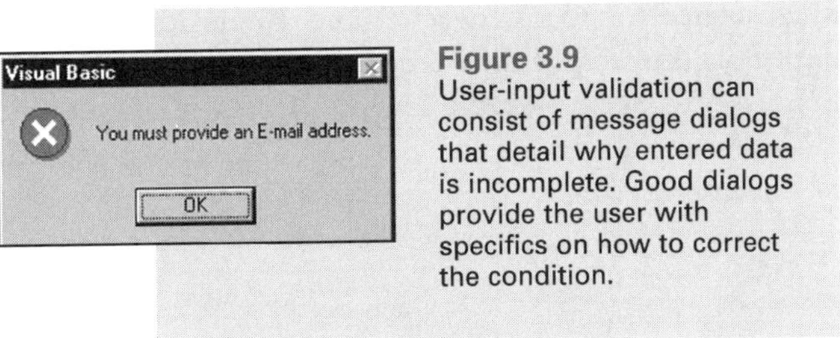

Figure 3.9
User-input validation can consist of message dialogs that detail why entered data is incomplete. Good dialogs provide the user with specifics on how to correct the condition.

Utilizing Other Events with VBScript

There may be times when it's necessary to trap as a user leaves a control. For example, you may want to warn the user immediately if he or she forgot to provide an e-mail account when leaving the e-mail account text box. The event that fires when focus moves away from a control is called `OnBlur()`. Therefore, adding the following sub will provide an immediate warning if the user leaves the e-mail text box blank:

```
Sub txtemail_onBlur
Dim lcemail
lcemail = frmGuestBook.txtemail.Value
If Trim(lcemail) = "" Then
        MsgBox "You must provide an E-mail address prior to
➥submitting comments.",16
Endif
End Sub
```

In addition to the objects that are placed in an HTML document through the use of various elements, other objects exist. IE itself has a rich object model, complete with exposed properties, events, and methods. The details of the IE object model are beyond the scope of this text. For more documentation, please refer to the texts mentioned at the beginning of this chapter.

Two objects that bear mentioning at this point are the window and document objects. The window object is actually IE itself. The document object refers to the HTML document loaded in the viewing area of the browser. There are two events associated with the window object: `OnLoad()` and `OnUnload()`. When a page is loaded into the browser and the Refresh button in the browser toolbar is pressed, the `OnLoad()` event fires. When a page is unloaded, usually as a result of navigating to a different page, the `OnUnload()` event fires. Just as VBScript code can be tied to events of objects placed in a document, code can be tied to window events as well. The following HTML code creates a randomly generated number between 1 and 16 and assigns the `BgColor` (background color) property of the document object via a `Select Case` statement:

```
<HTML>
<HEAD>
<SCRIPT LANGUAGE="VBSCRIPT">
<!-
Option Explicit
Sub Window_Onload
    Dim lnColor,lcColor
    Randomize
    lnColor = Int((16 - 1 + 1) * Rnd + 1)
    Select Case lnColor
        Case 1
            lcColor = "Aqua"
        Case 2
            lcColor = "Gray"
        Case 3
            lcColor = "Navy"
        Case 4
            lcColor = "Silver"
        Case 5
            lcColor = "Black"
        Case 6
            lcColor = "Green"
        Case 7
            lcColor = "Olive"
        Case 8
            lcColor = "Teal"
        Case 9
            lcColor = "Blue"
        Case 10
            lcColor = "Lime"
        Case 11
            lcColor = "Purple"
        Case 12
            lcColor = "White"
        Case 13
            lcColor = "Fuchsia"
        Case 14
            lcColor = "Maroon"
```

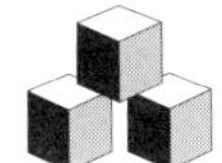


```
        Case 15
            lcColor = "Red"
        Case Else
            lcColor = "Yellow"
    End Select
    Document.BgColor = lcColor
End Sub
</SCRIPT>
<TITLE>An example of using the OnLoad event
    to provide a dynamic BgColor.</TITLE>
</HEAD>
<BODY>
</BODY>
</HTML>
```

When the document is loaded, and subsequently each time the Refresh button is pressed, the document object's `BgColor` property will be updated to reflect a new color.

For complete, up-to-date documents that detail the VBScript language, be sure to visit the Microsoft Web site at `http://www.microsoft.com/vbscript`.

Client-Side versus Server-Side Scripting

All of the material in this chapter to this point has focused on scripting at the client. Specifically, it's the Web browser that compiles the embedded scripts in the HTML document. Although scripting adds a great deal in terms of functionality, one major disadvantage exists, in that your code becomes browser-dependent. A scripting language such as JavaScript is natively supported by Microsoft Internet Explorer and Netscape Navigator. Suppose you've chosen VBScript as your standard scripting language—does this mean that only those clients that use IE or a third-party plug-in for Navigator can interact with your Web-based application? If you rely on client-side scripting, the answer is yes. However, if you rely on server-side scripting, your Web-based application will be client-independent, because the Web server does all the work. This concept is very similar to the client/server model of application development. In that model, two or more layers interact with each other, and at the same time are independent of each other.

What Is Server-Side Scripting?

Microsoft's implementation of server-side scripting is accomplished through a product called Active Server Pages (ASP). Microsoft has a number of Web server products: Internet Information Server (IIS) for Windows NT Server, Peer Web Services for NT Workstation, and Personal Web Server (PWS) for Windows 95/98. All of these products support server-side scripting through ASP. If you don't have access to IIS and/or NT, PWS can facilitate the local development and testing of ASP.

If you visit the Microsoft Web site, you'll encounter several pages that have an ASP extension—this stands for Active Server Page. Other than their respective extensions, ASP and HTM pages are essentially the same. Both use HTML code and have embedded scripts. The difference is in how they're treated by the Web server.

In an HTM page, the Web server ignores the scripts and leaves it up to the browser to compile and run the code. In an ASP page, the server compiles and runs the code, and the results of that code are merged with the existing HTML code in the ASP page. The final result is a document that's passed back to and displayed in the browser.

Comparing Client-Side and Server-Side Scripting

The following examples illustrate how the same functionality can be achieved by using either client-side or server-side scripting. In each of the previous scripting examples, the HTM pages were opened directly as files. When relying on client-side scripting, you can see the results of your scripts and debug them, if necessary, by opening each HTM page as a file in the browser. When a page is opened as a file, no interaction exists with a Web browser.

Because server-side scripting requires processing by the Web server, files must be opened through HTTP. On a local basis, the name of the Web server is the name of the machine in which IIS or PWS resides. On a remote basis, the name of the server is specified by the registered domain name of the Web site.

Client-Side Example

The following example is very simple in that its sole purpose is to display the date. This code block is an example of client-side scripting, the type of scripting that has constituted the majority of this chapter:

```
<HTML>
<HEAD>
<SCRIPT LANGUAGE="VBSCRIPT">
<!-
```

```
Option Explicit
Sub Window_OnLoad
Dim lcDate
lcDate = Date()
Document.Write "<H1>Today's date: " & lcDate & "</H1>"
End Sub
->
</SCRIPT>
<TITLE>An example of Client-Side Scripting</title>
</HEAD>
<BODY>
</BODY>
</HTML>
```

Figure 3.10 shows how the `HTM` page appears in the Web browser. Notice that the script code is tied to the window object's `OnLoad()` event. When this happens, the code is compiled and executed when the document is loaded into the browser. The code is also evaluated whenever the Refresh button is pressed.

Figure 3.11 shows the document in Netscape Navigator. Because Navigator cannot understand VBScript natively, nothing appears in the body of the document.

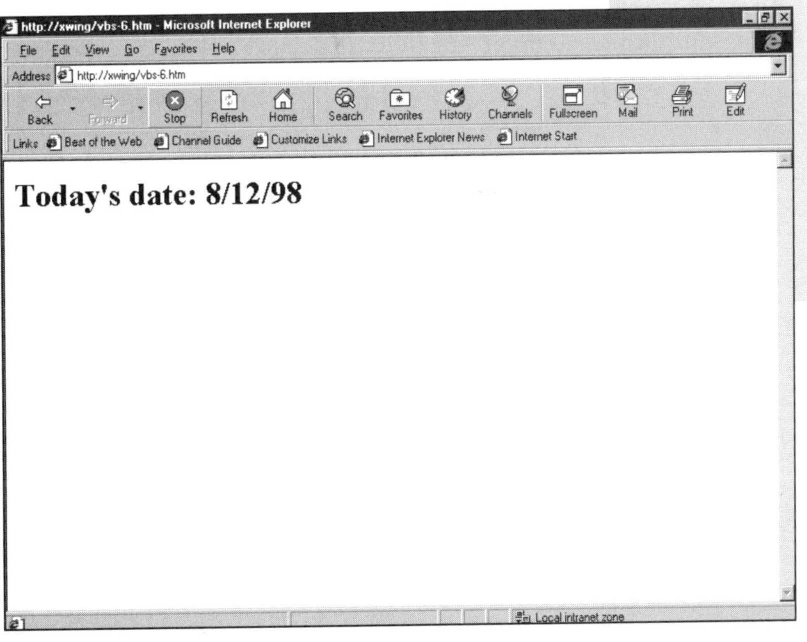

Figure 3.10
Code that doesn't reside in the confines of a subprocedure is compiled and executed when the document is loaded into the browser.

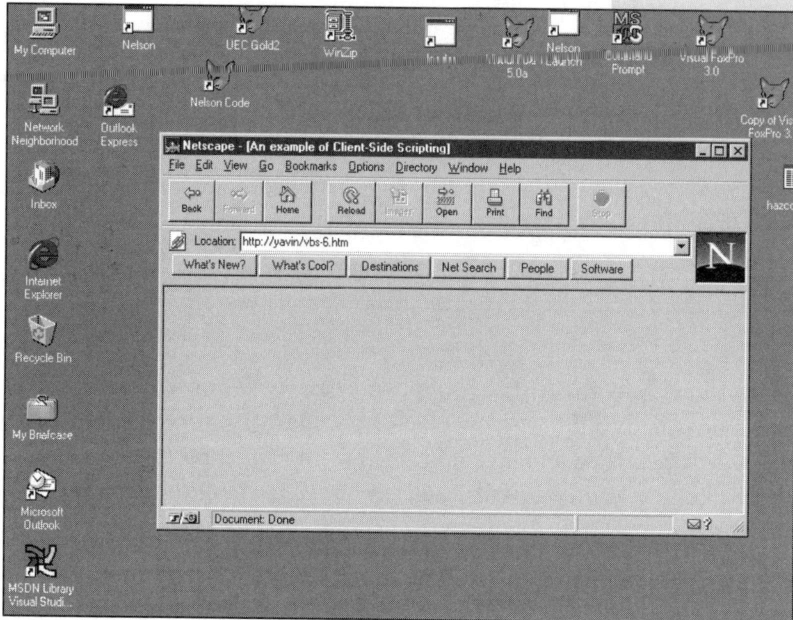

Figure 3.11 Without a third-party plug-in, the Navigator browser cannot interpret VBScript code.

Server-Side Example

Continuing with the date example, the following code block is contained in a file with an ASP extension:

```
<HTML>
<HEAD>
<TITLE>An example of Server-Side Scripting</TITLE>
</HEAD>
<BODY>
<%Dim lcDate%>
<%lcDate = Date()%>
<H1>Today's Date:  <%=lcDate%></H1>
</BODY>
</HTML>
```

This code is illustrated in Figure 3.12.

Because all processing occurs on the server, browsers like Navigator can be used. Figure 3.13 shows this ASP file being viewed in Navigator. Once the ASP file has been displayed in the browser, choosing to view the source HTML code yields the following:

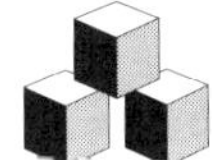


```
<HTML>
<HEAD>
<TITLE>An example of Server-Side Scripting</TITLE>
</HEAD>
<BODY>
<H1>Today's Date:  8/2/98</H1>
</BODY>
</HTML>
```

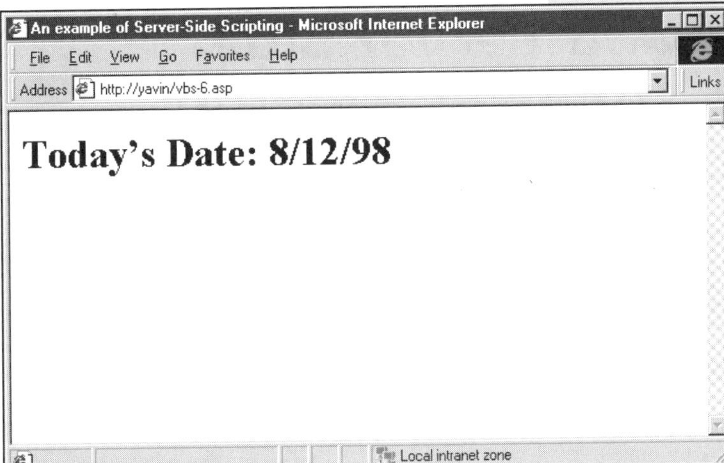

Figure 3.12
All processing required for an Active Server Page is performed by the server. The resulting HTML code is returned to the browser on the client.

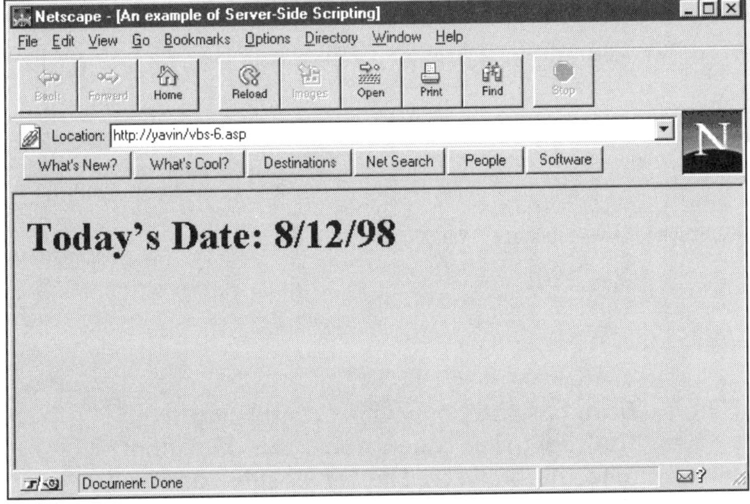

Figure 3.13
Server-side scripting makes your documents browser-independent.

ANALYSIS

ASP pages can be thought of as templates. An ASP file can have some or no static content (portions of the page that never change). An ASP file also can be composed partially or entirely of dynamic content (portions of the page that can change whenever the browser's Refresh button—or, for Netscape, Reload button—is pressed). In this example, the contents of the variable `lcDate`, which is a date, are merged with the static content of the ASP file. The resulting HTML code is passed back to the browser, yielding the results shown in Figures 3.12 and 3.13.

Client-Side and Server-Side Scripting—Working Together

You may be asking yourself, "Can I use a combination of client-side and server-side scripting?" The answer is yes. Remember that ASP files, once processed by the server, render HTML code back to the browser. This HTML code can contain scripts that are compiled and executed by the browser. The following code (shown in Figure 3.14) illustrates an ASP file that makes use of both client-side and server-side scripting:

```
<HTML>
<HEAD>
<SCRIPT LANGUAGE = "VBSCRIPT">
Option Explicit
Sub cmdDate_OnClick
   MsgBox "Today's Date: " & Date()
End Sub
</SCRIPT>
<TITLE>An example of combining Server-Side and Client-Side Scripting</TITLE>
</HEAD>
<BODY>
<%Dim lcDate%>
<%lcDate = Date()%>
<H1>Today's Date:  <%=lcDate%></H1>
<INPUT TYPE="button" NAME="cmdDate" VALUE="Today's date">
</BODY>
</HTML>
```

Note

The code from above has the possibility of returning two different dates. The client-side code returns the date from the machine running the browser. The server-side code returns the date from the Web server.

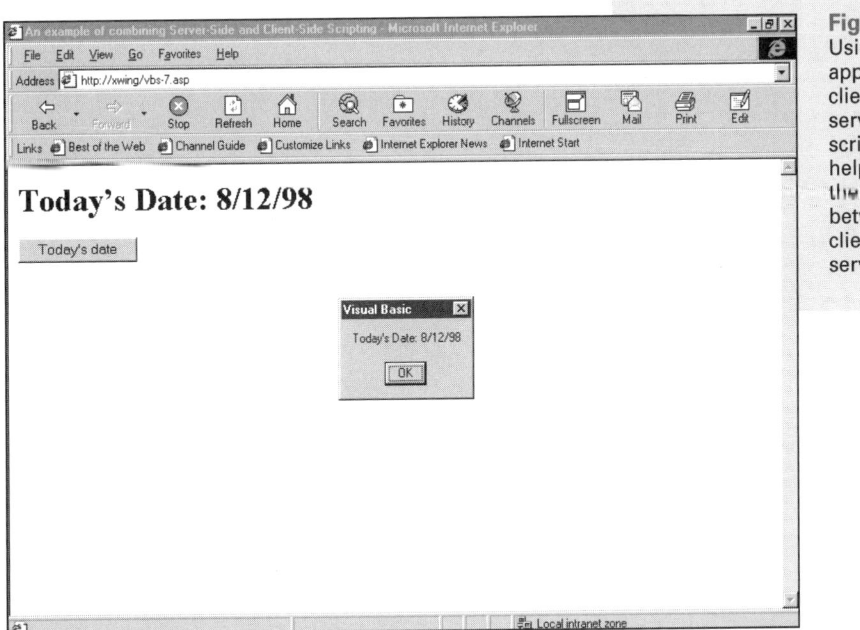

Figure 3.14 Using a hybrid approach of client-side and server-side scripting can help to balance the load between the client and the server.

Of course, by using a hybrid approach, a dependency is reestablished with the type of browser the client is running.

Summary

The goal of this chapter and the first section of this book has been to provide you with a basic understanding of the Internet and the basics of HTML and VBScript. This chapter has explored what VBScript is, how it can be implemented into HTML documents, and how scripting can be used to validate input captured by end users of your Web pages. This chapter also went into some detail to outline the similarities and differences between client-side and server-side scripting. With the basic skills under your belt, you are now ready to begin the process of creating Visual Basic-based Web applications!

Hands On Project 1

The VBBrowser

- Tracking system requirements
- Tracking system design information
- Using prototyping in your applications
- Understanding Internet functionality available in Visual Basic
- Using ActiveX controls
- Using other people's Web pages to your advantage
- Sending e-mail with SMTP
- Transferring files using FTP
- Testing your applications

Project Overview

This first project introduces you to the concepts of developing Visual Basic/Internet applications. You learn that the Internet is made up of many different levels, and you learn how you can develop browser-based applications using Visual Basic.

You begin this project by gathering system requirements. You learn how to gather requirements and the importance of documenting requirements. You learn how to identify the users of a system and how to assist them in prioritizing requirements.

Next, you take a look at the application-design process, and learn that there are two common approaches to design: the waterfall approach and the RAD approach. After learning about these approaches, you develop a prototype of your application.

Finally, you begin creating the actual Visual Basic forms for your application. The Web pages you work with use many different techniques for accessing data from the World Wide Web.

What Is the VBBrowser?

Up to this point in this book, you have been working with HTML, VBScript, and Visual Basic. It's essential that you have an understanding of these topics prior to developing an Internet application. This is necessary because the Internet introduces developers to large amounts of new terminology, techniques, and development methodologies.

Now it's time to get specific.

In this section, you're going to start your first project. This chapter starts this process by describing the project you're going to create and giving you an overview of the key topics presented in the remaining chapters for this project.

Describing the VBBrowser

The first project you're going to create is an Internet-enabled Visual Basic application. One of the most powerful features of Visual Basic is its ability to integrate with other applications. These other applications include applications on the client machine, applications on another machine connected via a LAN, and especially applications found on the Internet. The Internet contains vast amounts of information just waiting to be accessed by your applications.

The goal of the VBBrowser system is to create a coherent Internet desktop for accessing information from the Internet. The problem with most commercial browsers (Microsoft Internet Explorer, Netscape Navigator, and so on) is that they provide no simple way of organizing information—the user must know the workings of the browser and search engines to find any useful information. Also, once he finds information, the user needs to remember where he found it and then manually return to the source of the information.

Note

Most browsers have some method of storing bookmarks. But over time, these bookmarks tend to become cluttered and cannot be automatically retrieved.

The VBBrowser will solve these problems by creating a front-end application that can be used to access useful functions found on the Internet and encapsulate them into a simple, useful interface.

When you develop Internet applications, you commonly work at one of three layers. These are the client, middleware, and server layers. Figure 4.1 shows these three layers and the software that operates at each layer.

In this project, you'll be dealing with applications residing at the client layer. This means that you're going to add functionality found in browsers into your applications. The first task you'll need to accomplish is to gather the requirements for your system.

System Requirements of the VBBrowser System

The most important stage of the development process is the initial requirements-gathering stage. This stage is important because it defines the scope of your application. It's crucial to do a good job of accurately gathering the necessary requirements for systems, as the costs of development escalate as the system matures. This results in higher costs of fixing problems with missing features at later stages of the development process. Some studies say that it can cost up to 100 times more to fix a problem in the development stages of a project than in the requirements stage. Missing a crucial requirement can even result in project cancellation.

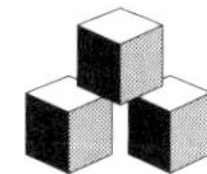

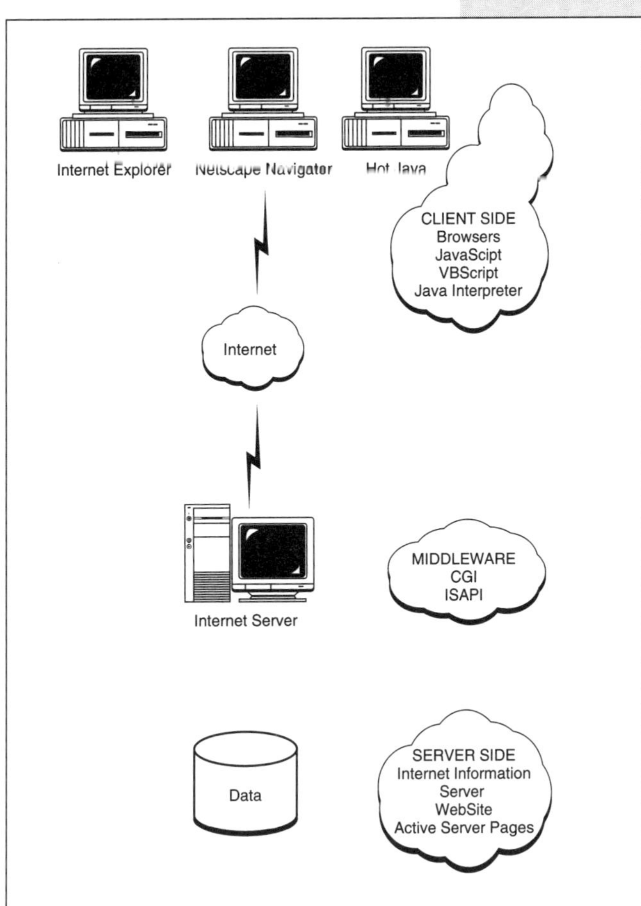

Figure 4.1
This illustration shows the three layers involved in developing Internet applications.

Now that you understand the need for good requirements, consider the list of requirements for the VBBrowser system. This system, when complete, will do the following:

- Provide information to financial management personnel
- Provide seamless connections to the Internet
- Provide the ability to pull stock quotes from the Internet
- Provide the ability to access currency values from the Internet
- Provide the ability to track Federal Express packages
- Provide the ability to transfer files from one site to another
- Provide the ability to access e-mail from the interface
- Provide the ability to bulk e-mail customers from the interface

Goals of the VBBrowser System

This project is designed to introduce Visual Basic developers to the tools necessary to access information from the Internet. This process introduces developers to numerous topics related to the integration of different applications. The following list describes some of the topics that are covered:

- **Internet client functionality present in Visual Basic**
  Visual Basic comes with a great deal of Internet functionality right out of the box. This project discusses the Internet client capabilities found in Visual Basic.
- **Connecting to the Internet**
  The first step in creating an Internet application is to connect your application to the Internet. This project discusses the tools and techniques necessary for connecting your application to the Internet.
- **Using ActiveX controls**
  When you add Internet functionality to your applications, you'll be using ActiveX controls. This project discusses adding ActiveX controls to your Visual Basic applications and using them to gain access to information found on the Internet.
- **How to use other people's Web pages to your advantage**
  The Internet is full of useful information. If you can figure out how to access this information, you can add functionality to your application that you never before thought possible.
- **How to send e-mail using SMTP**
  One of the more powerful features of the Internet is its ability to route e-mail easily and quickly. You'll learn how to incorporate e-mail using the SMTP protocol. You'll also learn how to integrate e-mail with databases.
- **How to transfer files using FTP**
  The Internet has a set of protocols that you can use to send and retrieve files from external sites. You'll learn how to use FTP to move files around on the Internet.

Summary

The most important aspect of any project is defining what it does. This chapter has described the functionality and components of the VBBrowser application. Now that you understand what this application is going to do, you can begin the process of creating your first Internet-enabled application.

Gathering Information for the VBBrowser

Chapter 4 examined the requirements for creating a useful Internet-enabled application. This chapter examines the steps necessary for gathering information about this project.

Finding Sources of Information

Before you can gather information about any system, you need to take a look at what information you're trying to gather. The purpose of the information-gathering stage is to further flesh out the requirements of your system. When gathering information for your system, you should concentrate your efforts on finding and documenting the following information:

- **The mission statement.** The purpose of the mission statement is to define at a very high level what the goal of the system is. This mission statement can be one sentence or one page. The goal of the mission statement is to set the focus of the project. A common practice of many system developers is to ask for one page (and only one page) describing the system they're being asked to create.

- **The system users.** For any system to be successful, you need to involve the direct users of the system. Users of a system have the power to make or break whatever developers throw at them. When dealing with users, you should attempt to learn what their job functions are and what impact the system will have on these users.
- **The system managers.** When developing a system, it's important to distinguish between managers and users. The needs of managers are very different from those of users. Users want to do their work and go home; managers are commonly responsible for much higher-level tasks. It's easy to fall into the trap of trying to cater your system to the managers. This is a surefire way to fail.
- **Required features.** This item can be the most difficult to quantify and is the most difficult to rein in. When developing a system, you want to make sure that you prioritize the required features and dedicate your resources to working on those features. The big question is how you derive these features. The easiest method of doing this is to ask a very direct question of the system users: "What are the three most important features to you?" Then force users to pick three and only three (or whatever your number may be), which forces them to prioritize.
- **Out-of-scope features.** When gathering information for a system, this item is commonly overlooked. All user-requested features should be documented. Once the first version of your software is complete, you can return to your out-of-scope features list and go right to work on your next version.
- **Other sources of information.** When you're dealing with Internet applications, you're faced with a sea of information that's available to you. This section should document where you intend to go for your information.

When looking at the information you're attempting to gather, you can break it down into five basic tenets of any project:

- **What.** What are you trying to do?
- **Why.** Why are you trying to do it?
- **Who.** Who is going to use or be affected by the system?
- **Where.** Where can you find the information you need?
- **When.** When is the information needed, or how often will it be accessed?

These items may seem obvious to you, but you'd be surprised how many people forget even the most basic development principles.

Beginning the Gathering Process

Now that you have an understanding of what you need to accomplish in the information-gathering stage of a project, you can begin breaking it down. The first task in the gathering stage is to define the mission statement of the system. The mission statement can be derived from the initial document or Request for Proposal (RFP) sent by the users. Chapter 4 explains that the system should do the following:

- Provide information to financial management personnel
- Provide seamless connections to the Internet
- Provide the ability to pull stock quotes from the Internet
- Provide the ability to access currency values from the Internet
- Provide the ability to track Federal Express packages
- Provide the ability to transfer files from one site to another
- Provide the ability to access e-mail from the interface
- Provide the ability to bulk e-mail customers from the interface

This list is nice for defining just what the system is supposed to do, but it falls short of defining *why*. This is your job as a system developer—to attempt to figure out why this project needs to do certain things.

The first item in this list probably says enough to become the beginning of the mission statement. It says that the purpose of the system is to "provide information to financial management personnel." The next items on the list provide even more information about just what this system should do ("provide seamless connections to the Internet") and go further in documenting specific information about the system—stock quotes, currency, e-mail, and so on. After analyzing the requirements list, you can derive the following mission statement:

Mission Statement

The purpose of the VBBrowser application is to provide our management personnel with financial and operational information, using the Internet as a resource.

The task that immediately follows the mission statement is the process of breaking the requirements document into functional areas. This allows you as a developer to concentrate your time into specific areas. In each area, the information you gather should answer the list of questions defined earlier: what, why, who, where, and when. From this list, you can even create a form that will serve as the source of your documentation. Your form can be as simple as the one in Table 5-1.

Table 5-1 Proposed Requirements-Gathering Form

Item	Notes
Project	
Name of Analyst	
Date Created	
Task Description (What)	
Item Purpose (Why)	
Responsible Party or Users (Who)	
Source of Information (Where)	
Access Requirements (When)	
Notes	

Now that you understand what information you need to gather, you can go to work. Using the proposed requirements form shown in Table 5-1, you can begin gathering information for each functional area of your project. In the next section, you begin the actual documentation of your system requirements.

Provide Seamless Connections to the Internet

This requirement can be broken down as shown in Table 5-2.

Table 5-2 Seamless Internet Connection Requirement

Item	Notes
Project	VBBrowser
Name of Analyst	Rod Paddock
Date Created	09/30/98
Task Description (What)	Provide seamless connections to the Internet.
Item Purpose (Why)	The company doesn't currently have a direct link to the Internet. The system should make it easy for the user to log on to the Internet.
Responsible Party or Users (Who)	System developers.
Source of Information (Where)	Consult Windows API documentation or purchase third-party tool.
Access Requirements (When)	Will be accessed each time user logs on.
Notes	Will use Dial-Up Networking feature of Windows 95/NT to perform this task.

Provide the Ability to Pull Stock Quotes from the Internet

The next item on the requirements list can be broken down as shown in Table 5-3.

Table 5-3 Stock Quote Requirement

Item	Notes
Project	VBBrowser
Name Of Analyst	Rod Paddock
Date Created	09/30/98
Task Description (What)	The system needs to be able to provide the user with stock quotes.
Item Purpose (Why)	Financial traders have the need to periodically check the price of stocks.

Table 5-3 Stock Quote Requirement *(continued)*	
Item	**Notes**
Responsible Party or Users (Who)	Financial traders.
Source of Information (Where) (Where)	NASDAQ has a good Web site for pulling stock and mutual fund information. This would be a good site to look at.
Access Requirements (When)	Periodic access throughout the day.
Notes	

Provide the Ability to Access Currency Values from the Internet

The next item on the requirements list can be broken down as shown in Table 5-4.

Table 5-4 Currency Value Access Requirement	
Item	**Notes**
Project	VBBrowser
Name of Analyst	Rod Paddock
Date Created	09/30/98
Task Description (What)	The system should be capable of requesting current currency valuations.
Item Purpose (Why)	Because the firm deals with clients both nationally and internationally, the system needs to be able to show currency rates in other financial markets.
Responsible Party or Users (Who)	Financial traders.
Source of Information (Where)	The CNN Financial Web site is the best site for accessing currency valuations.
Access Requirements (When)	Periodic access throughout the day.
Notes	When analyzing this requirement, it became clear that it's also important to know times in various financial centers throughout the world. Need to add another requirement.

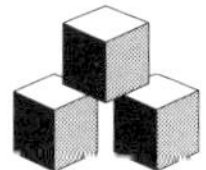

From reading this requirement, you learned that there's another requirement for finding the time in various financial markets. Equipped with this knowledge, you can add another requirement, as shown in Table 5-5.

Table 5-5 International Time Clock Requirement

Item	Notes
Project	VBBrowser
Name of Analyst	Rod Paddock
Date Created	09/30/98
Task Description (What)	The system should be able to provide the time in various financial centers.
Item Purpose (Why)	Because the firm deals with clients both nationally and internationally, the system needs to be able to show the time in other financial centers' financial markets.
Responsible Party or Users (Who)	Financial traders.
Source of Information (Where)	MIT has a server that provides the correct current Greenwich Mean Time (GMT).
Access Requirements (When)	Periodic access throughout the day.
Notes	

Provide the Ability to Track Federal Express Packages

The next item can be broken down as shown in Table 5-6.

Table 5-6 Federal Express Package Tracking Requirement

Item	Notes
Project	VBBrowser
Name of Analyst	Rod Paddock
Date Created	09/30/98
Task Description (What)	Provide ability to track packages sent by Federal Express.

Table 5-6 Federal Express Package Tracking Requirement *(continued)*

Item	Notes
Item Purpose (Why)	Many of the documents sent by this firm are critical and must be tracked at all times. The company uses Federal Express to send these packages. The system should be able to interface with Federal Express' system to provide tracking information.
Responsible Party or Users (Who)	Financial traders and shipping coordinators.
Source of Information (Where)	Federal Express has a Web site dedicated to tracking packages.
Access Requirements (When)	Periodic daily access by financial traders and shipping coordinators.
Notes	

Note

Many other shipping companies have Web sites. Consult your vendor to see whether these techniques will work for you.

Provide the Ability to Transfer Files from One Site to Another

The next item can be broken down as shown in Table 5-7.

Table 5-7 File Transfer Requirement

Item	Notes
Project	VBBrowser
Name of Analyst	Rod Paddock
Date Created	09/30/98
Task Description (What)	Need the ability to transfer documents between different companies.
Item Purpose (Why)	Sometimes it's necessary to send documents to or retrieve documents from other companies. These documents include contracts, proposals, and occasional graphics.

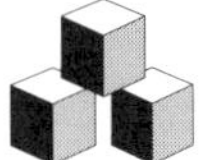

Item	Notes
Responsible Party or Users (Who)	Financial traders, managers.
Source of Information (Where)	The Internet provides protocols for sending files between different sites. We should use these protocols for sending files.
Access Requirements (When)	Periodic access.
Notes	

Provide the Ability to Access E-mail from the Interface

The next item can be broken down as shown in Table 5-8.

Table 5-8 E-mail Requirement

Item	Notes
Project	VBBrowser
Name of Analyst	Rod Paddock
Date Created	09/30/98
Task Description (What)	System should be able to send e-mail using the Internet.
Item Purpose (Why)	It's necessary to confirm orders with customers throughout the day. The company has standardized on an Internet e-mail system and so should VBBrowser.
Responsible Party or Users (Who)	All system users.
Source of Information (Where)	The Internet provides protocols for sending e-mail. This system should use these protocols.
Access Requirements (When)	Periodic daily access.
Notes	There may be a future requirement for reading e-mail information from the Internet. During the design phase, research protocols for reading e-mail.

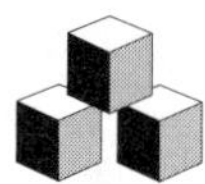

Provide the Ability to Bulk E-mail Customers from the Interface

The next item can be broken down as shown in Table 5-9.

Table 5-9 Bulk E-mail Requirement

Item	Notes
Project	VBBrowser
Name of Analyst	Rod Paddock
Date Created	09/30/98
Task Description (What)	System should be able to send e-mail messages from a list of people saved in a Microsoft Access database.
Item Purpose (Why)	It's necessary to send bulk e-mail messages to current clients.
Responsible Party or Users (Who)	Marketing Department.
Source of Information (Where)	The Internet provides protocols for sending e-mail. This system should use these protocols.
Access Requirements (When)	Periodic daily access.
Notes	Microsoft Access is the company standard database, and therefore should be used by this system.

Summary

As you can see, a lot of useful information can be gathered at this stage of development. It's at this stage that your system should begin to take shape. You should have a clear idea of what you're attempting to do and what tools you'll need to accomplish your objectives. Using this information, you can set your sights on the next step of the development process—design.

Chapter 6

Designing the VBBrowser

In Chapter 5, "Gathering Information for the VBBrowser," you completed a detailed list of requirements for the system. Upon gathering a completed set of requirements, you can proceed with the design process. In the design process, you begin putting together a list of detailed technical specifications for your system. These specifications then will be used to actually implement your system. This chapter looks at the process of creating the design documents for a system. In this chapter, you examine the following areas of system design:

- Goals of system design
- How to choose a design methodology—waterfall versus RAD
- How to document your design
- Information necessary for the VBBrowser design

Design Goals

The primary goal of the system design phase is to document your requirements in such a way that they can be handed to a developer and created with little or no extra communication necessary. The design phase of a project is responsible for five distinct components:

1. Identifying and documenting each system process.
2. Identifying and documenting the inputs for the application being developed.
3. Identifying and documenting the outputs for the application being developed.
4. Identifying and documenting the exact sources of information for the system inputs and outputs.
5. Creating a design document that will be used to create the system.

Identifying and Documenting System Processes

Your first job when creating your design document is to break down your system into a set of features that will be developed. The primary source of this information is your detailed requirements document.

This list will become the outline for your design document. Each of these processes must have its inputs and outputs defined, the sources for its information found—and finally, all of this information must be put into a design document of some type.

After identifying the components of your system, you need to go to work on defining the inputs, outputs, and sources of information for your system. These items will tell developers what information they can expect from users, what information needs to be returned, and where to get the information requested. The easiest way of documenting this information is to create a design template that can be used to record the inputs, outputs, and sources of information for the system. Table 6-1 shows a sample template.

Table 6-1 Design Documentation Template

Item	Notes
Project	
Name of Analyst	
Date Created	

Item	Notes
Task Description	
Task Inputs	
Task Outputs	
Source of Information	
Notes	

Now that you understand what information you're trying to document, you can go about designing your system. Prior to designing your system, though, you need to consider the methodology you're going to use.

Choosing a Design Methodology

Over the past twenty years, many development methodologies have been created. Some of these design methodologies have proven to be more successful than others. The two most prevalent design methodologies are the waterfall methodology and the rapid application development (RAD) methodology. Each methodology has a distinct set of advantages and disadvantages; this section examines each of these methodologies and explores their respective strengths and weaknesses.

The Waterfall Method

The oldest and probably most-used system design methodology is the *waterfall method*. This methodology says that a system goes through a set of established steps, one after the other. It's a linear design methodology consisting of five steps:

1. Requirements
2. Analysis
3. Design
4. Development
5. Implementation/testing

As the name implies, a project moves through each step like a waterfall—each step being completed in turn. Eventually, the waterfall method results in a completed system. This method has a problem, though: It doesn't involve the user until step 5 in the process. The user may be consulted early in the process, but in reality the user might not see the actual application until months—or, in some cases, years—later. This has been a primary source of failed systems throughout the years. During the development process, some users might be consulted with requirements/analysis and design documents, but these documents are commonly cryptic and difficult for the end user to understand. This is where the RAD method comes in.

The major advantage of the waterfall method is that it provides a consistent method for developing applications. You can use this methodology to create applications of any size and complexity. Also, it's a proven method for developing applications and consequently has a large number of tools and resources that can be used by developers.

The Rapid Application Development (RAD) Method

One of the newest methods of software development is the rapid application development method. RAD takes classic software development methodologies in a slightly different direction. It takes the classic steps of the waterfall method and accelerates them into a very rapid iterative development cycle. Where the waterfall method is a linear process (see Figure 6.1), the RAD method is a more circular process (see Figure 6.2).

This is the guiding principle of the RAD method: "Put as much functionality as possible in a user's hands as soon as possible." This means that developers don't necessarily need a full and complete set of requirements and design documents in their hands prior to developing software. What you commonly do in the RAD method is this:

1. Gather a set of system requirements.
2. Create a rough design document for these requirements. The template shown earlier (in Table 6-1) is a good start.
3. Design a prototype of the system. This prototype should have as much functionality as possible that can be assembled in a short period of time.
4. Once the prototype has been developed, get it into the hands of users ASAP.
5. Document any inconsistencies, problems, or necessary features requested by the user.
6. Return to step 1 and define more requirements, etc.

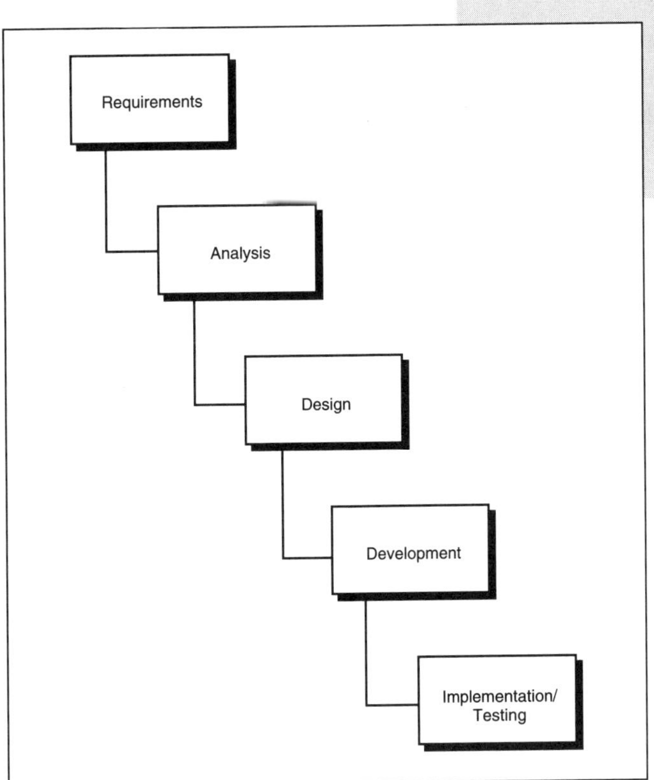

Figure 6.1
The waterfall method ends with implementation and testing.

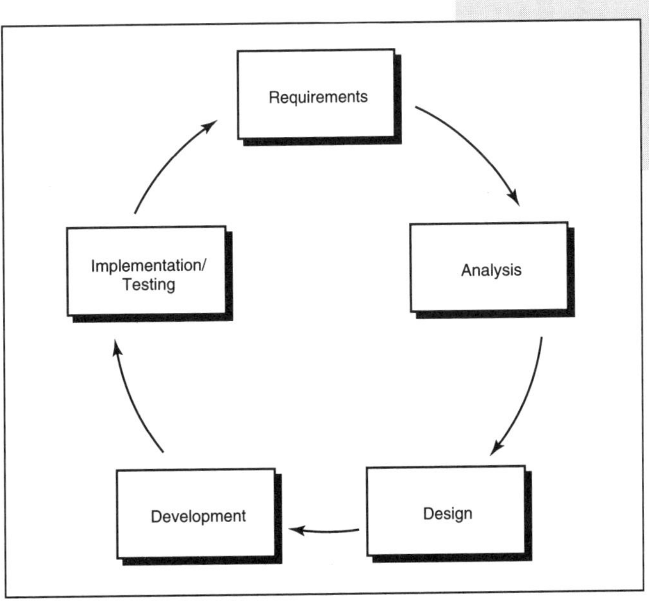

Figure 6.2
The RAD method continues in a circular fashion.

The effect of this new functionality can be summed up in one very familiar sentence: "A picture is worth a thousand words." What this means to a developer is that he can have his design validated by real-life users immediately, instead of waiting until the end of the development process. It also has another, even more important benefit: It causes "buy-in" from the users. If users can be involved in the development process from the earliest stages, they will take ownership of the system and will be great assets to the system developers.

However, this method does have its problems:

- The first problem is that developers may feel the temptation to just jump in and start coding. It's a bad practice to just jump in and code. For a system to be successful, a developer still must spend time doing a good job of defining requirements and designing a system.
- The second problem is that developers must have tools that allow them to develop and change systems rapidly. In the COBOL or C world, this method might not have been feasible. But with tools like Visual Basic, Visual FoxPro, and Delphi, this has become a realistic method of creating a system.

Now that you understand the different methodologies available, you can proceed with designing the VBBrowser.

Designing the VBBrowser Using the RAD Method

The VBBrowser system will be designed using the RAD method of development. We chose the RAD method because this is how most Visual Basic developers create applications. Visual Basic development usually is done by creating forms rapidly and giving them to the users for further evaluation and input.

Taking the requirements documents from Chapters 4 and 5, you can determine that you will be developing a Visual Basic application that will be used to access information from the Internet. This application will concentrate on functionality that's useful to financial trading companies and their personnel.

The first item in your documentation will be a list of features to be developed. From the requirements documented in Chapter 5, you'll find this list:

- Provide seamless connections to the Internet.
- Provide the ability to pull stock quotes from the Internet.
- Provide the ability to access currency values from the Internet.
- Provide the ability to see what time it is in various financial centers.

- Provide the ability to track Federal Express packages.
- Provide the ability to access e-mail from the interface.
- Provide the ability to bulk e-mail customers from the interface.
- Provide the ability to transfer files from one site to another.

After composing this list, you can go to work identifying the information for each component.

Designing the Main Menu/Screen

The first item on the requirements list dictates that the system should provide seamless access to the Internet. The common method of doing this is to provide some capability of logging into your system by using some type of menuing or login screen. Using the template shown earlier in Table 6-1, you can document the components of this feature as shown in Table 6-2.

Table 6-2 Startup Menu/Screen

Item	Notes
Project	VBBrowser
Name of Analyst	Rod Paddock
Date Created	09/30/98
Task Description	Create a main menu screen.
Task Inputs	Username/password
Task Outputs	None
Source of Information	N/A
Notes	

Visual Basic provides a tool known as the *Application Wizard* that makes creating a new application easy. You activate the Application Wizard by choosing File, New Project from the Visual Basic menu. Upon selecting this option, you're prompted with the New Project screen shown in Figure 6.3. From this screen, select the Application Wizard icon and click OK (or simply double-click the Application Wizard icon).

A series of screens prompts you for information on the style of application you want to generate. Some of the information requested includes:

- Whether to create an MDI, SDI, or Explorer-style interface
- Which menu bars to create for the application

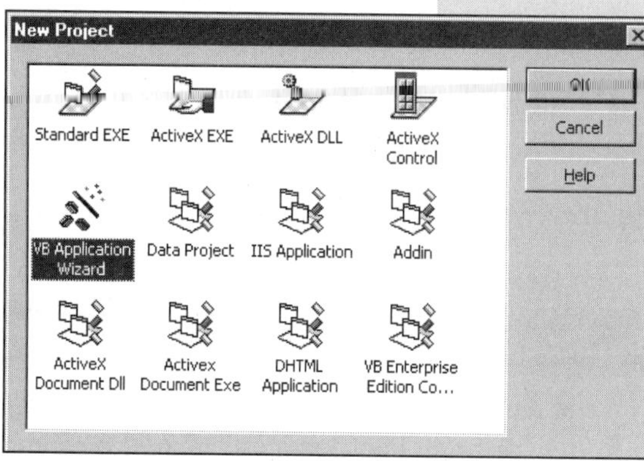

Figure 6.3
This illustration shows the Visual Basic New Project screen with the Application Wizard icon selected.

- Whether to use a resource file for system strings (this is useful for international apps)
- Whether to include a browser in your application
- Whether to include login screens, splash screens, etc.

This wizard is a handy tool for creating the framework for an application with a few simple steps. Figure 6.4 shows an application generated by the Application Wizard.

The next step in the design process is to create the individual screens that will represent your system. From the requirements document, you can determine

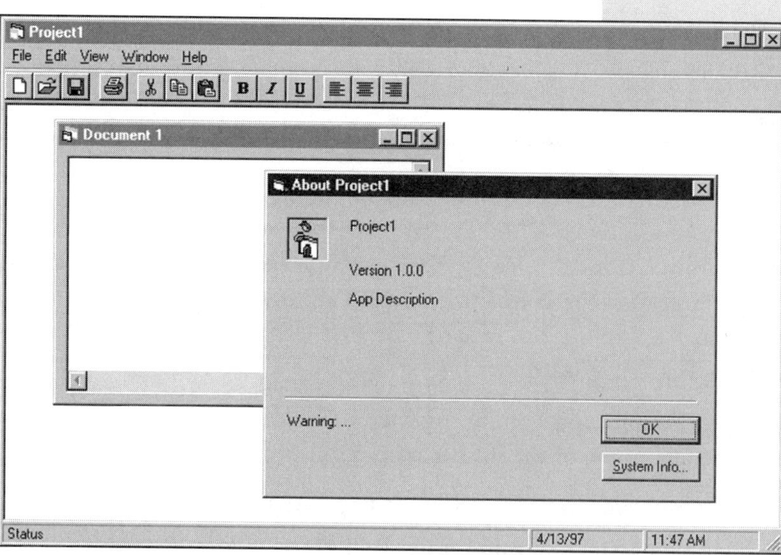

Figure 6.4
This illustration shows a framework generated by the Visual Basic Application Wizard.

that the next components to develop are the individual screens that will be used to access information from various Web sites.

Designing the Stock Quote Screen

The first component to be developed is a screen for requesting stock quotes. Table 6-3 shows the requirements for this form.

Table 6-3 Stock Quotes Tracking Screen

Item	Notes
Project	VBBrowser
Name of Analyst	Rod Paddock
Date Created	09/30/98
Task Description	This screen should allow brokers to track stock quotes.
Task Inputs	Ticker symbols for stocks needing tracking.
Task Outputs	Price(s) for the stocks being tracked.
Source of Information	NASDAQ provides a Web site for tracking stock quotes. Its URL is www.nasdaq.com.
Notes	

From this information, you can go to the NASDAQ Web site and find out what protocol that Web site uses to track information. The information you'll be concerned with as a designer is the URL that the Web site uses to request stock quotes. Figure 6.5 shows the NASDAQ Web site with the URL requesting a stock quote.

This URL is a piece of information that tells you how to incorporate stock quotes into your VB applications. Chapter 7 shows how to use this URL, accompanied by the Internet Web Browser control, to make a VB form capable of requesting stock quotes.

The next step in the design process is to create a prototype screen for accessing this information. Figure 6.6 shows a prototype screen for requesting stock quotes.

The process that you follow will be the same for each of the screens developed for your system. The following sections demonstrate the design requirements for the remaining components.

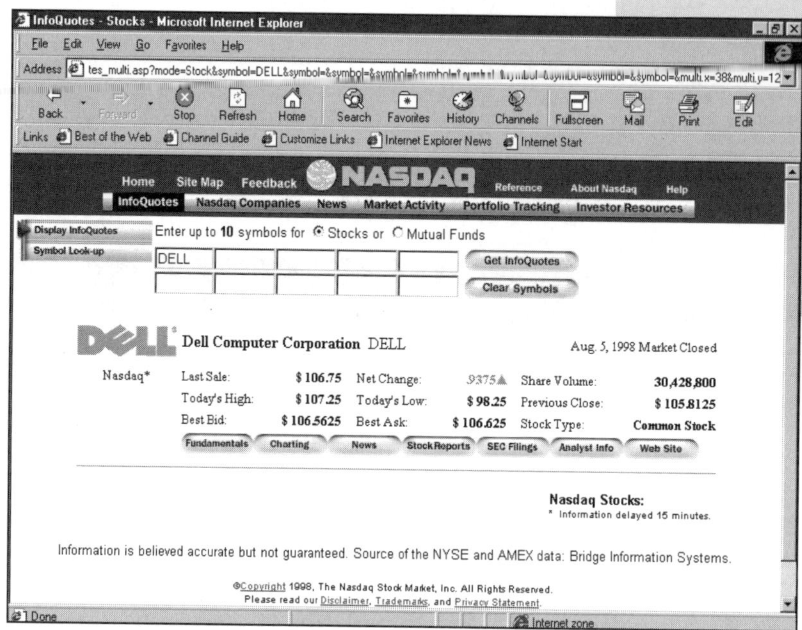

Figure 6.5 This figure shows the URL and corresponding Web page returned from the NASDAQ Web site after a stock quote request.

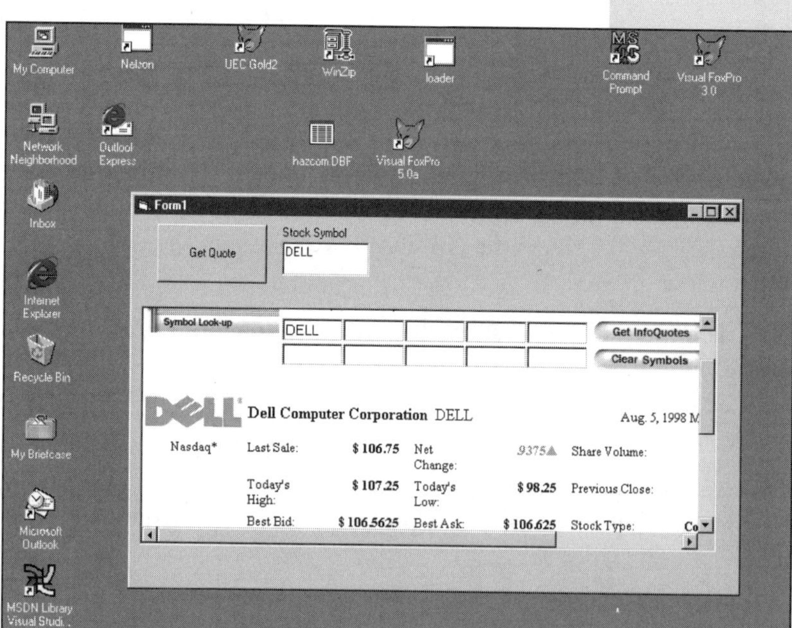

Figure 6.6 This figure shows a prototype VB form for accessing stock quotes.

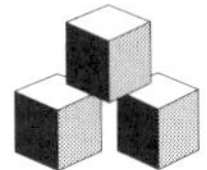

Designing the Currency Screen

The next task is to design the currency form. Table 6-4 shows the design information for the currency screen; Figure 6.7 shows the prototype screen.

Table 6-4 Currency Access Screen

Item	Notes
Project	VBBrowser
Name of Analyst	Rod Paddock
Date Created	09/30/98
Task Description	Access currency pricing information.
Task Inputs	None
Task Outputs	List of exchange rates for various international currencies.
Source of Information	The CNN Financial Web page found at `http://www.cnnfn.com/markets/currencies.html`
Notes	

Find it Online

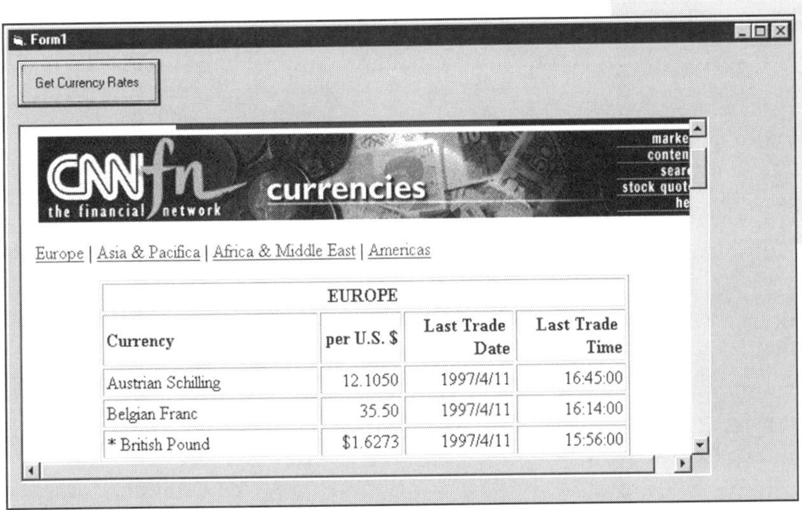

Figure 6.7 This illustration shows a prototype VB form for accessing currency information.

Designing the Clock Screen

The next task is to design the international time form. Table 6-5 shows the design information for the form; Figure 6.8 shows the prototype.

Table 6-5 Access Times in Different Financial Centers

Item	Notes
Project	VBBrowser
Name of Analyst	Rod Paddock
Date Created	09/30/98
Task Description	The system must be capable of accessing time information in various international financial centers.
Task Inputs	None
Task Outputs	Times in various time centers.
Source of Information	Web site found at `mit.edu`
Notes	

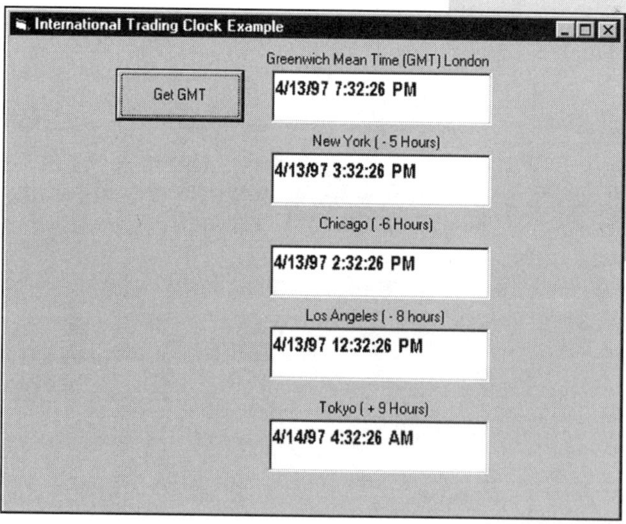

Figure 6.8 This figure shows a prototype VB form for accessing times in various financial centers.

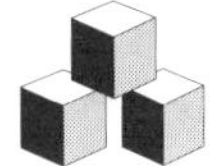

Designing the Federal Express Screen

The next feature to be designed is the form for tracking Federal Express packages. Table 6-6 shows the requirements; Figure 6.9 shows the prototype.

Table 6-6 Track Federal Express Packages Feature

Item	Notes
Project	VBBrowser
Name of Analyst	Rod Paddock
Date Created	09/30/98
Task Description	The system should be capable of tracking Federal Express packages.
Task Inputs	Package ID, Country Sent To, and Date package was sent.
Task Outputs	Tracking information for the FedEx package.
Source of Information	`www.fedex.com`
Notes	The Federal Express system uses a special URL to track packages. Need to substitute values into this URL.

Figure 6.9 Here is a prototype VB form for accessing the Federal Express package tracking system.

Designing the E-mail Sending Screen

The next feature to be designed is the form for sending e-mail. Table 6-7 shows the requirements for the e-mail form; Figure 6.10 shows the prototype.

Table 6-7 E-mail Capability Feature

Item	Notes
Project	VBBrowser
Name of Analyst	Rod Paddock
Date Created	09/30/98
Task Description	The system needs to be able to send e-mail messages.
Task Inputs	E-mail addresses, subject, text message, and address of SMTP server.
Task Outputs	E-mail message sent to specified address.
Source of Information	`smtp.ix.netcom`
Notes	Need to use the SMTP capabilities found at the company's ISP's SMTP server. System needs to obtain e-mail addresses and names from an Access database.

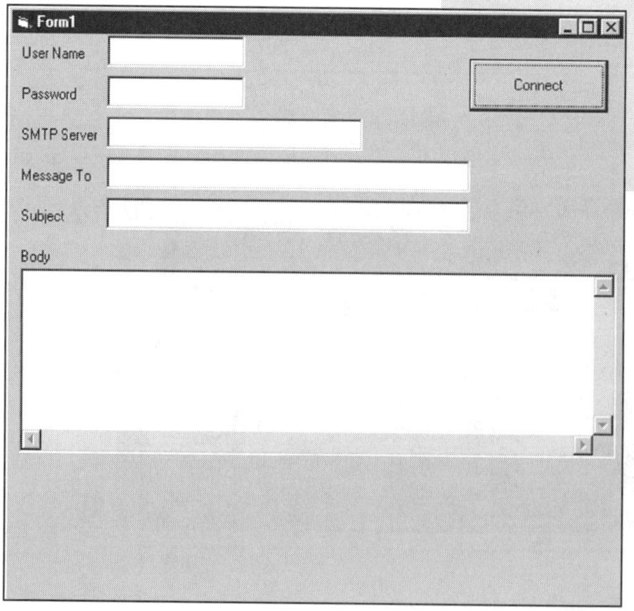

Figure 6.10 This is a prototype VB form for sending e-mail using SMTP.

Designing the Bulk E-mailer

The next feature to be designed is the form for sending bulk e-mail. Table 6-8 shows the requirements for the e-mail form; Figure 6.11 shows the prototype.

Table 6-8 Bulk E-mail Capability Feature

Item	Notes
Project	VBBrowser
Name of Analyst	Rod Paddock
Date Created	09/30/98
Task Description	The system needs to be able to send bulk e-mail messages.
Task Inputs	E-mail addresses, subject, text message, and address of SMTP server.
Task Outputs	E-mail message sent to specified addresses.
Source of Information	`smtp.ix.netcom`
Notes	Need to use the SMTP capabilities found at the company's ISP's SMTP server.

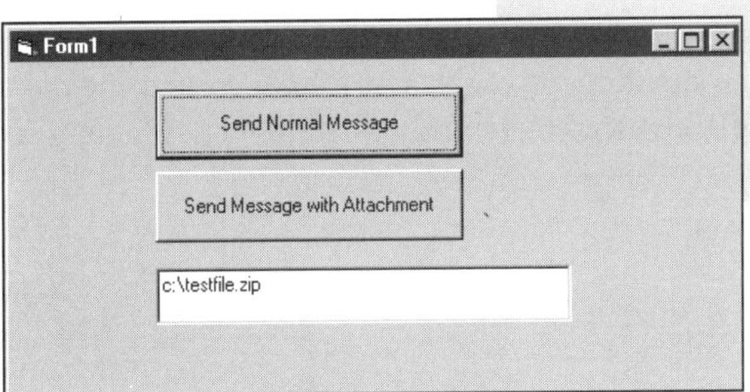

Figure 6.11
This is a prototype bulk e-mail form developed in Visual Basic.

Designing the FTP System

The next task is to design the system for transferring files. Table 6-9 shows the design information for the file transfer process.

Table 6-9 File Transfer Feature

Item	Notes
Project	VBBrowser
Name of Analyst	Rod Paddock
Date Created	09/30/98
Task Description	The system must allow for transmitting files between different systems.
Task Inputs	File to retrieve or send.
Task Outputs	Name of file on the respective system.
Source of Information	`ftp<url of FTP site you want to connect to>`
Notes	

Summary

The information documented at the design phase of your project will have long-term effects on your overall system development. When creating your designs, you need to take into account the fact that the developer of your system may not be you. With this in mind, you'll be sure to provide enough information to your developers so that they can go to work as soon as possible with few or no questions. Now that you have created the design documentation for the VBBrowser, you're ready to go to work building it in Chapter 7.

Building the VBBrowser

Earlier chapters looked at the process of gathering information for the creation of the VBBrowser application. This chapter takes you through the process of building that application. Where to begin? Return to your design document and find out what pieces you need to build for your application. Consulting the design documentation from Chapter 6, you can break down the application into a number of different components, as follows:

- The ability to view accurate time in multiple financial centers
- The ability to track Federal Express packages from the system
- The ability to track single and multiple stock quotes throughout the day
- The ability to access currency information
- The ability to send e-mail messages
- The ability to send e-mail messages from a database
- The ability to transfer files between sites

Connecting to the Internet

The first task for creating a Web-enabled application is to connect to the Internet, using your Internet service provider (ISP). There are many methods of connecting to the Internet. You can connect using the Dial-Up Networking facilities or using an automated method. In some companies, Internet access is provided as a basic service to the users of a corporate network. In any case, the examples from this chapter rely on having an Internet connection, so you should connect to the Internet *before* trying any of these examples.

Once you've connected to the Internet, you'll be ready to begin accessing information.

A Simple Internet Example: Getting the Time

When consulting the VBBrowser design documents, you'll find that one of the required systems to be developed is a mechanism for accurately displaying the time in various commerce trading centers throughout the world. How do you do this with any degree of accuracy? One method of providing the time in different time zones is to capture the local machine's time and do some basic math. This has a problem: How can you guarantee that the local machine has the correct time? You can't. That's where the Internet comes in. There are sites on the Internet that you can use to get the accurate time. Let's go to work.

Adding the Time Control

During the design process, you learned that there's an ActiveX control you can use to access Greenwich Mean Time from the Internet. This control can be added to your VB application very easily.

The first step in this process is to create a new VB application; then add the Mabry time control to your VB form. To install the Mabry control, follow these steps:

1. Choose Project, Components from the VB menu. The Visual Basic Components dialog opens.
2. Highlight the Mabry Internet Time Control (see Figure 7.1).
3. Click OK to add the control to your VB toolbox.

After adding the Internet time control to your application, you can drop it onto your form, and then use it to get the time from a specified Internet site.

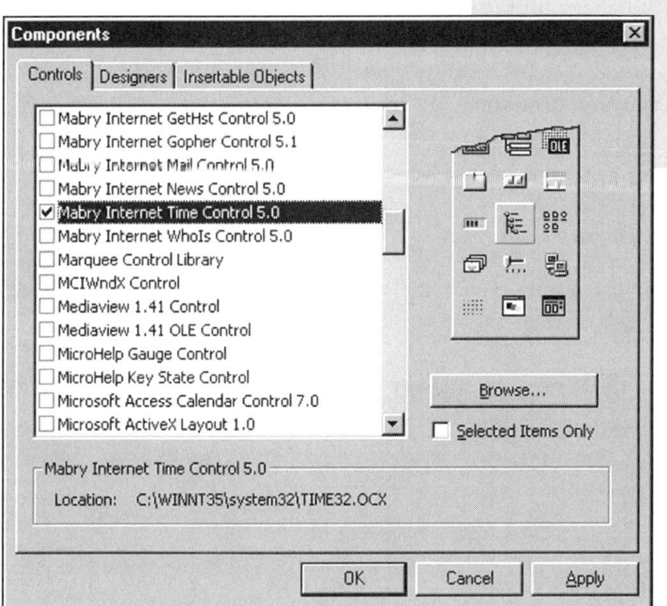

Figure 7.1
The Components dialog with the Mabry Internet Time Control selected.

To get the time from the Massachusetts Institute of Technology (MIT) site, open the Properties sheet for the time control object and specify `mit.edu` as the host (see Figure 7.2). `mit.edu` is the domain name for Massachusetts Institute of Technology. This is a server that keeps accurate time.

Figure 7.2
This illustration shows the Properties sheet for the Mabry Internet Time Control.

After adding the control to your form, you can retrieve the time by calling the `GetTime()` method. The `GetTime()` method retrieves the time from the specified host and stores it in the `GMTTime` property. Put the following code into a command button to show how the time control works:

```
' Retrieve Greenwich Mean Time
Time1.GetTime()
'Set The Text Box with GMT
Text1.Text = Time1.GMTTime
```

Figure 7.3 shows the form with the results of accessing the time control.

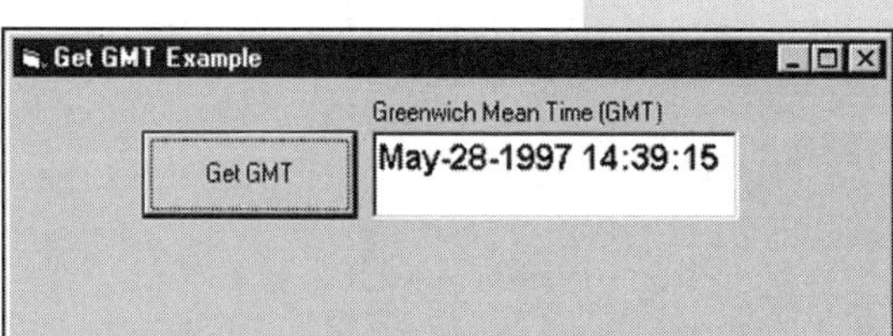

Figure 7.3
This figure shows the current Greenwich Mean Time as returned by the Mabry Internet Time Control.

Now that you have added a button capable of retrieving the time, you need to add a mechanism for updating the time automatically. You can do this by using a timer control. Add a timer control to your form and set its interval to `1000`. This will cause the timer to call the `Timer` event every second. Next, put the following code into the timer event:

```
'Call the get time button
    Call Command1_Click
```

This code causes the time object to be refreshed every second.

Consulting your design documentation again, you learn that you need the clock application to show the time in London, Tokyo, Los Angeles, Chicago, and New York. You also learn that the differences in hours (from Greenwich Mean Time) are 0, +9, –8, –6, and –5 hours, respectively. With this knowledge, you can create an international clock with different time zones represented. To do this, add a label and a text box object to your form for each time zone you want to display. Then add the following code to the command button you added earlier:

```
txtGMT.Text = DateAdd("h", 0, Time1.GMTTime)
txtNewYork.Text = DateAdd("h", -5, Time1.GMTTime)
txtChicago.Text = DateAdd("h", -6, Time1.GMTTime)
txtLosAngeles.Text = DateAdd("h", -8, Time1.GMTTime)
txtTokyo.Text = DateAdd("h", 9, Time1.GMTTime)
```

Figure 7.4 shows the finished clock.

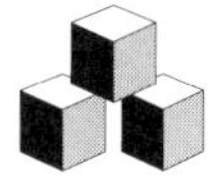

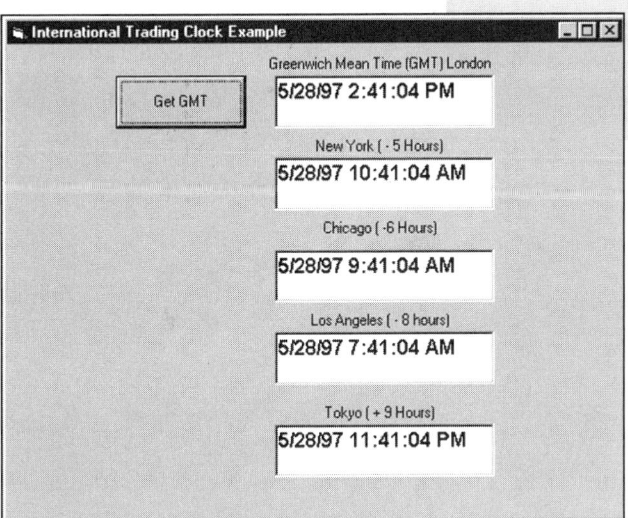

Figure 7.4 The finished international time clock.

Creating a Browser

As you can see from the first example, creating a Web-enabled VB application is pretty straightforward. Now let's get a little more elaborate. In this next set of examples, you'll learn how to add the functionality of a Web browser to your applications.

Creating a Browser with the Visual Basic Add Form Dialog

Visual Basic comes equipped with a set of tools that simplify the process of adding a Web browser to your application. To add a Web browser form to a VB application, choose Project, Add Form from the VB menu. This activates the Visual Basic Add Form dialog. Select the Web Browser icon from the dialog, as shown in Figure 7.5. VB then creates a Visual Basic form with a browser-style interface, as shown in Figure 7.6.

To run this form, you need to make a few minor modifications. By default, VB creates the browser form as an MDI child-style form. If you aren't creating MDI-style applications, you need to set the `MDIChild` property of the form to `False`. The next step is to specify the browser form as the startup object for your project. You do this by selecting Project, Properties from the VB menu. This brings up the Project Properties dialog. Specify `frmBrowser` as your startup object in the Startup Object list box (see Figure 7.7).

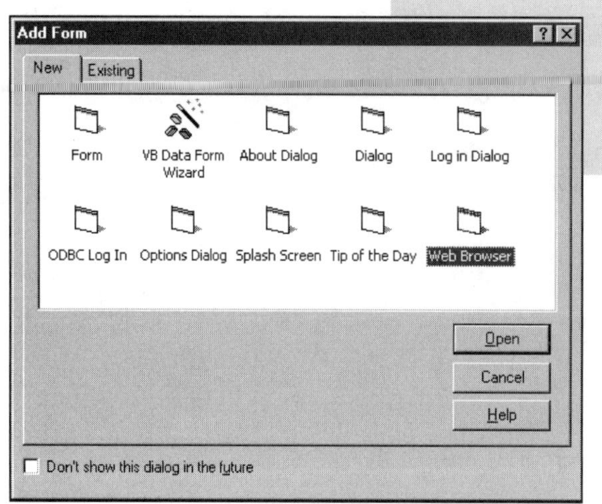

Figure 7.5
The Add Form dialog with the Web Browser icon selected.

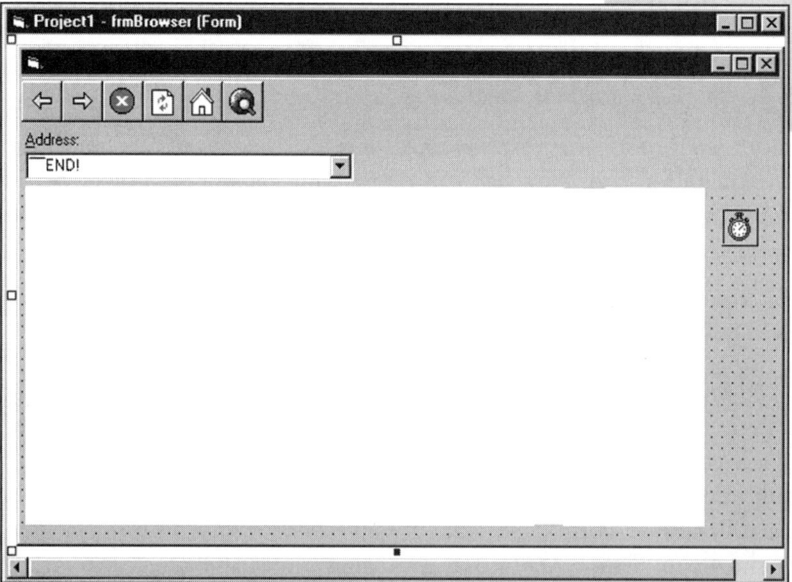

Figure 7.6
A browser form created by Visual Basic.

Now that you have created a browser for your VB application, you can run it and begin browsing the Web immediately. Figure 7.8 shows the form created by VB browsing the `www.microsoft.com` Web site.

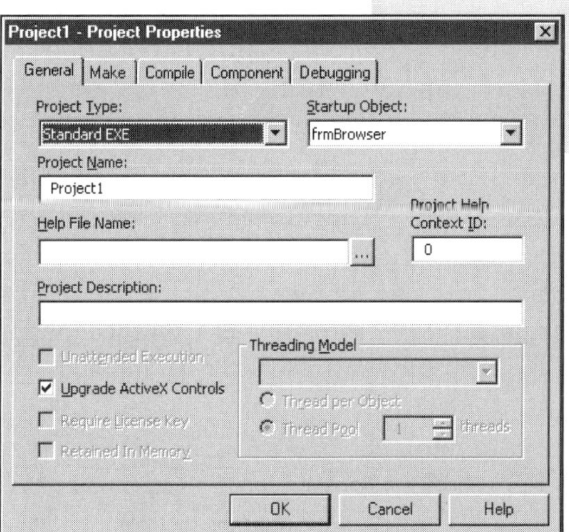

Figure 7.7
The `frmBrowser` form is specified as the startup object.

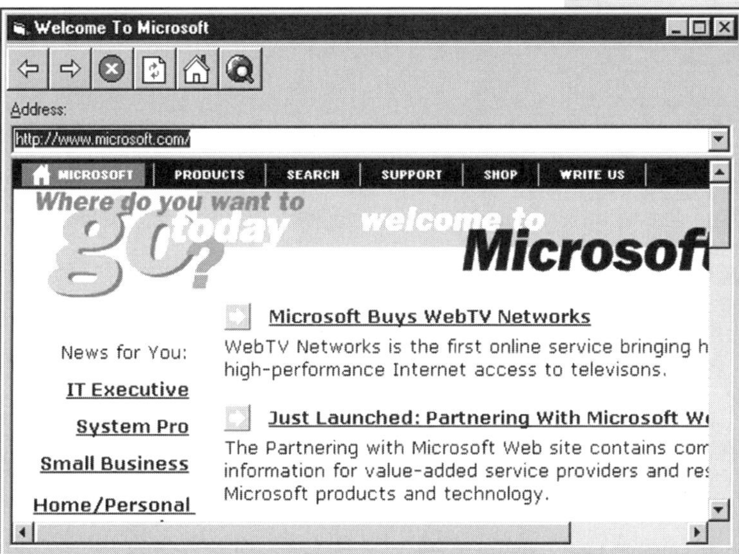

Figure 7.8
The form created by Visual Basic, shown browsing the Microsoft Web site.

As you can see, VB can create a fairly nice browser for you automatically. However, this is just a simple browser with very little functionality. If you want to create some very useful browser tools, you need to do more work, as described in the following section.

Creating a Browser by Hand

The browsers that VB can create natively are nice but not very powerful. In this section, you learn how to create a browser by hand, using some controls provided by VB.

To create your own Web browser in VB, you need to make sure that the Microsoft Internet controls that come with VB are available to your project. To install the Microsoft Internet controls, you need to add them to your project by selecting Project, Components from the VB menu. VB posts the Visual Basic Components dialog; highlight the Microsoft Internet Controls option (see Figure 7.9), and click OK. This adds the control to your VB toolbox.

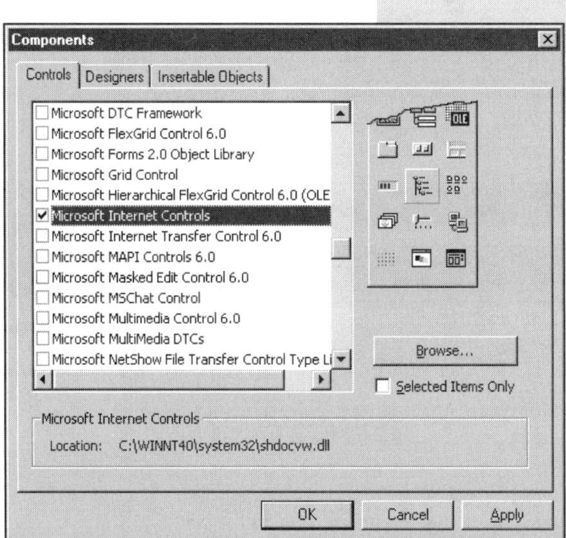

Figure 7.9
Adding the Microsoft Internet controls.

After adding the Internet controls to your project, you'll see a browser control in your toolbox. Figure 7.10 shows the VB toolbox with the Web browser control installed.

With the Web browser control added to your project, you're ready to create your own browser. Follow these steps:

1. Create a new standard project by selecting File, New Project from the VB menu.
2. Add the Microsoft Internet controls to your project.
3. Add a Web browser control to the form.
4. Add a command button to the form. Change its caption to `www.microsoft.com`.

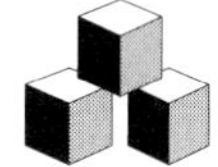

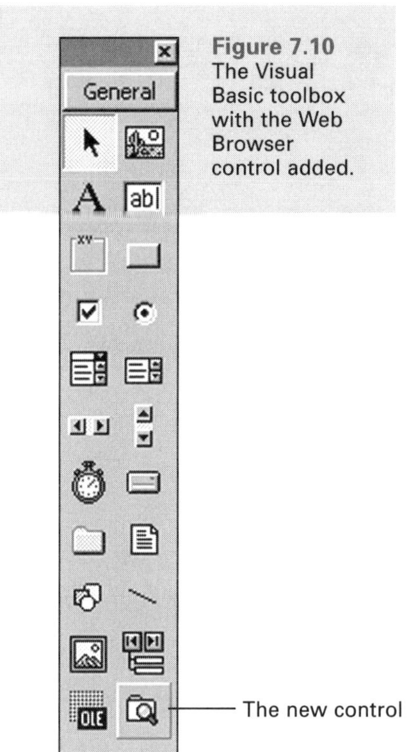

Figure 7.10 The Visual Basic toolbox with the Web Browser control added.

5. In the command button's `Click` event, add the following code:

   WebBrowser1.Navigate ("www.microsoft.com")

6. Run your VB program and click the button.

Assuming that you're connected to the Internet already, this item takes you to the Microsoft Web page.

Now that you have created your first Web browser, it's time to add more functionality. The first thing is to allow users to specify the Web page to which they want to navigate. To add this functionality, follow these steps:

1. Add a new text box to the form. Change its `Name` property to **`txtUrl`** and its `Text` property to **`www.microsoft.com`**.
2. Change the caption of the command button to **`Navigate`**.
3. Change the code in the command button to the following:

   WebBrowser1.Navigate (txtUrl.text)

Now that you have added this functionality to your Web page, change the text object to your favorite Web site and click the Navigate button. Figure 7.11 shows the new navigator (here displaying the Web site found at `www.pcweek.com`).

Figure 7.11
The `pcweek.com` Web site shown in the Visual Basic browser just created.

Here's an interesting feature of the Web browser control. Type C:\ in the `txtURL` text box, and click Navigate to see what happens.

Adding Functionality to Your Browser

Now that you understand the process of adding a Web browser to your VB forms, you can proceed to add useful functionality to your application. Looking at the system design documents, you'll find three components that need to have some type of interface. These are the components:

- The ability to track documents using the company's shipping provider, Federal Express
- The ability to receive stock quotes from the NASDAQ Web site
- The ability to request currency exchange rates

Accessing FedEx

The first item on the list is to track packages using Federal Express. From the design documents, you'll find that Federal Express uses the common gateway interface (CGI) for processing package-tracking requests. You can add this functionality to your application by logging onto their Web site using the proper URL. To create this interface, you need to know two pieces of information:

- What's the protocol for calling the Federal Express tracking system from a browser?
- What information is needed to track a package?

From the design documentation, you'll find that the protocol for calling the package-tracking system is to connect using the proper FedEx URL with package-tracking information embedded. The URL for tracking a package through FedEx looks like this:

```
http://www.fedex.com/cgi-bin/track_it?trk_num=2837510384&dest_cntry=
➥UNITED+STATES.&ship_date=072498
```

From this URL and from the Federal Express Web site (see Figure 7.12), you'll find that tracking a package requires three pieces of information:

- The package tracking number
- The country to which the package was shipped

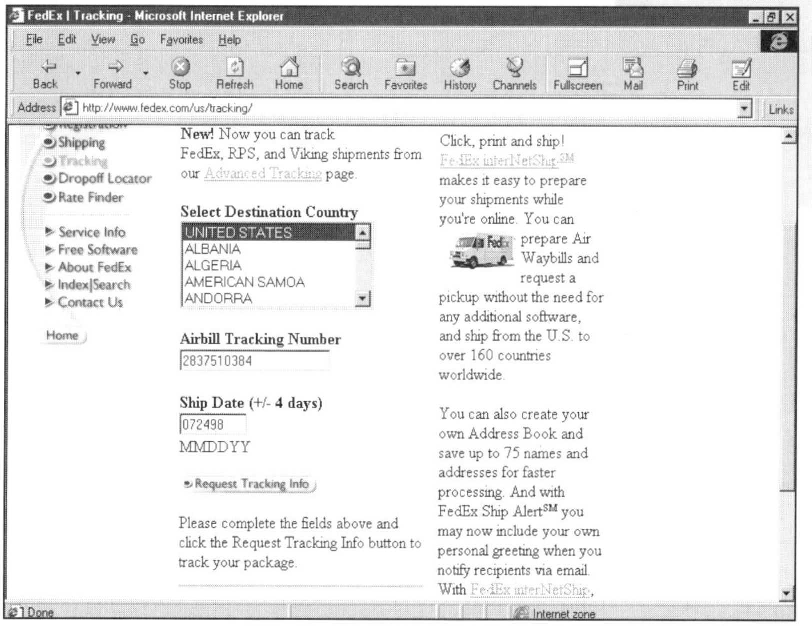

Figure 7.12 The Federal Express Web site, showing the page for tracking a package.

- The date of the shipment +/– four days in MMDDYY format

Now that you understand what information is necessary to track a package, you can create an interface for tracking a package from your application. To create the package tracker component, do the following:

1. Create a new VB project.
2. Add a Web browser control.
3. Add a command button to the form. Change its `Caption` property to **`Go FedEx`**.
4. In the `Click` event of the command button, add the following code:

```
WebBrowser1.Navigate ("http://www.fedex.com/cgi-bin/track_it?trk_num=
➥2837510384&dest_cntry=U.S.A.&ship_date=072498")
```

5. Run your form.

After running this project, click the button to return the tracking information for this package to your browser window, as shown in Figure 7.13.

Now that you've started your interface, you need to spruce it up. Return your form to design mode and do the following:

1. Add two text boxes with the names `txtPackageId` and `txtShipDate`. Set the `Text` properties to <*blank*> (in other words, nothing).
2. Add a combo box object with the name `cboCountry`. Add the following items to its `List` property: **`U.S.A.`**, **`Canada`**, and **`Germany`**. Set its `Text` property to **`U.S.A.`**.

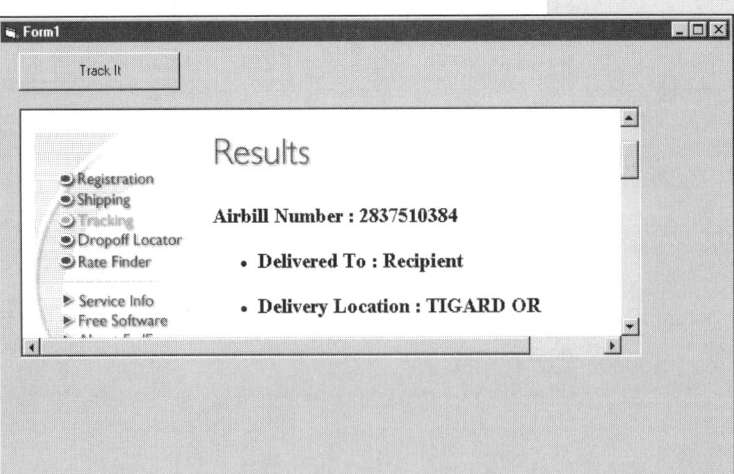

Figure 7.13 This illustration shows shipping information returned from the Federal Express Web site.

3. Add labels for each of the items you added in the preceding steps.
4. Change the caption of the button you added in the preceding exercise to **Track Package**.
5. Add the following code to the `Click` event of the command button:

```
Dim strUrl As String

' Create the URL for tracking a package
strUrl = "http://www.fedex.com/cgi-bin/track_it?trk_num="
strUrl = strUrl & Trim(txtPackageId.Text)
strUrl = strUrl & "&dest_cntry=" & cboCountry.Text
strUrl = strUrl & "&ship_date=" & Trim(txtShipDate.Text)

' Track the package
WebBrowser1.Navigate (strUrl)
```

6. Now that you have created the form, run it and enter the appropriate information for tracking your package. Figure 7.14 shows your package-tracking system with information from Federal Express.

Now that you have completed this first step, you could go in and add validation code to the form. But why do that when the FedEx site will handle it for you? Figure 7.15 shows what happens when users enter incorrect information.

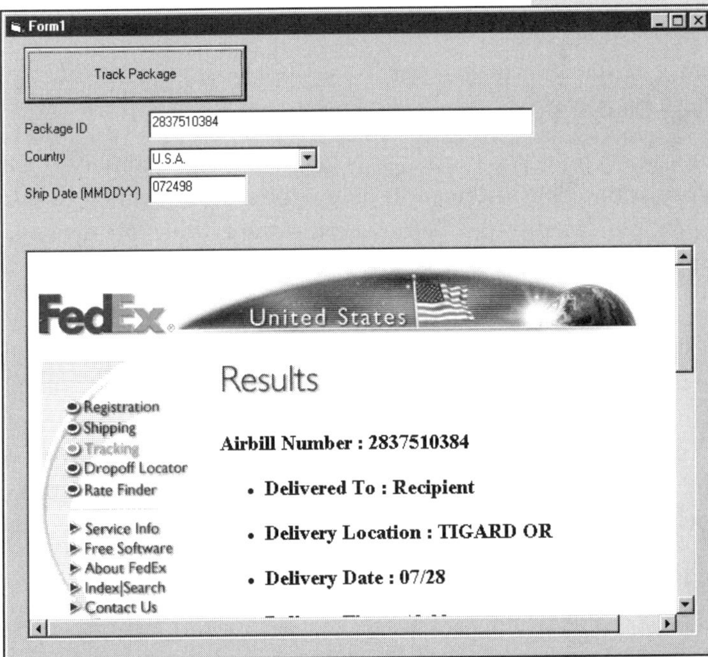

Figure 7.14
The finished Visual Basic package-tracking form.

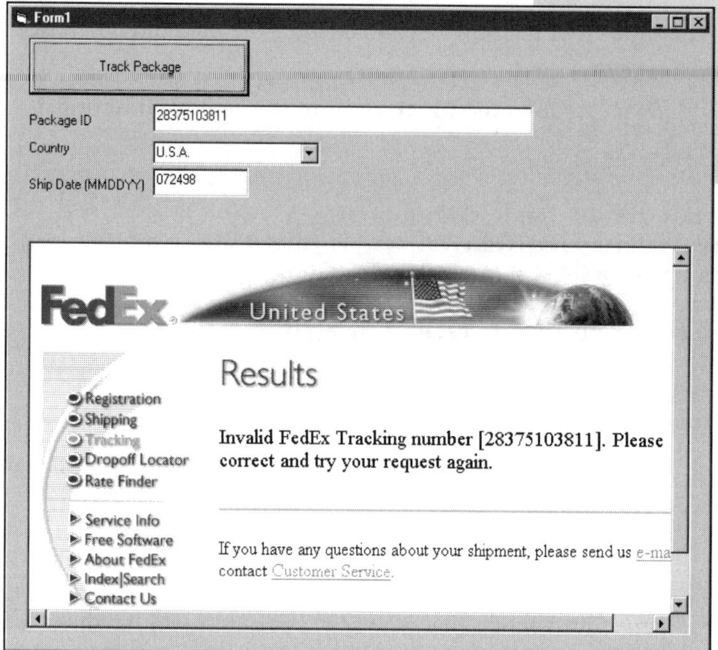

Figure 7.15
This illustration shows the information returned from the FedEx site when users enter incorrect data.

Now that this is done, you can move on to using the Web to track stock quotes.

Accessing NASDAQ

From the preceding example, you learned how to use a Web site to track some very useful information. This information doesn't need to be limited to just tracking packages. You can also track information that's a little more dynamic in nature, such as stock quotes.

One of the more useful sites on the Web is provided by NASDAQ. The NASDAQ site allows you to track financial information such as stock and mutual fund prices. To use the NASDAQ site, you follow the same set of steps you did with Federal Express. Go to the site and find out what type of URL you need to provide for tracking a stock. The easiest method of doing this is actually to visit the site and track a stock quote. As Figure 7.16 shows, the URL for tracking a single stock quote is as follows:

```
http://www.nasdaq.com/asp/quotes_multi.asp?mode=Stock&symbol=DELL
```

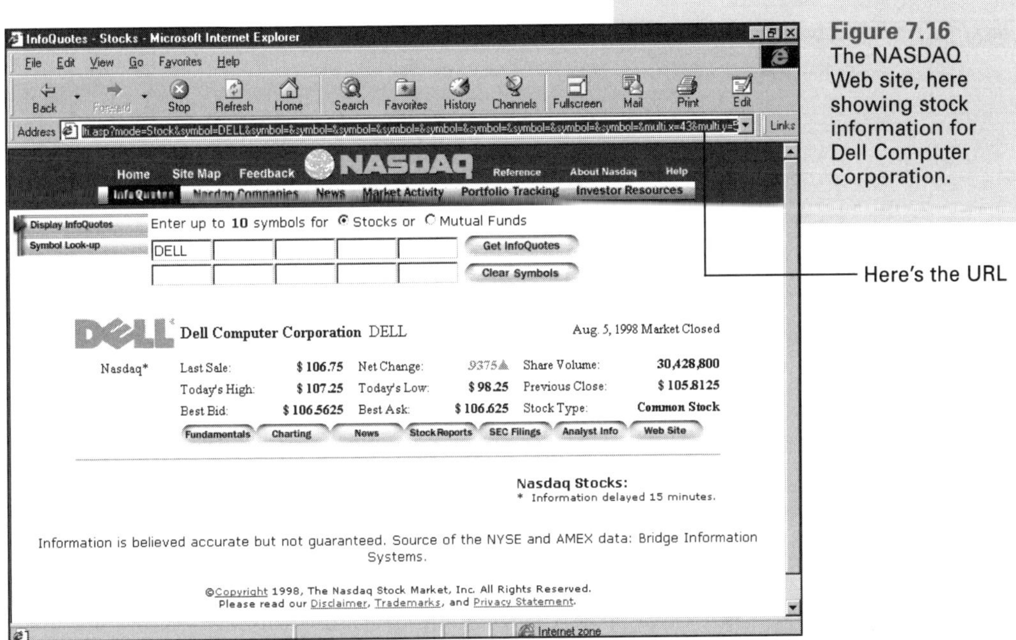

Figure 7.16 The NASDAQ Web site, here showing stock information for Dell Computer Corporation.

Now you can begin creating a VB form to track stock quotes. Follow these steps:

1. Create a new VB project.
2. Add a Web browser control.
3. Add a text box object to the form. Change its `Name` property to **`txtSymbol`**. Change its **`Text`** property to **`<blank>`**.
4. Add a command button to the form. Change its `Caption` property to **`Get Quote`**.
5. In the `Click` event of the command button, add the following code:

```
        ' Create NASDAQ URL
          Dim strUrl As String
strURL = "http://www.nasdaq.com/asp/quotes_multi.asp?mode=Stock&symbol="
strUrl = strUrl & txtSymbol.Text

          ' Go get the quote
          WebBrowser1.Navigate (strUrl)
```

6. Add a label for the text box.
7. Run your form.

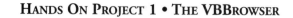

Figure 7.17
The Visual Basic form generated for tracking stock quotes.

After activating the form, enter the ticker symbol for your favorite stock (for example, **MSFT** for Microsoft or **ORCL** for Oracle). Figure 7.17 shows the stock information for Dell Computer Corporation.

One of the other nice features of the NASDAQ site is its ability to track multiple quotes. However, the URL for tracking multiple quotes is a little different. This is the URL for tracking three different stocks:

```
http://www.nasdaq.com/asp/quotes_multi.asp?mode=Stock&symbol=
➥DELL&symbol=MSFT&symbol=AAPL
```

As you can see, it's necessary to create an URL with different ticker symbols, delimited by an ampersand (&). This is much like the earlier Federal Express example. To request multiple quotes, make the following alterations to your stock quote form:

1. Change the name of the `txtSymbol` object to **`txtSymbol1`**.
2. Add three more text boxes to your form; name them **`txtSymbol2`**, **`txtSymbol3`**, and **`txtSymbol4`**.
3. Change the code in the command button to read like this:

ON THE CD

```
' Create NASDAQ URL
   Dim strUrl As String

   'Create beginning of URL
   strUrl = "http://www.nasdaq.com/asp/quotes_multi.asp?mode=Stock"

   'Add first symbol
```

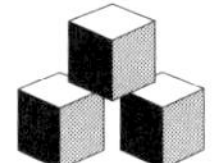


```
If Len(txtSymbol1.Text) > 0 Then
    strUrl = strUrl & "&symbol=" & Trim(txtSymbol1.Text)
End If

'Add the second symbol
If Len(txtSymbol2.Text) > 0 Then
strUrl = strUrl & "&symbol=" & Trim(txtSymbol2.Text)
End If

'Add the third symbol
If Len(txtSymbol3.Text) > 0 Then
        strUrl = strUrl & "&symbol=" & Trim(txtSymbol3.Text)
End If

'Add the fourth symbol
If Len(txtSymbol4.Text) > 0 Then
        strUrl = strUrl & "&symbol=" & Trim(txtSymbol4.Text)
End If


'Show us what we created
MsgBox (strUrl)

' Go get the quote(s)
WebBrowser1.Navigate (strUrl)
```

4. Save your project and run the form. Figure 7.18 shows the finished form with three requested stock quotes.

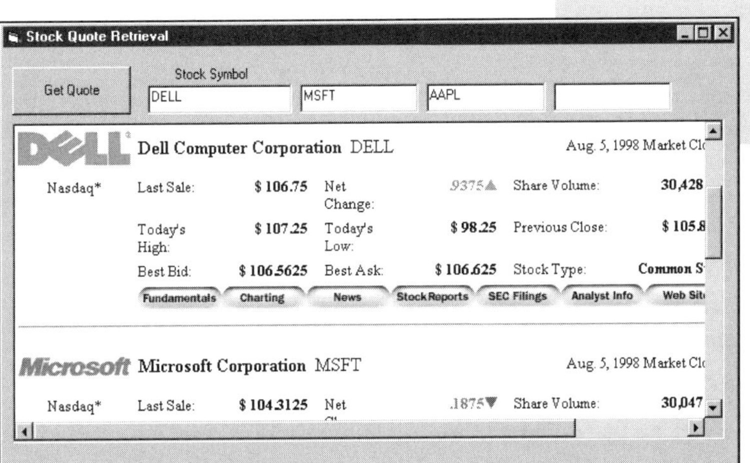

Figure 7.18
The multiple-request generator form with three stock quotes.

Accessing a Currency Forum

Until now you've been using the Web browser control to look at the data found on Web pages. This method is limited by the fact that it simply displays the contents of Web pages. What if you want to look at the actual HTML contents of the Web page and turn them into more useful data? This is where the *Microsoft Internet transfer control* comes in. The Microsoft Internet transfer control is an ActiveX control provided with Visual Basic that allows you to use some of the lower-level Internet protocols directly. The protocols supported by the Internet transfer control are as follows:

- File transfer protocol (FTP)
- Hypertext transport protocol (HTTP)
- Secure hypertext transport protocol (HTTPS)
- Gopher

In this example, you'll learn how to extract the raw HTML code from a Web page. You'll see the rendered page using the browser control, and in another window you'll see the raw contents of the HTML page. The raw contents are retrieved with the Internet transfer control using the HTTP protocol.

The first step is to find the URL for the currency exchange rates Web page. Consulting the design documentation, you'll find the currency page at this URL:

Find it Online

```
http://www.cnnfn.com/markets/currencies.html
```

After retrieving this information, you can begin creating your VB currency project, which requires two phases:

- Show the currency Web page in a Web browser control.
- Extract the information from that Web page, using the Internet transfer control.

The first step is to create the VB form for showing the Web page. To create this form, do the following:

1. Create a new VB project.
2. Change the caption of the form to **`Get Currency Rates`**.
3. Add a Web browser control.
4. Add a command button to the form. Change its `Caption` property to **`Get Currency Rates`**.
5. In the `Click` event of the command button, add the following code:

   ```
   WebBrowser1.Navigate ("http://www.cnnfn.com/markets/currencies.html")
   ```

6. Run your form (see Figure 7.19).

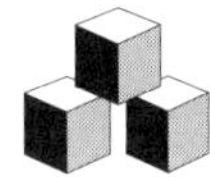

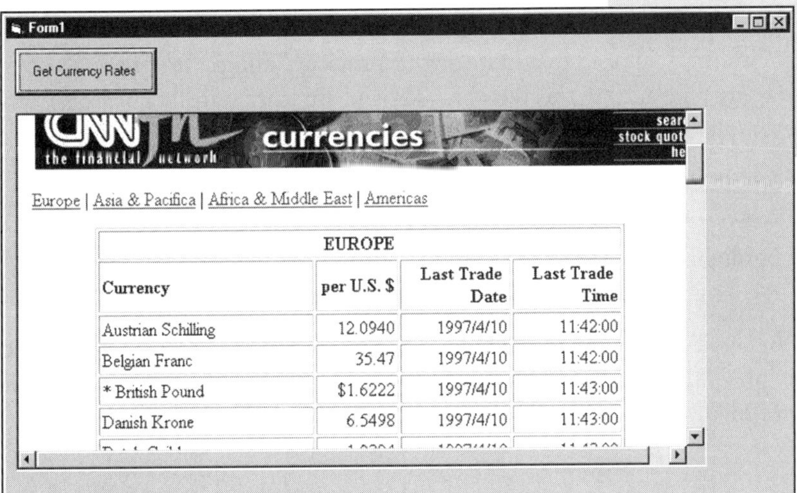

EUROPE			
Currency	per U.S. $	Last Trade Date	Last Trade Time
Austrian Schilling	12.0940	1997/4/10	11:42:00
Belgian Franc	35.47	1997/4/10	11:42:00
* British Pound	$1.6222	1997/4/10	11:43:00
Danish Krone	6.5498	1997/4/10	11:43:00

Figure 7.19
Displaying the contents of the currency Web page.

As you can see, you can retrieve the raw HTML code from a Web page. After retrieving the text, you are free to parse the text into a more usable format using text file manipulation routines found in Visual Basic.

Browser Components Summary

The Internet can be used to provide a wide range of information services. This section discussed only one of the facilities available to VB developers. In the next section, you learn how to use some of the other facilities provided by the Internet, including sending e-mail and transferring files with FTP.

Adding E-mail to Your Applications

Up to this point in the chapter, you were dealing with the Web-based components of the Internet. However, one of the most powerful components of the Internet is its ability to send and receive e-mail. In this section, you learn how to add e-mail facilities to your applications.

Using SMTP to Send E-mail

The first step to integrating e-mail into your applications is to add the ability to simply send e-mail. To send e-mail using the Internet, you use a protocol

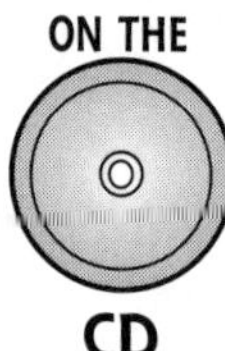

known as simple mail transfer protocol (SMTP). The CD accompanying this book contains a control from Mabry Software for creating e-mail messages. To use this control, you need to add it to your project. Adding the control to your project is just like adding the Web browser and Internet transfer controls from prior examples:

1. Choose Project, Components from the VB menu to open the Visual Basic Components dialog.
2. Highlight the Mabry Mail Control option (see Figure 7.20) and click OK. This adds the control to your VB toolbox.

Now that you've added the control to your project, you can go about the process of sending e-mail messages from your applications. Creating e-mail messages involves a specific set of steps:

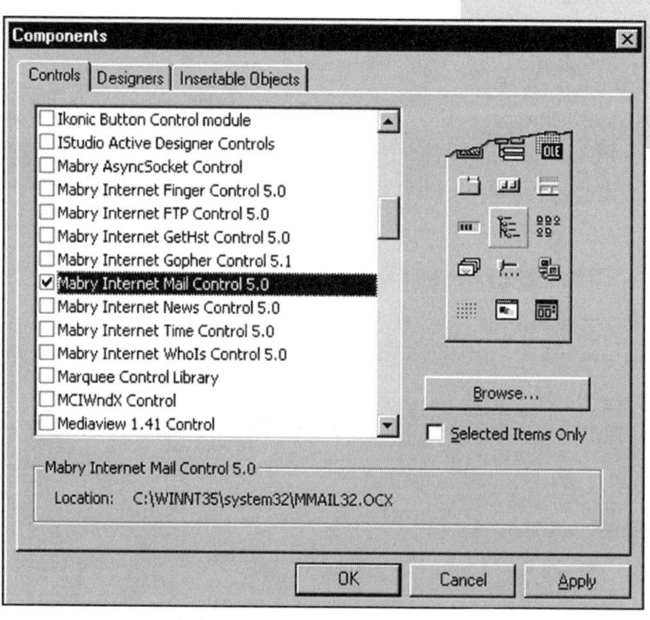

Figure 7.20 Adding the Mabry mail control.

1. Connect to the e-mail server.
2. Create a new message.
3. Assign the subject, recipient, and contents of the e-mail message.
4. Send the message.

As you can see, creating an e-mail message is a fairly simple set of tasks. Now let's create a message.

Connecting to the Server

The first step to creating an e-mail message is to connect to the server. To connect to the server, you need three pieces of information:

- The name of the SMTP server that you use for e-mail. You'll need to obtain this information from either your ISP or your system administrator.
- Your username.
- Your password.

Once you've gathered the information specified in this list, you're ready to begin the process of sending a message. To connect to the e-mail server, follow these steps:

1. Create a new VB project.
2. Add the Mabry mail control to your project.
3. Add a command button to your form. Change its caption to **`connect`**.
4. Add the following code to the `Click` event of the button:

ON THE CD

```
With mMail1
     .Host = "smtp.ix.netcom.com"
     .LogonName = "<your name>"
     .LogonPassword = "<your password>"
     .Connect
End With
```

5. Set the mail control's `ConnectType` property to **`MailConnectTypeSMTP`**.
6. Set the `Blocking` property to **`True`**. This makes the control behave in synchronous mode (one line at a time).
7. Run the form.

Once you've completed the connection process, you can create and send an e-mail message.

Creating and Sending the Message

After connecting to the server, you can create a new message by calling the `NewMessage` method of the mail control. Then you need to set the properties of the object to the contents of your new message. Table 7-1 describes some of the properties available.

Table 7-1 Mail Control Properties

Property	Description
`Subject`	Subject of the message
`To`	Whom to send message to
`From`	Who sent the message
`Body(n)`	Message content
`Emailaddress`	SMTP requires you to specify the e-mail address of the message sender.

After connecting to the server, add the following code to create and send a test message:

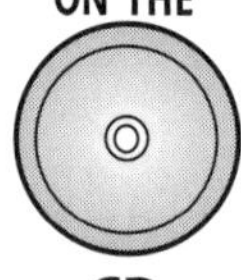

```
With mMail1
        ' Create new message
        .NewMessage

        ' Set the subject
        .Subject = "Rodman was here in VB"

        'Set the to address
        .To = "rpaddock@ix.netcom.com"

        'Set the from address
        .From = "rodman himself"

        'Set the e-mail address required by SMTP
        .EMailAddress = "rpaddock@ix.netcom.com"

        'Set the body of the message
        .Body(0) = "Hello this is a test"

        'Set the message's header
        .Headers(0) = "X-Mailer: Rpaddock"

        'Set the flag to send to SMTP host
        .Flags = MailDstIsHost

        'Send the message
        .Action = MailActionWriteMessage

        'We're done, disconnect
        .Disconnect
    End With
```

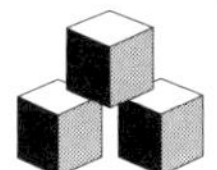

Now go to your browser and retrieve your mail. Figure 7.21 shows a mailbox with the test message from this code. After completing your test message, you should add an interface for sending e-mail. Figure 7.22 shows a completed e-mail form.

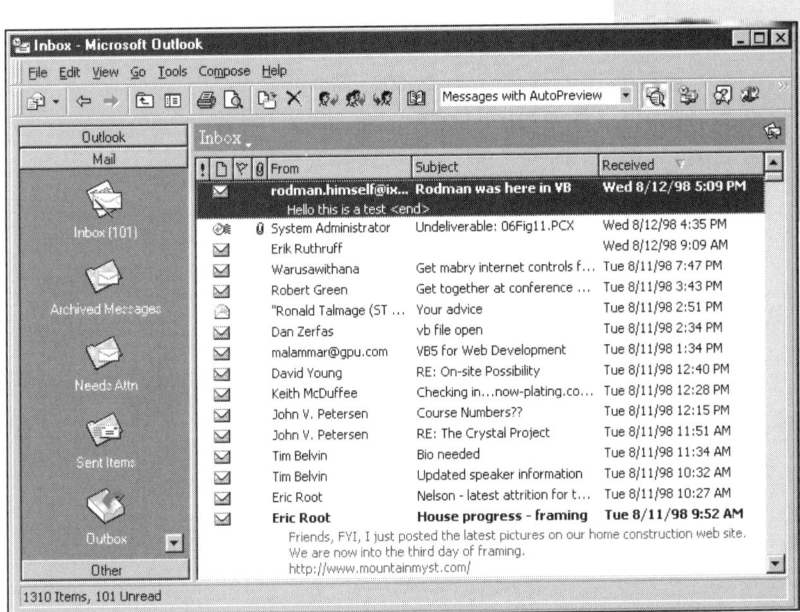

Figure 7.21
Microsoft Outlook with the message sent from the preceding code lines.

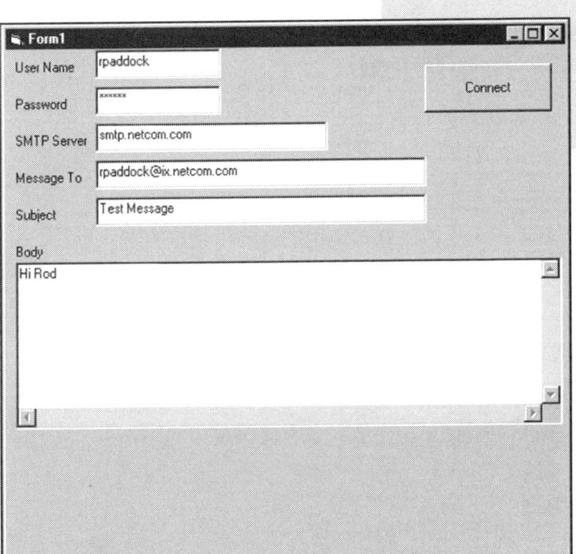

Figure 7.22
A Visual Basic form developed for sending e-mail with SMTP.

The process for creating this message is as follows:

1. Add text box controls to your form for each parameter.
2. Change the code in the command button to read as follows:

```
With mMail1
        ' Create new message
        .NewMessage

        ' Set the subject
        .Subject = txtSubject.Text

        'Set the to address
        .To = txtToName.Text

        'Set the from address
        .From = txtUserName.Text

        'Set the e-mail address required by SMTP
        .EMailAddress = "rpaddock@ix.netcom.com"

        'Set the body of the message
        .Body(0) = txtBody.Text

        'Set the message's header
        .Headers(0) = "X-Mailer: Rpaddock"

        'Set the flag to send to SMTP host
        .Flags = MailDstIsHost

        'Send the message
        .Action = MailActionWriteMessage

        'We're done, disconnect
        .Disconnect
    End With
```

3. Run the form and enter the appropriate information for your SMTP server, username, password, and e-mail message information.

Sending E-mail from a Database

Now that you've mastered sending e-mail using SMTP, you can further integrate some of your other VB experience into a more complex example. In this section you begin sending e-mail from a table of user information. To send e-mail from a database, you need to perform the following steps:

1. Establish a connection with a database. Upon connecting to the database, retrieve the users you want to e-mail.
2. Send e-mail to each of the people returned by your query.

Retrieving Your Mailing List

The first step to adding database functionality to your application is to create a connection to a database. Creating a connection to a database with VB involves the use of Microsoft Data Access Objects (DAO), version 3.5. DAO is a set of tools that you can use in VB and other applications to connect to databases. DAO version 3.5 has a type of connection called ODBCDirect. ODBCDirect is a light framework for accessing data by using ODBC drivers.

Creating a connection to a database with VB begins with referencing DAO 3.5 with your project. Follow these steps:

1. Select Project, References from the VB menu to open the VB References dialog.
2. Select Microsoft DAO 3.5 Object Library (see Figure 7.23).

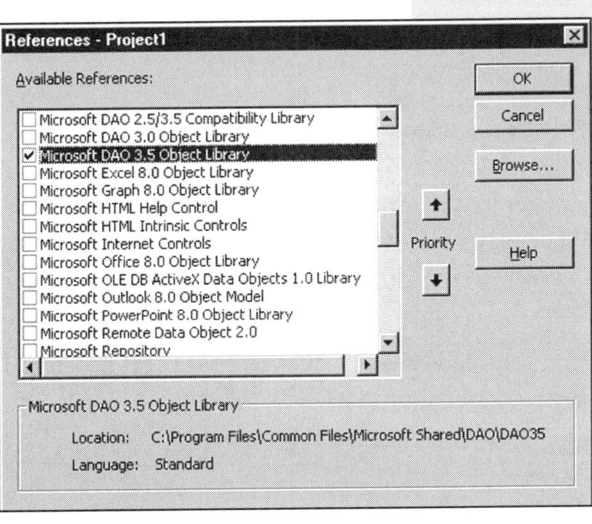

Figure 7.23
The VB References dialog shown here has the DAO 3.5 object library selected.

After creating your new project and related DAO, you can begin adding code to your class. The following code creates a connection to an ODBC data source named `EmailList`:

```
Dim oWorkspace As Workspace
    Set oWorkspace = DBEngine.CreateWorkspace("ODBCDirect", "", "",
➥dbUseODBC)

    Dim oConn As Connection
    Set oConn = oWorkspace.OpenConnection("EmailList",dbDriverNoPrompt,
➥False)
```

This code performs two functions. It first creates a database engine object with the `CreateWorkSpace` method. It then connects to the `EmailList` database with the `OpenConnection` method. Once you have created a connection to a database, you can begin querying that database.

Creating the Query

After establishing a connection to a database, you can begin querying that database by creating a `Recordset` object. A `Recordset` object is a collection of records returned from a database based on a query passed during its instantiation process. The following code demonstrates creating a `Recordset` object with all records from the `email_list` table:

```
Dim recRecordsSelected As Recordset
Set recRecordsSelected = oConn.OpenRecordset("Select *
➥from email_list", dbOpenForwardOnly)
```

Creating a recordset required two parameters:

- The first is a SQL `Select` statement. The `Recordset` object uses this parameter to determine which records it will return from the database.
- The second is a parameter that tells the database engine how this object will be used. This `Recordset` object will be one that can only be scrolled through using `MoveNext`. This allows the database engine to optimize for this action.

Now that you have accessed your database and queried `email_list`, you can begin sending e-mail to the selected list of users. The following code demonstrates sending e-mail to this list:

```
'Open the database query first
    Dim oWorkspace As Workspace
    Set oWorkspace =
➥DBEngine.CreateWorkspace("ODBCDirect", "", "", dbUseODBC)

        'Create connection
```

```
    Dim oConn As Connection
    Set oConn =
➥oWorkspace.OpenConnection("email_list", dbDriverNoPrompt, False)

         'Query records from e-mail database
    Dim oRecs As Recordset
    Set oRecs =
➥oConn.OpenRecordset("Select * from email_list", dbOpenForwardOnly)

         'Connect e-mail control to server
    With Form1.mMail1

              'We need to set the control to synchronous mode
              'when sending more than one e-mail message.
              .Blocking = True

              'Login to the e-mail server
              .Host = "smtp.ix.netcom.com"
              .LogonName = "rpaddock"
              .LogonPassword = "yoda4rod"
              .Connect
    End With

         'Scan the e-mail message
    Do Until oRecs.EOF

         With Form1.mMail1
              'Create a new message
              .NewMessage

              'Set subject
              .Subject = "Bulk-email test. Msg Sent:" & Now

              'Set e-mail address
              .To = oRecs.Fields("email_address").Value

              'Set From line and address
              .From = "rpaddock@dashpoint.com"
              .EMailAddress = "rpaddock@dashpoint.com"

              'Set body of e-mail message (could be a text box)
              .Body(0) = "Bulk email test"

              'Must send an e-mail header
              .Headers(0) = "X-Mailer: rpaddock"

              'We are sending to a host e-mailer
              .Flags = MailDstIsHost
```

```
        'Send the message
        .Action = MailActionWriteMessage
    End With

    'Move through the data
    oRecs.MoveNext
Loop

        'Close the e-mail connection
Form1.mMail1.Disconnect
```

Now that you know how to send e-mail messages, what good does that do you? Well, now you can write automated e-mail-sending systems that alert supervisors, systems administrators, and other concerned parties of events occurring within a system. Some ideas that come to mind include shipping status information for your customers, reorder messages for purchasing departments, and other information that needs periodic attention.

Transferring Files with FTP

The last step in this project is sending and retrieving files from external systems. In doing so, you learn how to use FTP, a protocol that allows users to send and retrieve files from Internet sites. This is how many companies distribute software updates and information.

Earlier in this chapter, you learned that the Internet transfer control supports multiple protocols. One of those protocols is File Transfer Protocol (FTP).

Note

To use the Internet transfer control, you need to add it to your project (refer to the instructions earlier in the chapter). After adding this control, you can begin using it in your application.

The following steps allow you to view a directory of files on an external site:

1. Add an Internet transfer control to your form. Set the `Protocol` property to **`icFTP`**, the `URL` property to **`ftp.microsoft.com`**, and the `Username` property to **`anonymous`**.
2. Add a text box control to your form. Give it the name **`txtContents`**.
3. Add a command button to your form. Set its `Caption` property to **`Get Contents`**.

4. Add the following code to the command button's `Click` event:

```
Call Inet1.Execute(Inet1.URL, "DIR *.*")
```

5. Add the following code to the `StateChanged` event of the Internet transfer control:

```
Select Case Ctato
        Case 12  ' Done
            txtContents.Text = Inet1.GetChunk(1024, isString)
    End Select
```

6. Run the form and click the button. Figure 7.24 shows the contents of the Microsoft FTP site.

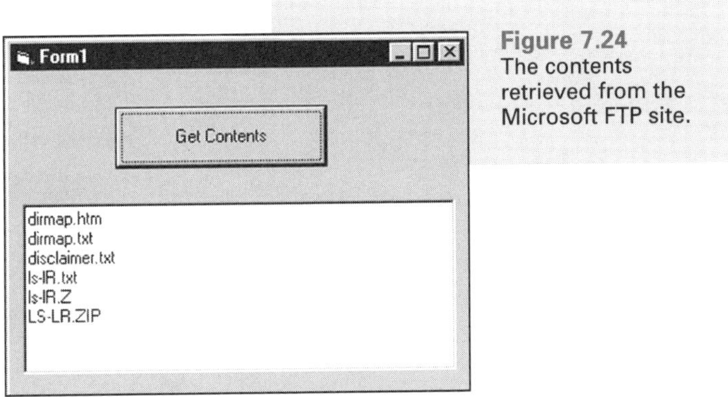

Figure 7.24
The contents retrieved from the Microsoft FTP site.

If you want to retrieve a file from this site, enter a command like the following in the command button's `Click` event:

```
Call Inet1.Execute(Inet1.URL, "GET disclaimer.txt c:\rodman99.txt")
```

This code copies the `disclaimer.txt` file to `c:\rodman99.txt`.

Besides retrieving files, you also can send files using the `SEND` command; however, many FTP sites are read-only. You'll need to contact the administrator of the site to which you want to send files, to learn whether that site is capable of receiving files or is a read-only site.

Summary

As you can see by this project, the Internet is fertile ground for information and cool features for your Web site. From now on, you'll look at each Web site you visit as a source of information for your programs, and thereby hopefully will gain greater use of the Web.

Project 1 Summary

The VBBrowser project introduced you to the concepts of developing Visual Basic/Internet applications. You examined the different levels of the Internet and learned how to develop browser-based applications using Visual Basic.

You gathered system requirements and then learned about two approaches to application design. After analyzing these approaches, you determined that Visual Basic is well-suited to the RAD approach. You then went about the business of prototyping your VB screens for the VBBrowser.

After creating the prototype of your application, you began creating the actual VB forms you needed. You created pages that use many different techniques for retrieving information from the Web. You created Web pages to track packages, extract currency information, retrieve stock quotes, get the time on different continents, and send e-mail. Each of these tasks presented its own set of challenges, which you learned to overcome while doing this project.

After creating your application, you learned techniques for testing and implementing the application.

HANDS ON PROJECT 2

THE VBRESEARCHER

- Tracking system requirements
- Tracking system design information
- Using prototyping in your applications
- Using Microsoft FrontPage to prototype HTML applications
- Creating Active servers with Visual Basic
- Building Active Server Pages
- Creating Active servers that query databases
- Integrating ASP with your Visual Basic Active servers
- Creating dynamic query pages with Visual Basic

Project Overview

The second project presents a set of tools that allow you to publish data from your Visual Basic applications. In these chapters, you combine Internet technologies such as HTML and Active Server Pages with Visual Basic Active servers.

You begin this project by gathering system requirements, then you generate a prototype application using Microsoft Front-Page. FrontPage allows you to develop the "look and feel" of your application without investing a large amount of time coding your Web pages by hand.

After creating the prototype, you learn about the technologies that will be used to present your databases on the Internet. You also learn about Active Server Pages and how you can retrieve information from the server and place it in your applications. You learn how to launch Active servers from your Web pages.

After learning how Active Server Pages work, you learn how to create Active servers with VB. You create servers that allow you to query data from databases; then you alter those servers so that they can be used to provide data to your Web pages.

After learning how to create Active Server Pages and Active servers, you learn how to integrate these two technologies to create an Internet solution. Finally, you learn techniques for testing Active servers, which present a new set of challenges to developers in terms of testing.

What Is the VBResearcher?

Up to this point in the book, you have been working with VB to create client-side Internet tools. It's important to understand the basics of VB development in order to build server-side components. In this chapter, you start your first server-side VB project. This chapter starts the process by describing the project you are going to create and giving you an overview of the key topics presented in the remaining chapters of this section.

Describing the VBResearcher

Project 2 is a VB server-based Internet application that will provide access to information stored in databases. This project focuses on providing information about a company's products. This information includes product descriptions, prices, and other relevant information. The product information will be stored in a set of databases that will be used to generate dynamic Web pages containing information from those databases. The system will be developed to facilitate access to this information from a Web browser.

Goal of the VBResearcher

As you may recall from Chapter 4, when developing Internet applications you commonly work at one of three layers—client, middleware, and server. Figure 8.1 shows these three layers and the software that operates at each layer.

In this project, you'll be dealing with applications residing at the server layer. This means that you're going to add functionality to your HTML pages that will communicate with an application running on the server.

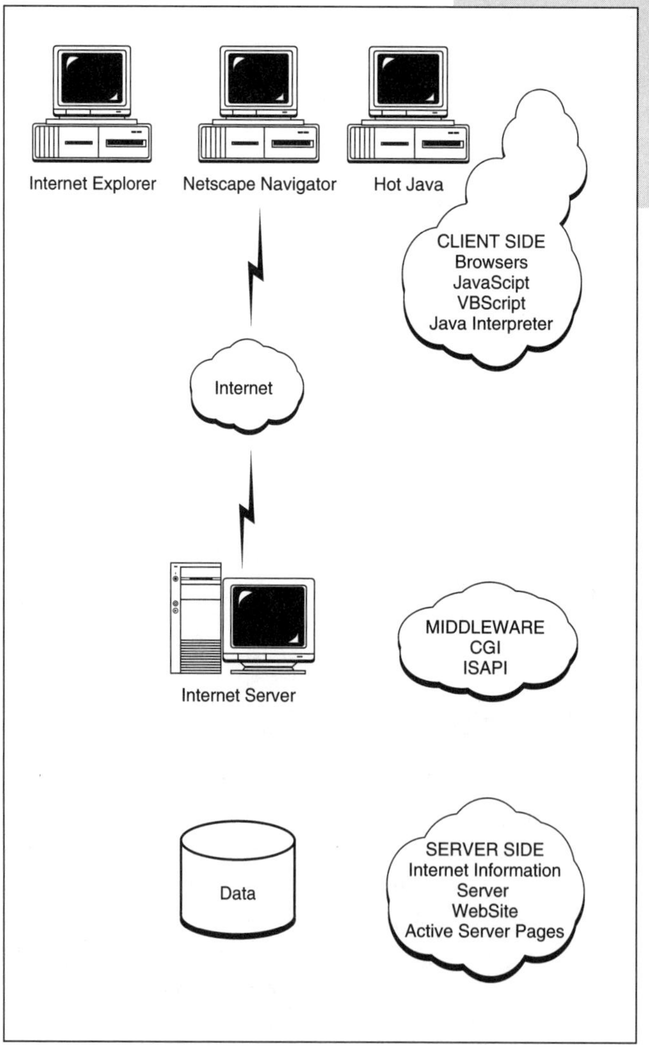

Figure 8.1
This illustration shows the three layers involved in developing Internet applications.

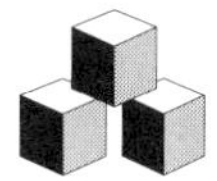

System Requirements of the VBResearcher

The most important stage of the development process is the requirements-gathering stage. This stage is important because it defines the scope of your application. It's crucial to do a good job of accurately gathering the necessary requirements for systems, as the costs of development escalate as the system matures. This results in higher costs of fixing problems with missing features at later stages of the development process. Some studies say that it can cost up to 100 times more to fix a problem in the development stages of a project than in the requirements stage. Missing a crucial requirement can even result in project cancellation.

Now that you understand the need for good requirements, you can begin gathering the requirements for the VBResearcher system. The VBResearcher system should do the following:

- Provide a list of products that is dynamically generated from a product database. The purpose of generating these pages dynamically is so that they'll always be current. Generating static Web pages causes the information to become "stale" rather quickly.
- Provide detailed information about the company's products. This information should be dynamically generated from the product information database.
- Provide a user-friendly search mechanism for finding information about products. This mechanism should allow users to find product information with an easy-to-use and powerful interface. It may be good to segment products by category or some other grouping criterion.
- Allow the company's art department to develop Web pages using standard HTML development tools such as FrontPage or PageMill.

Goals of the Project

This project is designed to introduce VB developers to the tools necessary to use the Internet to access information stored in databases. This process introduces developers to many topics related to the integration of different applications. Some of the topics you learn in this project include the following:

- **How to use Active Server Pages**

  One of the best technologies to ever appear on the Internet horizon is a technology known as *Active Server Pages (ASP)*. ASP is a protocol that allows browsers to launch programs on the server while at the same time remaining browser-independent. What this means to developers is that you can call your VB applications from the Web with little or no effort.

- **How to create Active servers**
  You integrate Web pages and VB through the use of Active servers. Active servers (formerly known as OLE Automation servers) allow developers to create components that can be called from numerous applications. You do this by creating servers that provide a set of properties and methods that can be accessed by developers. Active servers are going to be the mechanism that you use to integrate your VB applications into the Web.
- **How to collect data and present it to the Web**
  One of the very powerful abilities of VB is the robust set of mechanisms it provides for accessing data. You learn how to retrieve data from a database server and present it to users.
- **How to use standard Web development tools with VB**
  Developing effective Web applications takes a combination of two talents: technical and artistic. You already have the technical part covered—what about the artistic part? Generally, artists like to use tools they are familiar with to do Web development. ASP allows artists to create pages using standard tools (such as FrontPage) and then turn them over to developers for enhancement with code.
- **How to integrate ASP and VB**
  After learning about all of the subjects highlighted prior to this point, you can begin integrating your ASP pages with VB. You learn the basics of this integration, including creating a simple server and creating a database server component.

Summary

The most important aspect of any project is defining what it does. This chapter has described the functionality and components of the VBResearcher application. You're creating a system that allows users to query product information from a product database. This information will be kept current, as it will be retrieved directly from the database. Now that you understand what this application is going to do, you can begin the process of creating your first Internet server-enabled application.

Chapter 9

Gathering Information for the VBResearcher

The last chapter examined requirements for creating a useful Internet server-based application, which is what you're doing in Project 2. This chapter examines the steps necessary for gathering information about this project.

While working on Project 1 in Chapter 5, you learned about the different components of creating a requirements document. From that chapter you learned that, when creating an application, you need to find and document the following information:

- **The mission statement.** The purpose of the mission statement is to define at a very high level what the goal of the system is. This mission statement can be one sentence or one page. The goal of the mission statement is to set the focus of the project. A common practice of many system developers is to ask for one page (and only one page) describing the system they're being asked to create.
- **The system users.** For any system to be successful, you need to involve the direct users of the system. Users of a system have the power to make or break whatever developers throw at them. When dealing with

users, you should attempt to learn what their job functions are and what impact the system will have on these users.

- **The system managers.** When developing a system, it's important to distinguish between managers and users. The needs of managers are very different from those of users. Users want to do their work and go home; managers are commonly responsible for much higher-level tasks. It's easy to fall into the trap of trying to cater your system to the managers. This is a surefire way to fail.
- **Required features.** This item can be the most difficult to quantify and is the most difficult to rein in. When developing a system, you want to make sure that you prioritize the required features and dedicate your resources to working on those features. The big question is how you derive these features. The easiest method of doing this is to ask a very direct question of the system users: "What are the three most important features to you?" Then force users to pick three and only three (or whatever your number may be), which forces them to prioritize.
- **Out-of-scope features.** When gathering information for a system, this item is commonly overlooked. All user-requested features should be documented. Once the first version of your software is complete, you can return to your out-of-scope features list and go right to work on your next version.
- **Other sources of information.** When you're dealing with Internet applications, you're faced with a sea of information that's available to you. This section should document where you intend to go for your information.

You also learned in Chapter 5 that when looking at the information you're attempting to gather for any project, you can break it down into five basic tenets:

- **What.** What are you trying to do?
- **Why.** Why are you trying to do it?
- **Who.** Who is going to use or be affected by the system?
- **Where.** Where can you find the information you need?
- **When.** When is the information needed, or how often will it be accessed?

These items may seem obvious to you, but you'd be surprised how many people forget even the most basic development principles.

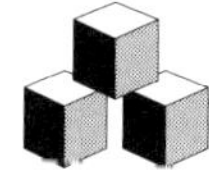

Beginning the Gathering Process

Now that you have an understanding of what you need to accomplish in the information-gathering stage of a project, you can begin breaking it down. The first task in the gathering stage is to define the mission statement of the system. The mission statement can be derived from the initial document or RFP sent by the users. Chapter 8 explained that the system should do the following:

- Provide a list of products that is dynamically generated from a product database.
- Provide detailed information about the company's products. This information should be dynamically generated from the product information database.
- Provide a user-friendly search mechanism for finding information about products.
- Allow the company's art department to develop Web pages using standard HTML development tools such as FrontPage or PageMill.

This list is nice for defining just what the system is supposed to do, but it falls short of defining *why*. This is your job as a system developer—to attempt to figure out why this project needs to do certain things. After analyzing the requirements list, you can derive the following mission statement:

Mission Statement

The purpose of the VBResearcher is to allow customers to find information about our company's products. It should do so in a simple and user-friendly manner.

The task that immediately follows the mission statement is the process of breaking the requirements document into functional areas. This allows you as a developer to concentrate your time into specific areas. In each area, the information you gather should answer the list of questions defined earlier: what, why, who, where, and when. From this list, you can even create a form that will serve as the source of your documentation. Your form can be as simple as the one in Table 9-1.

Table 9-1 Proposed Requirements-Gathering Form

Item	Notes
Project	
Name of Analyst	
Date Created	
Task Description (What)	
Item Purpose (Why)	
Responsible Party or Users (Who)	
Source of Information (Where)	
Access Requirements (When)	
Notes	

Now that you understand what information you need to gather, you can go to work. Using the proposed requirements form shown in Table 9-1, you can begin gathering information for each functional area of your project. The following sections discuss the process of formalizing the requirements for this project.

Provide a Dynamically Generated List of Products

Taking the proposed form from Table 9-1, this requirement can be broken down as shown in Table 9-2.

Table 9-2 Dynamically Generated Product List Requirement

Item	Notes
Project	VBResearcher
Name of Analyst	Rod Paddock
Date Created	09/30/98
Task Description (What)	Provide a list of products that is dynamically generated.
Item Purpose (Why)	The company has a rapidly changing number of products. Creating a Web site with static product information would be too costly. The system should be capable of managing this list.
Responsible Party or Users (Who)	System developers and product managers.
Source of Information (Where)	Corporate product information systems.
Access Requirements (When)	Will be frequently accessed by customers.
Notes	

Provide Detailed Information about the Company's Products

This requirement can be broken down as shown in Table 9-3.

Table 9-3 Company Products Information Requirement

Item	Notes
Project	VBResearcher
Name of Analyst	Rod Paddock
Date Created	09/30/98
Task Description (What)	Provide detailed information about company products.
Item Purpose (Why)	The specifications for the company's products are constantly changing. Styles, models, descriptions, and prices can change on a daily basis. Creating a Web site with static product information would be too costly. The system should be capable of providing detailed product information from a database.

Table 9-3 Company Products Information Requirement *(continued)*

Item	Notes
Responsible Party or Users (Who)	System developers and product managers.
Source of Information (Where)	Corporate product information systems.
Access Requirements (When)	Will be frequently accessed by customers.
Notes	

Provide a User-Friendly Search Mechanism for Finding Product Information

Table 9-4 shows the breakdown for this requirement.

Table 9-4 User-Friendly Search Requirement

Item	Notes
Project	VBResearcher
Name of Analyst	Rod Paddock
Date Created	09/30/98
Task Description (What)	Provide a user-friendly search mechanism for finding information about company products.
Item Purpose (Why)	The company has a large number of products and product categories, so it can be difficult to find information quickly. There should be a simple way of finding out about specific products.
Responsible Party or Users (Who)	System developers and product managers.
Source of Information (Where)	Corporate product information systems.
Access Requirements (When)	Will be frequently accessed by customers.
Notes	

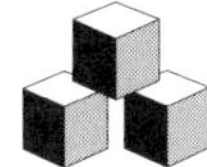

Allow Development of Web Pages Using Standard HTML Development Tools

Table 9-5 shows how to prepare for this requirement.

Table 9-5 Standard HTML Tools Requirement

Item	Notes
Project	VBResearcher
Name of Analyst	Rod Paddock
Date Created	09/30/98
Task Description (What)	Allow the company's art department to use standard HTML development tools.
Item Purpose (Why)	The company's art department is familiar with commercially-available HTML development tools. They should be able to use these tools to create the corporate Web site content.
Responsible Party or Users (Who)	System developers and art department.
Source of Information (Where)	Art department and Web developers.
Access Requirements (When)	Will be used by art department extensively.
Notes	Tools such as FrontPage or PageMill.

Summary

As you can see, a lot of useful information can be gathered at this stage of development. In this chapter, you've learned that you're going to develop a system that generates product information Web pages dynamically from a product database. You've also learned that one of the requirements is to create a user-friendly development environment. Using this information, you can set your sights on the next step of the development process—design.

Designing the VBResearcher

In Chapter 9, "Gathering Information for the VBResearcher," you completed a detailed list of requirements for the system. After gathering a completed set of requirements, you can proceed with the design process. In the design process, you begin putting together a list of detailed technical specifications for your system. These technical specifications will then be used to actually implement your system. This chapter looks at the process of creating the design documents for a system. In this chapter, you'll design the VBResearcher system.

Designing the VBResearcher Using the RAD Method

The VBResearcher system will be designed using the RAD method of development (explained in Chapter 6). Taking the requirements documents from Chapters 8 and 9, you can determine that you will be developing a server-based Visual Basic application. This application will be used to produce information about a company's products.

The first item in your documentation will be a list of features to be developed. From the requirements document developed in Chapter 9, you'll find that list of needs to be developed:

- Provide a list of products that is dynamically generated from a product database.
- Provide detailed information about the company's products. This information should be dynamically generated from the product information database.
- Provide a user-friendly search mechanism for finding information about products.
- Allow the company's art department to develop Web pages using standard HTML development tools such as FrontPage or PageMill.

After composing this list, you can go to work identifying the information for each component.

Designing the Products Page

The goal of the RAD methodology is to put as much functionality into the hands of users as possible. This application is a Web site, so you'll want to choose a tool that allows you to develop Web sites in a rapid manner. You could try to write the HTML code by hand, but that's an inefficient method of doing RAD when there are literally dozens of HTML tools. One of the best tools for creating Web sites rapidly is Microsoft FrontPage. (You aren't required to use FrontPage, of course; any Web development tool will suffice.)

The samples from this chapter were developed using Microsoft FrontPage, which comes on the Windows NT Server 4.0 CD (and is also available separately).

The first step to creating your prototype Web site is to install and launch Microsoft FrontPage. Upon running FrontPage, you'll be prompted with a dialog that allows you to create a new FrontPage Web page (which FrontPage just calls a *web*— see Figure 10.1). In this dialog, select Create a New FrontPage Web and click OK.

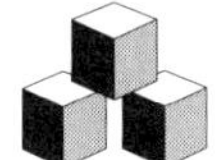

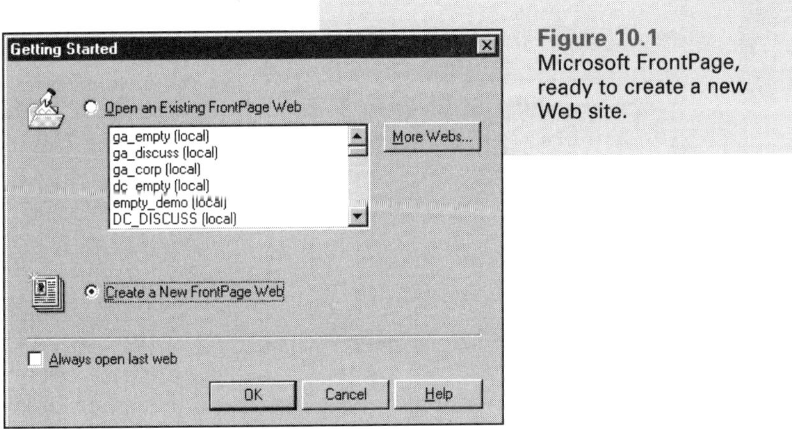

Figure 10.1 Microsoft FrontPage, ready to create a new Web site.

After instructing FrontPage to create a new web, you can specify the type of web you want to create, the name of your new site, and the Web server to which to install your new page (see Figure 10.2).

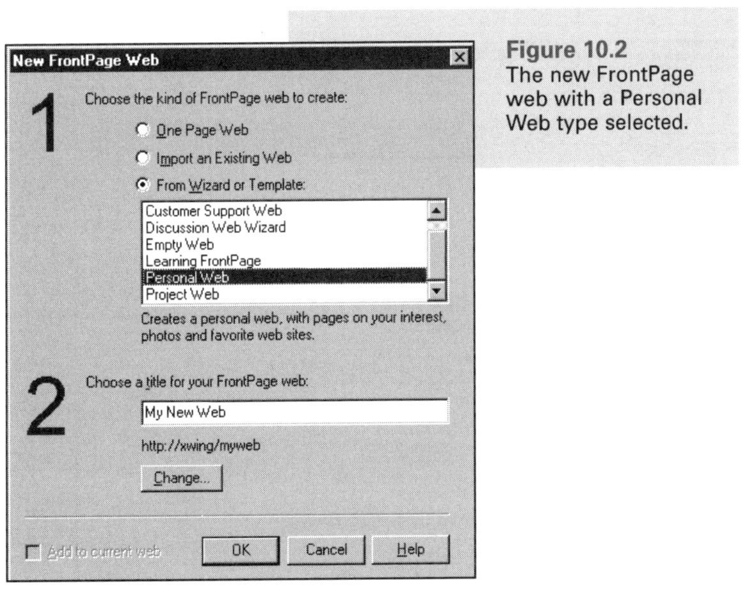

Figure 10.2 The new FrontPage web with a Personal Web type selected.

If you don't have your own Web server software, you can use Personal Web Server, which comes with Microsoft FrontPage (or can be downloaded from Microsoft's Web site at `http://www.microsoft.com`). You can use this "mini" Web server to prototype Web sites.

After you specify the options for your Web site, FrontPage installs your Web site on the specified server. After installing the structure for your site, you'll see the FrontPage Explorer (see Figure 10.3). The FrontPage Explorer shows your Web site and its various links, using a graphical metaphor. In Figure 10.3, you see a Home Page icon. This icon is the default form that will be shown on your Web site. Once you have added some links to your site, FrontPage will show this icon with other icons representing your links.

Once you have installed your Web site, you can go about the process of creating the prototype Web pages for your application. To find out what the first Web page should be, you need to consult your requirements documentation. From the list of requirements, you determine that the first requirement is to

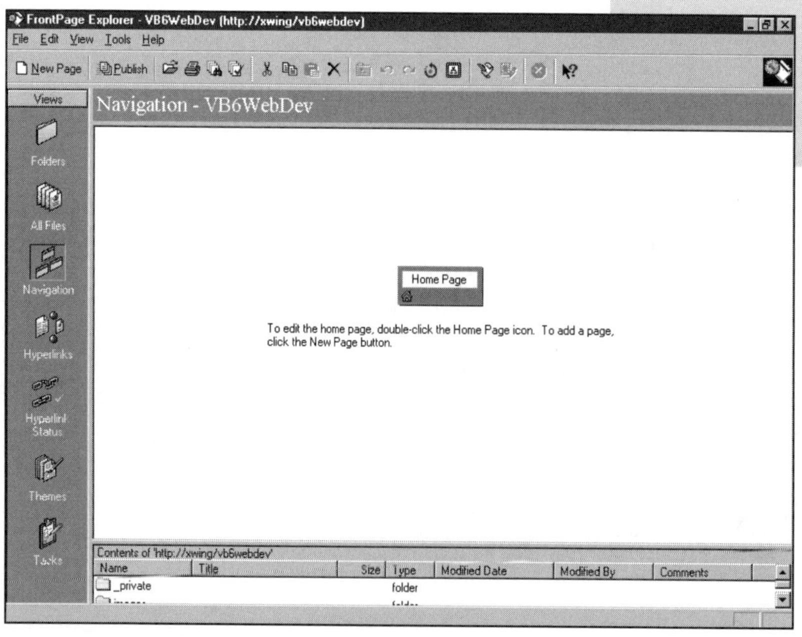

Figure 10.3 The new Web site in the FrontPage Explorer.

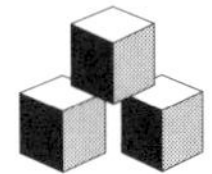

create a products list from the database. Using the template from Chapter 6, your design specification looks like Table 10-1.

Table 10-1 Create Products List from Database Requirement

Item	Notes
Project	VBResearcher
Name of Analyst	Rod Paddock
Date Created	12/31/99
Task Description	Create a product list
Task Inputs	Company products
Task Outputs	Web page with product list
Source of Information	Products database
Notes	

After creating the specification, you can go about the process of creating the prototype Web page. To create your first Web page, double-click the Home Page icon at the center of the FrontPage Explorer. The FrontPage Editor opens; this editor is like a combination word processor and form designer. It greatly speeds the development of Web sites. To add text to your Web page, you can simply begin typing into the Web page. Figure 10.4 shows the Web page you are creating with some very simple text.

As you may recall from Chapter 1, a good method of representing lists of items is to use an HTML table. HTML tables give developers great control over formatting data, and in general appear very nice on Web pages. Microsoft FrontPage provides mechanisms for adding tables with little or no effort. To add a table to your Web page, select Table, Insert Table from the FrontPage menu. The Insert Table dialog opens (see Figure 10.5). This dialog allows you to specify parameters for your table, including the following items:

- Number of rows for the table
- Number of columns for the table
- Alignment of the table on the Web page
- Width of the border for the table
- The size of the table in pixels

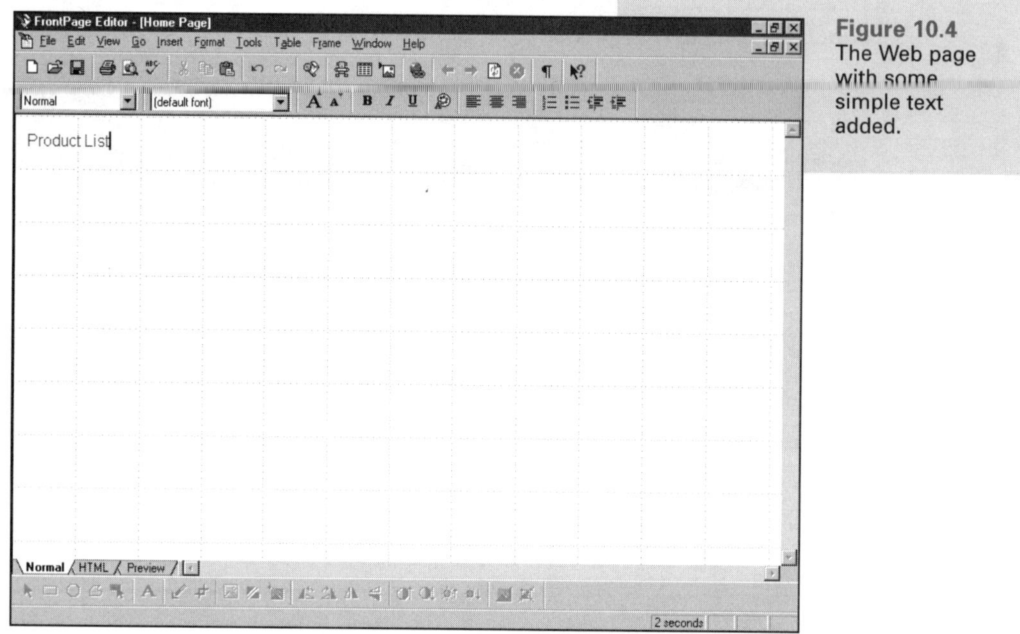

Figure 10.4
The Web page with some simple text added.

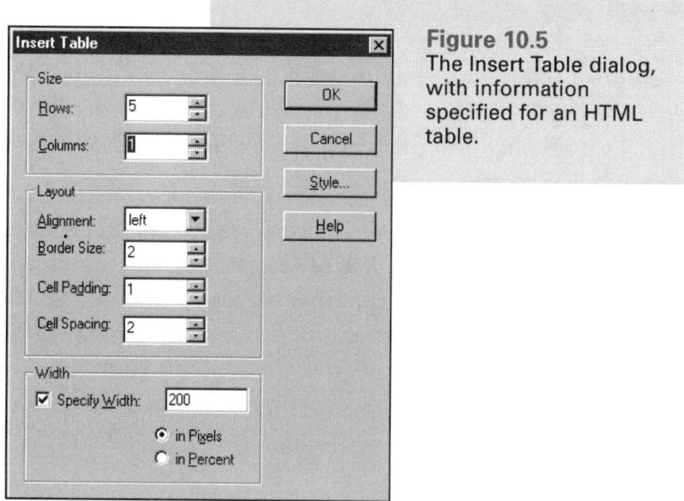

Figure 10.5
The Insert Table dialog, with information specified for an HTML table.

After you specify the information for your table and click OK, your table will be added to the FrontPage editor, as shown in Figure 10.6. You can now move your cursor into the individual cells of your table and begin adding information.

When editing an HTML table, you can add text, graphics, controls, and hyperlinks to the cells of your table. To add text to your table, you simply move to the

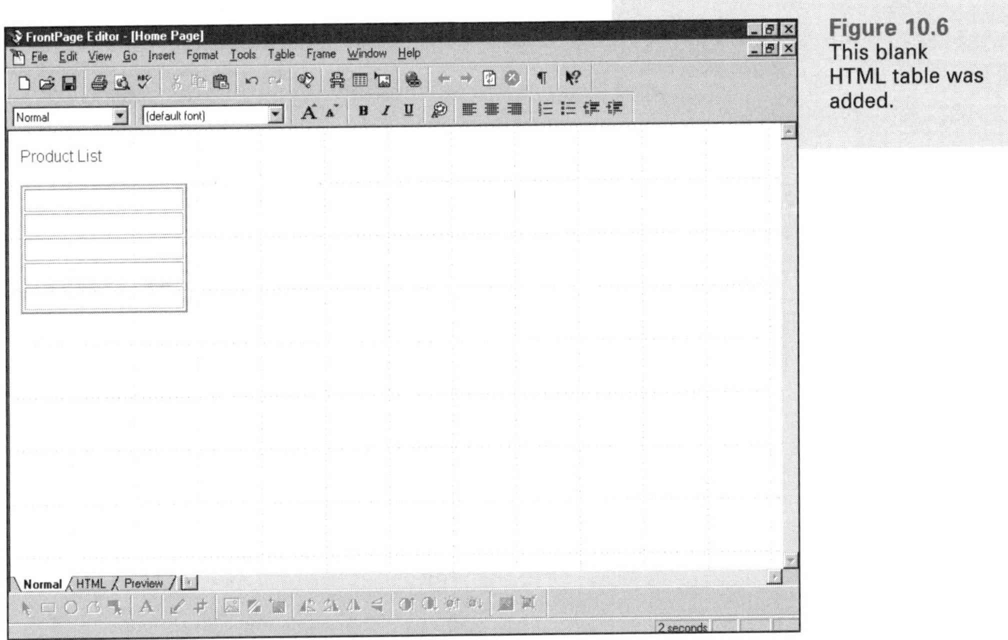

Figure 10.6
This blank HTML table was added.

appropriate cell and begin typing text into that cell. If you need to change the layout of the cell, simply right-click the cell and select Table Properties from the pop-up menu. The Table Properties dialog appears, as shown in Figure 10.7. This dialog allows you to change such table properties as rows, columns, and colors.

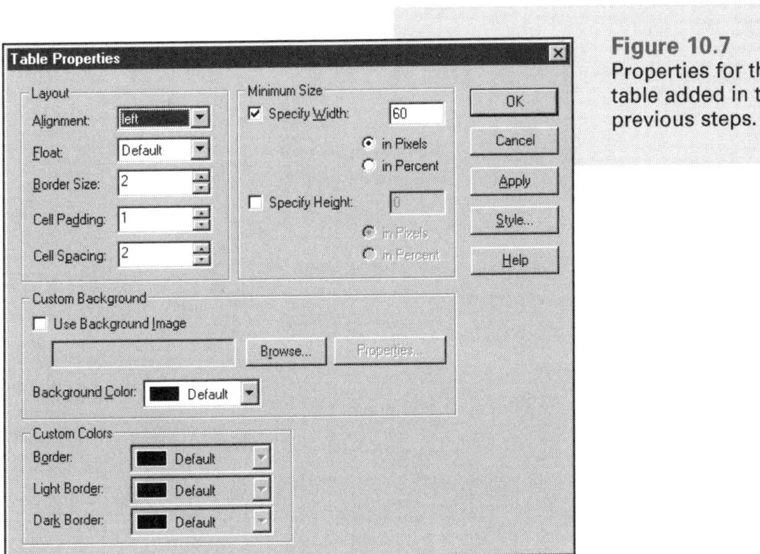

Figure 10.7
Properties for the table added in the previous steps.

To continue the development of the prototype, you should enter information into your HTML table directly. Figure 10.8 shows how the table should look.

After you have entered simulated product information into your table, you can look at the next requirement, as shown in Table 10-2.

Table 10-2 Detailed Information List Requirement

Item	Notes
Project	VBResearcher
Name of Analyst	Rod Paddock
Date Created	12/31/99
Task Description	Provide detailed product information.
Task Inputs	Company product detail information.
Task Outputs	Web pages with detailed product info.
Source of Information	Products database.
Notes	Access detailed product information by selecting hyperlinks from the product page.

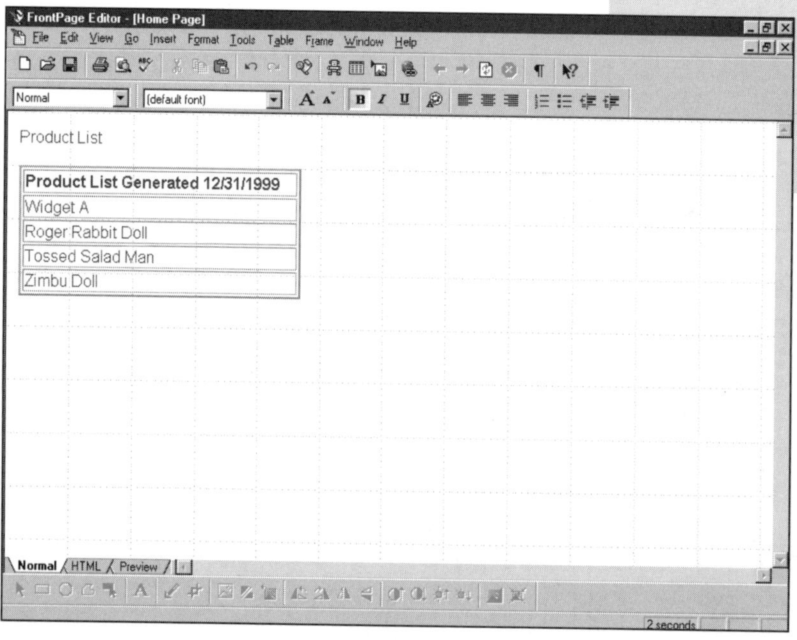

Figure 10.8 The HTML table you generated, with product information listed in it.

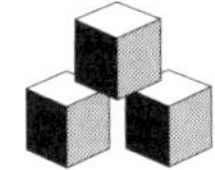

With this requirement in mind, you can return to your Web page and begin making some slight alterations. The first alteration is to add a hyperlink to a set of product information. To add a hyperlink to your document, follow these steps:

1. Highlight the text for which you want to create a hyperlink.
2. Select Insert, Hyperlink from the FrontPage menu. The Create Hyperlink dialog opens (see Figure 10.9).

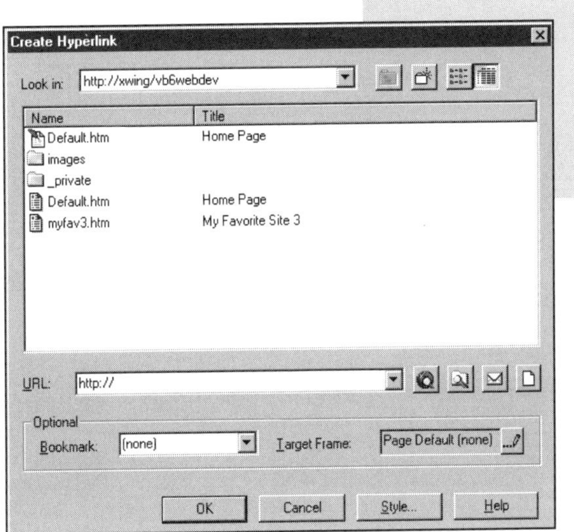

Figure 10.9
The Create Hyperlink dialog holds information specified for a new hyperlink.

3. Click the New Page icon.
4. Click OK. The New dialog appears (see Figure 10.10). This dialog allows you to create Web pages quickly from a set of standard templates.
5. Select `Product Description` and click OK. FrontPage generates your new page and presents it in the FrontPage editor (see Figure 10.11).

After completing these tasks, you can modify the Web page to meet your needs.

After specifying the options for your Web page, choose File, Save from the FrontPage editor.

It's a good idea to test your Web page in your favorite browser. Select File, Preview In Browser to open the Preview in Browser dialog (see Figure 10.12). This

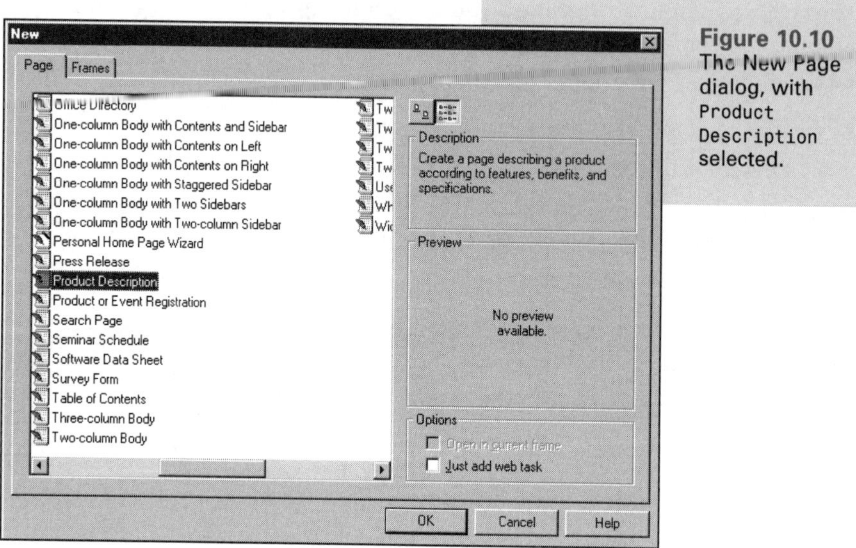

Figure 10.10
The New Page dialog, with `Product Description` selected.

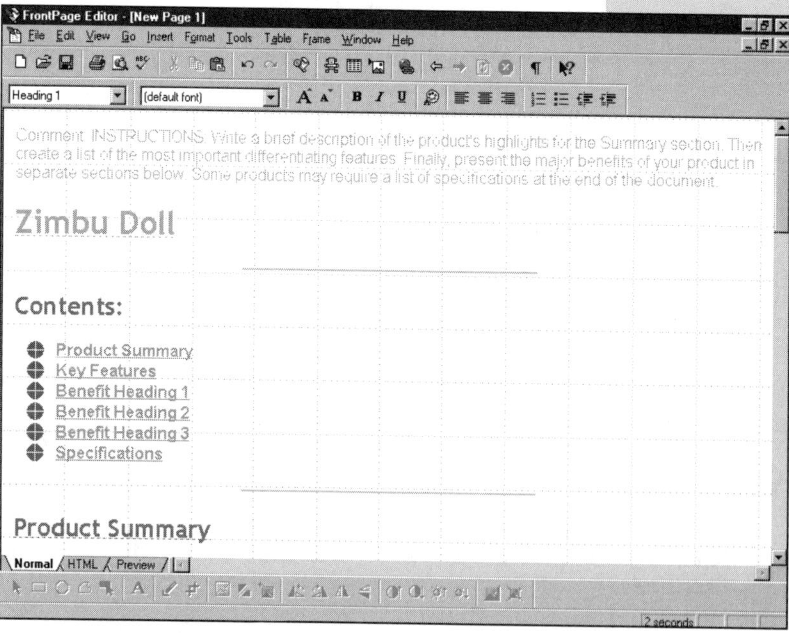

Figure 10.11
The product description Web page generated by FrontPage.

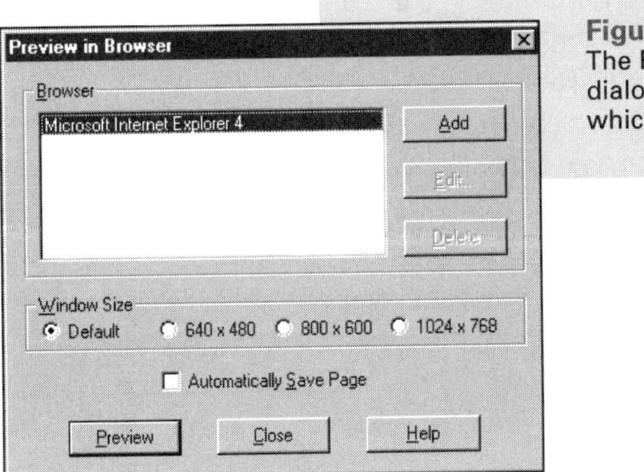

Figure 10.12
The Preview in Browser dialog lets you specify which browser to use.

dialog allows you to test your Web page in multiple browsers and at different resolutions. Select the desired settings and then click the Preview button. FrontPage displays your Web page in the selected browser. Figure 10.13 shows the prototype in the Microsoft Internet Explorer browser.

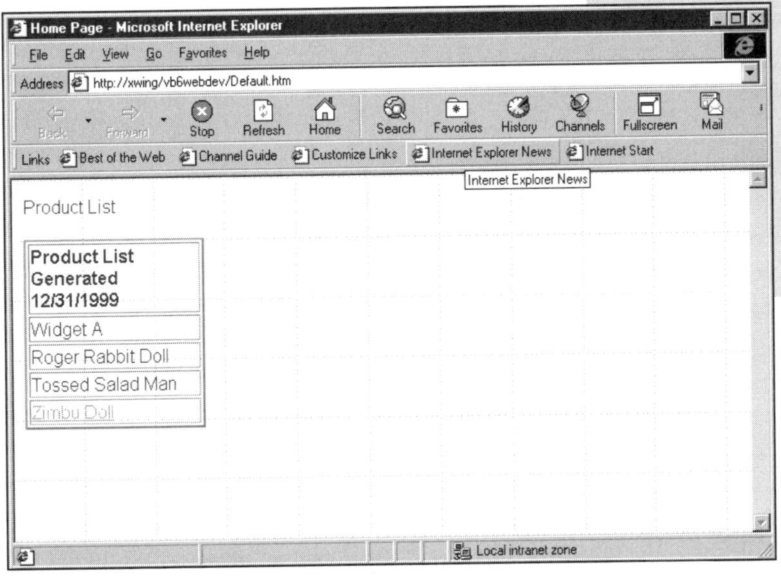

Figure 10.13
The Web page you've been creating, shown here in Microsoft Internet Explorer. As you can see, it's pretty close to the image shown in the FrontPage Explorer.

After finishing the first two requirements, you can set your sights on the requirement for creating a user-friendly search mechanism. This requirement can be detailed as shown in Table 10-3.

Table 10-3 User-Friendly Search Interface Requirement

Item	Notes
Project	VBResearcher
Name of Analyst	Rod Paddock
Date Created	12/31/99
Task Description	User-friendly interface to find products.
Task Inputs	User-specified criteria.
Task Outputs	List of products matching criteria.
Source of Information	Products database.
Notes	Search databases initially by product group. More criteria to be established later.

With this requirement in hand, you need to think about where to place this requirement in your Web page. The most obvious answer is to place another hyperlink onto your page; this hyperlink will take you to a search form. To add the search hyperlink to your form, do the following:

1. Add the text `Product Search` to your Web page.
2. Highlight the text.
3. Select Insert, Hyperlink from the FrontPage menu to open the Create Hyperlink dialog (refer to Figure 10.9).
4. Click the New Page icon.
5. Click OK to open the New dialog (refer to Figure 10.10).
6. Select Normal Page from the template dialog. This will take you into the FrontPage Editor with a blank page.

   Once you have opened your Web page, you can begin adding search criteria that can be selected by a user.
7. Most Web pages use drop-down lists to represent categories. To add a drop-down list item, select Insert, Form Field, Drop-Down Menu from the FrontPage menu. This will add a drop-down list to your page (see Figure 10.14).

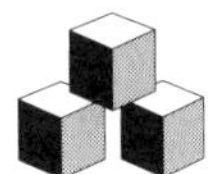

Note

You'll notice that whenever you add the first data entry control to a Web page, FrontPage automatically adds Submit and Reset buttons. These buttons (or some form of them) should be present on all Web page data entry screens to allow the user to submit his changes or reset the page to its beginning state.

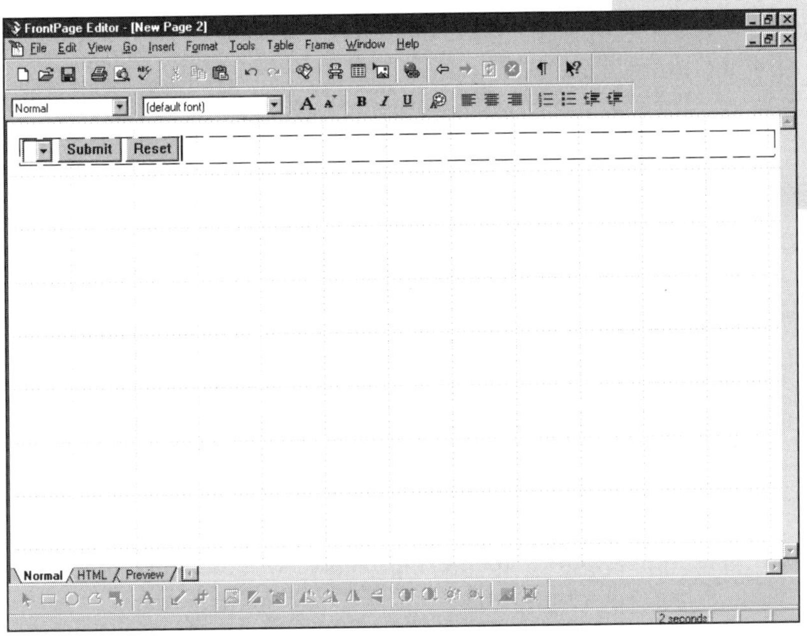

Figure 10.14
The new Web page with an empty drop-down list and two buttons on it.

8. After adding the drop-down list to the form, you need to add items to the list. You do this by right-clicking the object and selecting Form Field Properties from the pop-up menu.

   Selecting this option presents the Drop-Down Menu Properties dialog, as shown in Figure 10.15. This dialog allows you to add items to your drop-down lists.

9. Click Add to open the Add Choice dialog (see Figure 10.16). In this dialog, you add items to your drop-down list.
10. Add the desired text and then click OK.

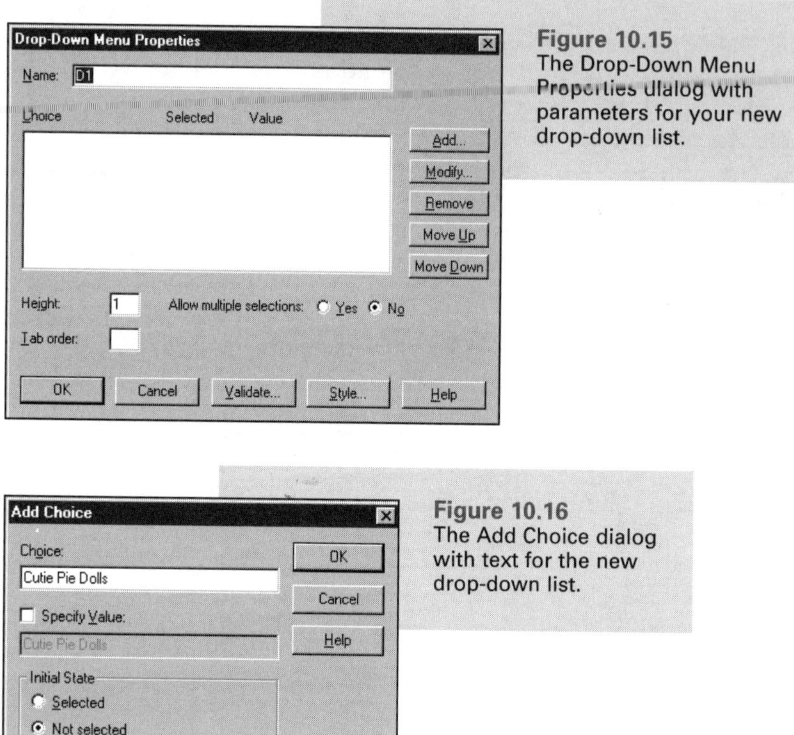

Figure 10.15 The Drop-Down Menu Properties dialog with parameters for your new drop-down list.

Figure 10.16 The Add Choice dialog with text for the new drop-down list.

11. Continue adding your prototype information with the Add Choice dialog. When you're finished, click OK. This completes your drop-down list and shows your options in the FrontPage Editor (see Figure 10.17).
12. The last step is to add a push button for your form. Select Insert, Form Field Object and set the properties for the button just like you did for the drop-down list.

Now that you've added your search form, you can return to the FrontPage Editor to look at the layout for your Web site. Figure 10.18 shows how your Web site looks with the links between your new documents. When you're on the home page of your Web site, you'll be able to link directly to product forms, or can use the Product Search page to find products.

When you have completed your Web site, you can preview it in your Web browser (see Figure 10.19).

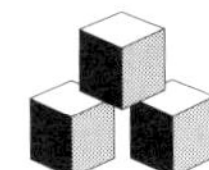

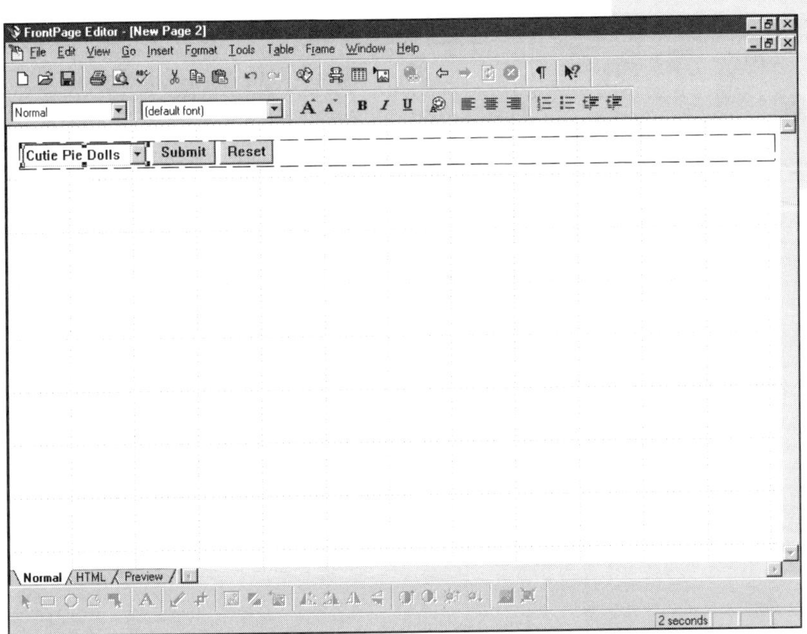

Figure 10.17 The FrontPage Editor shows the options specified in this lesson.

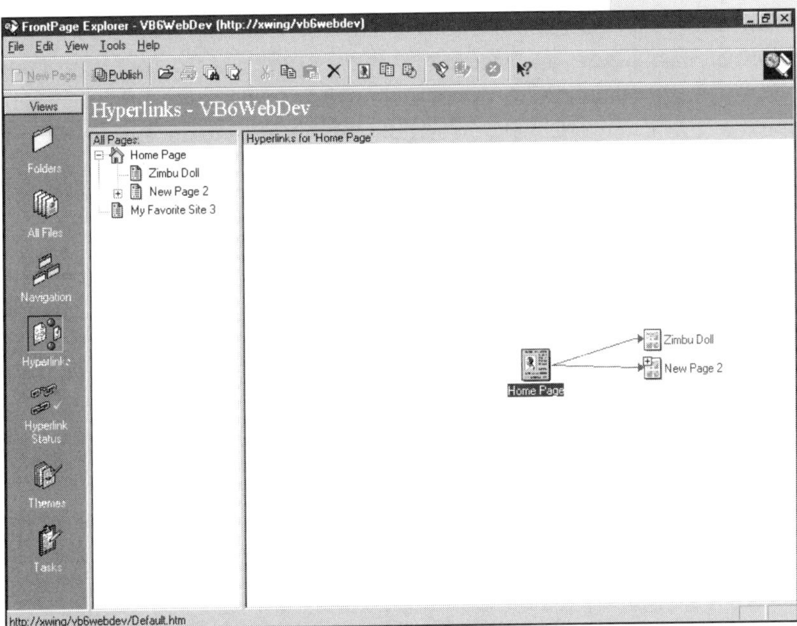

Figure 10.18 The new Web page in the FrontPage Explorer.

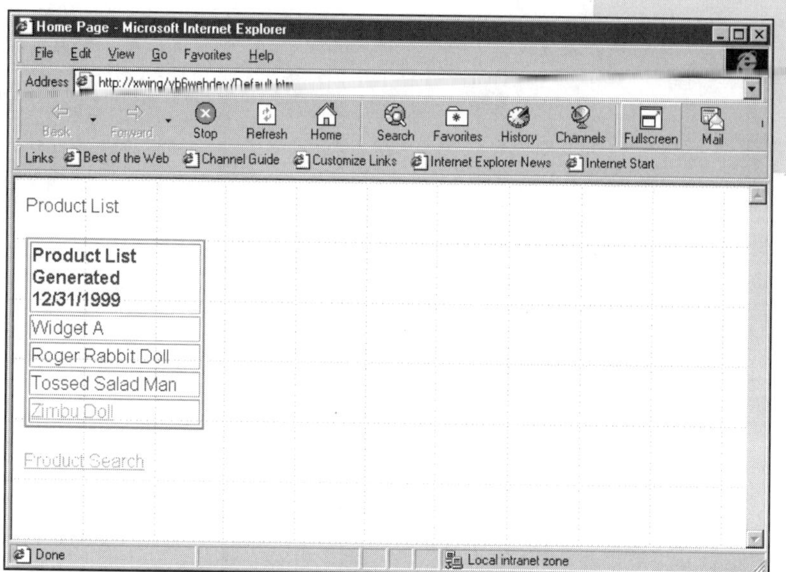

Figure 10.19 The Web site viewed in Microsoft Internet Explorer.

Summary

As you can see, developing applications for the Web is very similar to developing normal Visual Basic applications. Where it differs is the tools you may use. Because using VB in a Web development project is a little different from developing a run-of-the-mill VB application, you need to use a tool that facilitates this development. In this chapter, you have learned how to prototype a Web-based application using Microsoft FrontPage. This prototype will be the template for your final application. When you're done with the prototype, you can turn your sights to the development of VBResearcher, which will happen in the next chapter.

Chapter 11

Building the VBResearcher

In Chapter 10, "Designing the VBResearcher," you completed the design for your VB-enabled query tool. In this chapter, you take your requirements and design documents and create a Visual Basic query engine that can be accessed from the Internet. This chapter shows you the following:

- How to create Active Server Pages
- How to create ActiveX servers with Visual Basic
- How to access ActiveX servers from your Web pages
- How to access databases using ActiveX servers
- How to send parameters to an ActiveX server
- How to integrate dynamic queries and Web pages
- How to optimize Web servers for Internet access

What Are Active Server Pages?

It seem that almost every week a new technology is introduced that will revolutlonize the process of Internet development. One of the shining stars of Internet development is a technology known as *Active Server Pages* (*ASP*). Active Server Pages are unique in that they preprocess HTML pages at the server side. What this means is that when someone requests a Web page from your Web site, that Web page is first passed to the Web server for preprocessing and then sent on to the requesting Web browser. So what do you think is passed to the server for preprocessing? Well, guess what—it's Visual Basic code! What this means is that you can add Visual Basic code to your forms and then have the Web server process this code.

The implication of being able to add Visual Basic is that any information you can track or retrieve with Visual Basic can be tracked and retrieved from any Web browser. When consulting your requirements and design documents, you learn that you'll be retrieving corporate information from many company databases, including Personnel, Marketing, and Sales.

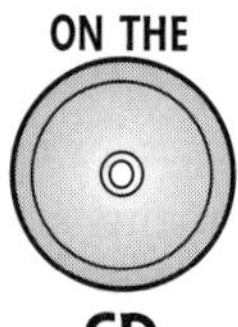

There are many Web servers that support Active Server Pages. You can run ASP with IIS 3.0 or higher, or O'Reilly WebSite 2.0. You also can run ASP on Netscape and Lotus servers with an add-on from a company named ChiliSoft. A demonstration of the ChiliSoft add-on is included on the CD that accompanies this book.

Creating an Active Server Page

Creating an Active Server Page is no different from developing a normal Web page; you just add a few special tags to your documents. These tags instruct your Web server to preprocess this page prior to returning it to the requesting Web browser. After you have installed the Active Server Pages add-in into your respective servers, you can begin the process of creating your own Active Server Pages. The following code represents an Active Server Page that returns the current time. Figure 11.1 shows the Web page returned by the Web server.

```
<HTML>
<TITLE>Chapter 11 Simple ASP Page</TITLE>
<H1>The time is: <%=now%> </H1>
</HTML>
```

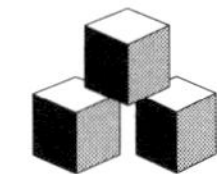

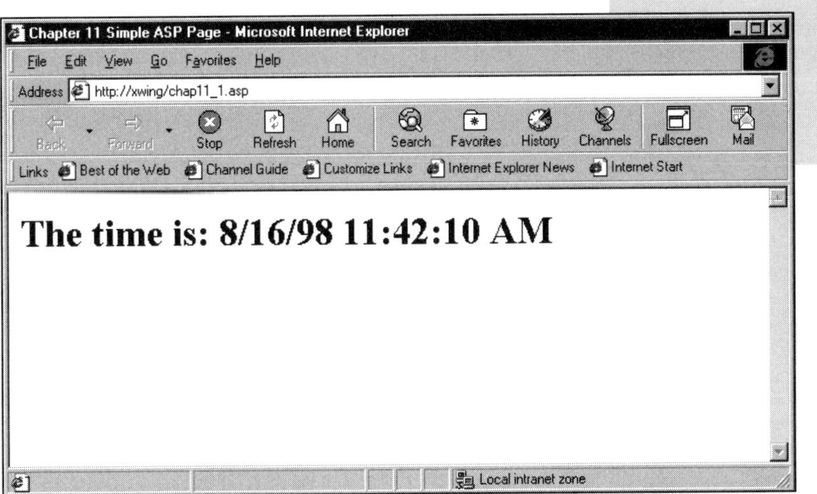

Figure 11.1
A Web page processed using Active Server Pages.

Active Server Page *Technology developed by Microsoft that allows Web developers to embed VBScript code into their Web pages. This code is preprocessed at the server side of the Web connection.*

Preprocess *Process code stored in a Web page prior to returning it to the client.*

The new tags you need to recognize are `<%= %>` and `<% %>`. These two types of tags instruct the Web server to preprocess the HTML prior to returning the Web page to the client. The difference between the two types of tags is that the tag with the notation `<%= %>` allows developers to retrieve information and place it in the Web page. The tag with the notation `<% %>` allows developers to process multiple lines of Visual Basic code. The following code and Figure 11.2 show how to create Web pages running multiple lines of Visual Basic code:

```
<HTML>
<TITLE>Chapter 11 Simple ASP Page</TITLE>
<H1>The time is: <%=now%> </H1>
<%For i = 1 to 10%>
  <%= "Item " & i & "<hr>"%>
<%Next%>
</HTML>
```

Retrieving Data from Active Server Pages

One of the features of Active Server Pages is its inclusion of a number of native objects that can be accessed from a Web page. These objects are present on the server and allow you as a developer to retrieve a number of useful facts about the current Internet session. Table 11-1 describes some of the objects and their purposes.

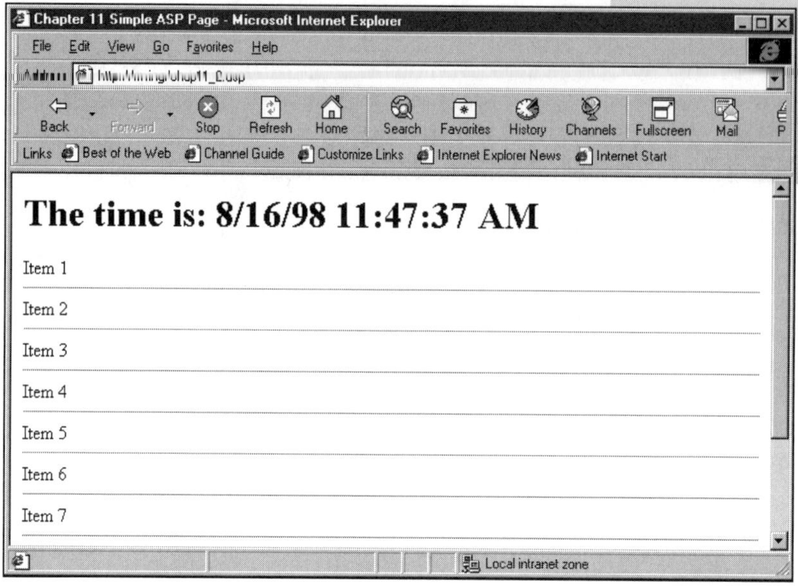

Figure 11.2 A Web page after processing multiple lines of Visual Basic code.

Table 11-1 Active Server Objects

Object	Description
`Request`	Allows you to retrieve information from a user.
`Response`	Allows you to manipulate the results of a Web page.
`Server`	Allows you to manipulate settings on the server.
`Session`	Allows you to retrieve specific user session information.
`Application`	Allows you to share information among different Internet users.

The purpose of these objects is to give developers a robust set of functionality for creating intelligent Web applications. One set of useful features available to developers comes from the `Response` object. The `Response` object has two capabilities. The first is that it allows you to manipulate the response being sent to the user. The second is that it allows developers to tailor Web page responses based on a number of parameters handed to the server. The following code and resulting Web page (see Figure 11.3) demonstrate information handed to the server:

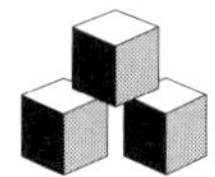

```
<HTML>
<TITLE>Chapter 11 Simple ASP Page</TITLE>
<%= "AUTH_TYPE=" & Request.ServerVariables("AUTH_TYPE") %><hr>
<%= "CONTENT_LENGTH=" & Request.ServerVariables("CONTENT_LENGTH") %><hr>
<%= "CONTENT_TYPE=" & Request.ServerVariables("CONTENT_TYPE") %><hr>
<%= "GATEWAY_INTERFACE=" & Request.ServerVariables("GATEWAY_INTERFACE") %><hr>
<%= "LOGON_USER=" & Request.ServerVariables("LOGON_USER") %><hr>
<%= "PATH_INFO=" & Request.ServerVariables("PATH_TRANSLATED") %><hr>
<%= "QUERY_STRING=" & Request.ServerVariables("QUERY_STRING") %><hr>
<%= "REMOTE_ADDR=" & Request.ServerVariables("REMOTE_ADDR") %><hr>
<%= "REMOTE_HOST=" & Request.ServerVariables("REMOTE_HOST") %><hr>
<%= "REQUEST_METHOD=" & Request.ServerVariables("REQUEST_METHOD") %><hr>
<%= "SCRIPT_NAME=" & Request.ServerVariables("SCRIPT_MAP") %><hr>
<%= "SERVER_NAME=" & Request.ServerVariables("SERVER_NAME") %><hr>
<%= "SERVER_PORT=" & Request.ServerVariables("SERVER_PORT") %><hr>
<%= "SERVER_PORT_SECURE=" & Request.ServerVariables("SERVER_SECURE") %><hr>
<%= "SERVER_PROTOCOL=" & Request.ServerVariables("SERVER_PROTOCOL") %><hr>
<%= "SERVER_SOFTWARE=" & Request.ServerVariables("SERVER_SOFTWARE") %><hr>
<%= "URL=" & Request.ServerVariables("URL") %><hr>
</HTML>
```

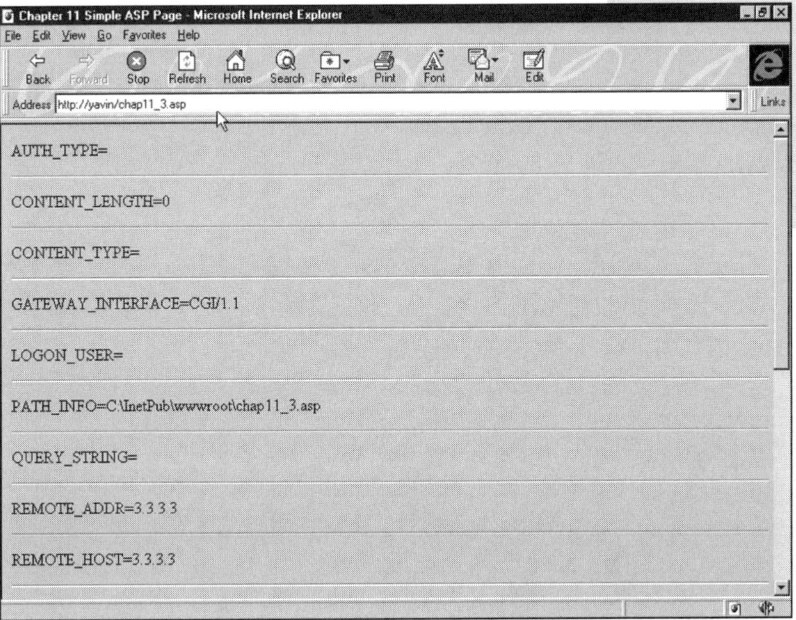

Figure 11.3 This illustration shows information that can be retrieved about a particular session.

As you can see, you can retrieve quite a bit of information from the server. This information can be used to tailor custom Web pages for users of your Web site. One new item you'll recognize is the familiar Visual Basic `object.property` syntax. The server objects behave just like Visual Basic objects in that you can retrieve the contents of properties and call methods from your Web pages. This leads you to the next step in using ASP, accessing Active servers.

Accessing ActiveX Servers from an Active Server Page

One of the most powerful capabilities of Active Server Pages is the ability to instantiate and access ActiveX servers. The following code shows examples of how to instantiate an ActiveX server and display information from that server on a Web page (see Figure 11.4):

```
<HTML>
<TITLE>Chapter 11 Simple ASP Page</TITLE>
<H1>Lets create a session of Excel</H1>
<% oExcel = Server.CreateObject("Excel.Application")%>
<%= oExcel.Caption %>
</HTML>
```

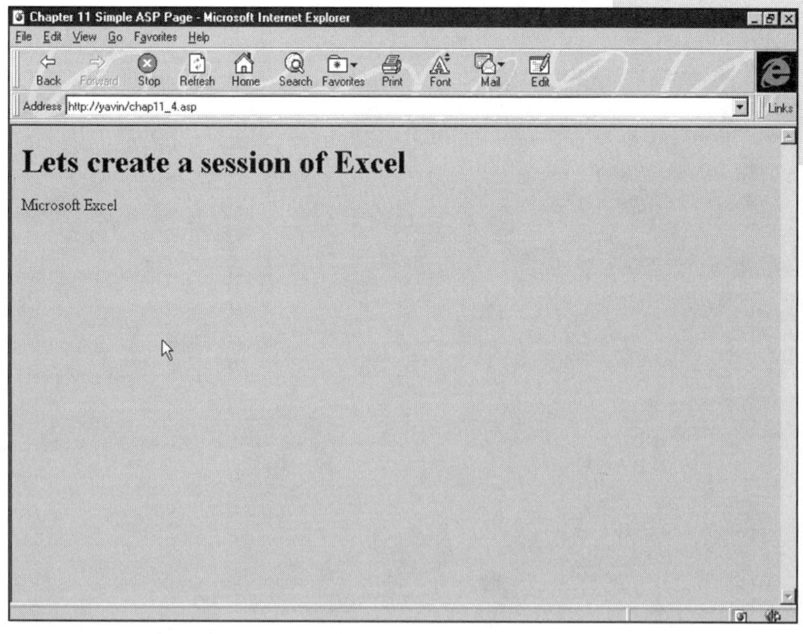

Figure 11.4 Information returned from a session of Microsoft Excel.

Instantiating ActiveX servers from Active Server Pages may require that you be able to instantiate out-of-process servers from the Web server. ActiveX servers run in two modes: in-process and out-of-process. An in-process server shares the memory space of the application launching it; out-of-process servers use their own memory spaces. To configure Active Server Pages to create out-of-process servers, you need to change a Registry setting by using the Registry Editor. In this case, you change the Registry entry `AllowOutOfProcCmpnts` to `1`. Figure 11.5 shows the Registry Editor with `AllowOutOfProcCmpnts` set to the correct value. Be aware that there may be more than one setting called `AllowOutOfProcCmpnts`. You should change all entries.

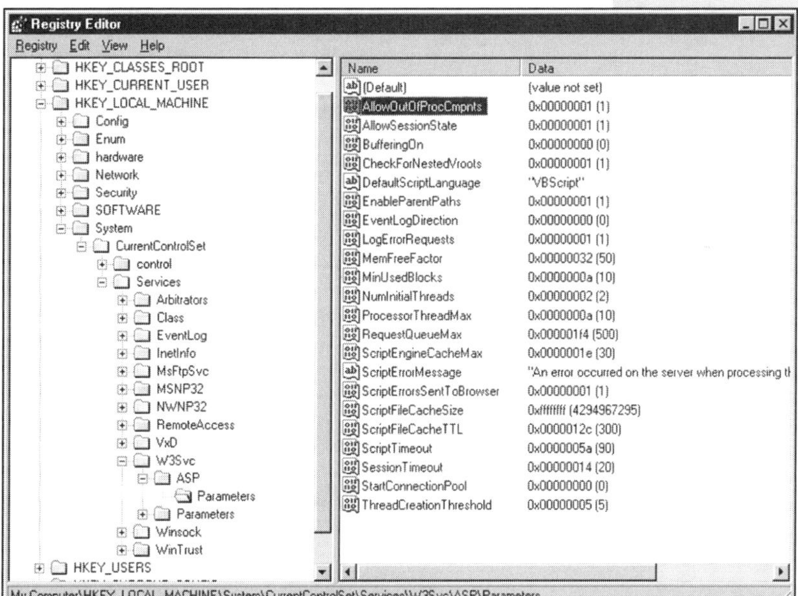

Figure 11.5 The Registry Editor with the setting changed.

Now that you understand how to instantiate a copy of Excel, let's make the example a bit more interesting. Figure 11.6 shows an Excel file containing data. The following code takes the data from the Excel spreadsheet and displays it in an HTML table (see Figure 11.7):

```
<HTML>
<TITLE>Chapter 11 Simple ASP Page</TITLE>
<H1>Lets create a session of Excel</H1>
<TABLE Border=2>
<% Set oExcel = Server.CreateObject("Excel.Application")%>
<% oExcel.WorkBooks.Open("c:\handsonvb\chap12\code\example.xls") %>
<%= "<TR><TD>" & oExcel.Cells(1,1).Value & "</TD><TD>"
➥& oExcel.Cells(1,2).Value & "</TD></TR>"%>
<%= "<TR><TD>" & oExcel.Cells(2,1).Value & "</TD><TD>"
➥& oExcel.Cells(2,2).Value & "</TD></TR>"%>
<%= "<TR><TD>" & oExcel.Cells(3,1).Value & "</TD><TD>"
➥& oExcel.Cells(3,2).Value & "</TD></TR>"%>
<%= "<TR><TD>" & oExcel.Cells(4,1).Value & "</TD><TD>"
➥& oExcel.Cells(4,2).Value & "</TD></TR>"%>
</TABLE>
<%= oExcel.Caption %>
</HTML>
```

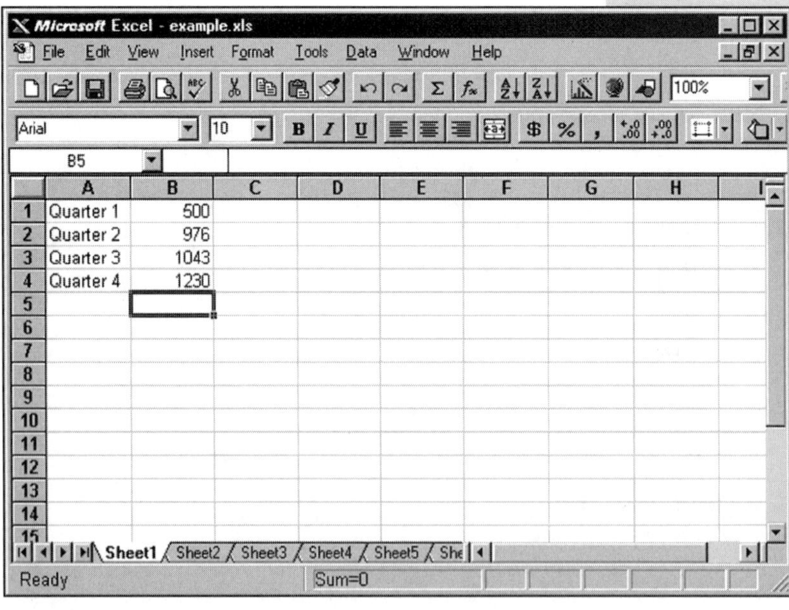

Figure 11.6 An Excel spreadsheet with data to be shown on an Active Server Page.

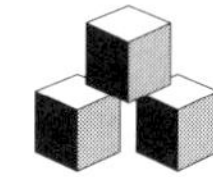

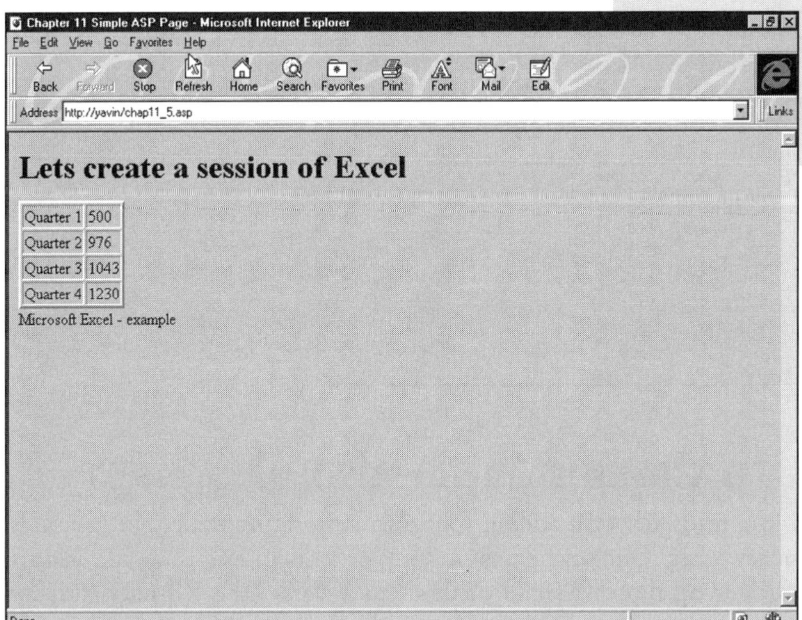

Figure 11.7
The contents of the spreadsheet in Figure 11.6 in an HTML page.

Creating ActiveX Servers

Visual Basic 4.0 introduced Visual Basic developers to the concept of creating OLE servers. You could create OLE servers in Visual Basic and call them from Visual FoxPro, Access, Excel, or any other application capable of launching OLE servers. Visual Basic allowed you to create your own objects with custom properties and methods.

Visual Basic now provides numerous tools that facilitate the development of ActiveX server components. To create an ActiveX server, follow these steps:

1. Choose File, New Project from the Visual Basic menu. The New Project dialog box opens.
2. Select the ActiveX EXE option and click Open (see Figure 11.8).

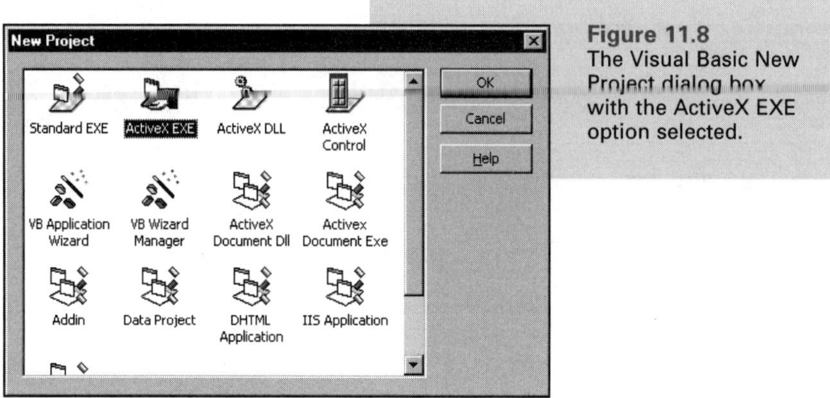

Figure 11.8
The Visual Basic New Project dialog box with the ActiveX EXE option selected.

Using the VB Class Builder Utility

Now you're ready to begin adding your own custom properties and methods to your new class. One of the new features of Visual Basic is an add-in that simplifies adding properties and methods to a class—the VB Class Builder utility. To use this add-in, you need to make sure that it's installed in your Visual Basic development environment. Follow these steps:

1. Choose Add-Ins, Add-In Manager from the Visual Basic menu to open the Add-In Manager dialog.
2. Select the VB Class Builder Utility and click OK (see Figure 11.9).

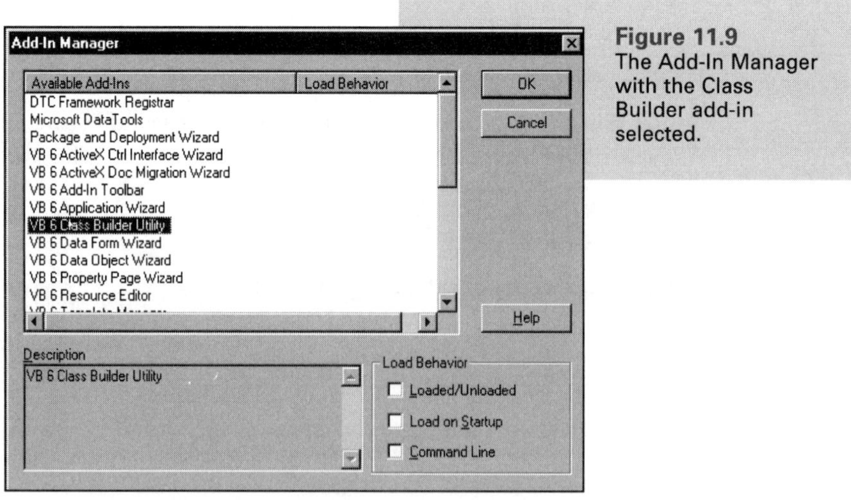

Figure 11.9
The Add-In Manager with the Class Builder add-in selected.

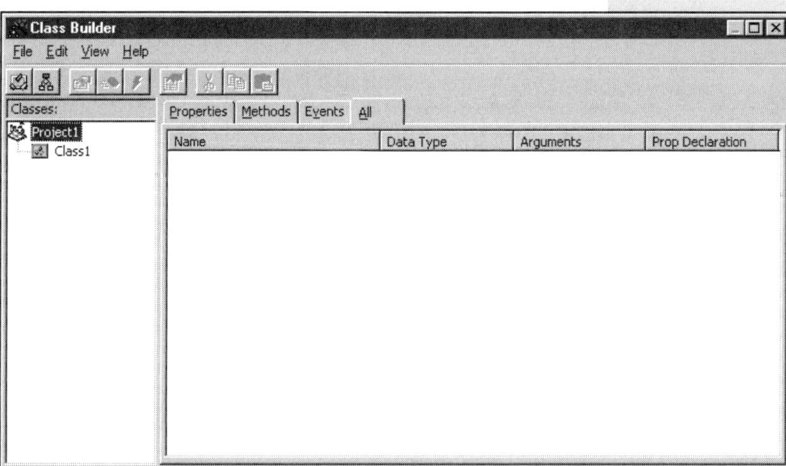

Figure 11.10 The Class Builder Utility maintaining the ActiveX server just created.

3. Choose Add-Ins, Class Builder Utility from the Visual Basic menu. Figure 11.10 shows the Class Builder.

Now that you've installed the Class Builder utility, you can begin maintaining your classes. The Class Builder allows you to add properties, methods, collections, and events to your classes. It also allows you to specify descriptive attributes for your classes. There are three aspects of this Class Builder that are of concern to Internet developers: adding properties, adding methods, and adding collections. The following sections describe methods for adding these items to your classes.

Adding Properties

When you create a class, you'll commonly begin by adding properties to that class. You usually define two types of class attributes: descriptive attributes and action attributes. Descriptive attributes are known as *properties*, action attributes are known as *methods*.

To add properties to your class, follow these steps:

1. Choose File, New, Property from the Class Builder menu. The Property Builder dialog appears (see Figure 11.11).
2. Specify the parameters for the class property. Some of the properties you can specify include:
   - The name of the property

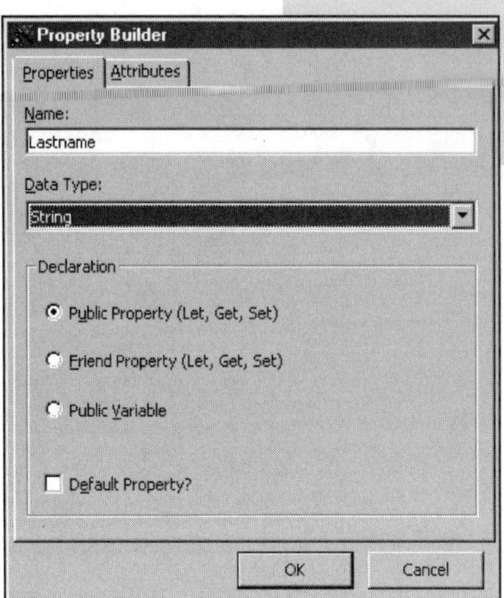

Figure 11.11
The Property Builder dialog box adding a property called `Lastname`.

- The property's datatype
- Scoping properties for the property
- Whether the property is the default property of the class
- A text description of the property
- Help Context IDs for the class

3. After specifying the properties that are applicable to this class, click OK. The new property is then displayed in the Class Builder Explorer window (see Figure 11.12).

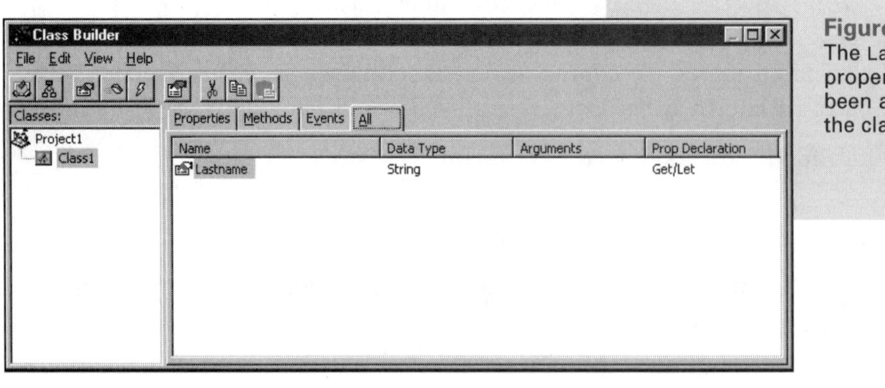

Figure 11.12
The `Lastname` property has been added to the class.

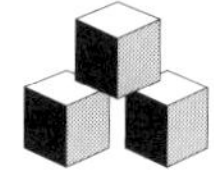

Adding Methods

In the preceding section, you learned that when you create classes you're commonly adding two types of attributes: descriptive and action attributes. Action attributes are known as *methods*. Designing methods is a little more difficult than defining properties. Properties are simply data elements of your attribute; methods can be passed data that they can then use internally to generate a return value or perform an action.

To add a method to your class, follow these steps:

1. Choose File, New, Method from the Class Builder menu. The Method Builder dialog appears, as shown in Figure 11.13.

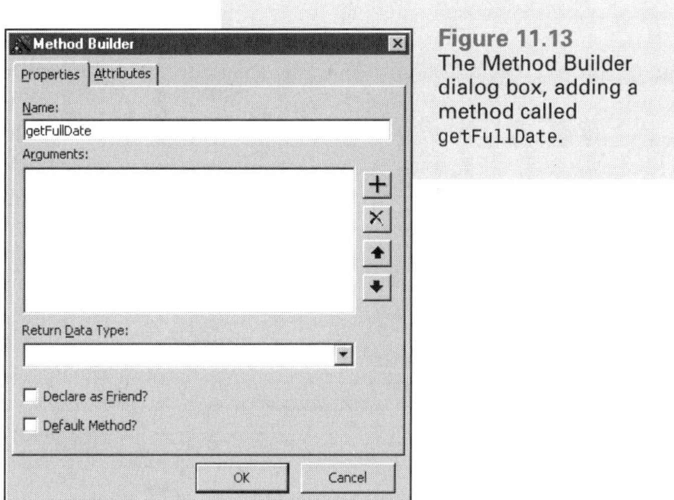

Figure 11.13
The Method Builder dialog box, adding a method called `getFullDate`.

2. Specify the parameters for your method. You can define the following attributes:
   - The name of the method
   - The return datatype of the method
   - Arguments that the method can accept from external applications or programs (selecting this option brings up a dialog that allows you to specify argument options, as shown in Figure 11.14)
   - Whether the method is the default method of the class
   - A text description of the method
   - Help context IDs for the method
3. After specifying the attributes of your method, click OK. Your method will be listed in the Class Builder Explorer window (see Figure 12.15).

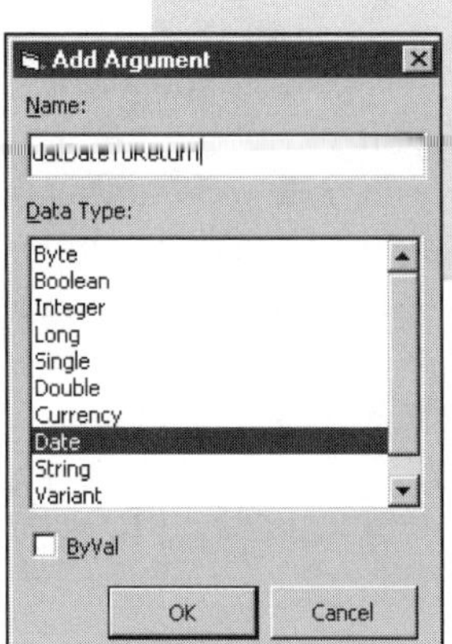

Figure 11.14 The Add Argument dialog box, with the date attribute of the `getFullDate` method.

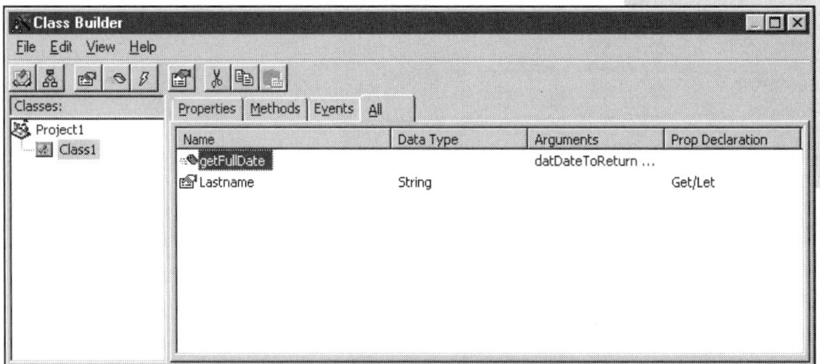

Figure 11.15 The result of adding a `getFullDate` method to the class.

Finishing the Code for the Class

Once you've finished defining the properties and methods of a class, choose File, Update Project from the Class Builder menu to add the property and method information you specified for the class. Figure 11.16 shows the Visual Basic IDE with the properties and methods defined in the preceding sections.

After updating your VB project, you can then add code to the methods you created. The next example creates a function that will return a formatted date from a passed-in date. Here's an example of what this function should return:

```
1/31/97 = January 31, 1997
```

To accomplish this, you change the `getFullDate` function to look like this:

```
Public Function getFullDate(datDateToConvert As Date) As String
    'Return fully expanded date
    getFullDate = Format(datDateToConvert, "mmmm d,yyyy")
End Function
```

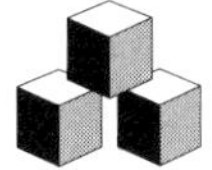

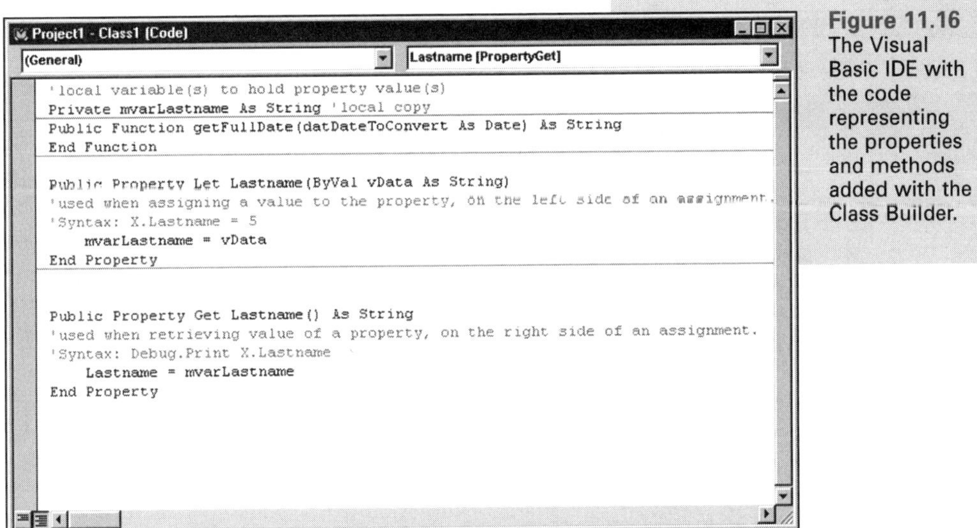

Figure 11.16 The Visual Basic IDE with the code representing the properties and methods added with the Class Builder.

Now the code for this class is complete. You can proceed to build and execute your ActiveX server.

Building the Server

After you finish defining the attributes of your ActiveX server, you need to build it. Generating the ActiveX server involves specifying two parameters—the name of the server and the name of the object that will be generated. By default, these parameters will be set to the name of the project and the name of the class you created.

To change the name of the server, follow these steps:

1. Choose Project, Properties from the Visual Basic menu. This step activates the Project Properties dialog, as shown in Figure 11.17.
2. Change the Project Name setting to your desired server name. For this example, use the name **ASPTest**.

The next step is to change the name of the class:

1. Open the property sheet for the class definition by right-clicking.
2. Specify the name of the object. For this example, use the name **ASPClass**, as shown in Figure 11.18.

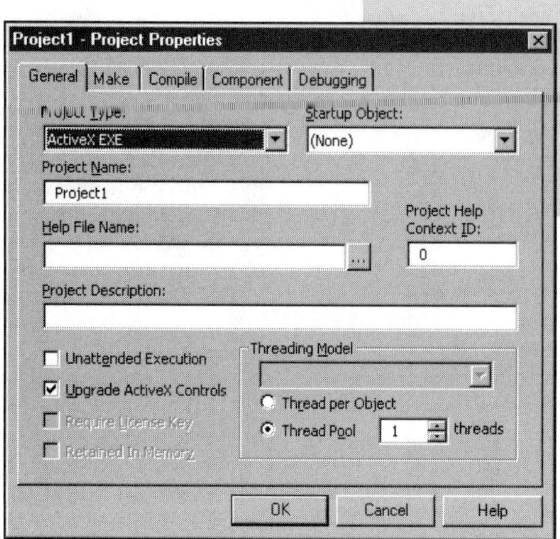

Figure 11.17 The Visual Basic Project Properties dialog, with the name of the ActiveX server defined.

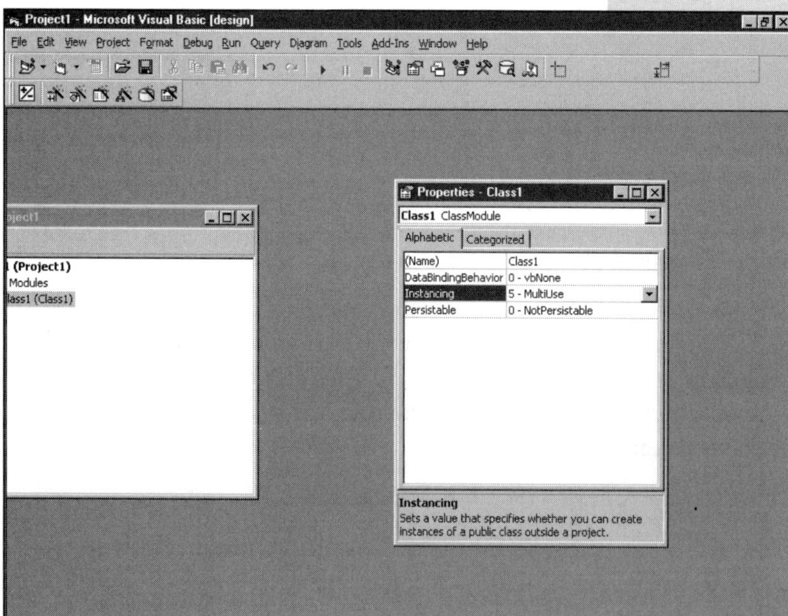

Figure 11.18 The property sheet for the `ASPClass` class.

After specifying the names for the project and the class, you can generate the server by choosing File, Make from the Visual Basic menu. Selecting this option creates the `EXE` file for your Active server. Now you can begin using this class.

Calling the ActiveX Server

After generating the ActiveX server, you can begin calling it. Before you install this class into your Active Server Pages, it's wise to make sure that it can be called from another ActiveX client. If you have Visual Studio, you can use Visual FoxPro, Visual Basic, or Visual C++ as testing tools; if you have Microsoft Office, you can use Excel as a testing tool. The following code shows calling the server just generated from Visual FoxPro or Visual Basic.

It's always a good idea to test your servers from as many platforms as possible — some servers may uncover unexpected behaviors of your object.

ON THE CD

```
*- FoxPro code to test ActiveX Server
Local oASPServ
oASPServ = CreateObject("ASPTest.ASPClass")
WAIT WIND oASPServ.getFullDate(DATE())
'VB Code to test object
    Dim oASP As Object
    Set oASP = CreateObject("ASPTest.ASPClass")
    MsgBox (oASP.getFullDate(Now))
```

After testing the code in different Active clients, you can proceed to install it into the Active Server Page. The following code demonstrates calling the ActiveX server you created from an Active Server Page. Figure 11.19 shows the server in a browser.

```
<HTML>
<TITLE>Chapter 11 Sample ASP Page</TITLE>
<H1>Lets create a session of the VB Server </H1>
<% Set oASPtest = Server.CreateObject("ASPTest.ASPClass") %>
<%= oASPtest.getFullDate(now) %>
</HTML>
```

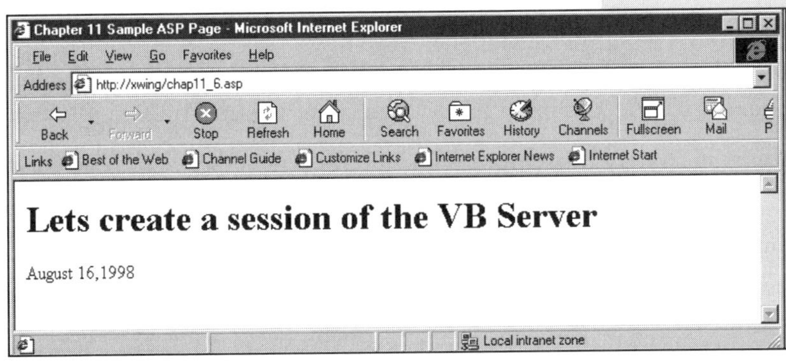

Figure 11.19
An Active Server Page with the contents of the call to the Active server created earlier.

Creating Database-Enabled ActiveX Servers

Until this point in this chapter, you've been creating ActiveX servers that have very limited functionality. You can set properties or call methods of these classes, but that's rather limited in value. The real value of using Visual Basic is its ability to access information from databases. What this means to developers creating Active Server Pages is that they can provide access to information stored in their databases from the Web.

Creating an ActiveX server with database capabilities involves a number of steps:

1. Create a connection to a database through ODBC.
2. Create a recordset, based on a set of selection criteria.
3. Create a collection of information that can be accessed from an external application.
4. Create an Active Server Page that calls the database server.

Recordset ***An object that returns a set of records from a table using a SQL query.***

The following sections show you how to connect to a database and return the information you collect to the Active Server Page.

Creating a Database Connection

The first step to adding database functionality to your application is to create a connection to a database. Creating a connection to a database with Visual Basic involves the use of Microsoft Data Access Objects (DAO) version 3.5. DAO is a set of tools that you can use in Visual Basic and other applications to connect to databases. Version 3.5 introduces a new type of connection called *ODBCDirect.* ODBCDirect is a light framework for accessing data by using ODBC drivers.

Creating a connection to a database with Visual Basic begins with referencing DAO 3.5 with your project. Follow these steps:

1. Select Project, References from the Visual Basic menu to open the Visual Basic References dialog box.
2. Select Microsoft DAO 3.5 Object Library (see Figure 11.20).

After adding this library to your project, you can begin coding. To create your data access class, do the following:

1. Create a new Active server project.
2. Activate the Class Builder add-in.

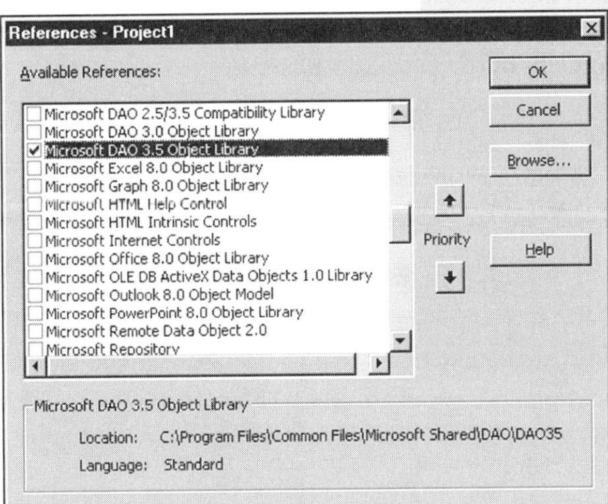

Figure 11.20
The VB References dialog box with the DAO 3.5 object library selected.

3. Add a method called **getDatabaseInfo**.
4. Update your project with the new information.
5. Add a reference to DAO 3.5 to the project.

After creating your new project and related DAO, you can begin adding code to your class. The following code creates a connection to an ODBC data source called `ProductList`:

ON THE CD

```
    Dim oWorkspace As Workspace
    Set oWorkspace = DBEngine.CreateWorkspace("ODBCDirect", "", "",
➥dbUseODBC)

    Dim oConn As Connection
    Set oConn = oWorkspace.OpenConnection("ProductList",dbDriverNoPrompt,
➥False)
```

This code performs two functions. It first creates a database engine object with the `CreateWorkSpace` method. It then connects to the `ProductList` database with the `OpenConnection` method. Once you have created a connection to a database, you can begin querying that database.

Creating the Query

After establishing a connection to a database, you can begin querying that database by creating a `Recordset` object. A `Recordset` object is a collection of records returned from a database based on a query passed during its instantiation process. The following code demonstrates creating a `Recordset` object with all records from the `products` table.

```
Dim recRecordsSelected As Recordset
    Set recRecordsSelected = oConn.OpenRecordset("Select * from
➥products", dbOpenForwardOnly)
```

This object is passed two parameters:

- First is a SQL `Select` statement. The `Recordset` object uses this parameter to determine which records it will return.
- Second is a parameter that tells the database engine how this object will be used. This `Recordset` object will be one that can only be scrolled through using `MoveNext`. This allows the database engine to optimize for this action.

Returning the Results in a Collection

After creating a recordset, you need to devise some method of returning it to the calling application. The most common method of doing this is to add a collection of information to your class. You do this by declaring a `Collection` object in the declarations section of your class. The following code demonstrates creating a collection object for the class:

```
Public oRecordsSelected As New Collection
```

After adding this `Collection` object, you can traverse through your recordset and add items to this collection. The following code shows the final result of the data access class:

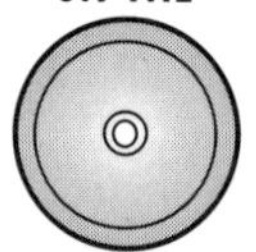


```
Public oRecordsSelected As New Collection

Public Function getDatabaseInfo() As String
    ' Create a handle to the database engine
    Dim oWorkspace As Workspace
    Set oWorkspace = DBEngine.CreateWorkspace("ODBCDirect", "", "",
➥dbUseODBC)

    ' Create a connection to the database
    Dim oConn As Connection
    Set oConn = oWorkspace.OpenConnection("ProductList",
➥dbDriverNoPrompt, False)

    ' Create and recordset object
```

```
    Dim recRecordsSelected As Recordset
    Set recRecordsSelected = oConn.OpenRecordset("Select * from
➥products", dbOpenForwardOnly)

    ' Put the contents of the records into a collection object
    Do Until recRecordsSelected.EOF
        oRecordsSelected.Add recRecordsSelected.Fields("product_name").Value
        recRecordsSelected.MoveNext
    Loop

    getDatabaseInfo = oRecordsSelected.Count
End Function
```

The last step in this process is to change the names of your server and class. The names should be `ASPData` and `ASPDataClass`, respectively. Now all you need to do is generate the `EXE` and call the server from your Web page. The following code demonstrates calling the ASP data server class from an Active Server Page. Figure 11.21 shows the results of calling this server.

```
<HTML>
<HEAD>
<TITLE>Autogenerated HTML</TITLE>
</HEAD>
<BODY>
<P>
Hello <%= Request.ServerVariables("REMOTE_USER") %><BR>
The Time Is <%= now %><BR>
Your browser is <%= Request.ServerVariables("http_user_agent") %><BR>
<TABLE WIDTH=400 Border = 1 >
<TR>
<TR><TH>Table Head</TH></TR>

<%
Set oMyObject = Server.CreateObject("ASPData.ASPDataClass")
oMyObject.getDatabaseInfo()
For i = 1 to oMyObject.oRecordsSelected.Count
    Response.Write "<TR><TD>" & oMyObject.oRecordsSelected(i) &
➥"</TD></TR>"
Next
%>
</TR>
</TABLE>
</BODY>
</HTML
```

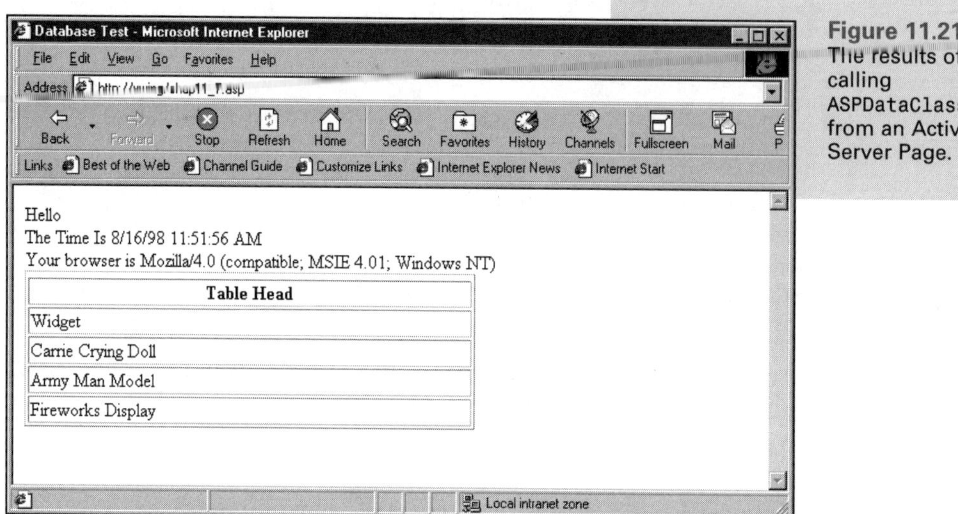

Figure 11.21 The results of calling `ASPDataClass` from an Active Server Page.

Testing the Server

Now that you've created the server, you need to test it. This introduces a new set of ideas. How can you test an ActiveX server? Testing forms is a pretty simple task, as you found in Chapter 4. However, ActiveX servers present a new set of problems. The first problem is that they have no visual interface; the second is that they can be called from multiple client interfaces. You should test your server against as many clients as possible.

The first problem to solve is that of testing a program that doesn't have an interface. There are two techniques that can be used here, known as *black box testing* and *white box testing*. The following sections describe these techniques.

Black Box Testing

Black box testing is a technique for testing the API of a particular object or function. It consists of instantiating the object and testing its inputs and outputs. Your goal here is to create an object that survives calls with bad parameters, and returns the correct values. There are many methods of black box testing in Visual Basic. You have the choice of either testing the code immediately in a screen known as the Immediate window, or creating a program that tests the code for you automatically. Each of these techniques has its place.

The first technique is using the Immediate window. The Immediate window allows you to type Visual Basic commands and see the results of those commands immediately. You activate the Immediate window by choosing View,

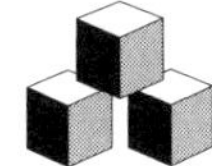

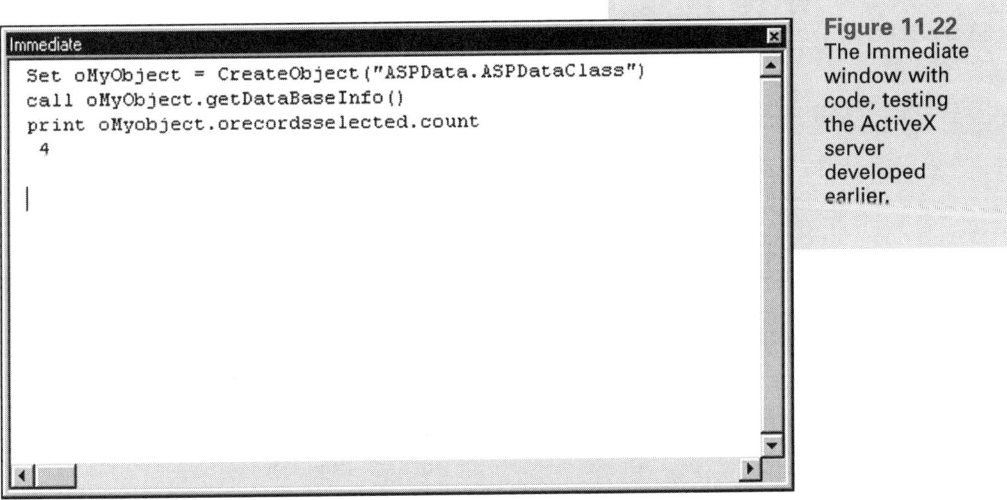
Immediate
Set oMyObject = CreateObject("ASPData.ASPDataClass")
call oMyObject.getDataBaseInfo()
print oMyobject.orecordsselected.count
4

Figure 11.22 The Immediate window with code, testing the ActiveX server developed earlier.

Immediate Window from the Visual Basic menu. Figure 11.22 shows the Immediate window with testing code in it.

Regression testing *Testing software in a manner that tests the same set of steps each time the software changes. This ensures that the software quality didn't regress.*

As you can see, the Immediate window allows you to test your code without the hassle of creating a form and a bunch of code to test your server. However, it does have one flaw: It's not repeatable. When you create applications, you should test the code repeatedly. This is a technique known as *regression testing.* Regression testing ensures that any new changes you make don't cause the system to *regress*—that is, get worse than when you started. This is where code comes in. To create regression tests, you need some method of calling code in a repeated manner. The best way to do this is to create "test suites" of Visual Basic code that test your objects. The easiest way of doing this is to test your objects using the Immediate window; then, after completing those tests, paste the code into a Visual Basic program with some slight alterations. The following code shows how your test can look:

```
on error goto TestFailed
Set oMyObject = CreateObject("ASPData.ASPDataClass")
call oMyObject.getDataBaseInfo()
debug.print oMyobject.orecordsselected.count
TestFailed:
debug.print "Test suite 001 failed"
```

This code installs an error routine that will trap if the test fails and return an error message to the Immediate window. You could get more elaborate and log the errors to a file or a set of databases for statistics tracking.

White Box Testing

White box testing looks at the inside of functions when they're called. The goal of this type of testing is to make sure that all lines of code are being executed, and in the correct manner.

Visual Basic provides a nice set of tools that can be used for this type of testing—the Visual Basic debugging tools. You can insert breakpoints into your code that allow you to stop your programs and step through them one line of code at a time. You can insert a breakpoint by right-clicking the line of code at which you want to stop. VB prompts you with a pop-up menu that allows you to toggle a breakpoint on a specific line of code (see Figure 11.23).

After specifying a breakpoint, you can run the VB project that calls this server; Visual Basic will stop the program at the place where you inserted the breakpoint. Then you can begin stepping through the code, testing the contents of variables and making sure that the code is running properly. Your goal here should be to test that all lines of code are called at least one time. This will require you to test your code using multiple scenarios. The result of this testing is a complete test of your code and assurance that all conditions are taken into account.

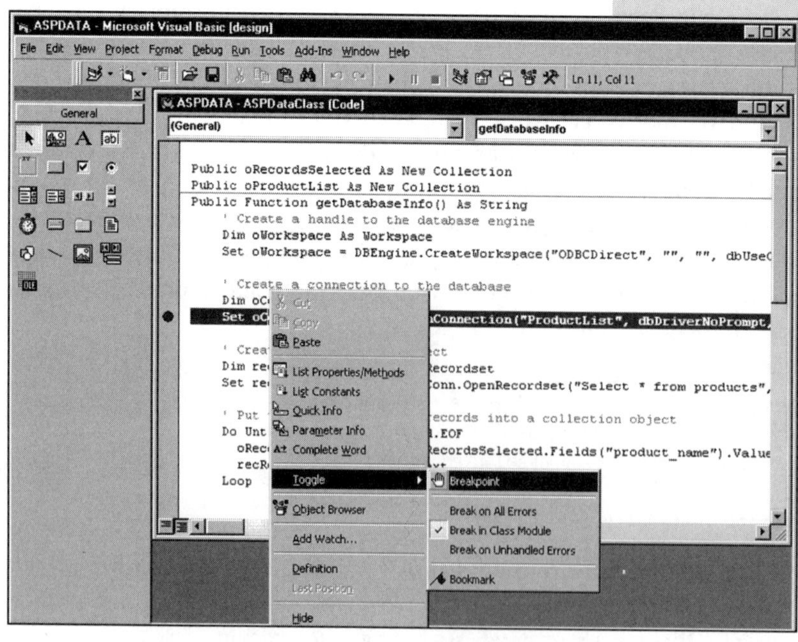

Figure 11.23
Toggling a breakpoint.

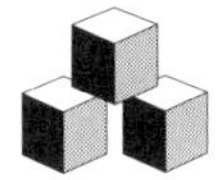

Creating a Query Active Server Page

Now that you understand the concepts involved in the development of ActiveX servers, you can begin creating the components specified in your design. Consulting the design, you find that the first requirement is to create a product listing page and a corresponding product details page. The product listing page will be an HTML table with hyperlinks to individual products.

Developing this set of Active Server Pages will involve two components:

- An object that will be used to generate the product list Web page
- An object that will accept a product ID code and return the information for that product

The following sections describe both components.

Creating the Product Listing Page

The first object to be generated is an object that will create a product list. This object will be an Active Server Page that will do the following:

1. Create a title for the Web page.
2. Create an HTML table.
3. Call an ActiveX server component to get the list of current products.
4. Format the data from the server and place it in the table.

The first item on the list is to create an Active Server Page that meets requirements 1 and 2. To do this, use the Active Server Page you created earlier in the chapter, with a few slight alterations. The HTML for this page is as follows:

ON THE CD

```
<HTML>
<HEAD>
<TITLE>Product Price List For Widget Inc. </TITLE>
</HEAD>
<BODY>
<P>
<H1>Product Price List</H1>
<H2>Generated<%=Now %></H2>
<TABLE WIDTH=400 Border = 1 >
<TR>
<TR><TH>Product List</TH></TR>

<%
```

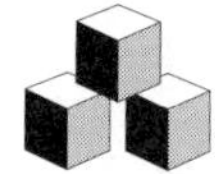


```
Set oMyObject = Server.CreateObject("ASPData.ASPDataClass")
oMyObject.getProductInfo()
For i = 1 to oMyObject.oRecordsSelected.Count
    Response.Write oMyObject.oProductList(i)
Next
%>
</TR>
</TABLE>
</BODY>
</HTML>
```

The next item on the list is to create an ActiveX server capable of returning the proper information for your Active Server Page. As you can see from the preceding code, you're going to create two new additions to your server:

- First is a new method called `getProductInfo`. This method will generate a list of products and the HTML code for putting these products into a Web page.
- The second component is a new collection object called `oProductList`. This collection will contain the product codes and the HTML tags to put in the page.

The following code shows the new functions for the ActiveX server:

```
Public Function getProductInfo() As String

    ' Create a handle to the database engine
    Dim oWorkspace As Workspace
    Set oWorkspace = DBEngine.CreateWorkspace("ODBCDirect", "", "",
➥dbUseODBC)

    ' Create a connection to the database
    Dim oConn As Connection
    Set oConn = oWorkspace.OpenConnection("ProductList",
➥dbDriverNoPrompt, False)

    ' Create and recordset object
    Dim recRecordsSelected As Recordset
    Set recRecordsSelected = oConn.OpenRecordset("Select
➥product_name, product_Id from products order by 1",
➥dbOpenForwardOnly)

    ' Put the contents of the records into a collection object
    Dim strUrl As String

    Do Until recRecordsSelected.EOF
        strUrl = "<TR><TD><A HREF=" & Chr(34) & "chap11_9.asp?prod_id="
```

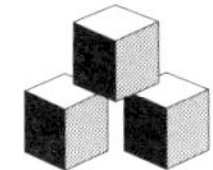


```
        strUrl = strUrl & recRecordsSelected.Fields("product_id").Value
        strUrl = strUrl & Chr(34) &
➥recRecordsSelected.Fields("product_name").Value
        strUrl = strUrl & "></A></TR></TD>"
        oProductList.Add strUrl
        recRecordsSelected.MoveNext
    Loop

    getProductInfo = oProductList.Count
End Function
```

ANALYSIS

The code of interest here is the lines that create the product records. These records use a combination of three tags: `<TR>`, `<TD>` and `<A HREF>`. `<TR>` and `<TD>` are tags used to create table rows. The `<A HREF>` tag lets you create links to other Web pages. The `<A HREF>` tag creates links to another ASP page that will loop up the appropriate document and show product information. This will be shown later.

After making the appropriate changes and generating a new executable for your server, you can test it in your browser. One item you should look at is the content of the Web page returned to the browser. ASP returns normal HTML pages. Figures 11.24 and 11.25 show the HTML source code generated and the page in a browser.

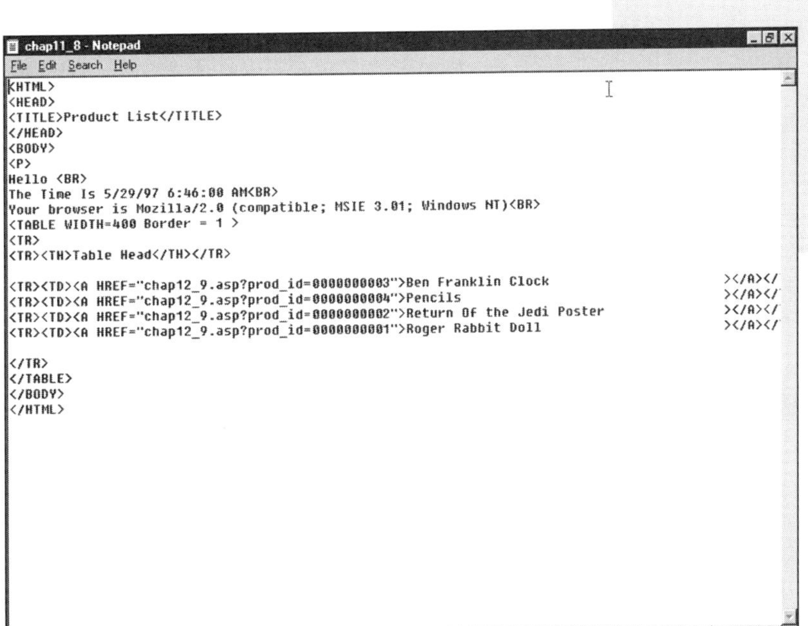

Figure 11.24
The HTML code resulting from the combination of the Active Server Page and the ActiveX server.

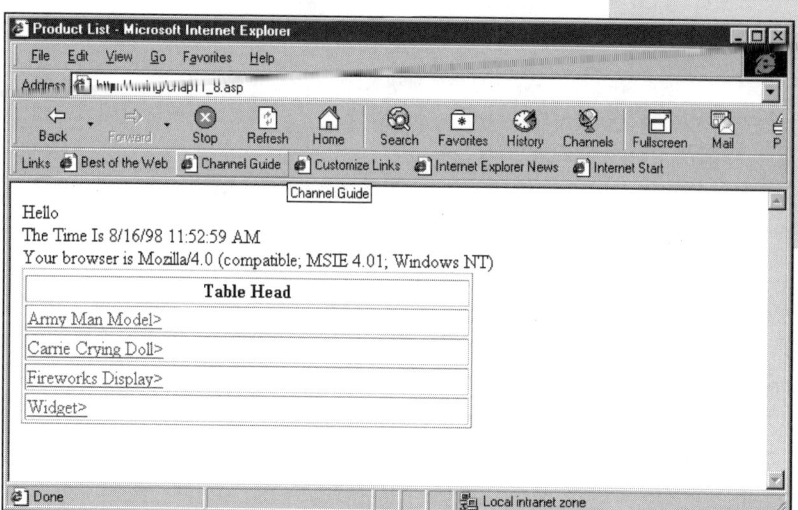

Figure 11.25 This illustration shows the Web page generated from the HTML code shown earlier in this section.

Adding Parameterized Functionality to Your Server

Looking at the <A HREF> tags from the page generated in the preceding section, you'll notice that they reference another Active Server Page with a parameter specified. This parameter will be sent to the `CHAP11_9.ASP` Active Server Page, which will then call another ActiveX server and return the information for the specified product.

As you may recall from earlier in this chapter, Active Server Pages provide an object known as the `Request` object. The following two sets of code show a Web page with an `<A HREF>` tag:

```
<HTML>
<A HREF="chap11_9.asp?cRodParameter=Rodman Was Here">Call Other Page</A>
</HTML>
```

and an Active Server Page with code that extracts the parameter passed by the `<A HREF>` tag:

```
<HTML>
<H1>And the parameter is<%=Request.Querystring("cRodParameter")%></H1>
</HTML>
```

This parameter is then displayed on the Web page. Figures 11.26 and 11.27 show the Web page with the parameterized hyperlink and the result of clicking that link, respectively.

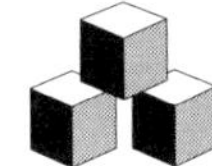

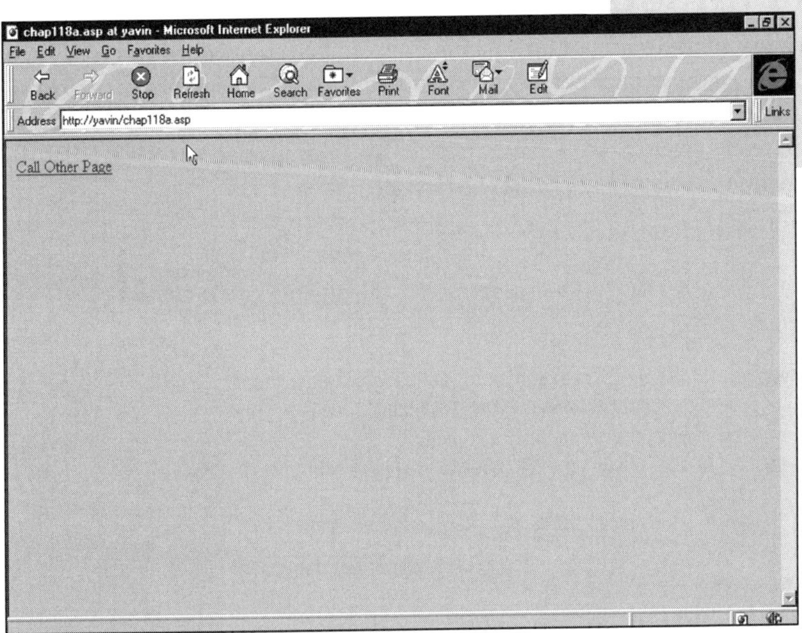

Figure 11.26 The Web page with a reference to an Active Server Page.

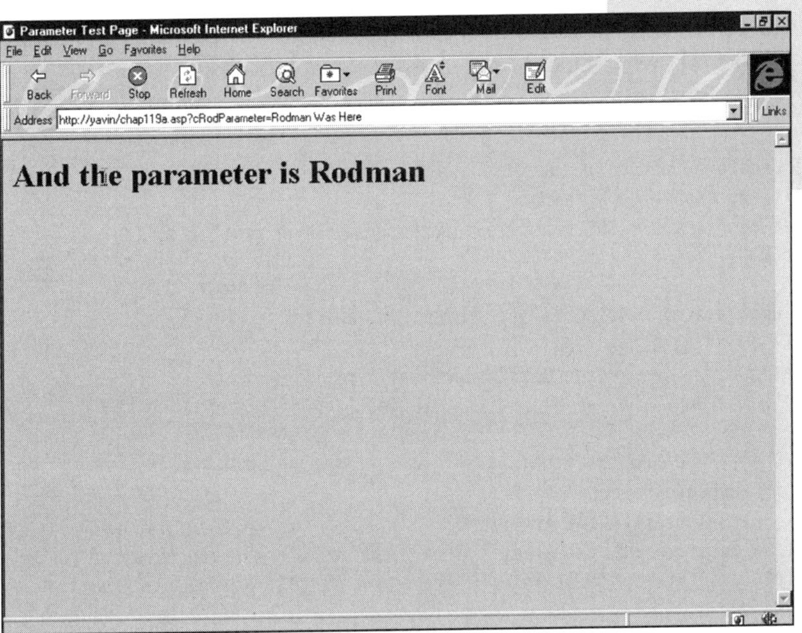

Figure 11.27 The value of the parameter passed to the Active Server Page.

Sending Parameters to the Server

With the understanding of how parameters can be extracted from a Web page, you can take those parameters and pass them to an Active server for information retrieval. The following code shows how you would retrieve the `product_id` code from a Web page, pass it to an Active server, and have the information formatted into an HTML page:

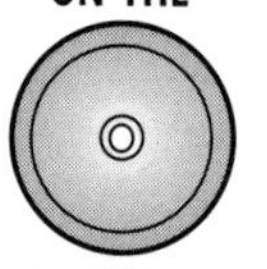

```
<TITLE>Product Information Page</TITLE>
<HTML>
<H1>And the parameter is <%=Request.Querystring("prod_id")%></H1>

<%
Set oMyObject = Server.CreateObject("ASPData.ASPDataClass")
oMyObject.getProductData(Request.Querystring("prod_id"))
For i = 1 to oMyObject.oProductData.Count
    Response.Write oMyObject.oProductData(i) & chr(10) & chr(13)
Next
%>

</HTML>
```

After creating the HTML code for your Active Server Page, you need to modify the server application to return product information. What this involves is creating a method that accepts `product_id` as an argument. This method then will look up the value passed and set some properties based on the information it finds. The following code shows how to accomplish this:

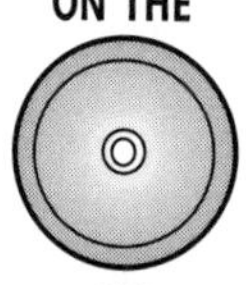

```
Public Function getProductData(strProductId As String) As String

    ' Create a handle to the database engine
    Dim oWorkspace As Workspace
    Set oWorkspace = DBEngine.CreateWorkspace("ODBCDirect", "", "",
➥dbUseODBC)

    ' Create a connection to the database
    Dim oConn As Connection
    Set oConn = oWorkspace.OpenConnection("ProductList",
➥dbDriverNoPrompt, False)

    ' Create and recordset object
    Dim recRecordsSelected As Recordset
    Dim strSelectStatement As String
    strSelectStatement = "Select * from products where product_id = "
    strSelectStatement = strSelectStatement & Chr(34) & strProductId &
➥Chr(34)
```

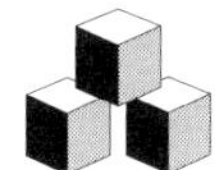


```
    Set recRecordsSelected = oConn.OpenRecordset(strSelectStatement,
➥dbOpenForwardOnly)

    ' Put the contents of the records into a collection object
    Dim strProductData As String

    Do Until recRecordsSelected.EOF
        strProductData = "<h1>"
➥& recRecordsSelected.Fields("product_name").Value & "</h1><br>"
        oProductData.Add strProductData
        strProductData = "<h2>Price: $" &
➥Str(recRecordsSelected.Fields("product_price").Value) & "</h2><br>"
        oProductData.Add strProductData
        recRecordsSelected.MoveNext
    Loop

    getProductData = oProductData.Count
End Function
```

Now that you've created the proper Active Server Pages for this process, you can test them in your browser. Figures 11.28 and 11.29 show the results of both operations.

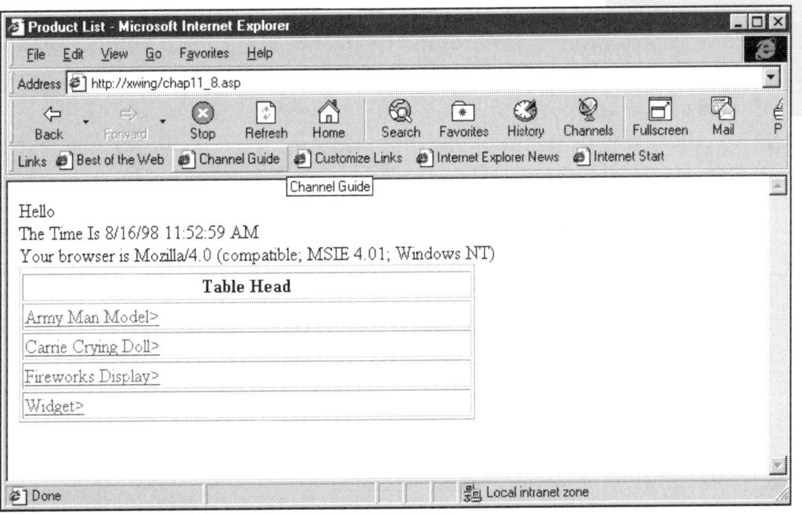

Figure 11.28
The product list Web page.

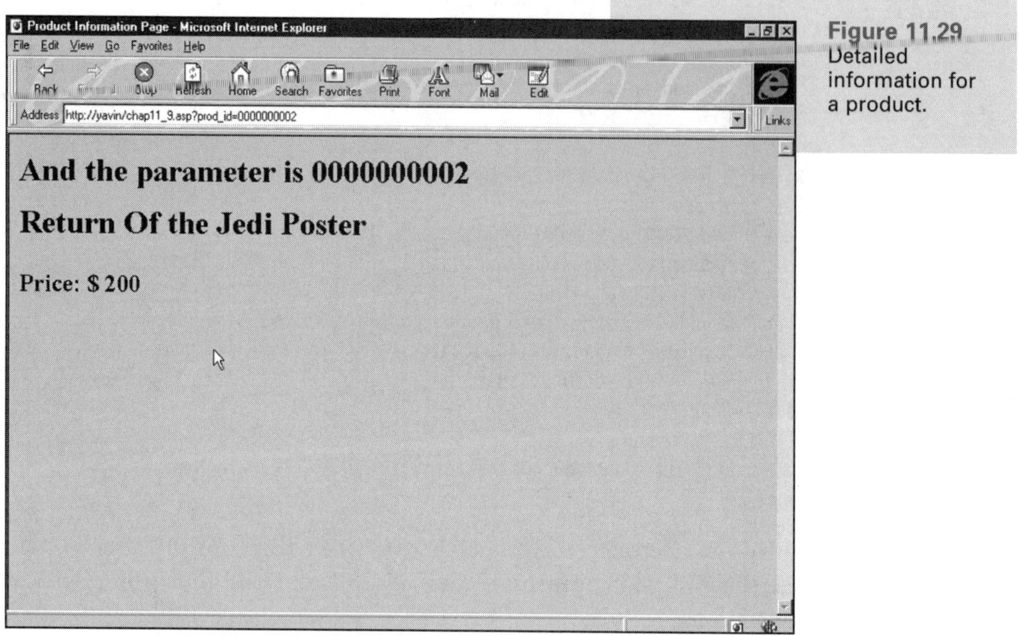

Figure 11.29 Detailed information for a product.

Creating a Search Screen

The final Active Server Page you'll create is the product category search screen. From the design chapter, you'll find that it's necessary to create a Web page that allows users to query products by product category. This task will be accomplished by creating a Web page with a drop-down list full of product categories. Once a user selects a category and selects the Search option, your program should query the database for that category of product and return the appropriate Web page with products for that category. This task will require that you do the following:

1. Create a Web page with a product category drop-down list. This list should be retrieved from the database.
2. Create an ActiveX server to generate a list of product categories.
3. Create an ActiveX server to generate a list of products based on a passed-in category.

The following sections describe this process.

Creating the Product Category Active Server Page

The first step in creating this set of Active Server Pages is to create the Web page that will display the product categories. The following code (extracted from the prototype created in the design chapter) shows the HTML for the product category Web page:

```
<HTML>
<BODY>
<TITLE>Product Search</TITLE>
<H1>Select Product Category</H1>1
<SELECT NAME="D1" SIZE="1">
        <OPTION>Cutie Pie Dolls</OPTION>
        <OPTION>Action Figures</OPTION>
        <OPTION>Stuffed Animals</OPTION>
</SELECT>
</FORM>
</BODY>
</HTML>
```

After extracting this code, you need to make some minor changes. The first change is to add code to call an ActiveX server to retrieve the product categories. With this change, the code for your HTML will look like this:

```
<TITLE>Product Information Page</TITLE>
<HTML>
<H1>And the parameter is <%=Request.Querystring("prod_id")%></H1>

<%
Set oMyObject = Server.CreateObject("ASPData.ASPDataClass")
oMyObject.getProductData(Request.Querystring("prod_id"))
For i = 1 to oMyObject.oProductData.Count
    Response.Write oMyObject.oProductData(i) & chr(10) & chr(13)
Next
%>

</HTML>
```

Creating the Product Category ActiveX Server

The next step to creating the product category page is to create the ActiveX server that will provide the list of product categories. This server will behave just like the product list Active server, except that it will extract data from the product categories table. The following code represents the code for the new ActiveX server:

```
Public oCategoryList As New Collection

Public Function getCategoryInfo() As String

    ' Create a handle to the database engine
    Dim oWorkspace As Workspace
    Set oWorkspace = DBEngine.CreateWorkspace("ODBCDirect", "", "",
➥dbUseODBC)

    ' Create a connection to the database
    Dim oConn As Connection
    Set oConn = oWorkspace.OpenConnection("ProductList",
➥dbDriverNoPrompt, False)

    ' Create and recordset object
    Dim recRecordsSelected As Recordset
    Set recRecordsSelected = oConn.OpenRecordset("Select
➥category_name from categories order by 1", dbOpenForwardOnly)

    ' Put the contents of the records into a collection object
    Dim strUrl As String

    Do Until recRecordsSelected.EOF
        strUrl = "<option>" & Chr(34) "
        strUrl = strUrl & recRecordsSelected.Fields("category_name").Value
        strUrl = strUrl & "></option>"
        oCategoryList.Add strUrl
        recRecordsSelected.MoveNext
    Loop

    getCategoryInfo = oCategoryList.Count
End Function
```

Figure 11.30 shows the results of the previous example. Once you've completed this server, all you need to do is modify the server that generates product data to retrieve the parameter from this Web page. We'll leave that one for you to practice on.

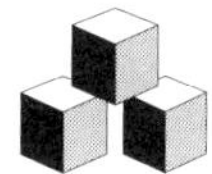

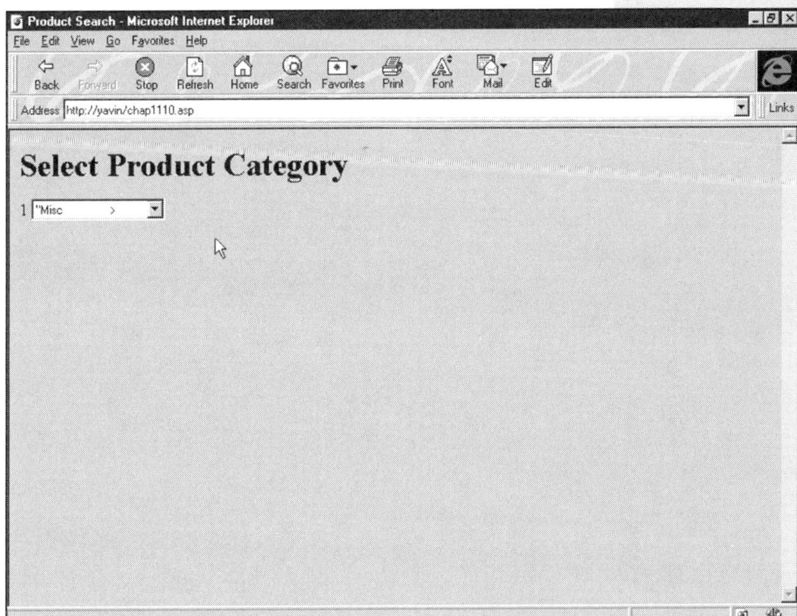

Figure 11.30 Web page with drop-down list of product categories.

Summary

As you can see, Active Server Pages and Visual Basic make two very powerful allies. In this chapter, you learned the basics of Active Server Pages, how to create ActiveX servers with Visual Basic, and how to integrate these two technologies together. You finished with a set of dynamic Web pages that allow you to query product information from a database. You can use the power of Visual Basic from your Web pages and create very powerful solutions. In later chapters, you'll explore more advanced tools for creating Active Server Pages.

Project 2 Summary

The second project presented you with a set of tools allowing you to publish data from your Visual Basic applications. You combined Internet technologies such as HTML and Active Server Pages with VB ActiveX servers.

You began this project by gathering system requirements, then generated a prototype application using Microsoft FrontPage, which required far less investment of time than coding the Web pages by hand.

After creating the prototype of your application, you began learning about the technologies that are used to present your databases on the Internet. You learned about ASP and how you can retrieve information from the server and place it in your applications. You also learned to launch ActiveX servers from your Web pages and create ActiveX servers with VB that allow you to query data from databases. You altered these servers so that they could be used to provide data to your Web pages, and created ActiveX servers that return data that can be displayed in your Web pages. Finally, you learned techniques for testing your ActiveX servers.

HANDS ON PROJECT 3

THE CUSTOMERTRACKER

- Designing a scalable Internet application
- Creating an ActiveX DLL server
- Defining public properties and methods
- Creating and using a collection object
- Using ODBCDirect
- Developing a test rig for an ActiveX DLL server
- Deploying an ActiveX DLL server
- Using HTML, VBScript, and Active Server Pages
- Developing mass e-mail tools

Project Overview

Microsoft has produced a large collection of products that provide a means for developers to leverage their existing skills in Internet development. The core of these products is the *common object model (COM)*, which isn't actually a product at all—it's an object specification. The implementation of COM is ActiveX. ActiveX components come in many forms—as controls, executables, and dynamic link libraries (DLLs). More variations are coming. Microsoft's Internet Information Server (IIS) can use ActiveX components in Web pages—called Active Server Pages. But the key change that Microsoft made was in the creation of ActiveX components.

It used to be that the only way to create an ActiveX (or OLE) component was using C++, which made component creation a difficult, time-consuming task for experts only. Visual Studio now has multiple products capable of creating ActiveX controls, including Visual Basic, Visual FoxPro, Visual J++, and of course Visual C++.

The combination of Visual Basic creating ActiveX components and Internet Information Server using Active Server Pages lets a Visual Basic programmer use his or her existing skills to develop for the Internet. The CustomerTracker application is an example of what you can do with these tools—build a real-world Internet application in a language you already know how to use.

What Is the CustomerTracker?

Many companies that have commercial Web sites collect information about the visitors to their site, using a form of some sort. This is an essential part of doing business—you must know as much as possible about your prospective customers, whether they are coming into your store or visiting your Web site.

The CustomerTracker is an automated solution in which customers fill out a form that's stored directly in a database. The form covers not only the customer's personal contact information, but a list of products as well. The customer can select what products he'd like to be notified about when new information is available.

After the record is created, the customer can return to the Web site to update his entry—perhaps to update his e-mail address, or to change his selection of product notifications.

Included as part of the CustomerTracker is an automated mechanism that's used by administration for sending out e-mail notices to all customers, based on their selection of products.

Describing the CustomerTracker

Most Web sites that have visitor forms use the common gateway interface (CGI) method for gathering data. A CGI script creates a text file or e-mail whenever a visitor fills in the form. This can create a tremendous amount of workload for the Web site operator—if the site is even moderately successful, the text files and/or inbox of the operator get stuffed full of prospective customers. Beyond that, a CGI script usually doesn't provide any method for a visitor to update his data—changing his e-mail address or removing himself from the mailing list.

To create a more sophisticated application, CustomerTracker utilizes a host of technologies. The central technology in CustomerTracker is Active Server Pages. Active Server Pages have *scripting*, a program written in VBScript or JavaScript, within the Web page. These scripts reference an ActiveX component built in Visual Basic. By using Active Server Pages, VBScript, and Visual Basic, you can build a far more sophisticated Web application than anything constructed using CGI.

The CustomerTracker is a much more advanced method of collecting and processing visitor information. Form entries are directly recorded into a database. The day-to-day operations of the form don't create any labor—visitors are able to add, edit, and delete their records themselves. Beyond this, there's the added attraction of e-mail notification—rather than the visitor doing you the "favor" of filling in your form, you are providing him a service. The visitor doesn't have to keep visiting your site to get additional information on your product; you'll contact him when that information is available. And if he doesn't want to be notified, he can indicate that himself.

Providing this service is not labor-intensive for your business at all—the customers fill in and maintain their own records. The only work you have to do is sending out the notification, which is done through an automated tool that's part of the application.

System Requirements of the CustomerTracker System

The overall goal of the CustomerTracker system is to create the largest database of prospective customers possible. To achieve that goal, the system has to work with as many different systems as possible. Remember that this is the Internet, and the mix of technology is huge. As well, the system has to provide value to the customer—he has to have a reason to want to fill in the form.

Beyond these requirements, the internal requirements involve being able to manage what should be a rapidly growing system—so it can't involve much labor to operate, and it needs to be scalable. No matter how busy the system gets, it has to minimize the amount of work involved to keep it running, and has to be able to handle the ever-growing loads without having to start over.

In summary, the CustomerTracker requirements are as follows:

- Provide the ability for customers to create their own records.
- Provide the ability for customers to request updates on products.
- Provide the ability for customers to update their own records.
- Provide the ability to e-mail customers automatically.
- Work with as many browsers as possible on the World Wide Web.
- Minimize the internal labor required to operate the CustomerTracker on a routine basis.
- Provide the ability to scale the system up to high-traffic loads.

Goals of the Customer Tracker System

This project is designed as a real-world application using Visual Basic with the Internet. Understanding this project and putting it to work should result in an application that you can use at any commercial site—to the benefit of the company. The Internet has a lot of potential for making profit. Using the tools available today, you can tap that profit. Here are some of the things you can expect to learn in this project:

- **Creating ActiveX servers in Visual Basic**
  Visual Basic is not only effective as a client-end application development tool; it also is effective at creating the back-end components of an application. ActiveX servers are applications that encapsulate functionality for other applications. Visual Basic can create ActiveX servers, so that you can use the language you're familiar with to create tools for other languages to use.

- **Creating Active Server Pages**
  Instead of having to learn all the unique technology of the Internet, Active Server Pages (ASP) provides a method for providing sophisticated features to a Web site without adding functionality at the browser level. With ASP, all the functionality is on the server—nothing new gets sent to the browser. So a standard HTML 2-compliant

browser can work just as effectively on your Web site as the latest browsers can. Maximum audience means maximum returns.

- **Using ODBCDirect**
  Building a scalable database application means being prepared to switch to a high-performance database engine in the future. ODBCDirect provides the ability to write database code in Visual Basic that can be switched to any ODBC-compliant database with virtually no changes in code.
- **Planning for upsizing**
  The design techniques used in the CustomerTracker system are specifically oriented for scaling up. ODBCDirect is part of the plan, but using ActiveX servers also allows for other tools, such as Microsoft Transaction Server (MTS), to be implemented with a minimum of redesign.

Summary

As you can see, an essential part of a real-world application is planning for its future. One of the key reasons to develop the CustomerTracker is that existing CGI techniques for data collection don't scale well. Many of the choices made in the specifications of the CustomerTracker have to do with being able to grow the application to whatever size it eventually ends up. Planning the future of an application makes certain that the application will have a future—no more dead-end legacy applications.

The next step in developing the CustomerTracker application, like developing any application, is to gather details on what exactly the CustomerTracker should do. The gathering and organizing of this information is discussed in Chapter 13.

Gathering Information for the CustomerTracker

In the previous projects, discussions on how to gather information on a development project provided certain insights as where and how this information can be gathered. The process of gathering additional information stems from the basic requirements that were outlined in Chapter 12. In addition, we need an overall mission statement, which is really the basic measuring stick by which the success of the project can be determined.

This is the mission statement for the CustomerTracker:

Mission Statement

To provide a system for gathering information about customers and prospective customers via the company Web site. Besides collecting information for the company, the system also should help bring our company to the attention of previous visitors by contacting them via e-mail. The system must have value to our

> customers by providing them with additional information, without creating unnecessary 'junk mail' that might create a negative image for our company. Ideally, the system should be maintenance-free and be considered an asset to our company, not a liability.

Chapter 12 outlined the requirements of the system. The additional information gathered fills out those requirements, detailing exactly what each requirement entails. Each requirement needs to be measured against the mission statement—how the requirement is fulfilled should be determined by how it can best support the overall mission. Once all the information about the requirements is gathered, the design of the system can be made.

Provide the Ability for Customers to Create Their Own Records

By letting customers create their own records, the labor that's normally involved in adding new prospects to a prospect database is saved. This requirement supports the overall mission statement because it minimizes the ongoing labor costs of the Web site. In fact, it's superior to any other collection method, Internet-based or otherwise, because the customer does a task that is normally an employee task. In this sense, the Web-collection tool is superior to any other method available to the company, and the asset value of the Web site is improved—you would rather have prospective customers filling in their own data records. The typical alternative is a customer on the phone talking to a customer representative, who has to fill in the data for the customer. Done correctly, the CustomerTracker system can actually save money for the entire company—an asset indeed.

So the value of gathering data by using the Web-collection tool is understood. What data should be gathered from a customer?

- Name of customer
- E-mail address
- Street address
- City

- Province/State
- Postal/ZIP code
- Country

The only information in this list that's really essential is the name and e-mail address—in the design of the application, these two elements must be specified as required for a valid record to be created. The mailing address information must be in a form that can accept a wide variety of address formats—this is an Internet application, and likely customers from all over the world will be using it. You can't count on what the style, format, or length of the address data will be like when entered.

Provide the Ability for Customers to Request Updates on Products

This requirement fulfills the mission statement's need to provide value to the customer for filling in the form. By offering the ability to request updates, the customer is giving you permission to e-mail him or her on a periodic basis. Rather than just having a simple tick box that says "Go ahead and e-mail me with any old thing you think I might be interested in," the CustomerTracker can send targeted e-mail. To best fulfill this requirement, you need to provide a list of products from which the customer can choose—only updates to those products the customer is interested in will result in e-mail.

Because the CustomerTracker system is able to work with a relational database, it's relatively simple to send e-mail to only those customers who indicate their interest in a product. Using this design will support another aspect of the mission statement—to avoid being a nuisance to customers by sending "junk mail." The e-mail sent to customers should be targeted to their needs, based on what they asked for. With these features, the e-mail sent by the CustomerTracker system becomes a service, rather than an annoyance.

To provide the facility for selecting products, the database needs a list of products from which to select. Hard-coding the products on to the Web page isn't the right solution—it incurs more long-term labor costs, because the Web page itself has to be altered each time the product line changes. Instead, the Web page should be built dynamically, based on the database of products. Then the administrators need only change the database of products to change the Web page and the list of e-mail options available to customers.

The customer table also needs a connection to the products table, in order to indicate what products the customer is interested in. This should be a separate table so that there's no limit to what products a customer can select.

Provide the Ability for Customers to Update Their Own Records

One of the key weaknesses of many Web-based entry forms is that once entered they're unchangeable, except by the operators of the Web site. This is a serious problem for two reasons:

- It frustrates prospective customers, who may not want to get your mail anymore, or have changed e-mail addresses and want to redirect the mail to the new address.
- It creates a labor cost—customers who have used your Web site and filled in your form are forced to call your customer support lines to ask for changes to be made. This ties up your people and makes the Web site an expense, rather than an asset.

Adding the ability for a customer to retrieve her record and modify it solves all the problems—the customer is satisfied that she can control what happens to her record, including removing it. And the labor cost involved in maintaining the database is minimized—the customer does the work for you.

To provide this ability safely, it's necessary to add security features to the system. You need a way to identify the customer with some certainty. As a result, part of the design has to include a unique customer identification code of some kind, and a password.

Provide the Ability to E-mail Customers Automatically

Automating the e-mail system ties two elements of the mission statement together—it offers a customer service at the same time as minimizing labor costs. With the proliferation of junk e-mail and the general outcry against it, it's essential that any e-mail sent to a prospective customer be seen in as positive a light as possible. Consequently, the e-mail system must be set up to be a service to the customer—which means that he or she wants to receive and read the e-mail sent by the company.

By automating the e-mail within the CustomerTracker system, the tools for targeting the mail are easily available—the relational database allows the operators to easily select only the appropriate group of customers for the e-mail. The customers themselves specify what groups they should be in. Ultimately, specific information about the customer can be collected from the entry form and used as filtering criteria for other targeted mailings.

The e-mail mechanism should be as simple to use as the entry system itself—point and click. The operators need only type in the actual body of the e-mail, select the customer group to send to, and go. By implementing the e-mail mechanism in this fashion, this feature also supports the mission statement by minimizing labor costs.

Work with as Many Browsers as Possible on the World Wide Web

The Internet is a wildly diverse place, with prospective customers all over the world. To best fulfill the mission statement and attract the largest customer contact list possible, as many people as possible have to be able to use the Web site. This is one of the key reasons that CGI scripts are used so often in customer data collection—they work with almost every kind of graphical browser available.

Active Server Pages have the same strength as CGI scripts, without many of the weaknesses. An Active Server Page requires nothing extra from a browser beyond what any CGI script needs. All the additional processing is done at the server end, where the company has control.

> **Note**
>
> **There are many Web servers that support Active Server Pages. You can run ASP with IIS 3.0 or higher, or O'Reilly WebSite 2.0. You also can run ASP on Netscape and Lotus servers with an add-on from a company named ChiliSoft. A demonstration of the ChiliSoft add-on is included on the CD that accompanies this book.**

Any Visual Basic code developed for the Web site executes only on the Web server as an ActiveX executable. The Web pages themselves contain references to the ActiveX objects, but the Web server processes them itself—the entire process is transparent to the client browser. The result is not only a very compatible execution method, but also extremely fast—no plug-ins or other data-heavy forms have to be sent to the client.

Minimize the Internal Labor Required to Operate the CustomerTracker on a Routine Basis

The labor involved in operating a Web site is often a hidden cost that undermines the success of the company's Web site in the long term. When labor resources aren't allocated to the Web site, the site stagnates and its performance suffers. By minimizing the ongoing labor costs—that is, the labor required to answer e-mail, process forms, and update records—more labor should be available to improve the quality of the site overall. This reduces the operating costs of the Web site and increases its value and productivity, because most of the labor time expended on the site is value-added time—the quality of the site is improved by the labor expended.

By allowing customers to add and maintain their own customer records, all of the entry-processing labor costs are eliminated—the customers take care of the data themselves. Likewise, the e-mailing system built into the CustomerTracker should be highly automated, using the database features of the system to retrieve appropriate customer records for a targeted e-mailing.

Minimizing operating costs, by reducing labor does more than just free up labor for other tasks—it can actually save the Web site from failing due to its own success. A maintenance-intensive Web site requires more and more labor as it gets busier. The more customers using the site, the worse the situation gets until, ultimately, the site fails. This failure can come in many forms: The costs involved to maintain the site get so high that it's no longer economical to support it; the customers are disappointed by the slow response of the site itself as well as the slow response of the support people through e-mail; too many people get `Site too busy` or `Site not responding` messages. So by keeping the amount of operating labor required to a minimum at the very beginning of the site's deployment, the long-term growth prospects look bright.

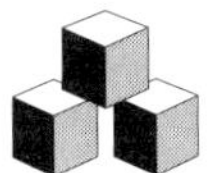

Provide the Ability to Scale the System Up to High-Traffic Loads

Although a company Web site might start small, ultimately the goal is to have a huge Web site, generating lots of revenue for the company with a minimum of expense. But many Web site designs don't include a plan for long-term growth, and the site fails from its own success—it gets busier, and demands more and more maintenance. Gradually, the quality and performance of the site declines as the system strains under the load of so many hits, and the personnel are too busy patching holes to make things better. In many ways, the failure of a good Web site is more damaging to a company than having no Web site at all —potential customers become disillusioned with the company. ("If they can't manage their own Web site, how can I expect them to take care of me?")

To build a successful Web site in the long term is to plan for growth—serious growth. The Internet is a massive place, and growing more massive by the day. Literally millions of new users are entering the World Wide Web every year, and they are all prospective customers. Your Web site has to be able to accept an ever-increasing number of "hits"—that is, simultaneous requests from your Web server.

ActiveX servers *ActiveX components that provide specific capabilities to other applications. ActiveX servers typically don't have user interfaces — the application utilizing the server provides the client interface.*

There are a variety of limiting factors on the growth of a Web site. A number of these issues have to do with hardware and the chosen method of Internet connection. While these elements are beyond the scope of this book, the application that runs on the Web server also has to scale up to the ultra-high velocities of a successful site.

Active Server Pages has the distinct advantage of minimal bandwidth requirements when serving to a client. What that means, basically, is that more customers can read the pages simultaneously, because a huge amount of data isn't being sent to each one when they request it.

Microsoft Transaction Server (MTS) *A Microsoft application that provides object brokerage services. MTS handles application requests for ActiveX server components.*

Using ActiveX servers is also a critical feature of the design. As usage grows on the Web site, Microsoft Transaction Server (MTS) can assist the ActiveX servers in handling literally thousands of simultaneous requests to read and write data. MTS acts as an object broker, controlling the number of instances of a given object (the ActiveX server), so that the system doesn't just break down under its own weight. Because Visual Basic can make ActiveX servers, you can use VB to create your initial versions of the servers when the load is light. As the system gets busier, you can add MTS to help broker the use of your VB-based ActiveX server. More information on MTS is available from Microsoft's Web site.

Ultimately, should your Web site hit the pinnacle of usage, the servers can be rewritten in a language such as Visual C++, for optimum performance with MTS.

Summary

The resulting details developed by the information-gathering process are the key ingredient for designing the application. The mission statement is the stick by which each feature of the application will be measured. The better the design supports the mission statement, the better the application will fulfill its goal. By mixing the mission statement and detailed requirements with an experienced developer, the result is a useful application.

CHAPTER 14

Designing the CustomerTracker

Chapter 13, "Gathering Information for the CustomerTracker," completed a detailed list of requirements for the system. Now you can proceed with the design process. In the design process, you begin putting together a list of detailed technical specifications for your system. These technical specifications will then be used to actually implement the CustomerTracker system.

The mission statement written in Chapter 13 still applies when designing the application, as do the original requirements outlined in Chapter 12. When writing up the technical design of the project, we must keep these elements in mind.

Mission Statement

To provide a system for gathering information about customers and prospective customers via the company Web site. Besides collecting information for the company, the system also should help bring our company to the attention of previous visitors by contacting them via e-mail. The system must have value to our customers by providing them with additional information, without creating unnecessary 'junk mail' that might create a negative image for our company. Ideally, the system should be maintenance-free and be considered an asset to our company, not a liability.

These are the requirements:

- Provide the ability for customers to create their own records.
- Provide the ability for customers to request updates on products.
- Provide the ability for customers to update their own records.
- Provide the ability to e-mail these customers automatically.
- Work with as many browsers as possible on the World Wide Web.
- Minimize the internal labor required to operate the CustomerTracker on a routine basis.
- Provide the ability to scale the system up to high-traffic loads.

Some Notes on Design Methodology

Previous chapters included some discussion on waterfall versus rapid application- development (RAD) design methodology. Both methods are rather similar, because the goal of each is basically the same—developing the application. Although all the projects in this book have been developed using the RAD methodology, because of the nature of books—where the entirety of the development is laid out for the reader—you're effectively seeing a waterfall development.

We consider the RAD method superior for several reasons—one is that in business development, the more you can involve the users, the easier the transition is. Another has more to do with billing and keeping the client happy—the RAD method takes an application down to smaller chunks, so that you can make gradual progress and regular "deliveries" of operating code. Because the design phase of the waterfall method tends to be all-encompassing, it takes a lot of work before any results—that is, working code—are delivered.

But there is another significant aspect of RAD methodology to be aware of—it's an admission that no program is ever truly "finished." Developing an application is an ongoing process—businesses change, and their programs have to change with them. If you develop with the waterfall method, you're presuming that your assessment of the business requirements at that time is how it will always be in that business—if the business changes, the development process must start over.

The same basic rule applies to RAD, but with RAD you presume that the business *will* change, and that part of the application's success is that it too *must* change. An essential part of the RAD methodology is repeatedly returning to the specifications and design phases. New ideas, new requirements, and new abilities are going to be brought to your application. Part of RAD is anticipating changing the application substantially over time. With RAD, there are no more legacy applications *per se*, because the application never gets abandoned in light of a new development. Applications grow and change with the business, and are designed from the outset to do so.

All the applications in this book were built with the RAD methodology, and also with the RAD philosophy—there's always more to be done.

Breaking Down the CustomerTracker Application to Components

So far, the CustomerTracker application has been defined only in terms of requirements. Now these detailed requirements have to be turned into logical components—the individual building blocks of an entire application. In Internet-related applications, good component design is absolutely critical—because the application may have to scale up to such massive performance requirements, only excellent component design will make this possible.

The CustomerTracker application breaks down into five components:

- The database, which provides storage and processing for the data
- The ActiveX server, which provides communication to the database
- The ActiveX Server Tester, which proves the functionality of the server
- The Web pages, which use the ActiveX server to retrieve and update data
- The Administration utility, for data maintenance and generating e-mail

All these components come together to make the CustomerTracker application.

The Database

The database used in this application is an Access database. Typically, Access databases are controlled using the Jet database engine. Since VB3, Visual Basic has provided data access objects (DAO) to communicate with Access databases using the Jet database engine. And also since VB3, there have been complaints about how the DAO works with Jet to communicate with Access databases.

The primary problem with this method of database communication has been speed, especially when the system gets large. The Access database is an *indexed sequential access method (ISAM) database*, like dBASE and Paradox databases. While it's true that Access provides more relational database features, such as querying in SQL, the fundamental fact is still there—the underlying architecture of an Access database is ISAM.

So why use ISAM databases at all? Well, they're simple to implement, included with the programming language, and make great test beds. In fact, they'll work for a product system until it starts to get really busy. Then you need to hand the database duties over to a SQL-based relational database, such as Microsoft SQL Server.

Open database connectivity (ODBC) ***ODBC is a specification designated by Microsoft and generally accepted by the database community. The ODBC API provides a common method for any database product to connect to any database application.***

SQL servers are more robust than ISAM databases—they run as an application service on a network server, such as NT Server. They're more expensive, but by using NT Server they can be scaled up to incredible size—massive amounts of memory, multiple processors, and large RAID hard-drive arrays are utilized by large-scale SQL servers to provide thousands of transactions per second.

Since VB3, Microsoft has said that the Access-to-SQL Server upgrade path was logical and simple. In practice, the process is more complicated than it's worth. The Jet database engine, while simulating some of the features of a SQL server, doesn't emulate its performance. In fact, the methods used to get the best performance out of the Jet database engine are literally the slowest methods for using a SQL server, and vice versa. Developing code in Visual Basic that will run equally well using Jet or SQL Server used to be virtually impossible.

With the release of Visual Basic 5, Microsoft introduced a new method of communicating with databases, called *ODBCDirect. ODBC*, short for *open database connectivity*, has been available for several years, and is a widely accepted standard for working with databases. It's *middleware*—that is, it resides between databases and database products, providing a common interface for both. A database vendor develops an ODBC driver for its database, knowing that then any ODBC-compliant application can work with that database. Application developers create their database applications working with ODBC, so that their application can work with all of the ODBC-compliant databases.

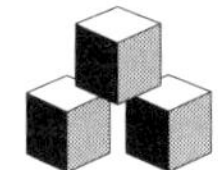

Data access objects (DAO)
A DAO can be configured to connect to a particular database, either as a query or (in the case of Access databases) a direct connection to a table. The object then exposes the columns of the database for the application to work with.

Until VB5, there was no good way to work directly with ODBC. The easy way involved working with the *data access objects* (DAO), and the performance was always disappointing. The fast way to work with ODBC was through the ODBC API, but that was extremely difficult and fraught with serious crash risks.

ODBCDirect offers an efficient and easy way to work directly with ODBC. Using ODBCDirect, a developer can write using familiar DAO functions, creating recordsets and using add, edit, delete, and move methods. The performance is excellent, and the commands are literally identical whether you're using an Access database, SQL Server, or any other type of ODBC-compliant database.

Because a critical part of the CustomerTracker application is scalability, it's anticipated that, under real-world conditions, the application will be switched up to SQL Server. Using ODBCDirect makes this extremely simple. When the time comes to switch, the data is converted to SQL Server, and a new ODBC connection is created for the SQL server. The only code changes involve the actual connect strings for the database—all queries, data objects, and methods remain the same.

The CustomerTracker system database is called `CTrack`. `CTrack` contains four tables: `Customers`, `Products`, `CustomerItems`, and `Config`. Each of these tables stores particular elements of the CustomerTracker system; their relationship is shown in Figure 14.1. Notice that the `Config` table has no connection to the other tables—it's used as storage for e-mail reference data.

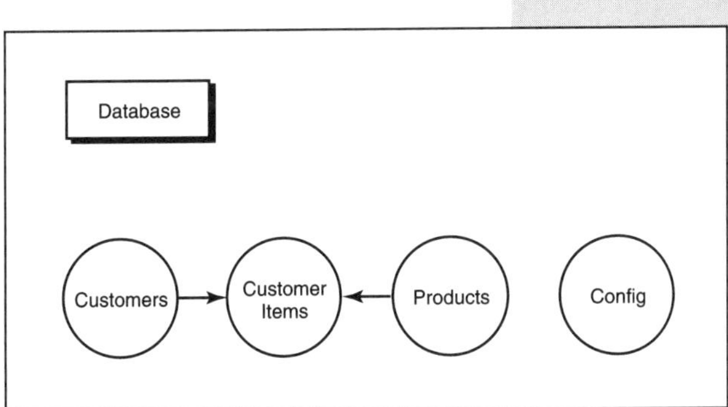

Figure 14.1
The relationship between the tables in the `CTrack` database.

Customers Table

The bulk of the data stored about a customer is stored in the `Customers` table (see Table 14-1). The `ID` field is used as the primary key, and therefore must be unique for each customer. Note that the `ID` field is different from the `Name` field—`ID` is used for logging in, along with the password. The `ID` field also acts as the connection from the `Customers` table to the `CustomerItems` table.

Note

In this project and the last project, you're using database technologies found in Visual Basic versions 5 and 6. The current "recommended" standard for data access is ActiveX Data Objects (ADO), which is discussed in the next project. It is the position of the authors of this book that people need to know more than one method for getting at data — hence the inclusion of both "old" and "new" methods in this book.

Table 14-1 Customers Table

Name	Type	Size
ID	Text	30
Password	Text	30
Name	Text	50
Email	Text	50
Address1	Text	50
Address2	Text	50
City	Text	40
State	Text	30
ZipCode	Text	20
Country	Text	30

Products Table

In a production application, it's likely that there would be far more information in the `Products` table than in this example (see Table 14-2). The `Products` table contains only two fields—`ProductName` and `Description`. `ProductName` is used as the link field to the `CustomerItems` table. In a production system, this table would contain information such as price, current inventory, supplier, and so forth. `ProductName` is the primary key, and so has to be a unique name— no duplicates allowed.

Table 14-2 Products Table

Name	Type	Size
ProductName	Text	30
Description	Text	120

CustomerItems Table

The CustomerItems table creates the relationship between the Customers table and the Products table (see Table 14-3). Using this table, any customer can indicate his interest in any or all of the products the company has. There are only two fields in the CustomerItems table, and likely will never be more. The sole purpose of this table is to provide a connection between the Customers and Products tables—hence, one indexed field from each table.

Table 14-3 CustomerItems Table

Name	Type	Size
CustomerID	Text	30
ProductName	Text	30

Config Table

The Config table is a bit of an oddball compared to the rest of the tables in the database (see Table 14-4). This table has no relationship with the other tables in the database; it's used as a storage space for certain programmable e-mail information. In a production system, it would likely have much more configuration information. The Class field sorts the configuration data into logical groups—in the sample application, there's only one Class: Email.

Table 14-4 Config Table

Name	Type	Size
Class	Text	20
Item	Text	30
Data	Text	50

The CustomerTracker ActiveX Server

The ActiveX server component of the CustomerTracker system provides access to the database for the Active Server Pages. When developing a server component in Visual Basic, there are actually two types—ActiveX server EXE and ActiveX server DLL. These two servers used to be known as *out-process* and *in-process OLE servers.*

ActiveX server EXEs (or out-process OLE servers) are stand-alone applications, although they have no user interface code. Other applications can communicate with these servers—including remote communications across networks. They execute in their own memory space and task thread. Because they're separate applications, they're not as fast as ActiveX server DLLs.

ActiveX server DLLs (or in-process OLE servers) are called upon by an application directly, and execute within the memory space and thread of the calling application. As a consequence, they're substantially faster than ActiveX server EXEs, but can't be called remotely. For the CustomerTracker application, the ActiveX server used is a DLL.

The CustomerTracker ActiveX server is actually composed of three objects: the publicly exposed `CustomerData` object, the `CustomerItems` collection, and the `CustomerItem` object. The relationship between these objects and how they connect to the database components is shown in Figure 14.2.

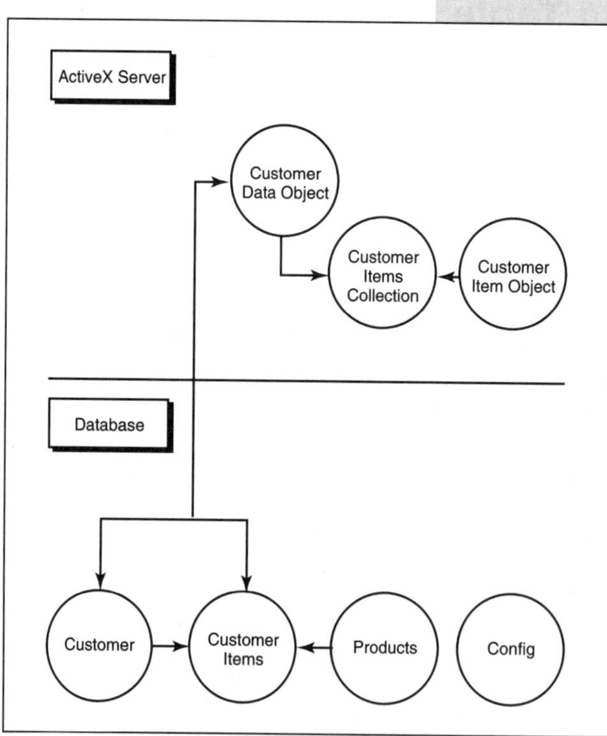

Figure 14.2 The relationship between the three CustomerTracker classes and the `CTrack` database. Notice that the `CustomerData` class is the only component of the CustomerTracker ActiveX server that's exposed to other applications.

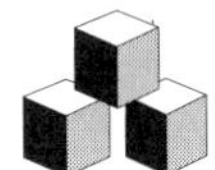

If you're not that familiar with object-oriented programming, classes and objects can be a bit boggling. Put simply, a *class* is the framework by which an object is created. The class describes the object; the *object* is the instantiation of that class. A good example of this is the difference between a blueprint and a house. The blueprint is the abstract representation of the house—a blueprint is a class. The house is what was constructed from the blueprint—the house is the object, an instantiation of the class.

The CustomerData Class

The `CustomerData` class is the interface through which other applications communicate with the CustomerTracker ActiveX server. The `CustomerData` class controls the database component to fulfill the requests of the other components. When an application calls the `CustomerData` class, a `CustomerData` object is instantiated. The data from the database is made available to the other applications using the `CustomerData` object's properties (see Table 14-5). Note that one of the properties of the `CustomerData` object is a `CustomerItems` collection, which contains `CustomerItems` objects.

The `CustomerData` object's methods listed in Table 14-6 are how another application gives instructions to manipulate data in the database. Each method passes the same parameters to the object—the ID of the customer and his or her password. The methods all return the same type of integer value, indicating success or failure.

Table 14-5 `CustomerData` Class Properties

Name	Datatype
`Name`	`String`
`Email`	`String`
`Address1`	`String`
`Address2`	`String`
`City`	`String`
`State`	`String`
`ZipCode`	`String`
`Country`	`String`
`Items`	`CustomerItems`

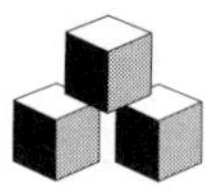

Table 14-6 CustomerData Class Methods

Method	Description
Create	Create a new customer record, based on ID and password
Retrieve	Retrieve a record from the database and fill the properties with it
Update	Apply the properties list to the database

The CustomerItems Collection Class

The CustomerItems collection class contains, logically, CustomerItem objects. When a CustomerData object is instantiated by an application, a CustomerItem object is also instantiated, as one of the properties of the CustomerData object. The CustomerItems collection class has no properties—only methods.

Table 14-7 lists the methods in the CustomerItems collection. These methods are the same methods available to any other collection in Visual Basic. This method of collection creation is complex, but has significant benefits to the user—it's by far the most powerful and flexible way to define collections of data together.

Table 14-7 CustomerItems Collection Class Methods

Method	Description
Add	Adds a new CustomerItem to the collection
Count	Returns the total number of CustomerItems in the collection
Delete	Deletes a CustomerItem from the collection
Item	The default property — it returns the currently selected CustomerItem in the collection
NewEnum	A special type of method, it provides the ability to walk through a collection using For Each... code

The CustomerItem Class

The CustomerItem class describes the products that a customer is interested in. CustomerItem objects are referenced by the CustomerData class through the CustomerItems collection class. A CustomerItem object only has properties (see Table 14-8). All methods for acting on the CustomerItem object are in the CustomerItems collection class.

In practice, the `CustomerItems` collection is populated with `CustomerItem` objects indicating every product, its description, and a flag indicating whether the customer is interested in the item. By bringing all products back into the class, a dynamically created list can be displayed, containing all the products. In the CustomerTracker application, this list is used in the Web pages and testing system for selecting which products the customer is interested in.

Table 14-8 `CustomerItem` Class Properties

Name	Datatype
`ProductName`	`String`
`Description`	`String`
`Selected`	`Boolean`

The CustomerTracker Tester

Developing ActiveX servers is a complex process. To make successful development easier, a testing rig is needed. The testing application utilizes every property and method exposed by the CustomerTracker ActiveX server. In the development process, two copies of Visual Basic run at the same time; one has the ActiveX server running, and the other has the test application. Using this development method, you can quickly test and debug all the features and functions of the ActiveX server.

Figure 14.3 shows the relationship of the testing application to the ActiveX server.

The Web Pages

The true user interface of the CustomerTracker application is the Web pages—it's through the Web pages that the customer communicates with the ActiveX server, which then accesses the database. In a typical production application, the CustomerTracker application would be only one small part of the total Web site. A complete Web site would include detailed descriptions of the products sold, information about the company, and so forth.

The Web pages for the CustomerTracker are actually of two varieties—standard HTML pages and Active Server Pages (ASP). It's the ASP Web pages that communicate with the ActiveX server on the Web server. ASP Web pages include VBScript or JavaScript programming code to provide the functionality to communicate with the ActiveX component. VBScript is very similar to

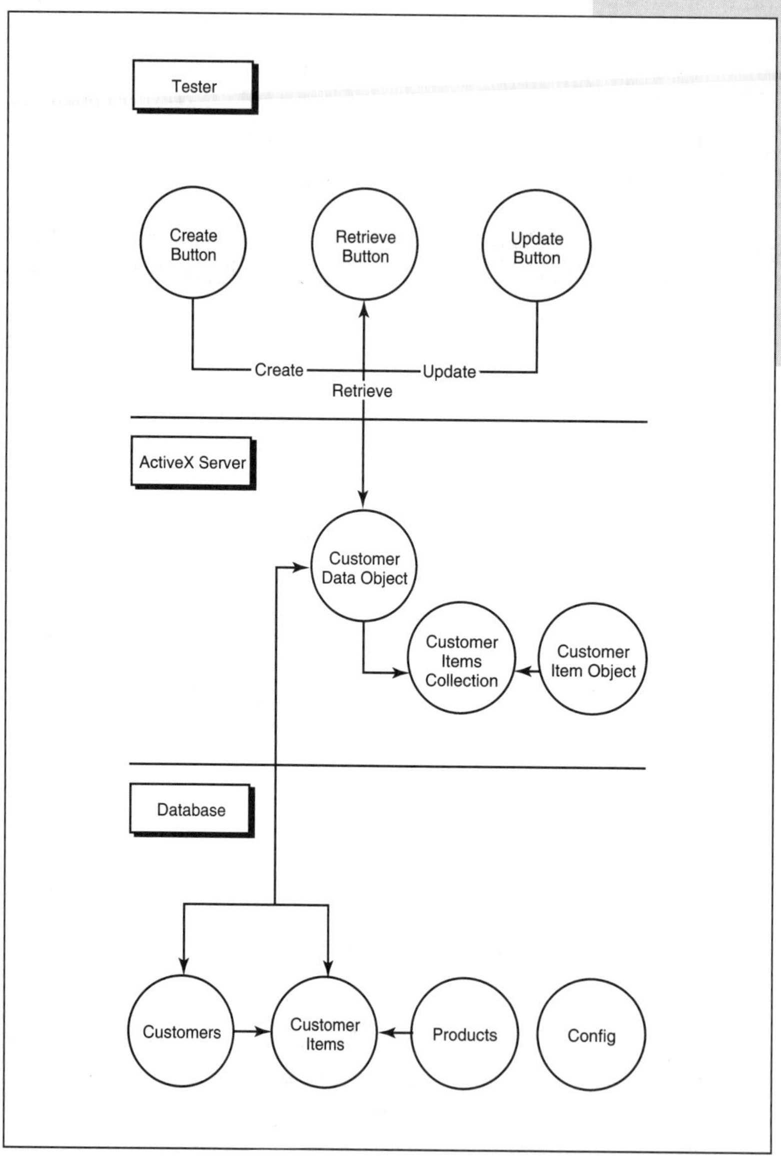

Figure 14.3 The relationship between the testing application, the ActiveX server, and the database. Using the testing application greatly simplifies the development process of an ActiveX server.

Visual Basic, with some limitations. (For more details on the differences and similarities of VB, VBA, and VBScript, see Chapter 3, "A VBScript Primer.")

Figure 14.4 shows the relationship between the Web pages and the ActiveX server.

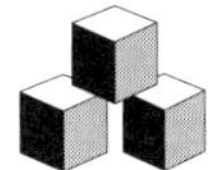

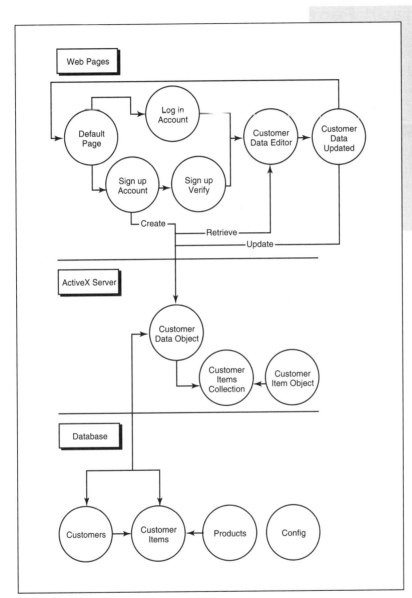

Figure 14.4
How the Web pages connect with the ActiveX server and database. Web pages that aren't involved with communication to the ActiveX Server are regular HTML; the pages connected to the ActiveX server are Active Server Pages (ASP).

In a production Web site, the pages in Figure 14.4 would be only a small part of a much larger whole. But the pages all work together here to make the CustomerTracker application.

Default Page

The opening page of the CustomerTracker application, the default page is standard HTML. The default page offers two links—one to the Log in Account page, for users who already have a record in the database; the other link to the Sign up Account page, for new users to create their records.

Log in Account

The Log in Account page is still a standard HTML page—it contains only HTML 2.0 form code for logging into the CustomerTracker system. When the user clicks the Submit button, the page automatically links to the Customer Data Editor, passing the login information along.

Sign up Account

Also a standard HTML page, the Sign up Account page looks almost identical to the Log in Account page—it has only a form for the ID and password that the user wants. But when the Submit button is clicked, it passes the information along to the Sign up Verify page.

Sign up Verify

The Sign up Verify page is an Active Server Page, as all are all subsequent pages in the list. It receives the ID and password form data from the Sign up Account page, and attempts to create an account. A `CustomerData` object is instantiated and the `Create` method is used, passing the ID and password to the CustomerTracker ActiveX server.

The `Create` method returns a success or failure. A failure displays a page indicating that the account can't be created and the user should go back and try again. Success displays a page saying that the user can proceed to the Customer Data Editor by clicking the Continue button.

Customer Data Editor

There are two ways to get to the Customer Data Editor page—through the Log in Account page or the Sign up Verify page. Either way, the same form data is passed along—an ID and password. The Customer Data Editor calls the CustomerTracker ActiveX server to create an instance of the `CustomerData` object. It then uses the `Retrieve` method, passing the ID and password along, to cause the CustomerTracker ActiveX server to populate the properties of the `CustomerData` object with data for the customer.

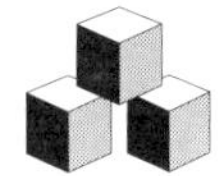

Should the retrieve fail, it's possible that the ID and/or password are incorrect—a failed login. If this happens, an "Uh oh" page is displayed, and the customer is told to go back and try again. If the `Retrieve` succeeds, the properties list of the `CustomerData` object is populated with the data of the customer.

This population includes a `CustomerItems` collection, which has a list of the products available for selection, as well as indicators as to what products the customer has selected.

All the properties of the `CustomerData` object are displayed in a form, including a series of special dynamically generated check boxes for each product in the `CustomerItems` collection. The check boxes are checked or not, depending on what `CustomerItem` objects are indicated as selected.

Once the page is displayed, the customer can add or remove data, change her product selection, and, when finished, click the Update button to bring up the Customer Data Updated page.

Customer Data Updated

The Customer Data Updated page retrieves all the customer information from the Customer Data Editor page, including the customer's product selections. The first thing the Customer Data Updated page does is check to make certain that the most critical information fields—the name and e-mail address—are entered. If they aren't, a page is displayed indicating that they're required, and the user should go back and enter them. Otherwise, the Customer Data Updated page creates an instance of the `CustomerData` object and populates its properties (including the `CustomerItems` collection) with the data entered by the customer. It then invokes the `Update` method.

In normal operation, the `Update` method should not fail—in order to get this far, the customer record exists, and everything should be fine. However, there is the possibility of something going wrong, so there's a trap for the `Update` method. If it fails, a message is displayed to the customer, explaining that there's a problem and suggesting that she go back and try again.

If the `Update` succeeds, the success page is displayed, along with one of two other options, based on whether the customer selected any products for which to be notified. Because one of the key features of the CustomerTracker system is the e-mail-based notification, a check is made as to whether the customer selected any products.

If the customer didn't select any products, a page is displayed suggesting that she might want to take advantage of this feature, and she can go back and do so. If she has selected products, the page thanks her for doing so, mentions that they'll be in touch, and offers a link to send her back to the default page. In a production system, this link would probably point to the home page of the Web site.

The Administration Utility

The Administration utility of the CustomerTracker system provide two useful capabilities—the ability to add and delete products, and the ability to generate e-mail to customers who have selected specific products.

The utility is a standard Visual Basic executable. It could have been made a Web page, but for simplicity and security reasons it's a stand-alone executable. The Administration utility uses the Mabry mail control to provide SMTP mail capabilities. Figure 14.5 shows how the Administration utility works with the database components.

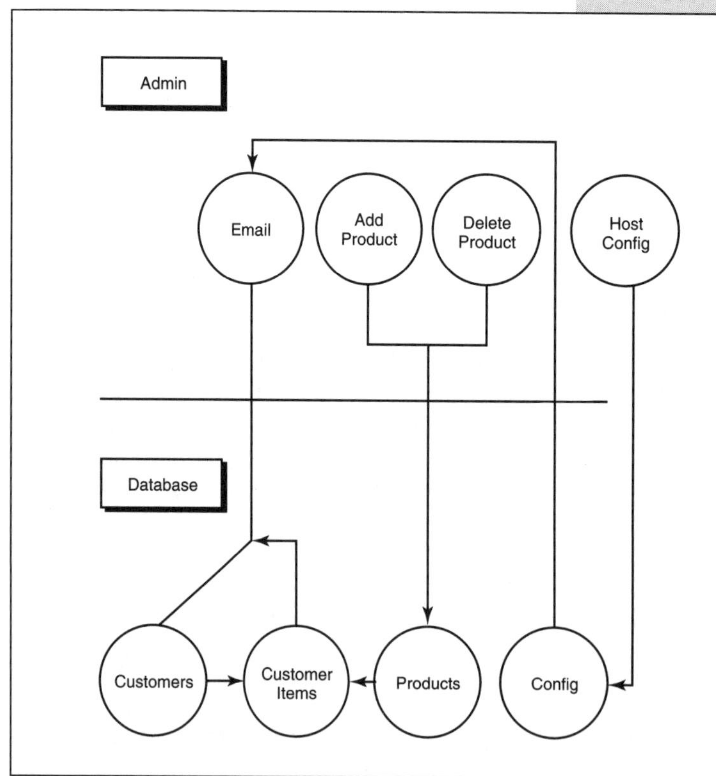

Figure 14.5 The connections between the Administration utility and the database components. Note that the ActiveX server isn't involved in this connection — it isn't needed. The Administration utility stands on its own, secure and isolated from the Web system.

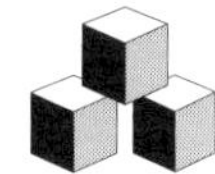

With the Administration utility, new products can be added and old products deleted. New products are instantly a part of the Web site. Because all lists of products are built dynamically, once a new product is added, the very next request of a Web page containing a list of products will show the new product.

Caution

> **When an old product is deleted, all references are removed from the `CustomerItems` table as well. For this reason, a production system should be careful of deleting products—you might be deleting some valuable information.**

The e-mail facility allows an operator to quickly select from a list of products, and then type the subject line and body of an e-mail message to send to all customers who have selected that product on the Web site. The e-mail is sent using SMTP, through a standard Dial-Up Networking (DUN) connection. Provision for entering the e-mail configuration data, such as e-mail address, POP host, username, and password, are part of the Administration utility. E-mail configuration data is stored in the `Config` table of the `CTrack` database.

Summary

Careful component design of a Web-based system is critical to the long-term success of the Web site. For this reason, every component has to be detailed during the design phase. Granted, as part of the RAD philosophy these components are likely to grow and change with time, but it's the initial separation, as much conceptual as physical, that must be determined in the design.

This design includes the Web pages—they're a key component of the application, and so must be carefully orchestrated as well. As a developer, you don't have to be a great Web page creator—stay focused on the coding and functional aspects; other people can make the pages pretty after you're done.

With the design specifications clearly laid out, it's time to start coding. Chapter 15 leads you through that process.

Building the CustomerTracker

As discussed in Chapter 14, there are five components of the CustomerTracker system. The design of the system has been top-down—that is, the high-level user interface features determine the specifications of the back end. To actually develop the project, you have to develop from the ground up; the low-level components are built first, like a foundation. The high-level components are built on top of the foundation.

The order of the components is as follows:

- The database, which provides storage and processing for the data
- The ActiveX server, which provides communication to the database
- The ActiveX Server Tester, which proves the functionality of the server
- The Web pages, which use the ActiveX server to retrieve and update data
- The Administration utility, for data maintenance and generating e-mail

So the development of a multi-component project begins at the bottom, with the lowest-level component.

The Database

The core of the entire CustomerTracker system is the database. For initial development, an Access database is used. As the system grows and gets busier, this will eventually be replaced with a SQL Server database.

While it's possible to create the tables programmatically using Visual Basic, there's an easier way. Included with Visual Basic is an add-in called *Visual Data Manager*. This tool is written in Visual Basic and provides all the functions necessary to build the `CTrack` tables, design the fields, and create indexes (see Figure 15.1). This screenshot shows the VisData table-entry window, where the fields and indexes can be defined.

When you create the database, store it on your Web server for maximum performance. The name of the database in the sample application is `CTrack.MDB`.

Of course, if you have Access, you can use it to create the tables. Table details are listed in Tables 15-1 to 15-4.

Once the tables are created, the tree view of Visual Data Manager allows you to inspect and modify the configuration of the tables, as shown in Figure 15.2. Fields, indexes, and the properties of the tables can be displayed and edited. On the right is the SQL query edit window, for testing custom queries.

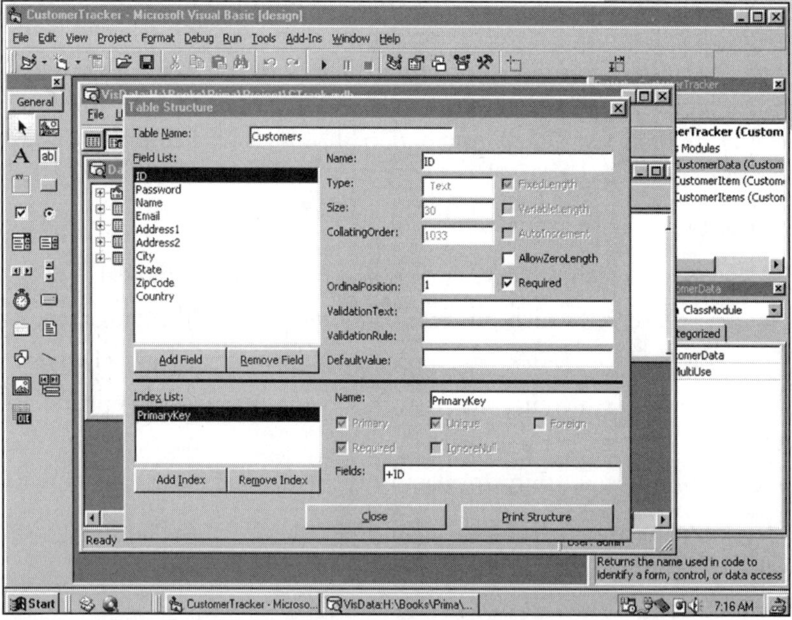

Figure 15.1
Using the VB add-in Visual Data Manager.

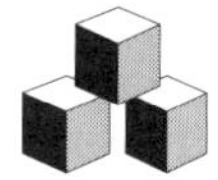

Table 15-1 Customers Table

Name	Type	Size
ID*	Text	30
Password	Text	30
Name	Text	50
Email	Text	50
Address1	Text	50
Address2	Text	50
City	Text	40
State	Text	30
ZipCode	Text	20
Country	Text	30

Table 15-2 Products Table

Name	Type	Size
ProductName*	Text	30
Description	Text	120

Table 15-3 CustomerItems Table

Name	Type	Size
CustomerID*	Text	30
ProductName	Text	30

Table 15-4 Config Table

Name	Type	Size
Class*	Text	20
Item*	Text	30
Data	Text	50

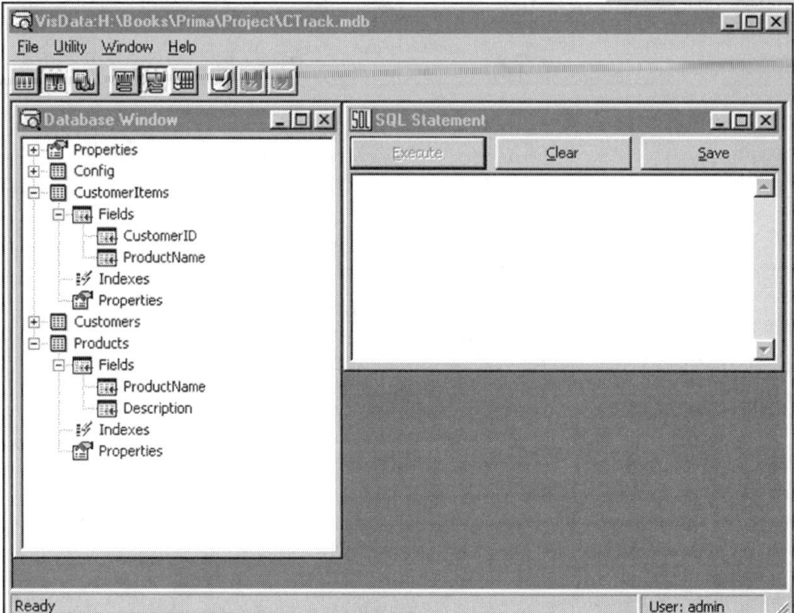

Figure 15.2 The database tree view of Visual Data Manager.

Caution

Be sure to create the primary keys for the `CTrack` tables. In Tables 15-1 to 15-4, the fields used in the primary keys are marked with an asterisk.

Testing the Database

Part of the rapid application-development process is testing each component of the application as it's developed. To test the integrity of the database structures, you must populate the tables with test data and run a query to make certain that the table names, key fields, and structure of the database work the way they were designed to work. Being certain of the functionality of the data itself simplifies debugging in the later components.

To create the test data to check the query against, follow these steps:

1. To open the Visual Data Manager, open the Add-Ins menu in Visual Basic and select Visual Data Manager.
2. When Visual Data Manager appears, choose File, Open Database, Microsoft Access.

3. Select CTrack.MDB in the Open File dialog box and click Open.

CTrack.MDB may already be in the File menu as a recently used file.

4. Click the second button on the toolbar, which selects a dynaset type recordset.
5. Double-click the Customers table. A dynaset type recordset is created, and a form appears with blank fields, because there are no records in the table.
6. Click the Add button to add a record, and fill in the fields with a dummy record (see Figure 15.3).

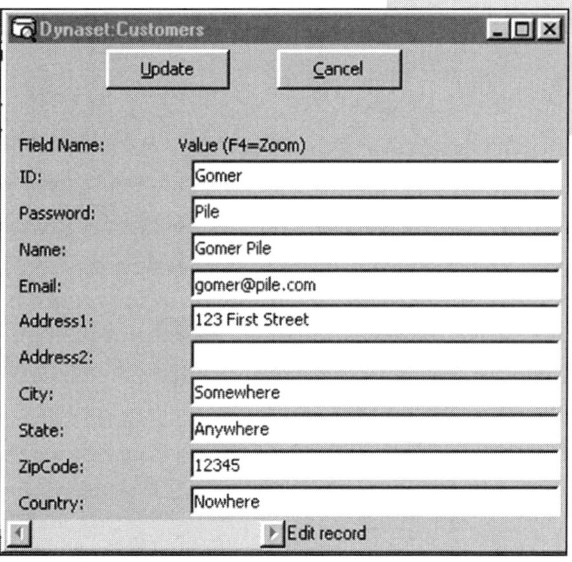

Figure 15.3
Adding records to the customer table.

7. Click the Update button to save the new record.
8. Add a second record, if you want.
9. When finished, click the Close button to close the dynaset.

Make note of the ID fields of the records you add—you'll need them for the CustomerItems table.

10. Next, return to step 5 and create a dynaset of the `Products` table. Add a few records and make note of the `ProductNames` you enter; you'll need them for the `CustomerItems` table.
11. Finally, repeat this process again to add some `CustomerItems`. The `CustomerID` in `CustomerItems` must match the `ID` from the `Customers` table, and the `ProductName` must match the `ProductName` from the `Products` table.

Dynaset
In VB, the DAO creates three types of recordsets. Table type recordsets can only be created against Access databases—they don't work with relational databases like SQL Server. Snapshot type recordsets are queries—typically joining and filtering several tables together. Snapshots aren't updateable—they're one-time "snapshots" of the data. Dynasets are created the same way Snapshots are, but are updateable. Dynaset type recordsets work with all types of databases, and are the best way to interactively add and edit data.

With all the sample data now entered, use the SQL statement window to build the following query:

```
SELECT Customers.Name, CustomerItems.ProductName,
➥Products.Description FROM ((Customers INNER JOIN
➥CustomerItems ON Customers.ID =
➥CustomerItems.CustomerID) INNER JOIN Products ON
➥CustomerItems.ProductName = Products.ProductName)
➥ORDER BY Customers.Name, CustomerItems.ProductName
```

Click the Execute button to execute the query. A message box pops up, asking whether this is a pass-through query; click No, because this database is an Access database, and the Jet engine must do the processing. The query results will appear almost instantly—one row for each record in the `CustomerItems` table that matches both a customer from the `Customers` table and a product from the `Products` table. You can make this list appear in a grid by clicking the DBGrid button on the toolbar (see Figure 15.4).

Check the results of the query to make sure that the tables are working together properly. If the query doesn't return the number of rows you think it should, check the following potential sources of problems:

- Check that the data in `JOIN` fields (`ID` in `Customers` with `CustomerID` in `CustomerItems`, and `ProductName` in both `CustomerItems` and `Products`) is identical—the join will not work unless the data is exactly the same.
- Make certain that the `JOIN` field data types and sizes are identical.
- Check the query itself—the `JOIN` conditions must have been entered exactly as provided.

Once the query behaves normally, you can proceed to the next stages of development. Don't delete the sample data you created—it will be used throughout the development process for testing the various functions of the application.

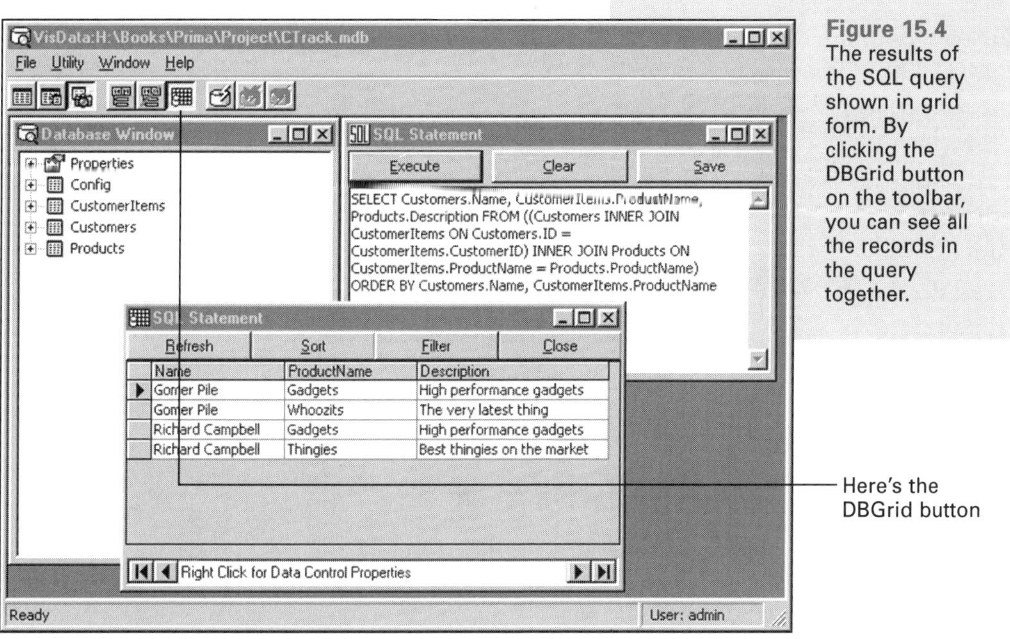

Figure 15.4 The results of the SQL query shown in grid form. By clicking the DBGrid button on the toolbar, you can see all the records in the query together.

Setting Up ODBC

Once the tables are set up, the next step is to configure the middleware—open database connectivity (ODBC). As specified in the design phase of the project in Chapter 14, the ideal method for communicating with a database that's intended to upgrade to SQL Server is ODBCDirect. ODBCDirect uses ODBC to build a common interface for any database, including Access. With a few minor code changes, the CustomerTracker system will be able to switch databases. To use ODBCDirect, you must configure an ODBC system data source for the `CTrack` database (see Figure 15.5).

To create an ODBC system data source, follow these steps:

1. Open the Windows Control Panel.
2. Double-click the 32-Bit ODBC applet.
3. Click the System DSN tab.
4. Click the Add button.

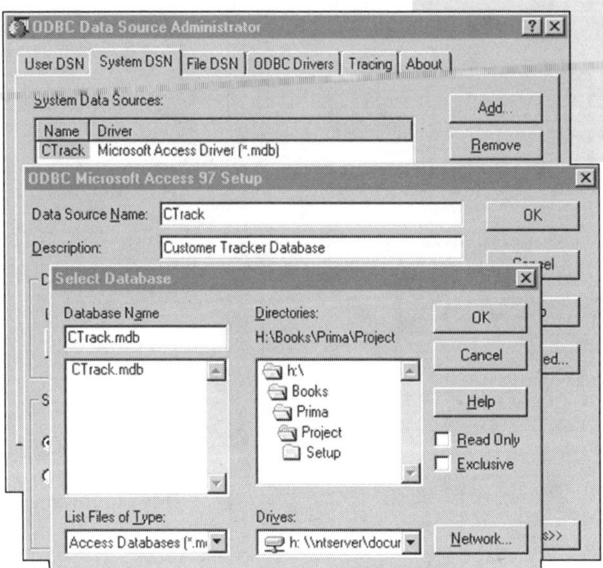

Figure 15.5
Setting up the ODBC system data source for the CTrack Access database.

5. From the Driver List, select the Microsoft Access Driver and click Finish.
6. Enter the Data Source Name as **`CTrack`**.
7. Enter the Description as **`Customer Tracker Connection`**.
8. Click the Select button. Use the File Open dialog box to locate and select `CTrack.MDB`.
9. Click the OK buttons and close down the ODBC applet.

The 32-bit ODBC drivers don't ship with Windows 95, but they ship with virtually everything else—Office, Visual Basic, SQL Server, and so forth. Just remember when deploying applications that use ODBC that you may need to ship ODBC with your application.

There is no easy way to test an ODBC connection to an Access database. Testing of the ODBC connection to the database will be done in the ActiveX Server Tester.

With the database created and the ODBC system data source set up, you're ready to start building the CustomerTracker ActiveX DLL.

The ActiveX Server

The interface between the database and the Web pages is the CustomerTracker ActiveX server component. The development of the ActiveX server is where Visual Basic really shines as an Internet development tool. Using Visual Basic, you can quickly develop the fundamental architecture of the server, and then add the functionality gradually.

There's a perception that the development of ActiveX servers of any kind is difficult. And it can be—the key to success in the development of ActiveX servers is planning. It's absolutely critical to have a clear picture of what you're trying to achieve with your server. Failing to plan out your server is a good way to guarantee disaster.

Fortunately, the specifications of the CustomerTracker ActiveX server were detailed in Chapter 14. Now to the task of actually developing the server in Visual Basic. Follow these steps:

1. Start Visual Basic.
2. If the New Project dialog doesn't automatically appear (see Figure 15.6), select File, New Project.

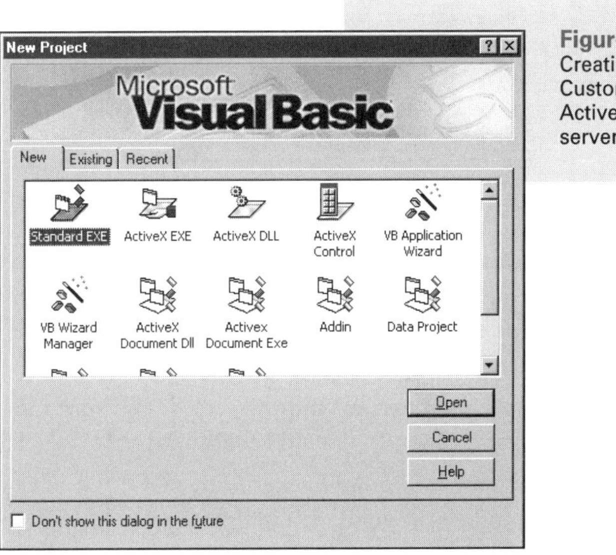

Figure 15.6
Creating the CustomerTracker ActiveX DLL server project.

3. The opening dialog of Visual Basic offers a variety of new projects to create. For the CustomerTracker ActiveX DLL project, select an ActiveX DLL. Select the ActiveX DLL project type and click Open. By default, the new project is called Project1.
4. In the Project window, right-click `Project1` and select `Project1 Properties`.
5. In the Project Properties window, change the name of the project to **`CustomerTracker`**.
6. Change the project description to **`Customer Tracker ActiveX DLL for Active Server Pages`** (see Figure 15.7). While the reason to set the project name is obvious, the purpose of the project description is more obscure. The project description is the text displayed in the component lists—it identifies the component.

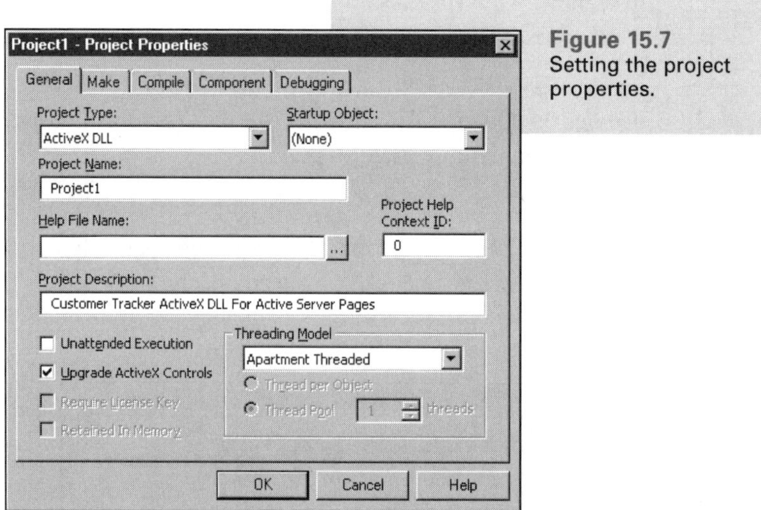

Figure 15.7 Setting the project properties.

7. Back to the Project window. Because the project is an ActiveX DLL, the default structure of the project includes a single class module called `Class1`. Select `Class1` and, in the Properties window, change the name of this class to `CustomerItem`—the first component of the CustomerTracker ActiveX DLL.
8. Also in the Properties window, change the `Instancing` property of `CustomerItem` to `2 - PublicNotCreatable` (see Figure 15.8).
9. Because the CustomerTracker ActiveX DLL uses ODBCDirect, there needs to be a reference to the data access object library. DAO 3.5 is the latest available from Microsoft, and supports ODBCDirect.

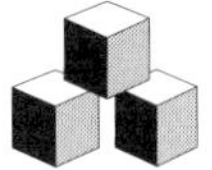

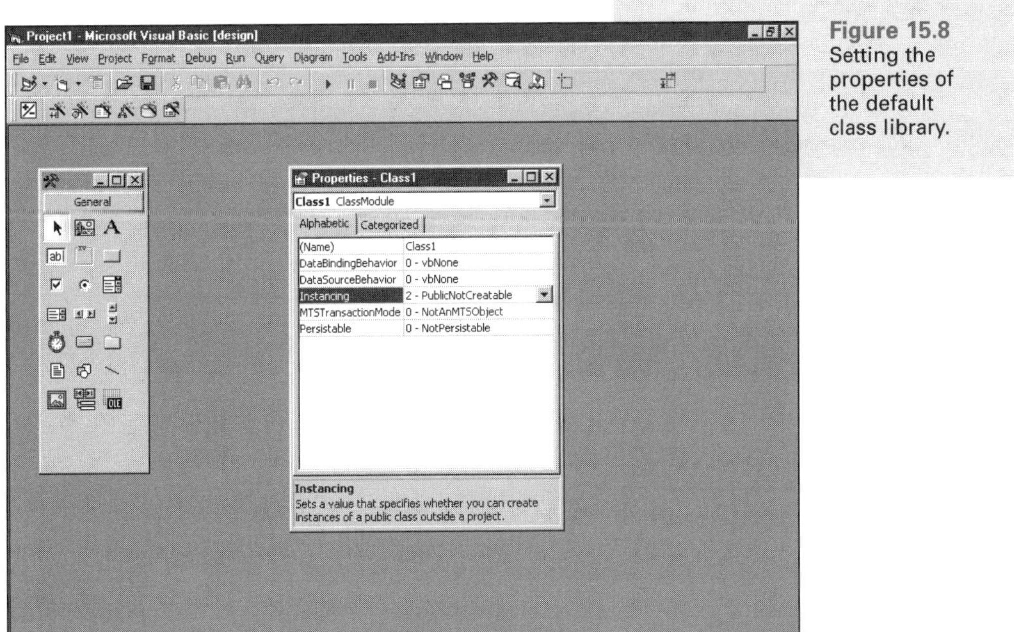

Figure 15.8
Setting the properties of the default class library.

Choose Project, References to open the References dialog box. Add a reference to the Microsoft DAO 3.5 object library to provide database access for the project (see Figure 15.9). Click OK to close the dialog box.

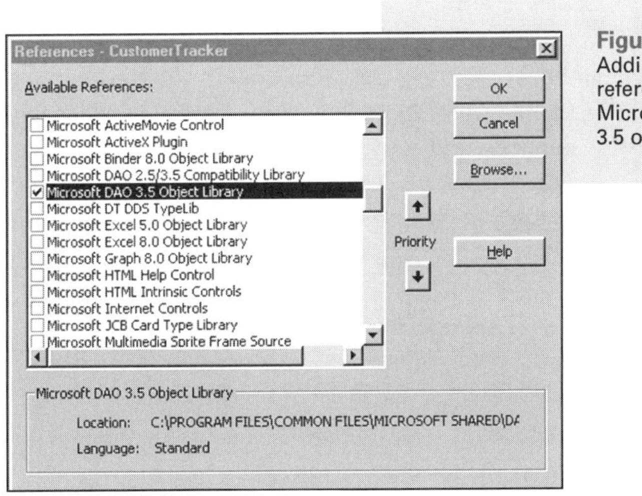

Figure 15.9
Adding a reference to the Microsoft DAO 3.5 object library.

Now the classes for the CustomerTracker ActiveX DLL are built, from the bottom up, like the rest of the project. The lowest or most "primitive" components are built first, and the more advanced built on top. There are three classes in the CustomerTracker project—from lowest to highest, the `CustomerItem` class, `CustomerItems` collection class, and `CustomerData` class. This is the order in which these classes must be constructed, because the next class in the sequence depends on the previous class.

The `CustomerItem` Class

As detailed in Chapter 14, the `CustomerItem` class is used to store the selection of products that the customer wants to be notified about when new information is available. `CustomerItem` objects are contained in the `CustomerItems` collection object. The `CustomerItems` collection is one property of the `CustomerData` class.

At this point, the `CustomerItem` class exists only in name—it has no properties, methods, or events defined. While it's possible to create all these characteristics directly in the code of the class, it's easier to use the Class Builder utility add-in that comes with Visual Basic. The Class Builder utility normally resides under the Add-Ins menu option. If it isn't there, use Add-In Manager to select the VB Class Builder utility. The Add-In Manager will add the Class Builder utility to the Add-Ins menu.

When you select the Class Builder utility, a dialog pops up, warning you that the project contains class modules not created by the Class Builder—it's talking about the `CustomerItem` class that already exists. Click OK to ignore the warning; it doesn't affect the project at all. You can also set the flag in the box to stop that dialog from ever appearing again.

When the Class Builder window appears, you'll see the CustomerTracker project and `CustomerItem` class displayed in the Classes frame on the left side of the Class Builder window. The larger right side of the window lists the properties, methods, and events of the class. There are tabs on the right side frame to filter the attributes selected. The default tab is All, which displays all attributes. Because the class was just created, this window is blank.

Time to reference the design notes. In the specifications for the `CustomerItem` class outlined in Chapter 14, there are only three properties of the class, as listed in Table 15-5.

Table 15-5 CustomerItem Class Properties

Name	Datatype
ProductName	String
Description	String
Selected	Boolean

To configure the CustomerItem class and add the properties from Table 15-5, follow these steps:

1. Select the CustomerItem class from the Classes frame on the left.
2. Right-click the CustomerItem class and select Properties from the menu. The Class Module Builder dialog box displays the name of the class and its instancing (both of which were set earlier).
3. Click the Attributes tab and enter the description of the class as **Items that a Customer may or may not have selected**.
4. Click OK to save the changes. The basic information about the CustomerItem class is set.

In the toolbar in the Class Builder window, three grouped buttons for adding properties, methods, and events will be enabled. Click the button with the ToolTip name Add New Property to Current Class. The Property Builder dialog appears.

Properties have a name, datatype, declaration, and some attributes. The first property is ProductName:

1. Type the name of the property from Table 15-5: **ProductName**.
2. Select the datatype (also from the table): **String**.
3. Set the declaration: **Public Property**, which identifies the property as available for use outside of its own class.
4. Indicate whether this property is the default or not—for ProductName, it is the default (see Figure 15.10).
5. Select the Attributes tab.
6. Enter a description of the property: **Name of the Product the Customer selected**.

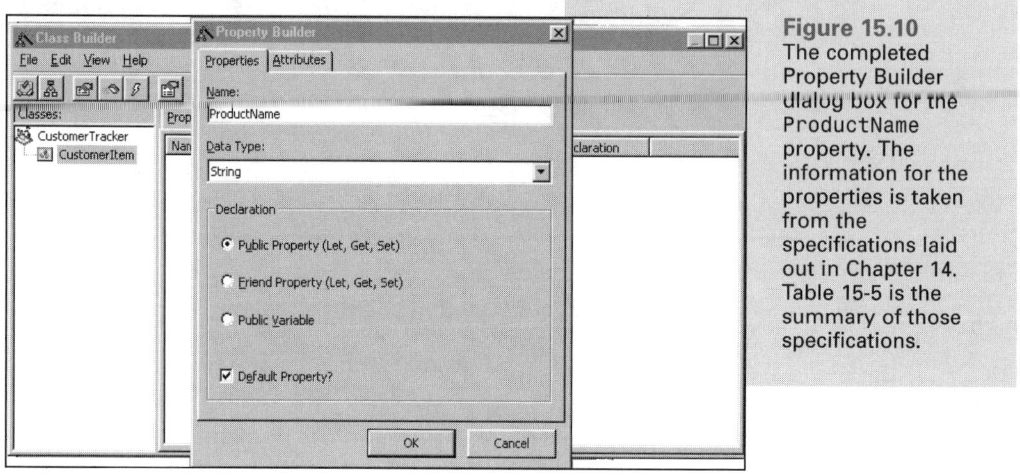

Figure 15.10 The completed Property Builder dialog box for the `ProductName` property. The information for the properties is taken from the specifications laid out in Chapter 14. Table 15-5 is the summary of those specifications.

7. If there's a help file for the project, you can specify the Help Context ID (there is no help file in this case).
8. Click OK to complete the creation of the property. When the Property Builder dialog box disappears, the new property is displayed in the right-hand frame (see Figure 15.11).
9. Add the other properties in the same way, based on Table 15-5.
10. Once all the properties are added, choose File, Exit in the Class Builder window. A prompt will appear, asking whether you want to update the project—click the Yes button.

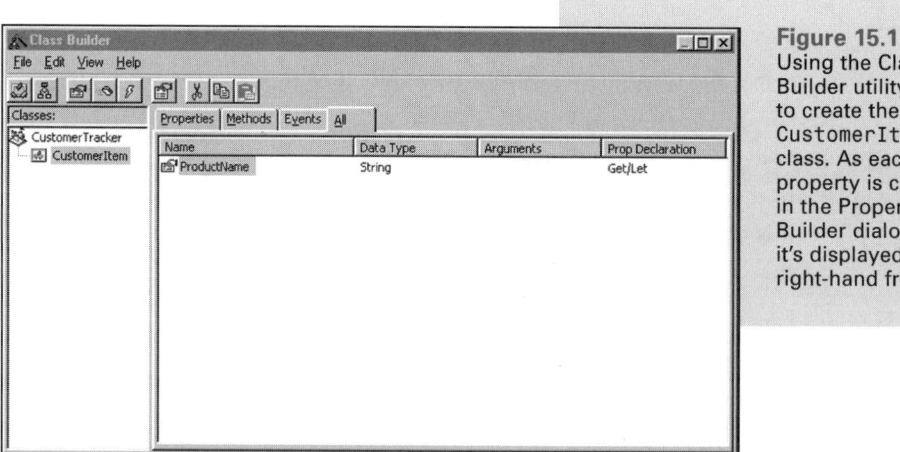

Figure 15.11 Using the Class Builder utility to create the `CustomerItem` class. As each property is created in the Property Builder dialog box, it's displayed in the right-hand frame.

When you complete the last step, the Class Builder Utility automatically writes the code for the class (the file on the CD is called `CustomerItem.cls`, as you might guess). Here's the code:

```
' Class for CustomerItem - what the CustomerItems collection is
based on
' All code in this module is generated by the Class Builder

'local variable(s) to hold property value(s)
Private mvarProductName As String 'local copy
Private mvarDescription As String 'local copy
Private mvarSelected As Boolean 'local copy

Public Property Let Selected(ByVal vData As Boolean)
'used when assigning a value to the property, on the left side
'of an assignment.
'Syntax: X.Selected = 5
    mvarSelected = vData
End Property

Public Property Get Selected() As Boolean
'used when retrieving value of a property, on the right side
'of an assignment.
'Syntax: Debug.Print X.Selected
    Selected = mvarSelected
End Property

Public Property Let Description(ByVal vData As String)
'used when assigning a value to the property, on the left side
'of an assignment.
'Syntax: X.Description = 5
    mvarDescription = vData
End Property

Public Property Get Description() As String
'used when retrieving value of a property, on the right side
'of an assignment.
'Syntax: Debug.Print X.Description
    Description = mvarDescription
End Property

Public Property Let ProductName(ByVal vData As String)
'used when assigning a value to the property, on the left side
'of an assignment.
'Syntax: X.ProductName = 5
    mvarProductName = vData
End Property
```

```
Public Property Get ProductName() As String
'used when retrieving value of a property, on the right side
'of an assignment.
'Syntax: Debug.Print X.ProductName
    ProductName = mvarProductName
End Property
```

ANALYSIS

The code generated by the Class Builder utility handles the basic functions of properties—storing the value set to the property, and returning the value when requested. This is accomplished using the `Let` and `Get` functions, respectively. The declaration prefix (`Public` or `Private`) indicates whether the property is exposed to the rest of the application. The datatype of each variable for each property is determined in the `Let` function, inside the parentheses. You could write this code by hand, but it's much easier to let the Class Builder utility write it for you. This is all the code required for the `CustomerItem` class.

The `CustomerItems` Collection Class

The `CustomerItems` collection class, as the name implies, is used to contain a collection of `CustomerItem` objects. A `CustomerItem` object is contained in the `CustomerData` class, which is detailed in the next section. The reason for using a `CustomerItems` collection is to allow for any number of `CustomerItems` to be associated with a given customer.

There are several ways to approach this goal—the method used here is generally considered the best way, although it's rather complex. The advantage of using this method is that you create a collection object that's functionally identical to any of the predefined collections in Visual Basic, with all the same capabilities. This means that you are able to use (and will use) such object-manipulating functions as `For Each`.

Note

The MSDN Library that comes with Visual Basic has a great tutorial on the various methods of using objects and collections. In the MSDN Library, look under Visual Basic Documentation, Getting Started with Visual Basic, Topics on Programming with ActiveX/OLE, Topics on General ActiveX Programming, Programming with Objects. There are code examples included with Visual Basic that explain in detail the various methods and techniques involved.

The CustomerItems collection class has only methods—the only "property" *per se* is the CustomerItem object that the collection references in its methods. The steps involved in creating the CustomerItems collection class are very similar to those for the CustomerItem class.

One new step is that the class itself has to be created. With the CustomerItem class, a class already existed when the project was created; all that had to be done was rename it. For the CustomerItems collection class, it has to be created from scratch. Again, the design specifications are referenced to get the list of methods used by CustomerItems (see Table 15-6).

Table 15-6 CustomerItems Collection Class Methods

Method	Parameters	Returns
Add	ProductName (*string*), Description (*string*), Selected (*string*)	CustomerItem
Count	None	Long integer (number of items)
Delete	Index (*variant*)	Nothing (none)
Item	Index (*variant*)	CustomerItem
NewEnum	Special (see text)	N/A

Follow these steps:

1. Choose Add-Ins, Class Builder Utility to open the Class Builder. Click the Add New Class button on the toolbar. The Class Module Builder dialog box opens.
2. Enter the Name of the new Class: **CustomerItems**. Leave the Based On list set to (New Class).
3. Set the Instancing of the class to Public Not Creatable (see Figure 15.12). The Public Not Creatable instancing allows other classes to use the class without exposing the class to applications outside the CustomerTracker ActiveX Server.
4. Click the Attributes tab.
5. Enter a description of the class: **Collection of CustomerItem objects**.
6. Leave the Help Context ID blank.

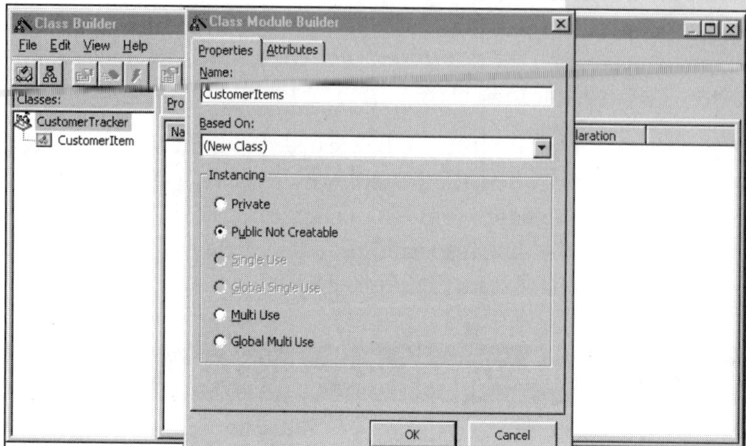

Figure 15.12 Creating the `CustomerItems` collection class in the Class Builder Utility.

7. Click OK to complete the creation of the class.

Adding methods to a class is much like adding properties. Start with the `Add` method:

1. Click the Add New Method to current Class button on the toolbar. The Method Builder dialog box appears.
2. Enter the Name of the new method: **`Add`**.
3. Enter the Arguments for the `Add` method by clicking the plus (+) button beside the argument list. For each argument, enter the name and data type. Each argument in the `Add` method corresponds to a `CustomerItem` property, so the arguments are `ProductName` (`string`), `Description` (`string`), `Selected` (`Boolean`). Unless you're modifying the values in the arguments (which you shouldn't do anyway), all the arguments should be flagged as `ByVal`.
4. Set the Return Data Type. For the `Add` method, set it to `CustomerItem`.
5. Set the Declare as Friend and Default Method settings as appropriate. For the `Add` method, both flags are blank (see Figure 15.13).

   The `Add` method receives the values of a product—the `ProductName`, `Description`, and whether the customer `Selected` the product. If the add is successful, it will return a `CustomerItem` object.
6. Click the Attributes tab.
7. Enter a description of the method: **`Add a CustomerItem to the collection`**.

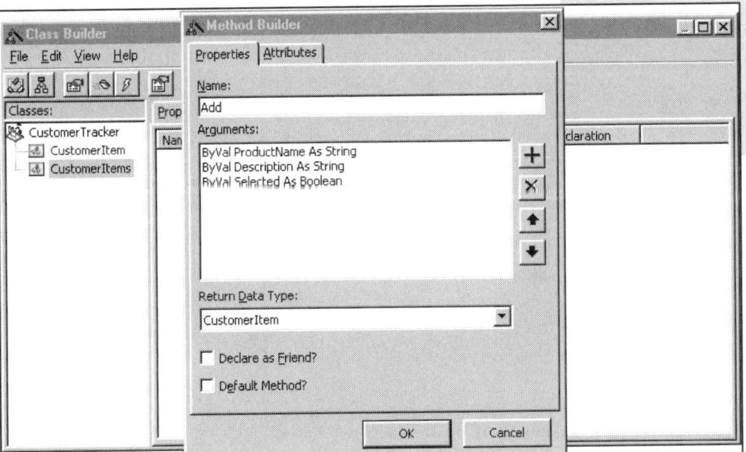

Figure 15.13 Creating the Add method in the `CustomerItems` class.

8. Leave the Help Context ID blank.
9. Click OK to complete the creation of the method.

Repeat the sequence for each method from Table 15-6. The `Item` method is the default method. When entering the `NewEnum` method, leave the argument and return data type blank. The `NewEnum` method is a special method that's utilized by a collection class to give an index value to an item of the collection. Visual Basic must be told that this method is to be used for this purpose. The settings for the `NewEnum` method are done when the methods are being coded.

Once the entry of the methods is complete, there's only one step left:

1. Right-click the `CustomerItems` entry in the Classes frame.
2. Click the last item on the shortcut menu, Set as Collection. This step identifies the `CustomerItems` class as a collection.

Once the entry of the methods is completed, it should look much like Figure 15.14.

While the Class Builder was able to add all the code needed for the properties of the `CustomerItem` class, it can't do the same for the methods of the `CustomerItems` collection class. You must enter the code yourself. Close the Class Builder and update the project with the new class information. The basic function structures—just the parameters and return values—will be created automatically.

The methods used in the `CustomerItems` collection correspond to the methods in every other collection, although you may not be aware of some of them.

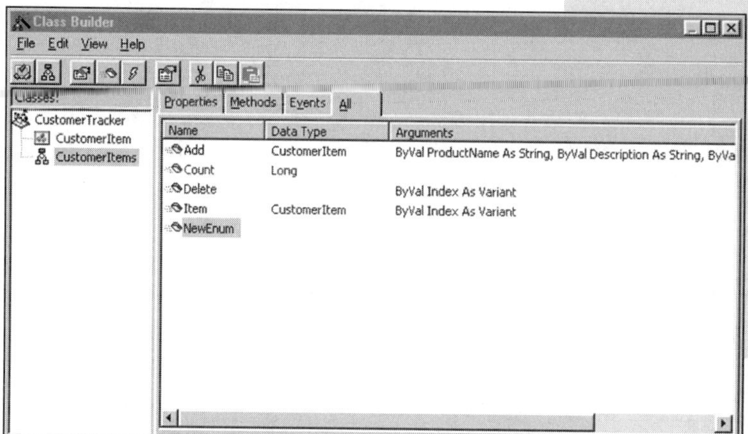

Figure 15.14 The completed list of methods for the `CustomerItems` collection. Notice that the symbol identifying the `CustomerItems` collection is different from the `CustomerItem` class in the Classes frame.

Methods such as `Item`, because it's usually the default method, are used implicitly rather than explicitly—the `Item` method is used when you reference an object in the collection. So even though you might never use `.Item` in your code, you do use the `Item` method. The same is also true of the `NewEnum` method—it's called whenever an iteration of a `For Each` construct executes.

General Declarations

The general declarations section of the `CustomerItems` code identifies the class and defines the collection object that's used for storing the `CustomerItems`. Each time a `CustomerItems` collection object is initialized, a new collection is created:

```
' Collection class for CustomerItems
' Private collection does all the work of storing the collection
'of CustomerItem
Private colCustomerItems As New Collection
```

Add Method

The `Add` method is used for adding a new `CustomerItem` to the collection. The properties of the `CustomerItem` are passed as parameters of the `Add` method, just like any other collection add. The `Add` method should return a copy of the object added (in this case, a `CustomerItem` object).

In the `Add` method, a `CustomerItem` object is created within the function and populated with the values passed as parameters. This `CustomerItem` object is then used to add the object to the collection created in the general declara-

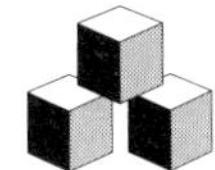

tions. The `ProductName` is used as the key value for identifying and sorting the object in the collection.

Once the `CustomerItem` object is added to the internal collection, it's set as the return value for the function:

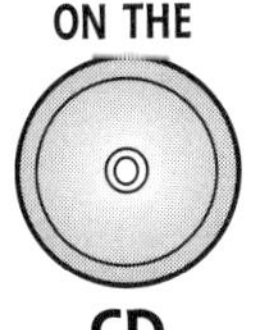

```
' Adding items to the collection - all values for item are passed
in
Public Function Add(ByVal ProductName As String,
➥ByVal Description As String, ByVal Selected As Boolean)
➥As CustomerItem
    ' Declare a local CustomerItem for populating
    Dim citemNew As New CustomerItem

    ' Using With construct for clarity, populate the item
    With citemNew
        .ProductName = ProductName
        .Description = Description
        .Selected = Selected
        ' Item is added to the collection, the product name being
        ' the key value
        colCustomerItems.Add citemNew, .ProductName
    End With

    ' Return the CustomerItem that was constructed, although
    ' it likely won't be used
    Set Add = citemNew

End Function
```

Count Method

The `Count` method is a standard collection function—it returns the number of objects in the collection. The function itself is simple; it just uses the `Count` method of the internal collection object to determine the count of the `CustomerItems` collection:

```
' Provide count ability in collection
Public Function Count() As Long
    Count = colCustomerItems.Count
End Function
```

Delete Method

The `Delete` method is also a standard method of all collections. The CustomerTracker ActiveX DLL never uses the `Delete` method; it's included here for the sake of completeness. If you're creating your own collections, you should create *all* the methods a collection has, whether you use them or not.

After all, if your collection and objects are truly useful, other programmers will want to use them again, and they may need those standard functions.

The Index value that's passed as a parameter of the Delete method in normal use would be the ProductName of a CustomerItem. The standard collection Remove method actually deletes the item from the internal collection:

```
' Standard delete function for collection - not used at all
Public Sub Delete(ByVal Index As Variant)
    colCustomerItems.Remove Index
End Sub
```

Item Method

The default function of any collection, the Item method isn't normally directly referenced—because it's the default function, it's invoked automatically whenever a reference to the collection is made without a method specified.

The Index parameter of the Item method normally contains the ProductName of a CustomerItem. The Item function returns the CustomerItem retrieved by the Item method of the internal collection:

```
' Default function - specifies item by index - returns the item
' referenced
Public Function Item(ByVal Index As Variant) As CustomerItem
    Set Item = colCustomerItems.Item(Index)
End Function
```

NewEnum Method

The NewEnum method is a bit different from an ordinary collection method, although all collections have a NewEnum method. This method is used by Visual Basic to enumerate the next object in the collection as each is requested. Because this is, in effect, a "system" method, there are special settings to be set on the method. The return value is also a unique datatype, called IUnknown:

```
' This enumeration function provides For Each functionality
' to the custom collection
' The advanced procedure attributes show the Procedure ID
' as -4, and the member is hidden
' For more information on enumeration and custom collections,
' see the MSDN library.
Public Function NewEnum() As IUnknown
    ' Delegate to the private Collection
    '   object's _NewEnum method.
    Set NewEnum = colCustomerItems.[_NewEnum]
End Function
```

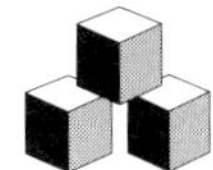

After entering the code for the method, you set certain procedure attributes:

1. While the cursor is still in the `NewEnum` function, choose Tools, Procedure Attributes. A small dialog box appears, displaying the basic information about the `NewEnum` function.
2. Click the Advanced button to display more details about the procedure.
3. Set the Procedure ID to **-4**, to identify the function to Visual Basic as the collection enumerator.
4. Select the Hide This Member option, because the `NewEnum` method shouldn't be displayed in an object browser (see Figure 15.15).

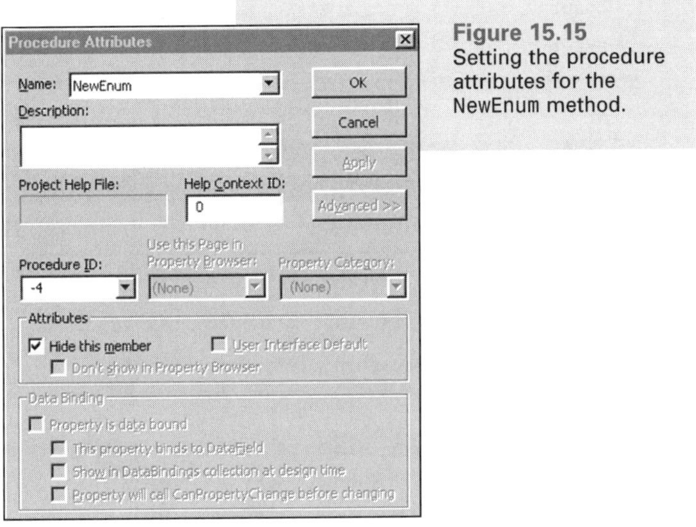

Figure 15.15
Setting the procedure attributes for the NewEnum method.

5. Click OK to save the changes.

Creation of the `CustomerItems` collection class is finished. The final step in constructing the CustomerTracker ActiveX DLL server is the publicly exposed `CustomerData` class.

The `CustomerData` Class

The interface through which other applications communicate with the CustomerTracker ActiveX server is the `CustomerData` class. The `CustomerData` class contains both properties and methods. The properties are the data of the customer; the methods are the ways in which the data in the properties can be manipulated. Table 15-7 lists the properties and Table 15-8 the methods of the `CustomerData` class.

Table 15-7 CustomerData Class Properties

Name	Datatype
Name	String
Email	String
Address1	String
Address2	String
City	String
State	String
ZipCode	String
Country	String
Items	CustomerItems

Table 15-8 CustomerData Class Methods

Method	Parameters	Returns
Create	ID *(string)*, Password *(string)*	*Integer* (success/fail)
Retrieve	ID *(string)*, Password *(string)*	*Integer* (success/fail)
Update	ID *(string)*, Password *(string)*	*Integer* (success/fail)

Use the Class Builder utility to create the properties and methods of the `CustomerData` class, the same way in which the `CustomerItem` class and `CustomerItems` class were created. The resulting list should appear much the same as Figure 15.16. The only unusual aspect of this list is the `Items` property, and only because its datatype is one created earlier—the `CustomerItems` collection. Note that none of the properties or methods in the `CustomerData` class are set as default—they must all be explicitly specified when used.

After exiting the Class Builder and updating the project, the code for the properties, including the `Items` property, is complete. Only the method code has to be written.

Create Method

The `Create` method creates new customer entries. It uses the `ID` and `Password` parameters for the new record, and checks to see whether the customer already exists. If the customer exists, it returns a failure. If the customer doesn't exist, it creates the customer using the ID and password, and returns success.

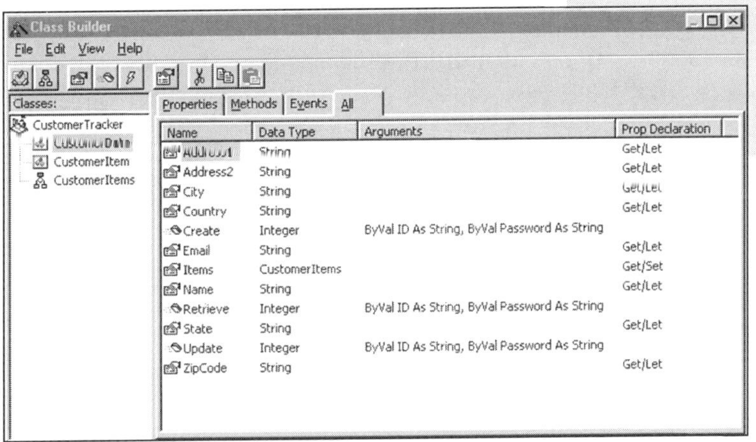

Figure 15.16 The properties and methods of the `CustomerData` class.

After the declarations of the function are done, a basic test of the ID and password are done. The ID and password cannot be zero length; if either value is zero length, the function returns immediately as a failure. If the parameters are valid, a flag is used to indicate the success of the creation attempt:

```
' Checking for the existence of a particular customer record
' If record does not exist, it is created
Public Function Create(ByVal ID As String,
➥ByVal Password As String) As Integer
    Dim wrkCust As Workspace
    Dim conCustTrack As Connection
    Dim rstCustomers As Recordset
    Dim Success As Integer
    Dim SQLString As String

    ' Check for valid data first
    If Len(ID) = 0 Or Len(Password) = 0 Then
        Create = False
        Exit Function
    End If

    ' Set Success flag to true - any failure results in it being
    ' set to false.
    Success = True
```

The `CustomerData` class does all the data access of the CustomerTracker ActiveX DLL. The access method (as specified in the design documents of Chapter 14) is ODBCDirect. The ODBCDirect data access method in Visual Basic offers the best way to upgrade databases with a minimum of code rewriting and consistent, reliable performance.

As with all code-based data access methods in Visual Basic, the first step is to create and define a `Workspace` object. It's in the `CreateWorkspace` function that the `dbUseODBC` parameter identifies the `Workspace` object as an ODBCDirect workspace. ODBCDirect workspaces use a `Connection` object as the connection to the ODBC database. With Jet workspaces, the connection to the database is a `Database` object, much as it was in Visual Basic 4. The `OpenConnection` method references the ODBC system data source created when the database was set up:

```
    ' Set up WorkSpace and Connection
    Set wrkCust = CreateWorkspace("CTrack", "", "", dbUseODBC)
    Set conCustTrack = wrkCust.OpenConnection("CustTrack",
➥dbDriverNoPrompt, , "ODBC;DSN=CTrack")
```

Once the connection is established, the test to see if the ID already exists is done. A snapshot query is run to check for the existence of a record in the database with the ID specified in the parameters. If there already is an ID, the `Success` flag is set to false, indicating a failure—you can't create an ID that already exists:

```
    ' Check to see if ID already exists - if it does, return a
    ' failure.
    SQLString = "SELECT Customers.ID FROM Customers
➥WHERE Customers.ID = '" & ID & "'"
    Set rstCustomers = conCustTrack.
➥OpenRecordset(SQLString, dbOpenSnapshot)
    If rstCustomers.RecordCount <> 0 Then Success = False
    rstCustomers.Close
```

If the ID doesn't exist, the customer record can be created. An `INSERT INTO` query is constructed and sent to the `Connection` object to add the record to the database. If the `.RecordsAffected` property of the `Connection` returns a one (`1`), the add was successful. Any other return would be considered a failure, and the `Success` flag set accordingly:

```
    ' If Success Flag is still true, then add the record
    If Success Then
        SQLString = "INSERT INTO Customers (ID, Password)
➥VALUES('" & ID & "', '" & Password & "')"
        conCustTrack.Execute SQLString
        ' Check to see if the record was added
        ' by checking the RecordsAffected...
        If conCustTrack.RecordsAffected <> 1 Then Success = False
    End If
```

Regardless of whether the `Add` query was attempted, the `Connection` and `Workspace` objects have to be closed down. Finally, the state of the `Success` flag is returned:

```
    ' Close up
    conCustTrack.Close
    wrkCust.Close

    ' Return the state of the success flag to indicate
    ' success or failure
    Create = Success
End Function
```

Retrieve Method

The `Retrieve` method populates the properties of the `CustomerData` object, based on the `ID` and `Password` parameters. The same data tests are done at the beginning of the `Retrieve` function as in the `Create` function. Once the ID and password are proved valid, a query is created to retrieve the record. If the record is not retrieved successfully, the `Success` flag is set to fail. If the record is retrieved, the internal property values are loaded with the fields of the record:

ON THE CD

```
' Retrieve record, based on ID and password
SQLString = "SELECT Customers.*
➥FROM Customers WHERE "
SQLString = SQLString & "Customers.ID =
➥'" & ID & "' "
SQLString = SQLString & "AND Customers.Password =
➥'" & Password & "'"
Set rstCustomers = conCustTrack.
➥OpenRecordset(SQLString, dbOpenSnapshot)
If rstCustomers.RecordCount = 0 Then
    ' If there's no record, return a failure -
    ' could be that it doesn't exist, or wrong password
    Success = False
Else
    ' If there is a record, fill the local
    ' variables with the contents of the record
    If Not IsNull(rstCustomers("Name")) Then
➥mvarName = rstCustomers("Name")
    If Not IsNull(rstCustomers("Email")) Then
➥mvarEmail = rstCustomers("Email")
    If Not IsNull(rstCustomers("Address1")) Then
➥mvarAddress1 = rstCustomers("Address1")
    If Not IsNull(rstCustomers("Address2")) Then
➥mvarAddress2 = rstCustomers("Address2")
    If Not IsNull(rstCustomers("City")) Then
➥mvarCity = rstCustomers("City")
    If Not IsNull(rstCustomers("State")) Then
➥mvarState = rstCustomers("State")
    If Not IsNull(rstCustomers("ZipCode")) Then
➥mvarZipCode = rstCustomers("ZipCode")
```

```
    If Not IsNull(rstCustomers("Country")) Then
➥mvarCountry = rstCustomers("Country")
End If
rstCustomers.Close
```

Populating the regular properties is simple, but the `Items` collection is a little more complicated. To populate the collection, the entire list of products needs to be retrieved first. This list is loaded into the `Items` collection, setting the `Selected` property to false:

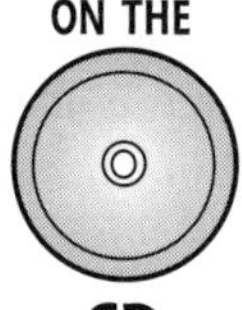

```
' Get all the products
SQLString = "SELECT Products.ProductName,
➥Products.Description "
SQLString = SQLString & "FROM Products
➥ORDER BY Products.ProductName"
Set rstCustomers = conCustTrack.
➥OpenRecordset(SQLString, dbOpenSnapshot)
' If there are records, add them
' to the CustomerItems collection
If rstCustomers.RecordCount <> 0 Then
    Do While Not rstCustomers.EOF
        Set CItem = mvarItems.Add(rstCustomers("ProductName"),
➥rstCustomers("Description"), False)
        rstCustomers.MoveNext
    Loop
End If
rstCustomers.Close
```

Why fill the `Items` collection with all the products whether the customer has selected them or not? For simplicity's sake. When using the ActiveX server against the testing application or Web pages, you'll need a list of *all* products, so that a customer will be able to select the products he's interested in. You could create two collections—one for products, one for selected products—but why? Instead, make a single collection that has a `Selected` flag. The list is populated with all products, plus the flag.

Once the `Items` list is populated with all products, the products selected by the customer can be marked on the list by setting the `Selected` flag. The second query retrieves a list of the products selected by the customer and then walks through the collection, matching the products. If a product matches, the `Selected` flag is set to `true`.

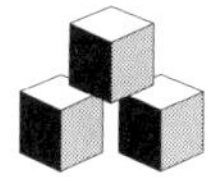

Doesn't it seem logical that you should be able to populate the list with a single query? I thought so, too. Using SQL Server, it wouldn't be a problem. But when I built the query using a left join to retrieve all the products and a field indicating which ones were selected by the customer, something went wrong. The query didn't return the values I wanted. I suspect this was a problem with the 3.5 DAO Engine, but I can't be sure. Doing a two-step query works for certain.

```
' Get products selected by customer
SQLString = "SELECT CustomerItems.ProductName
➥FROM CustomerItems "
SQLString = SQLString & "WHERE CustomerItems.
➥CustomerID = '" & ID & "'"
Set rstCustomers = conCustTrack.
➥OpenRecordset(SQLString, dbOpenSnapshot)
' If there are records, match them
' to the CustomerItem collection
If rstCustomers.RecordCount <> 0 Then
    For Each CItem In mvarItems
        rstCustomers.MoveFirst
        Do While Not rstCustomers.EOF
            If rstCustomers("ProductName") =
➥CItem.ProductName Then CItem.Selected = True
            rstCustomers.MoveNext
        Loop
    Next
End If
rstCustomers.Close
```

Wrap up of the function is identical to that of the `Create` method—where the `Connection` and `Workspace` objects are closed, and the function returns the state of the `Success` flag.

Update Method

The `Update` method writes the properties back to the database. Again, the method uses two parameters: `ID` and `Password`. The setup of this method is identical to the others—after the declares, the ID and password are checked for validity. If they're valid, the `Workspace` and `Connection` objects are set up.

The initial query writes the simple properties out to the database. Checking the `.RecordsAffected` property of the `Connection` object determines whether the query was successful:

```
' Build and execute update query for Customer data
SQLString = "UPDATE Customers SET Password = '" & Password & "', "
SQLString = SQLString & "Name = '" & mvarName & "', "
SQLString = SQLString & "Email = '" & mvarEmail & "', "
SQLString = SQLString & "Address1 = '" & mvarAddress1 & "', "
SQLString = SQLString & "Address2 = '" & mvarAddress2 & "', "
SQLString = SQLString & "City = '" & mvarCity & "', "
SQLString = SQLString & "State = '" & mvarState & "', "
SQLString = SQLString & "ZipCode = '" & mvarZipCode & "', "
SQLString = SQLString & "Country = '" & mvarCountry & "' "
SQLString = SQLString & "WHERE Customers.ID = '" & ID & "'"
conCustTrack.Execute SQLString

' Check to see if the record was added
' by checking the RecordsAffected...
If conCustTrack.RecordsAffected <> 1 Then
➥Update = False Else Update = True
```

If the query is successful, the `Items` collection can be written to the database. The first step is to delete the existing `CustomerItems` records for the customer. Then the `Items` collection is walked through, and if the `.Selected` flag is set, a query inserting the record is executed:

ON THE CD

```
' If that update succeeded, update the customer items
If Update Then
    ' Delete all existing items from CustomerItem table
    conCustTrack.Execute "DELETE * FROM CustomerItems
➥WHERE CustomerID = '" & ID & "'"
    For Each CItem In mvarItems
        If CItem.Selected = True Then
            SQLString = "INSERT INTO CustomerItems
➥(CustomerID, ProductName) "
            SQLString = SQLString & "VALUES ('" & ID &
➥"', '" & CItem.ProductName & "')"
            conCustTrack.Execute SQLString
        End If
    Next
End If
```

The `Connection` and `Workspace` objects are closed, and the `Update` method is complete.

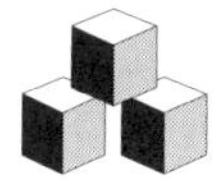

Testing an ActiveX server is a complex process, but an essential one. One of the components of the CustomerTracker application is the ActiveX Server Tester, which is developed specifically as a testing rig for the ActiveX server—see the next section.

The ActiveX Server Tester

Creating an ActiveX server isn't particularly difficult—it's making it work that's the hard part. A testing rig for your ActiveX server is an essential part of the development process. The ActiveX Server Tester utilizes all the properties and methods of the ActiveX server. If you can make the ActiveX Server Tester work perfectly, you can confirm that your ActiveX server, ODBC configuration, and database are correctly set up. Any development problems you have after that are related to the higher-level components, such as the Active Server Pages.

To test an ActiveX server, you need to have the server compiled and available for the test rig to work with. You could compile and install the server, but then if there are any problems with it you'll get an error message and have to start over. To test and debug an ActiveX server, you need to run two copies of Visual Basic. One has the ActiveX server running, the other has the test rig. Any errors that occur in either module stop the execution of the module and bring up an error message that can be fixed on-the-fly.

Building the Tester Application

The `CTrackTester` is composed of a single form (see Figure 15.17). The form has a text box for each property—the `Items` collection is displayed in a list box. There are four buttons, three of which correspond to the CustomerTracker ActiveX DLL server methods: `Create`, `Retrieve`, `Update`, and `Exit`. Each property and method of the CustomerTracker ActiveX DLL server is tested using this form. The only code in the application is in the `Click` event of each button.

Create Button

The Create button utilizes the `Create` method of the CustomerTracker ActiveX DLL server. In order to use the method of the ActiveX server, an instance of the server object must be created. This involves creating a reference to the server, which won't actually be done until it's time to test the application.

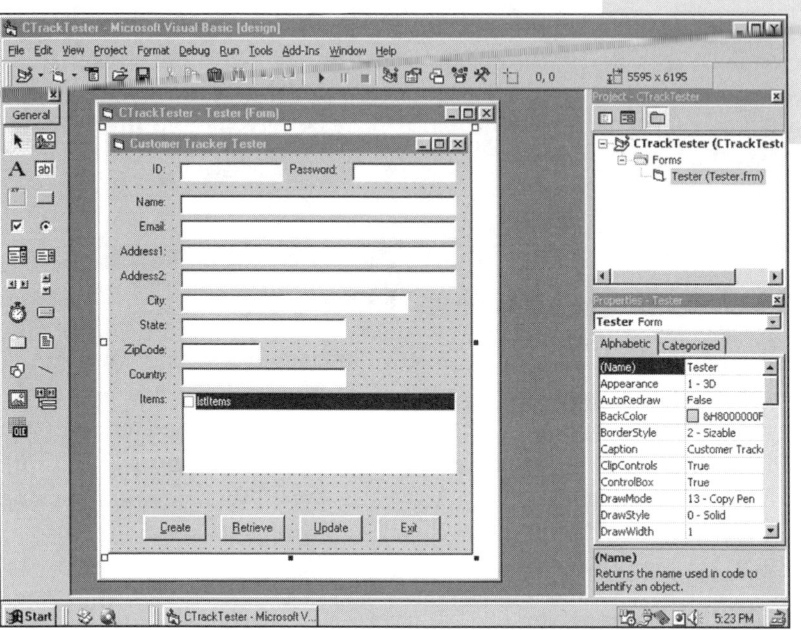

Figure 15.17 The form of the CTrackTester application.

The generic `Object` datatype can be used for any kind of ActiveX server. The `CreateObject` function actually sets up the `Object` datatype as an instance of the ActiveX server object. Once the object is created, all the features in the ActiveX server are available to the object—properties, methods, and events:

```
' Execute create function from Active Server DLL
' This function uses only the Customer ID and password
' Function succeeds if the Customer ID does not exist -
' the function creates a new ID and password
Private Sub cmdCreate_Click()
    Dim CTrack As Object
    Dim intSuccess As Integer

    ' Create an instance of the CustomerData object
    Set CTrack = CreateObject("CustomerTracker.CustomerData")
```

After the object is created, you can invoke and utilize its methods. For the Create button, the `Create` method is used—passing the ID and password from their respective text boxes. The `Create` method returns a success or failure flag, which determines which message box is displayed:

```
' Execute the Create Method on the CustomerData
' object, passing the ID and password
```

```
intSuccess = CTrack.Create(txtID.Text,
➥txtPassword.Text)

' Indicate success or failure
If intSuccess Then MsgBox "Create Succeeded!"
➥Else MsgBox "Create Failed."
```

After the message box is displayed, the object is set to nothing, releasing the instance of the ActiveX server, and the procedure is finished:

```
    ' Clean up after ourselves by setting the object to nothing
    Set CTrack = Nothing

End Sub
```

Retrieve Button

The Retrieve button utilizes the `Retrieve` method of the CustomerTracker ActiveX DLL server. Like the Create button, the initial parts of the code involve creating an instance of the ActiveX server in an `Object` datatype.

Once the instance is created, the `Retrieve` method is used, passing the ID and password. If the method returns `Success`, the text boxes of the Tester form are populated with the properties. The `Items` collection populates the list box using the `For Each...` command. The `ProductName` and `Description` are loaded as the item text of the list box, and the `Selected` flag sets the check box for each item in the list box:

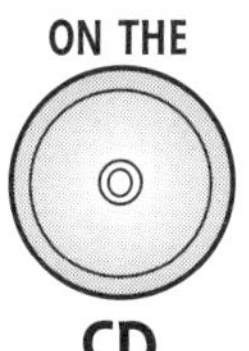


```
' Execute Retrieve method passing the ID and password
intSuccess = CTrack.Retrieve(txtID.Text, txtPassword.Text)

' If Retrieve succeeds, populate the
' text boxes with the data from the object
If intSuccess Then
    txtName.Text = CTrack.Name
    txtEmail.Text = CTrack.Email
    txtAddress1.Text = CTrack.Address1
    txtAddress2.Text = CTrack.Address2
    txtCity.Text = CTrack.City
    txtState.Text = CTrack.State
    txtZipCode.Text = CTrack.ZipCode
    txtCountry.Text = CTrack.Country
    ' Populate list box
    lstItems.Clear
    For Each CItem In CTrack.Items
        With CItem
            lstItems.AddItem Trim$(.ProductName) &
➥" (" & .Description & ")"
```

```
            lstItems.Selected(lstItems.NewIndex) = .Selected
        End With
    Next
    MsgBox "Retrieve Successed!"
Else
    MsgBox "Retrieve Failed."
End If
```

And, like the Create button code, once the process is finished, setting the object to nothing destroys it, and the subroutine is complete.

Update Button

Finally, the Update button uses the `Update` method of the CustomerTracker ActiveX DLL server to update the database record with the contents of the properties of the `CustomerData` object. Like the previous buttons, an `Object` datatype is turned into an instance of the `CustomerData` object using `CreateObject`.

The process of populating the properties of the object is simple—the property equals the text box for the given field:

```
' Populate the properties of the CustomerData
' object with the data from the text boxes
CTrack.Name = txtName.Text
CTrack.Email = txtEmail.Text
CTrack.Address1 = txtAddress1.Text
CTrack.Address2 = txtAddress2.Text
CTrack.City = txtCity.Text
CTrack.State = txtState.Text
CTrack.ZipCode = txtZipCode.Text
CTrack.Country = txtCountry.Text
```

Populating the `Items` collection is a little more complicated—remember that the `CustomerData` object has just been instantiated, so it's blank. All data has to be retrieved from the Tester form. For updating, the `Items` collection needs only the items selected by the customer, and only the `ProductName` and the `Selected` flag (set to `true`) need to be filled in.

The code in the Update button walks the entire list, parses the `ProductName` and `Description` from the list box text, and the `selected` flag from the `.Selected` property of the list box item. The `.Add` method of the `Items` collection adds the parsed list box items to the `Items` collection. When the `Update` method is invoked, the CustomerTracker ActiveX server records only the items with the `Selected` flag set and completely ignores the `Description`:

```
' Walk through the list box, adding the
' item selections to the list box
```

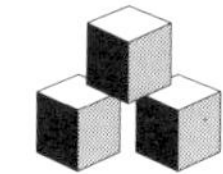

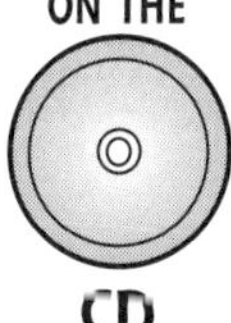


```
lstItems.ListIndex = -1
Do While lstItems.ListIndex <> lstItems.ListCount - 1
    lstItems.ListIndex = lstItems.ListIndex + 1
    ' Strip out the Product name and description
    ' from the list box
    StrPos = InStr(1, lstItems.List(lstItems.ListIndex), "(")
    ProdName = Trim$(Left$(lstItems.
➥List(lstItems.ListIndex), StrPos - 1))
    ProdDesc = Mid$(lstItems.List(lstItems.ListIndex),
➥StrPos + 1, Len(lstItems.List(lstItems.ListIndex)) - StrPos - 1)
    ' Add the CustomerItem to the Items
    ' collection of the CustomerData object
    Set CItem = CTrack.Items.Add(ProdName,
➥ProdDesc, lstItems.Selected(lstItems.ListIndex))
Loop
```

Now that the `CustomerData` object properties are fully populated, the `Update` method can be invoked to cause the ActiveX server to update the customer record. The `Update` method returns success or failure, a message box is displayed saying what happened, and the object is destroyed by setting it to nothing.

```
    ' Use the Update method of the CustomerData
    ' object to send the data back to the database
    intSuccess = CTrack.Update(txtID.Text, txtPassword.Text)

    ' Indicate success or failure
    If intSuccess Then MsgBox "Update Succeeded!"
    Else MsgBox "Update Failed."

    ' Clean up the objects
    Set CTrack = Nothing

End Sub
```

Caution

If you read this code carefully, you'll realize that it isn't bulletproof. You could change the password or ID between an `Update` and a `Retrieve` and the record would not be updated. In a regular application, you wouldn't allow this to happen, but this isn't a regular application—it's a test bed. It's not apathy that leaves off the safety devices, it's testing flexibility—you want to be able to come up with any method of crashing the ActiveX server possible. Ideally, it should be impossible.

Exit Button

Every form needs an Exit button; the Tester is no exception. The code for the Exit button is pretty simple—`Unload Me`:

```
Private Sub cmdExit_Click()
    Unload Me
End Sub
```

Using the Tester Application

Once the Tester application is written, it's ready to do testing—testing of itself, and of the ActiveX server, ODBC connection, and database.

Before the Tester application can be run, the ActiveX server has to exist. While you can compile the ActiveX server and install it into your system, this isn't conducive to rapid debugging. Visual Basic will write the Registry entries for an ActiveX server just by running the application from within the IDE. Better still, if (and when) an error occurs in the ActiveX server, the Visual Basic IDE will pop up, displaying the error and the location where it occurs.

Using two copies of Visual Basic—one running the ActiveX server and the other running the Tester application—is the best way to test and debug the server.

To get started, load Visual Basic, open the CustomerTracker Active DLL application, and run it. Nothing much will happen, but actually Visual Basic has added the CustomerTracker Active DLL to the Registry of your workstation—it's now available for use.

Switch to (or load) the other copy of Visual Basic that has the CTrackTester application loaded. Open the References dialog by choosing Project, References from the menu. Select the reference `CustomerTracker ActiveX DLL for Active Server Pages` (see Figure 15.18). The name of the ActiveX reference comes from the project description of the ActiveX DLL server application. Obviously, it's important to set the project description when you create the project, and use a description that will help identify the project among the others.

With the reference in place, the CTrackTester application will start. When the application runs, the `Tester` form will appear, with all the text boxes and list box blank. Test each method of the ActiveX server—each is connected to a button on the `Tester` form:

1. Enter an ID and password in the form—one that doesn't already exist.
2. Click the Create button—a message box should appear, saying that the `Create` succeeded.

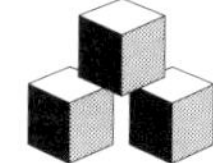

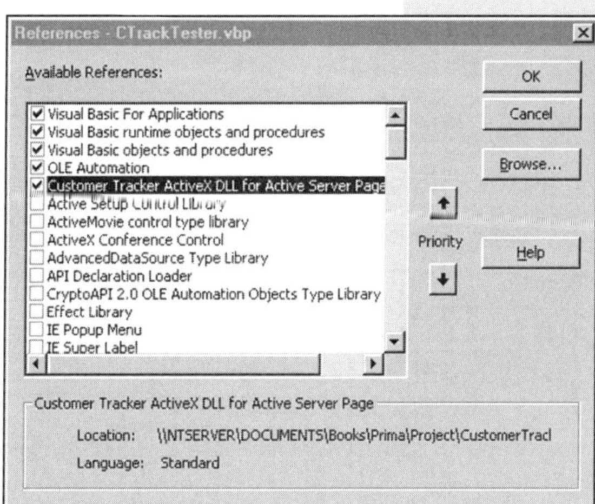

Figure 15.18 Selecting the CustomerTracker ActiveX server reference for the CTrackTester application.

3. Click the Create button again—a message box should appear, saying that the `Create` failed.
4. Click the Retrieve button—because there's no data in the form, the text boxes should stay blank, but the list fills in with all the products, albeit unselected. A message box will appear, saying that the `Retrieve` succeeded.
5. Fill in the text boxes and select some products from the list (see Figure 15.19).
6. Click the Update button—a message box should appear, saying that the `Update` succeeded. Clicking the Update button tells the ActiveX server to write the record to the database.
7. Click the Retrieve button—no data should change on the form, and a message box should appear, saying that the `Retrieve` succeeded.
8. Try retrieves and updates with invalid IDs and passwords, to test the trapping.
9. Click the Exit button when finished.

During the testing, you may turn up a few bugs. If the error exists in the Tester application, it will pop up an error dialog and the code window, showing where the error is. If an error occurs in the ActiveX server, the other Visual Basic IDE (containing the Server application) will pop up, showing the error dialog and code window there.

Once the Tester works completely, you can be certain that the ActiveX server, ODBC connection, and database are working according to plan. You're ready to move on to development of the Web portion of the application.

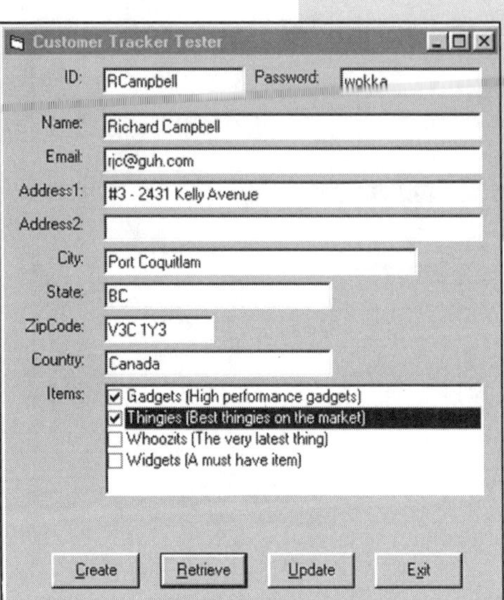

Figure 15.19
Filling in the `Tester` form and updating a record. The completed form includes selecting some of the products from the `Items` collection.

Caution

If you should have to stop the execution of the ActiveX server, the Tester application will also have to be stopped and restarted. Just make sure that you don't run the Tester application before you run the ActiveX server application, because the reference to the ActiveX server becomes invalid when execution of the Server stops (Visual Basic unregisters the Server when it's stopped). Should you attempt to run the Tester without the ActiveX server, the reference will be considered invalid and you'll have to remove it and add it again to the Tester application—after starting the ActiveX server again, of course.

The Web Pages

The Web pages of the CustomerTracker application are the user interface that will most often be used against the database. It's likely that these Web pages are to be integrated with an existing Web site—quite possibly replacing an existing visitor entry form. The sample Web pages in this application are basically the minimum required to make the CustomerTracker application run. If you intend to deploy this application, you'll want to modify the pages to make them fit with the "look" of your Web site, and use consistent language and style.

But before the Web pages can be developed, a Web server has to be set up. In Project 2, the Web server used was the Personal Web Server for Windows 95.

For this application, the Web Server is Internet Information Server (IIS) 3.0, running on a Windows NT 4 server (with Service Pack 2). The basic installation and configuration of IIS isn't complicated—if you can install Windows NT, you can install IIS.

When IIS is running, the CustomerTracker ActiveX DLL server has to be set up on the NT Server, so that the Web pages (Active Server Pages) can reference it. To set up the ActiveX server, you need to use the Setup Wizard to create an installable version of the CustomerTracker ActiveX DLL server.

Using the VB5 Setup Wizard on the CustomerTracker ActiveX DLL Server Application

This section discusses the Visual Basic Setup Wizard. If you are using Visual Basic 5, you will use the Setup Wizard to deploy your applications. In Visual Basic 6, the Setup Wizard has been replaced with the Package and Deployment Wizard. For more information on the Package and Deployment Wizard, see Chapter 19, "Building the Real Estate Companion."

In earlier versions of Visual Basic, the Setup Wizard had many problems. In Visual Basic 5, the Setup Wizard works as advertised—in most cases. Fortunately, the CustomerTracker ActiveX DLL server application is one application that has no problems with the Setup Wizard.

To install the ActiveX server on the NT Server, an installable version needs to be created. Here are the steps to create an installable version of the CustomerTracker ActiveX DLL server:

1. Start the Visual Basic 5 Application Setup Wizard—a shortcut should exist in the Visual Basic 5 group.
2. Enter (or browse) the path of the CustomerTracker application. Select the Rebuild the Project and Create a Setup Program options (see Figure 15.20). Click Next.
3. In the next window, set the Distribution Method to Single Directory, and click Next.
4. Now select the directory in which the setup version of the application will be stored (see Figure 15.21). This directory should be on the NT server, because the application will be installed there. Click Next.

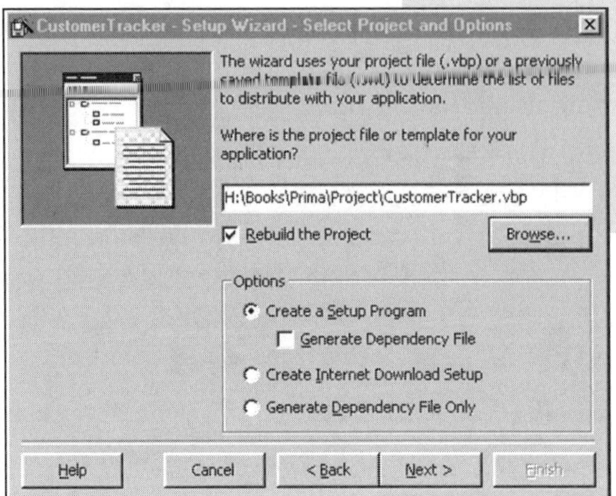

Figure 15.20 Creating an Installable version of the CustomerTracker ActiveX DLL server.

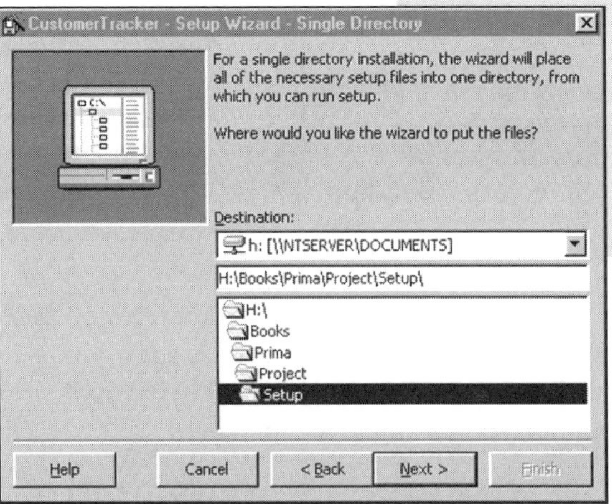

Figure 15.21 Selecting the directory for saving the setup version of the CustomerTracker ActiveX DLL server application.

5. Set the data access properties of the application (see Figure 15.22). The application doesn't use any installable ISAMs, but it does use ODBCDirect—select the dbUseODBC flag. Click Next.
6. The next screen specifies any ActiveX server components not detected by the Setup Wizard. There aren't any, so click Next.
7. There's only one dependency in the CustomerTracker ActiveX DLL server application—the `DAO350.DLL`. The wizard automatically detects the dependency, so nothing needs to be changed. Click Next.
8. A dialog appears while the Setup Wizard works for a few moments, determining runtime file requirements. Then it displays a file summary

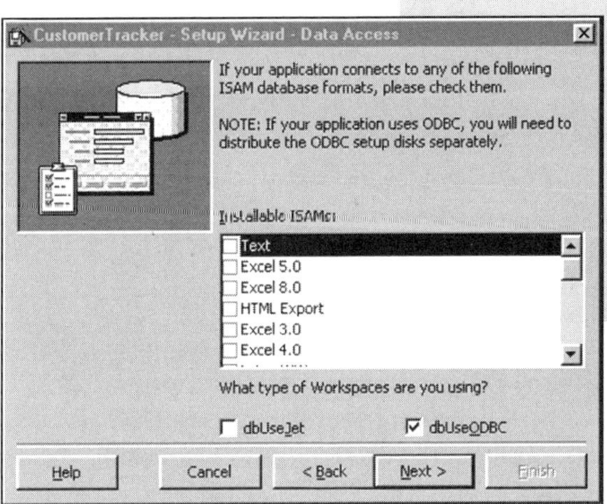

Figure 15.22 Setting the data access parameters of the CustomerTracker ActiveX DLL server application.

for all the files required in the setup. Again, there are no changes—click Next.

9. The Setup Wizard is finished and ready to begin creating the setup installation for the CustomerTracker ActiveX DLL server. Click the Finish button to begin.

Each file required for the setup application is compressed and copied to the installation directory you specified. The wizard also creates the actual Setup program for doing the installation on the NT server. A dialog box appears, listing each file and the time left to complete (see Figure 15.23). When it's finished, the CustomerTracker ActiveX DLL server is ready to be installed on the NT Server.

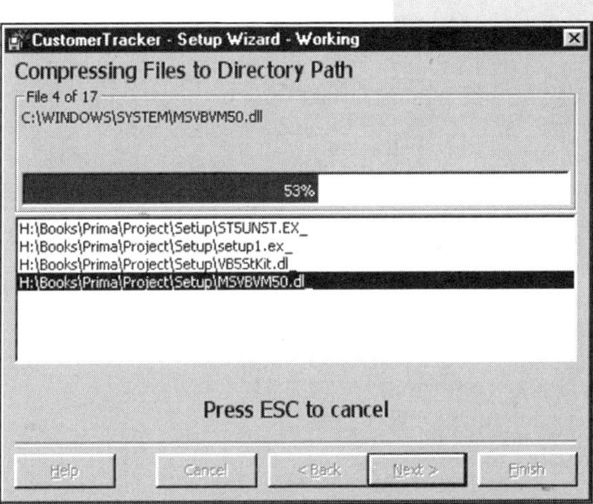

Figure 15.23 The Setup Wizard creating the setup application version of the CustomerTracker ActiveX DLL server.

Installing the CustomerTracker ActiveX DLL Server Application on the NT Server

To install the CustomerTracker ActiveX DLL server on your NT server, you need to run the Setup program created by the Application Setup Wizard. The Setup program guides you through the rest of the process. With an ActiveX DLL server, you don't need to specify in which directory the application is installed—all DLLs go to the `System32` directory in the `Windows` directory on the NT server.

Once you click the big button to begin the install, the rest of the process is automatic—the Setup program copies the appropriate files (see Figure 15.24) and creates the Registry entries for the server. You're ready to move on to the next step—setting up the ODBC connection to the database that the ActiveX server will use.

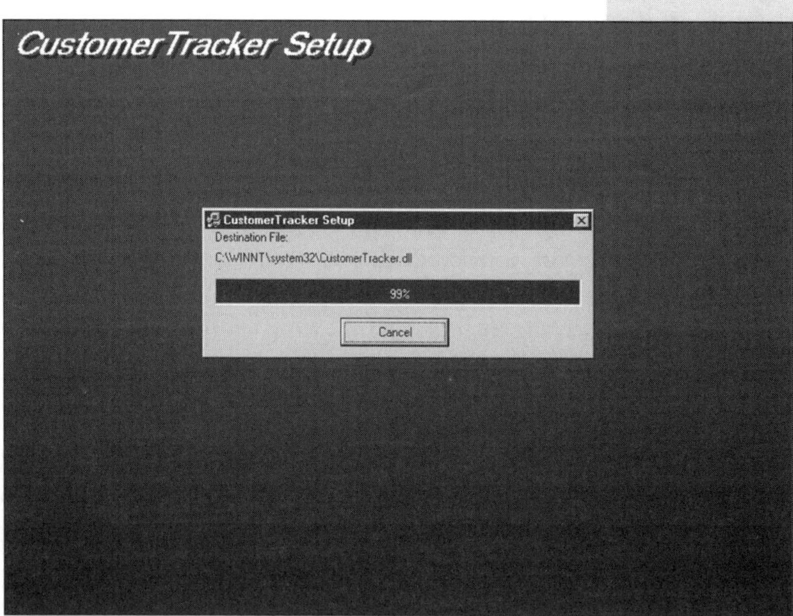

Figure 15.24 Because all ActiveX DLLs are installed in the `System32` directory automatically, there's very little to do with the Setup program for the CustomerTracker ActiveX DLL server.

Setting Up an ODBC Entry on the NT Server

Creating an ODBC entry on the NT server is much like creating a 32-bit ODBC entry on Windows 95 (see Figure 15.25):

1. Open the Windows NT Control Panel.
2. Double-click the ODBC applet.
3. Click the System DSN tab.

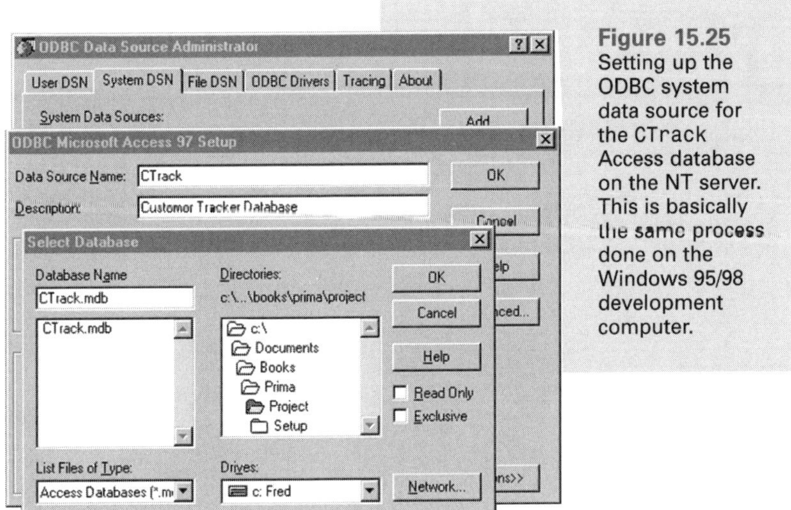

Figure 15.25
Setting up the ODBC system data source for the CTrack Access database on the NT server. This is basically the same process done on the Windows 95/98 development computer.

4. Click the Add button.
5. From the Driver List, select the Microsoft Access Driver and click Finish.
6. Enter the Data Source Name as **CTrack**.
7. Enter the Description as **Customer Tracker Connection**.
8. Click the Select button, and use the File Open dialog box to locate `CTrack.MDB`.
9. Click the OK buttons and close down the ODBC applet and Control Panel.

Configuring Internet Information Server for the CTrack Web Pages

Although eventually you'll want to integrate the CustomerTracker Web pages with your company's Web site, you don't want to have the pages on the site during testing. Creating a new virtual directory and path on your Web server allows you to use the production Web server platform without actually deploying the pages before you're ready.

Once you're ready, it's relatively simple to transfer the pages to the production area of the Web site—after the pages are made beautiful, of course:

1. To create a new virtual directory, run the Internet Service Manager and double-click WWW Services.

2. The WWW Services dialog box appears, listing the services parameters. Click the Directories tab to display the virtual directories already defined.
3. Click the Add button to add a new directory.
4. Browse and create a new directory for the CustomerTracker Web pages, called **CTrack**.
5. Select Virtual Directory and enter the name of the directory as **/CTrack**.
6. Set both the Read and Execute check box options (see Figure 15.26).

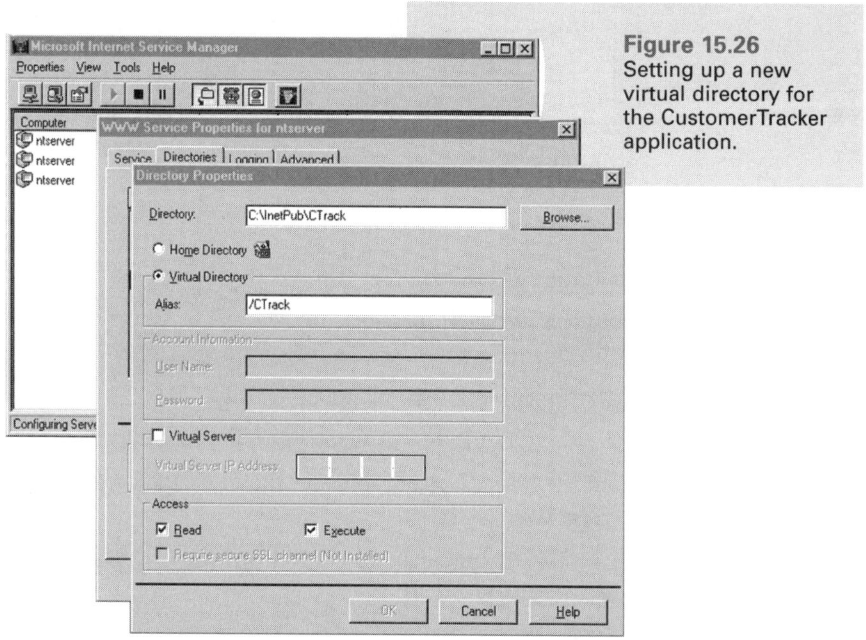

Figure 15.26
Setting up a new virtual directory for the CustomerTracker application.

Caution

Be certain to turn on the Read and Execute check boxes when creating the new virtual directory for the CustomerTracker. Active Server Pages require both Read and Access rights on the Web pages. Without Access rights, the Active Server Pages can't access the CustomerTracker ActiveX DLL server. It's very easy to miss setting this parameter and drive yourself crazy trying to figure out why your Web pages don't work.

The ActiveX server is set up, the ODBC connection is done, and a virtual directory is ready—time to make some Web pages.

Building the Web Pages

There are a variety of tools you can use to make a Web page. In the end, it's very much a case of personal preference. For simplicity, as well as the fact that there is very little decoration in the sample pages, the sample pages here are developed using Windows Notepad. HTML pages are, after all, just ASCII text.

Notepad doesn't seem like a very glamorous development tool, but it works great, with no problems. If you choose to use this functional tool, be sure to answer the question, "Which Web page development tool do you use?" with "Visual Notepad." That will keep those prying developers searching for your cool development product for a while.

There isn't much of a tutorial on HTML in this document—the process of creating Active Server Pages is complex enough. (Chapter 2 has some basic information about creating HTML pages, in case you're just starting out.) Of the six pages in the CustomerTracker application, three are standard HTML and three are Active Server Pages.

The Default Page

The starting page of the CustomerTracker application, the default page is standard HTML and offers two links—one for customers who have already signed up, the other for new customers (see Figure 15.27). The links lead to the Log in Account page and the Sign in Account page, depending on whether the customer has signed in previously or not.

The Log in Account Page

Linked from the default page, the Log in Account page is also standard HTML, although it has a form on it for entering the ID and password of the customer (see Figure 15.28). Forms are still part of standard HTML, although the form provides information to the Customer Data Editor page, which is an Active Server Page. The Submit button is a standard form button for completing the link to the Customer Data Editor page; it is renamed Login to make its use more apparent to the user. The Reset button clears the form for reentry.

```
<! Login form - input type password displays
asterisks when the user types >
<! The submit button posts the data from this
page to the CustData page >
```

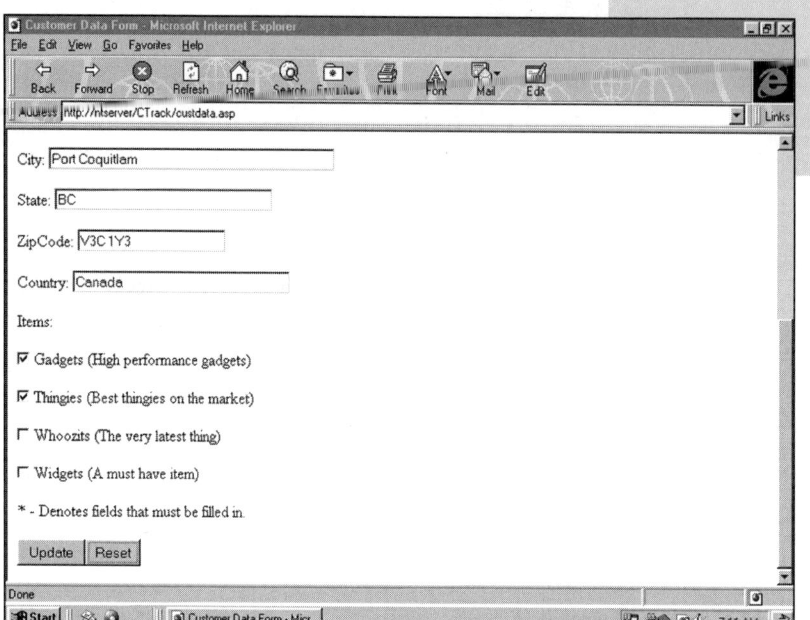

Figure 15.27
The default page for the CustomerTracker application.

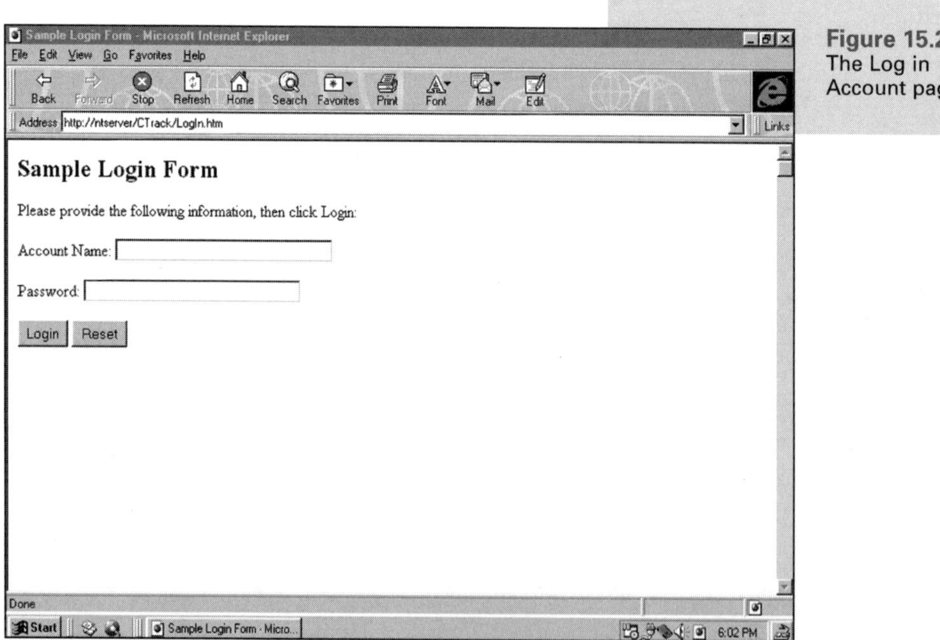

Figure 15.28
The Log in Account page.

```
<form action="custdata.asp" method="POST">
    <p>Account Name: <input type="text"
size="30" name="ID"> </p>
    <p>Password: <input type="password"
size="30" name="Password"> </p>
    <p><input type="submit" value="Login">
<input type="reset" value="Reset"> </p>
</form>
```

The Sign in Account Page

The Sign in Account page (see Figure 15.29) is virtually identical to the Log in Account page, except that the HTML form links to the Sign in Verify page:

```
<! Form for signing up - pressing submit
sends the data to the TestSign form >
<form action="TestSign.asp" method="POST">
    <p>Account Name: <input type="text"
size="30" name="ID"> </p>
    <p>Password: <input type="password"
size="30" name="Password"> </p>
    <p><input type="submit" value="Sign Up">
<input type="reset"> </p>
</form>
```

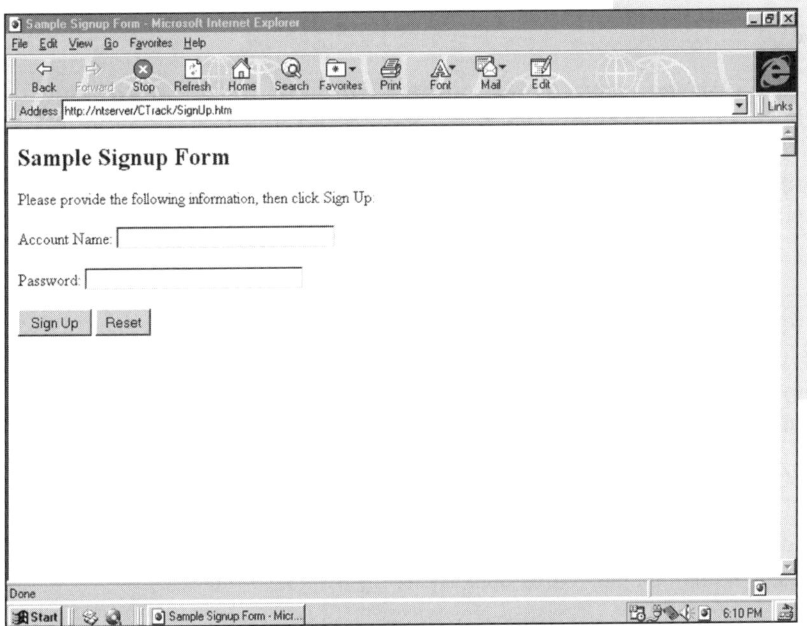

Figure 15.29 The Sign in Account page works virtually identically to the Log in Account page, except that the Sign Up button passes along the ID and password information to the Sign in Verify page.

The Sign in Verify Page

When the Sign Up button on the Sign in Account page is clicked, the Sign in Verify page is loaded. This page is an Active Server Page—it has VBScript code in it, and references the CustomerTracker ActiveX DLL server. Although the VBScript is on the Web page, it isn't sent to the client browser—it executes on the Web server. So it makes no difference what browser the client uses—as long as it supports standard HTML 2.0, it can use an Active Server Page.

The first step of `TestSign.ASP` is to create an instance of the `CustomerData` object, and use the `Create` method. The parameters of the `Create` method are retrieved from the Sign in Account page, using the `Request` object—part of VBScript. Based on whether the `Create` method succeeds, the Web page will display different information:

```
<%
    ' Create an instance of the
CustomerData object
    Set CTrack = CreateObject
("CustomerTracker.CustomerData")
    ' Use create method to create the record -
a failure means the record already exists
    intSuccess = CTrack.Create(Request.Form("ID"),
Request.Form("Password"))
    If intSuccess Then
%>
```

All of HTML uses tags to start and end settings. To start a VBScript code block, the opening tag is <%. To end the VBScript code block, the tag is %>. VBScript code is executed on the server, and doesn't appear on the Web page at all. Hence, anything you want to display on the page must come outside of the <% %> tags.

If the `Create` method succeeds, the customer record has been created, and execution can continue to the Customer Data Editor page. The Web page displays a happy welcoming message, and an odd form (see Figure 15.30). This form does not have any text boxes—only a button for continuing.

The form is used to pass along the ID and password information to the Customer Data Editor form, but the information shouldn't be changed and doesn't need to be displayed. So the input type of the form is `hidden`. The submit button has its name changed to `Continue`:

```
<! Create succeeded, welcome the new customer >
<h2>Welcome to our Customer database!</h2>
```

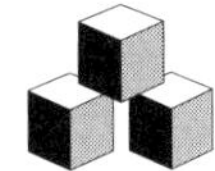


```
<p>Press Continue to move to the Customer
editor and fill in the rest of your information.
You can also specify what products
you'd like to be kept posted on.</p>

<! A funny form - the inputs are hidden to pass them
on to the next page, only the Continue button is displayed >
<form action="custdata.asp" method="POST">
    <input type="hidden" name="ID"
value="<%=Request.Form("ID")%>">
    <input type="hidden" name="Password"
value="<%=Request.Form("Password")%>">
    <p><input type="submit" value="Continue"> </p>
</form>
```

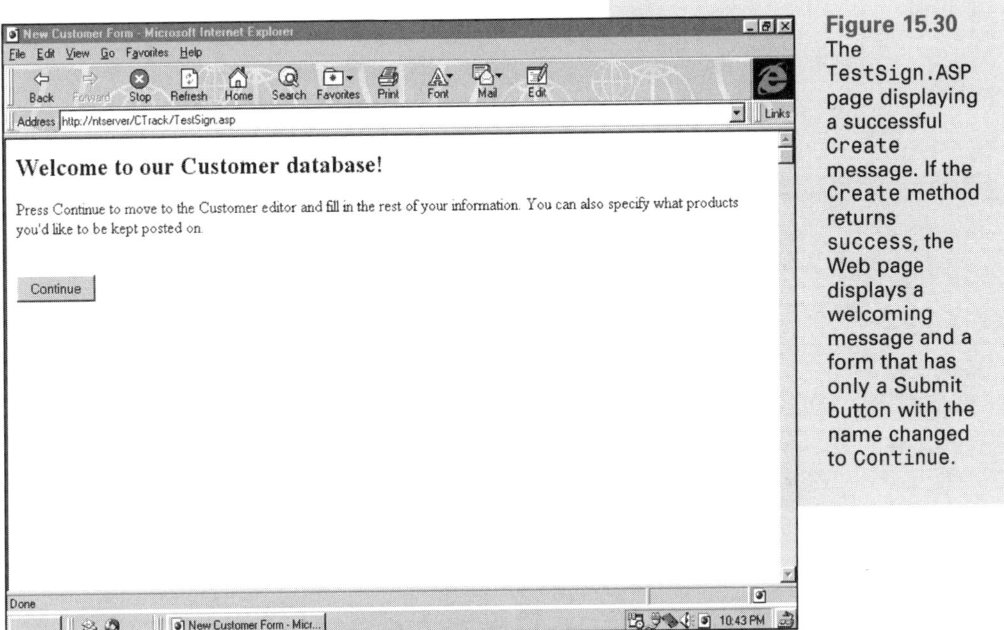

Figure 15.30 The TestSign.ASP page displaying a successful Create message. If the Create method returns success, the Web page displays a welcoming message and a form that has only a Submit button with the name changed to Continue.

If the `Create` method doesn't succeed, the ID must already exist, and the new customer needs to select a different ID. The Web page displays an "Uh oh" message and suggests that the customer use the Back button to reenter the data (see Figure 15.31):

```
<% Else %>

<! Create failed - explain it to the customer >
<h2>Uh oh! Couldn't create your account. </h2>
<p>Your choice of account code already exists. </p>
<p>Press 'Back' and enter a new account name. </p>
```

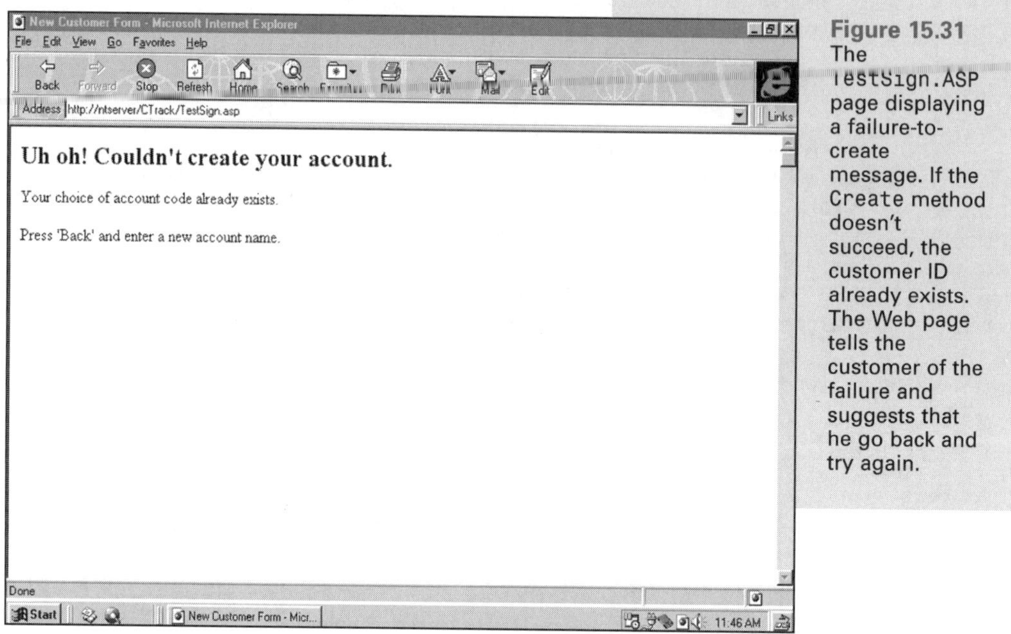

Figure 15.31 The `TestSign.ASP` page displaying a failure-to-create message. If the `Create` method doesn't succeed, the customer ID already exists. The Web page tells the customer of the failure and suggests that he go back and try again.

At the end is the same sort of clean up process that the ActiveX Server Tester application did—the `CTrack` object is set to `Nothing`:

```
<%
End If

' Clean up
Set CTrack = Nothing
%>
```

The Customer Data Editor Page

Whether the customer used the Log in Account page or the Sign in Account/Verify pages, all links lead to the Customer Data Editor page. The Customer Data Editor page uses the `Retrieve` method of the `CustomerData` object to display the customer's data, including the `Item` collection. When the `Retrieve` method is called (using the ID and password from the previous form, whichever form that might be), it may not succeed—the usual reason would be entering the ID and/or password incorrectly in the Log in Account page:

```
<%
' Create an instance of the CustomerData object
Set CTrack = CreateObject("CustomerTracker.CustomerData")
```

```
' Use the Retrieve method to populate the object
intSuccess = CTrack.Retrieve(Request.Form("ID"),
Request.Form("Password"))
' Check that the retrieve succeeded -
' if it did not, we have an invalid login.
If intSuccess Then
%>
```

If the `Retrieve` succeeds, the page is displayed as a form, so that the customer can edit the data himself. The ID and password are also on the form, but hidden—the parameters will be needed by the Customer Data Update page (see Figure 15.32):

```
<! Header and ID are displayed normally >
<h2>Customer Data Editor</h2>

<p> </p>

<p><font size="4">Account:
<%=Request.Form("ID")%> </font></p>

<! The form allows for entry/edit of data -
the form is populated with existing data from object >
<form action="custupd.asp" method="POST">
    <! Hidden input types preserve the
ID and password for the next form >
    <input type="hidden" name="ID"
value="<%=Request.Form("ID")%>">
    <input type="hidden" name="Password"
value="<%=Request.Form("Password")%>">

    <! Text input boxes populated
with object properties >
    <p>Name: <input type="text" size="50"
name="Name" value="<%=CTrack.Name%>">*</p>
    <p>Email: <input type="text" size="50"
name="Email" value="<%=CTrack.Email%>">*</p>
    <p>Address1: <input type="text" size="50"
name="Address1" value="<%=CTrack.Address1%>"></p>
    <p>Address2: <input type="text" size="50"
name="Address2" value="<%=CTrack.Address2%>"></p>
    <p>City: <input type="text" size="40"
name="City" value="<%=CTrack.City%>"></p>
    <p>State: <input type="text" size="30"
name="State" value="<%=CTrack.State%>"></p>
    <p>ZipCode: <input type="text" size="20"
name="ZipCode" value="<%=CTrack.ZipCode%>"></p>
    <p>Country: <input type="text" size="30"
name="Country" value="<%=CTrack.Country%>"></p>
```

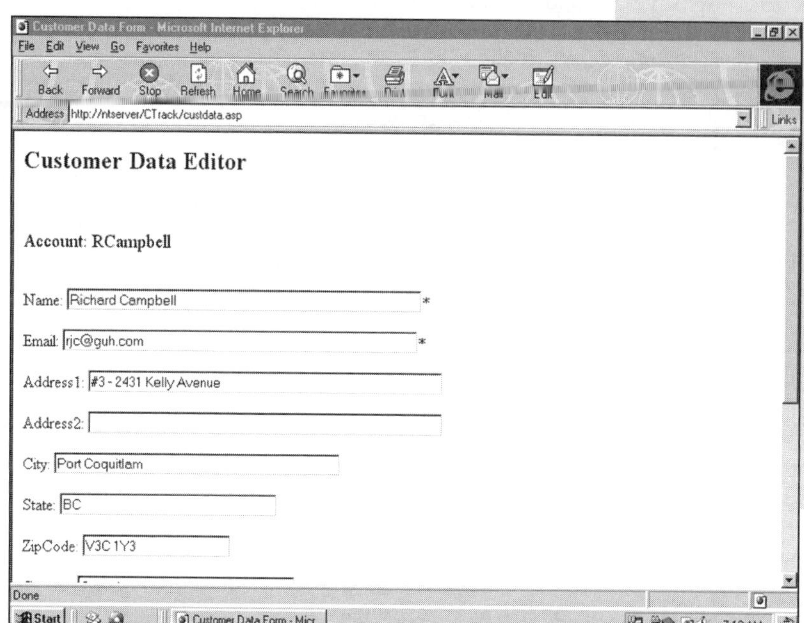

Figure 15.32 The `CustData.ASP` page is very long—this figure shows only the top half, displaying the account name and the form for editing the customer record. Hidden on the form are the `ID` and `Password` fields for the Customer Data Update page.

To display the `Items` collection on the Web page, the `For Each...` function is used to walk through the `Items` collection. Each `Item` becomes a check box line on the Web page (see Figure 15.33). The entire set of check boxes goes under the name of `Items`. The values of the check boxes are set to the `ProductName`. Beside the check box, the `ProductName` and `Description` are displayed.

After all the items are displayed, the buttons on the form offer the option of updating the record, loading the Customer Data Update page, or resetting the form to the settings it had when the page was loaded. At the end of the code block is the cleanup code—setting the object to `nothing`:

```
    <! Item check boxes are filled in by walking
through the Items collection of the CustomerData object >
    <p>Items: </p>
    <% For Each CItem In CTrack.Items %>
        <! The name of the check boxes stay the same
so that they are retrieved as one item on the CustUpd page >
        <! The value of each item is the ProductName,
which identifies what items are selected >
        <! If the .Selected property is true,
the check box is checked >
        <p><input type="checkbox" name="Items"
```

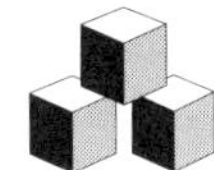


```
value="<%=CItem.ProductName%>"
        <% if CItem.Selected then %>
            checked
        <% else %>
            unchecked
        <% end if %>>
        <%=CItem.ProductName%> (<%=CItem.Description%>)</p>
    <% Next %>
    <p> * - Denotes fields that must be filled in.</p>
    <! Display the submit button with text 'Update'
- pressing the button submits the form to CustUpd >
    <! Note that the reset button resets the values
to what they were initially displayed as - not blank >
    <p><input type="submit" value="Update">
<input type="reset" value="Reset"></p>
</form>
<% Set CTrack = Nothing ' Clean up
```

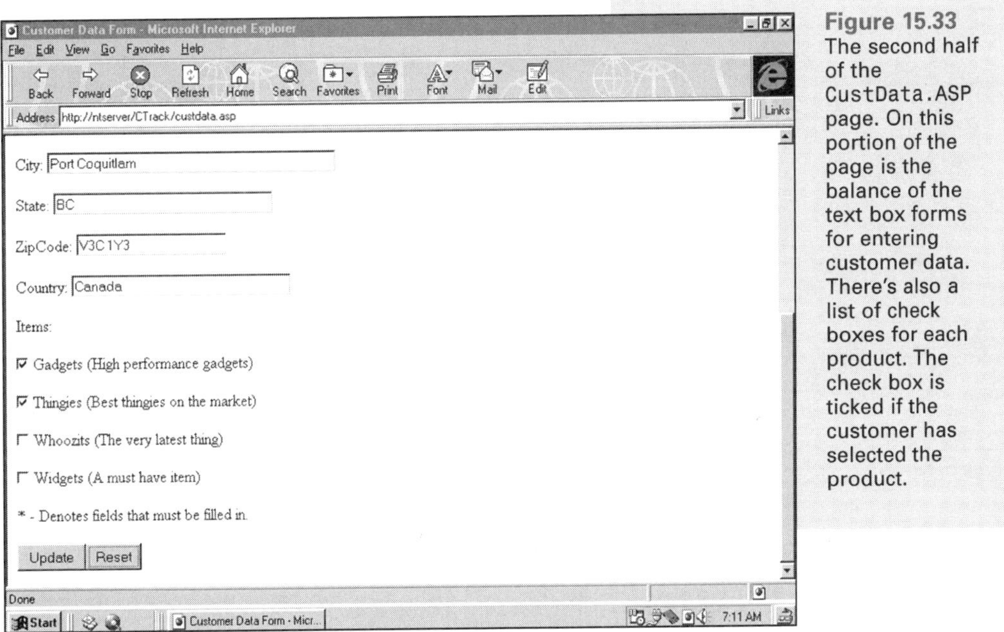

Figure 15.33 The second half of the CustData.ASP page. On this portion of the page is the balance of the text box forms for entering customer data. There's also a list of check boxes for each product. The check box is ticked if the customer has selected the product.

But what if the `Retrieve` method fails? Then the Web page has to display a failure message (see Figure 15.34). The usual reason for a failure is that the login parameters are invalid. The failure page offers the choice of going back to log in again, or linking to the Sign up Account page:

```
Else %>
    <! Invalid login - either the account
```

```
doesn't exist or the password is wrong >
    <h2>Can't Log In!</h2>

    <p> </p>

    <p>We're sorry - either the account you
entered doesn't exist or the password is incorrect.</p>
    <p>Press 'Back' on your browser to attempt
to log in again, or you can
    <a href="http://ntserver/CTrack/SignUp.htm"
>sign up a new account.</a> </p>

<% End If %>
```

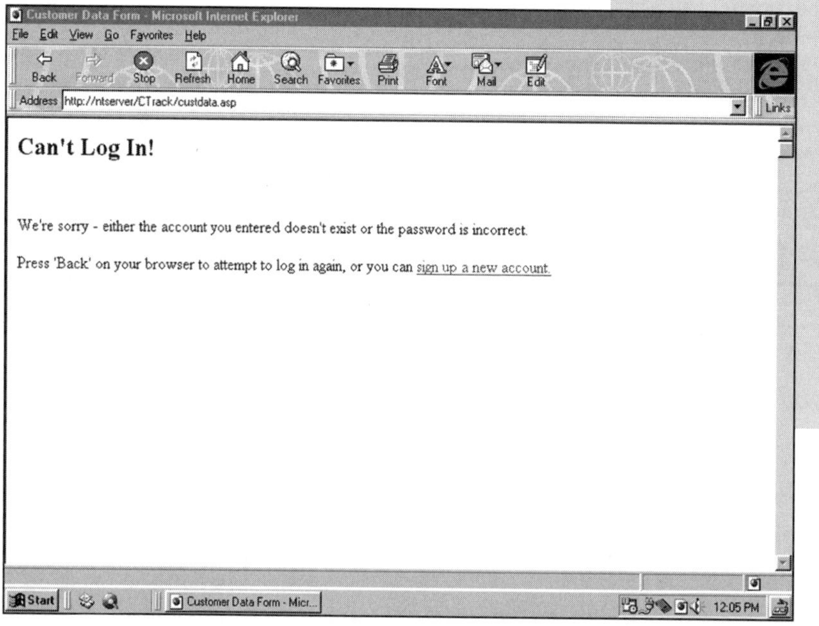

Figure 15.34 The failure message of the `CustData.ASP` page. If the `Retrieve` method doesn't work, this page is displayed. The usual reason for a `Retrieve` method failure would be invalid login parameters.

The Customer Data Updated Page

When the customer clicks the Update button on the Customer Data Editor page, the page links to the Customer Data Updated page. This page uses the `Update` method of the `CustomerData` object to write out the contents of the form on the Customer Data Editor page to the database.

Before creating the `CustomerData` object, the data received from the Customer Data Editor form needs to be checked for critical information—the name and e-mail address. If either of these elements is missing, the page displays a warning message and asks that the customer use the Back button and fill in the information:

```
<%  If Len(Trim(Request.Form("Name"))) = 0 Or
Len(Trim(Request.Form("Email"))) = 0 Then %>
        <! Missing name or email. >
        <h2>Can't Create Record!</h2>
        <p> </p>
        <p>Your customer record must include a name and
email address. Please press 'Back' and try again. </p>
```

If all the critical information exists, the `CustomerData` object is created, and the properties of the object are populated with the contents of the Customer Data Editor form:

```
<%  Else

    ' Create an instance of the CustomerData object
    Set CTrack = CreateObject("CustomerTracker.CustomerData")

    ' Populate the properties of the object
with the contents of the CustData form
    CTrack.Name = Request.Form("Name")
    CTrack.Email = Request.Form("Email")
    CTrack.Address1 = Request.Form("Address1")
    CTrack.Address2 = Request.Form("Address2")
    CTrack.City = Request.Form("City")
    CTrack.State = Request.Form("State")
    CTrack.ZipCode = Request.Form("ZipCode")
    CTrack.Country = Request.Form("Country")
```

Populating the `Items` collection is a little more complicated, especially in an Active Server Page. The check boxes from the Customer Data Editor form return a single value, which is a comma-delimited list of all of the `ProductNames` checked. The product names are broken from the `Items` list by parsing through the commas. The list contains only the products selected—these products are added to the `Items` collection of the `CustomerData` object, along with the `Selected` property being set to `True`:

```
' Parse the Items string that has the names of
each product whose check box is selected
' Each item in the string is separated by a comma
' First step is to test that there are items
in the string - if it's blank, set a flag
If Len(Trim(Request.Form("Items"))) = 0 then
    noitems = True
Else
    ' Start at the beginning of the string,
keep looping as long as there are commas
    startpos = 1
    Do While Instr(startpos,
```

```
Request.Form("Items"), ",") <> 0
        ' Get the position of the next comma
        endpos = Instr(startpos,
Request.Form("Items"), ",")
        ' If there is no comma, it's the last item,
set the value to the length of the string
        If endpos = 0 Then endpos = Len(Request.Form("Items"))
        ' Put the parsed item name into a separate string
        productname = Trim(Mid(Request.Form("Items"),
startpos, endpos - startpos))
        ' Position ahead of the last comma
        startpos = endpos + 1
        ' Write the product and flag to the Items
collection in the CustomerData object
        ' Note that the description is blank -
we don't actually need it
        Set CItem = CTrack.Items.Add(productname, "", True)
    Loop
    ' Once the loop is exited, only the
last item in the string remains
    productname = Trim(Mid(Request.Form("Items"),
startpos, Len(Request.Form("Items")) - startpos))
    ' Write the last product to the Items collection
    set CItem = CTrack.Items.Add(productname, "", True)
End If
```

Note

If the `Items` list is blank, the customer selected no items. A flag is set for a special variation of the Web page to display.

Once the `CustomerData` object is fully populated, the `Update` method is called, using the `ID` and `Password` parameters. While normally the update would always succeed, there's the possibility that it won't, so let's trap for it:

```
' Finally, the Update method of the CustomerData
object writes the data changes to the database
intSuccess = CTrack.Update(Request.Form("ID"),
Request.Form("Password"))

' Check to see if the update succeeded
If intSuccess Then %>
```

If the update succeeds, a success page is displayed. There are two variations on the success page. If the customer selected no products from the check box list on the Customer Data Editor form, the Web page says so, and suggests that the customer go back and select some items (see Figure 15.35).

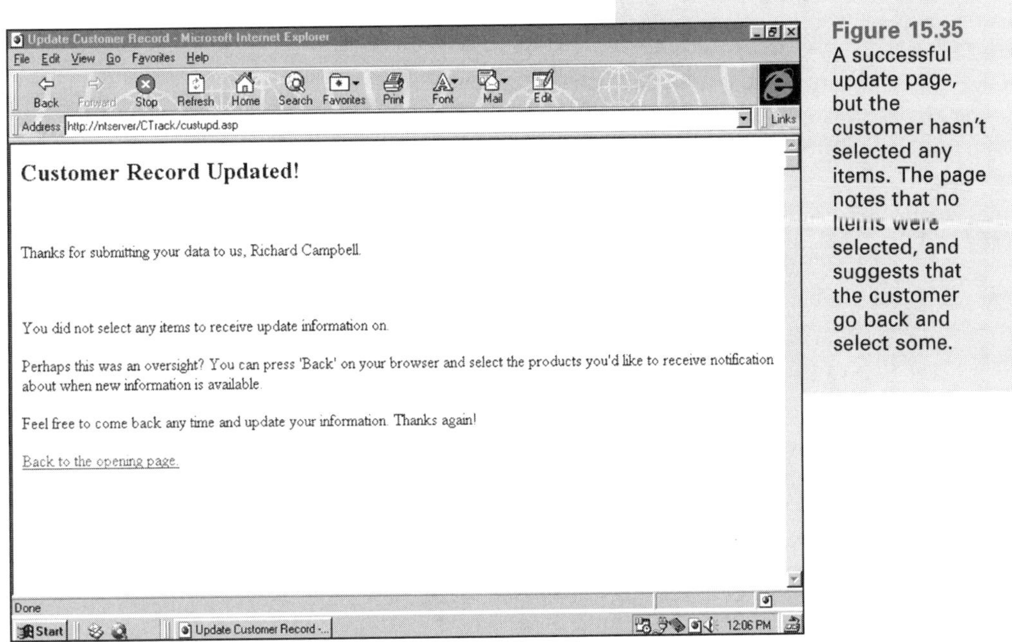

Figure 15.35 A successful update page, but the customer hasn't selected any items. The page notes that no items were selected, and suggests that the customer go back and select some.

When the customer selects products, the Web page says that the company will notify the customer whenever new information is available about those products (see Figure 15.36). Either way, a link is provided back to the opening (default) page:

```
<! Update succeed - say nice things>
<h2>Customer Record Updated!</h2>

<p> </p>

<p>Thanks for submitting your data to us,
<%= Request.Form("Name") %>.</p>
<p> </p>

<! If there were no items selected, mention it and suggest that the
customer go back >
<% If noitems Then %>
    <p>You did not select any items to
receive update information on.</p>
    <p>Perhaps this was an oversight? You can press 'Back'
on your browser and select the products you'd
like to receive notification about
when new information is available.</p>
<% Else %>
    <p>As soon as there is some new information
```

```
on the products you've selected, we'll let you know.</p>
<% End If %>
<p>Feel free to come back any time and
update your information. Thanks again!</p>
<p><a href="http://ntserver/CTrack/Default.htm"
>Back to the opening page.</a> </p>
```

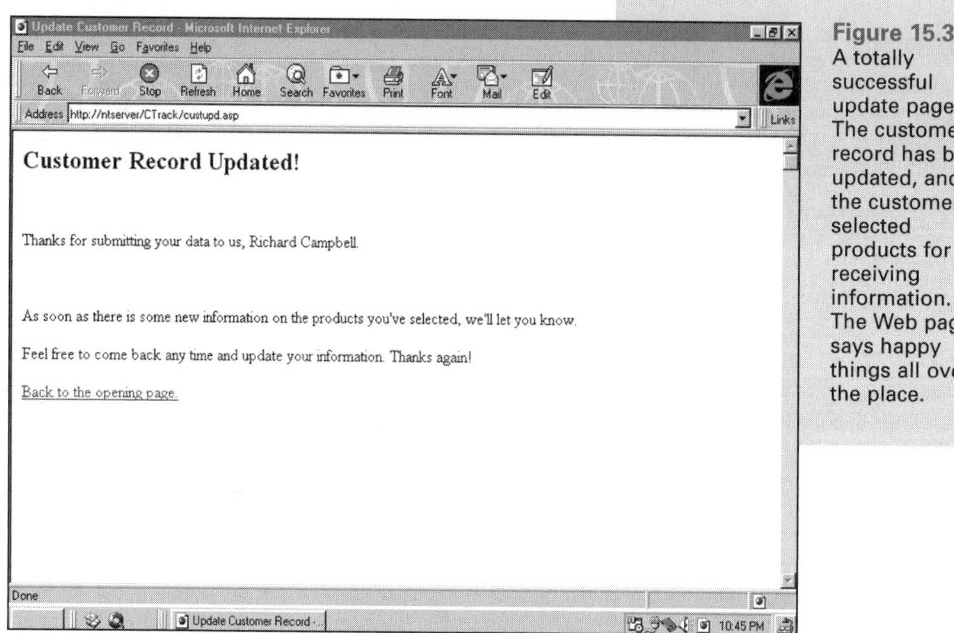

Figure 15.36 A totally successful update page. The customer record has been updated, and the customer selected products for receiving information. The Web page says happy things all over the place.

There's the possibility that the update fails—it isn't likely, because the previous page is always the Customer Data Editor page, which invokes the `Retrieve` method. But, just in case, there needs to be a trap and warning. If the `Update` method fails, the Web page says that something went wrong, and suggests that the user might want to try again by going back, or link to the opening (default) page:

```
<% Else %>
    <! Update failed. >
    <h2>Uh oh...</h2>
    <p> </p>
    <p>Something bad happened. The record wouldn't
update. You can press 'Back' and try again,
or go <a href="http://ntserver/CTrack/Default.htm"
>back to the opening page.</a> </p>
<% End If
    Set CTrack = Nothing ' Clean up
End If %>
```

The Administration Utility

The final component of the CustomerTracker application, the Administration utility, provides two functions. The first is the ability to add products to and delete products from the database. The second is the e-mailing tool—one of the key functions of the CustomerTracker application.

As customers add records to the `CTrack` database, they indicate which products they're interested in. The company can utilize this information to send e-mail to customers about developments in those products. The e-mailing system is simple, fast, and as automated as possible. To send e-mail, you specify which customers you want to mail to by selecting which products to send to; then you type the subject and body of the e-mail. The rest is automatic—the database is queried, e-mail addresses gathered up, and e-mail sent.

The Administration utility doesn't use the ActiveX server component of the CustomerTracker system—there's no need to do so. Nor is the Administration utility a set of Active Server Pages stored on a Web server, although it could be. The Administration utility is a conventional Visual Basic application. There are several reasons for developing the utility this way:

- The application is complex enough—the primary CustomerTracker Active Server Pages demonstrate the technology effectively enough.
- The Mabry mail control used to provide mail services to the application is the unregistered version that pops up a "nuisance" dialog whenever executed. This dialog would wreak havoc on the NT server.
- When sending bulk e-mail, you might not want to tie up your Web server with the work—it's likely busy enough as is. Using a separate utility application allows you to spread the workload around.
- Putting the Administration utility on the Web server is a security risk. The best way to secure a sensitive component like the Administration utility from unauthorized use is simply to make it unavailable. The only way to get access to the Administration utility is to be on the network where the database resides.

As an experienced Visual Basic developer, you're likely to be familiar with the process of creating a standard executable Visual Basic application. The development process focuses on the details of the application.

`AdminCode` Module

When developing database applications in Visual Basic, I prefer to keep my database-related code encapsulated in a code module. That being said, in the

Administration utility I deviate from this behavior by putting database-related code directly into the `Email` form. The reason is to simplify the interfacing between the database and the Mabry mail control.

The `AdminCode` module also has the `Main Sub`, which the project uses for starting up. The `Main Sub` only calls the `FillProductList` subroutine and then shows the `Admin` form.

The `AdminCode` module also includes the global constants for the Mabry mail control, and these three subroutines:

- `FillProductList`, which fills the list box on the `Admin` form with all the products in the database.
- `AddProduct`, for adding a new product to the database.
- `DeleteProduct`, for deleting a product from the database. Any references to the product are also deleted from the `CustomerItems` table.

As with all database access in the CustomerTracker application, the method used for controlling the database in the Administration utility is ODBCDirect. To use ODBCDirect, you must include the DAO 3.5 object in the references list. For more details on ODBCDirect, check the earlier section "The ActiveX Server," and the Visual Basic Books Online.

`Admin` Form

The starting point of the Administration utility, the `Admin` form, has a list box for the products and four buttons: Add, Delete, Email, and Exit (see Figure 15.37).

The code in the `Admin` form is in the `Click` events of the buttons:

- The Add button uses input boxes to prompt for the information necessary to create a new product. It then invokes the `AddProduct` subroutine to add the product to the database, and refills the product list to display the new item.
- The Delete button checks to see whether any products have been selected for deletion. If so, it displays a message box warning that the product and any references to it by a customer will be deleted. If the operator chooses yes, the `DeleteProduct` subroutine is called for each product.
- The Email button displays the `Email` form, providing that a product is selected—without a selected product, there's no one to e-mail to.

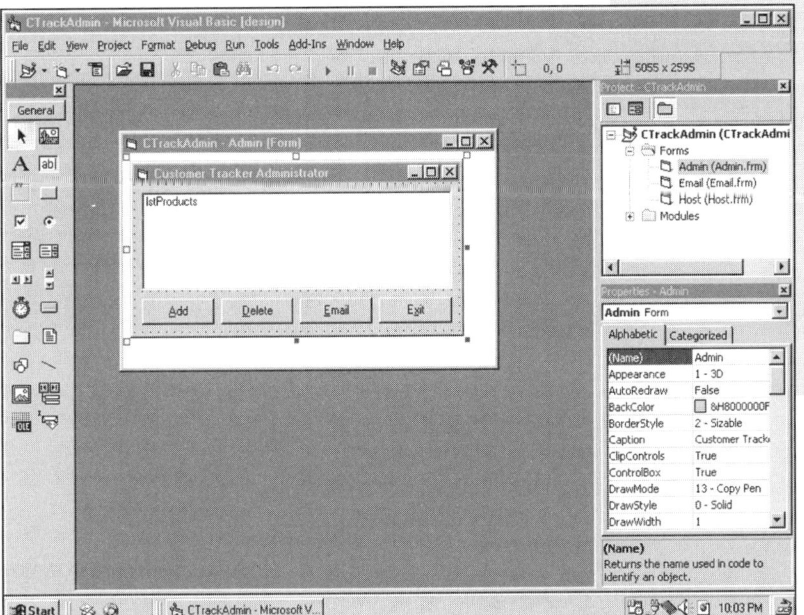

Figure 15.37 The Admin form. The main form of the Administration utility, this form displays the list of products for adding and deleting, and provides access to the e-mail subsystem through the Email button.

- The Exit button does something rather obvious—it exits the application, with an `Unload Me`.

Email Form

The `Email` form contains the bulk of the complexity of the Administration utility. When a product is selected on the `Admin` form and then the Email button clicked, the `Email` form is displayed (see Figure 15.38). This form has a label for displaying a description of the query to be used to select customers, the subject line, body of the e-mail, and a Mabry mail control. If you've worked through the second project in this book, you've already had some experience with the Mabry mail control.

Also on this form are three buttons: Send, Host Config, and Cancel. The Cancel button is pretty self-evident—it unloads the `Email` form and sends control back to the `Admin` form. The Host Config button displays the `Host Config` form, which provides access to the `Config` table in the `CTrack` database. The `Config` table stores the parameters for sending e-mail.

It's the Send button that has all the neat functions.

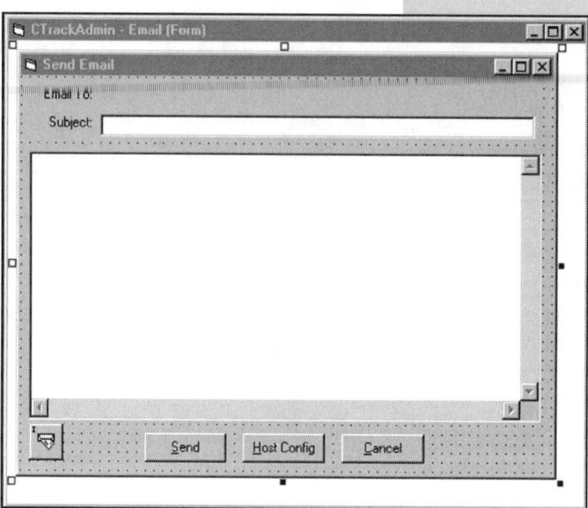

Figure 15.38
The Email form. When a product is selected from the Admin form and the Email button clicked, the Email form is displayed. This form is where the bulk e-mail for customers is actually created and sent.

The first part of the `Send_Click` subroutine sets up access to the `CTrack` database through an ODBCDirect connection:

```
Private Sub cmdSend_Click()

    Dim wrkAdmin As Workspace
    Dim conCustAdmin As Connection
    Dim rstEmail As Recordset
    Dim SQLString As String, TempString As String,
➥m_Name As String, m_Email As String
    Dim ConfigCnt As Integer, x As Integer

    Screen.MousePointer = vbHourglass

    ' Set up WorkSpace and Connection
    Set wrkAdmin = CreateWorkspace("CTrack",
➥"", "", dbUseODBC)
    Set conCustAdmin = wrkAdmin.OpenConnection("CustTrack",
➥dbDriverNoPrompt, , "ODBC;DSN=CTrack")
```

After the connection is established, the `Config` table is retrieved and the e-mail parameter data loaded into the Mabry mail control. Note that the user name and e-mail address are retained in a string, because they're used several times in several ways. The `ConfigCnt` flag is used to make certain that *all* of the e-mail parameters are entered—if any are missing, `ConfigCnt` won't equal zero, and a message box displays an error:

```
' Retrieve configuration data for email - counter is to check for
' all data
ConfigCnt = 5
```

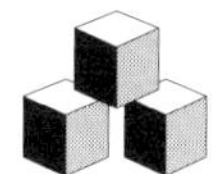


```
SQLString = "SELECT Config.Item, Config.Data
FROM Config WHERE Config.Class = 'Email'"
Set rstEmail = conCustAdmin.
OpenRecordset(SQLString, dbOpenSnapshot)
If rstEmail.RecordCount <> 0 Then
    ' If there are records, loop
through and fill the appropriate strings
    Do While Not rstEmail.EOF
        Select Case rstEmail("Item")
            Case "Name"
                m_Name = rstEmail("Data")
                ConfigCnt = ConfigCnt - 1
            Case "Email"
                m_Email = rstEmail("Data")
                ConfigCnt = ConfigCnt - 1
            Case "POPHost"
                mMail1.Host = rstEmail("Data")
                ConfigCnt = ConfigCnt - 1
            Case "POPUser"
                mMail1.LogonName = rstEmail("Data")
                ConfigCnt = ConfigCnt - 1
            Case "POPPassword"
                mMail1.LogonPassword = rstEmail("Data")
                ConfigCnt = ConfigCnt - 1
        End Select
        rstEmail.MoveNext
    Loop
End If
rstEmail.Close

' If ConfigCnt does not equal zero, then abort email.
If ConfigCnt <> 0 Then
    MsgBox "Email configuration information missing. Press
➥'Host Config' button to set up data.", vbOKOnly + vbCritical,
➥"Need Host Configuration Data"
    conCustAdmin.Close
    wrkAdmin.Close
    Exit Sub
End If
```

Ready to build an e-mail. The Mabry mail control has its properties loaded with the various elements of the e-mail (most of this code is taken directly from the excellent examples provided with the control from Mabry):

```
mMail1.Subject = txtSubject.Text
mMail1.From = m_Name & " <" & m_Email & ">"
mMail1.Headers(mMail1.HeadersCount) = "X-Mailer: Mabry"
mMail1.EMailAddress = Chr(34) & m_Name & Chr(34) & "<" & m_Email &
➥">"
mMail1.MessageID = Year(Now) & Month(Now) &
```

```
Day(Now) & Fix(Timer) & "_MabryMail"
mMail1.Body(0) = txtBody.Text
```

The query to retrieve the names and e-mail addresses of the customers allows for multiple product selections. The product selections have to be parsed from the product list box on the `Admin` form:

```
' Build query for names and email addresses of customers
SQLString = "SELECT DISTINCT Customers.Name,
Customers.Email FROM Customers "
SQLString = SQLString & "INNER JOIN CustomerItems ON
Customers.ID = CustomerItems.CustomerID "
SQLString = SQLString & "WHERE "
ConfigCnt = False
For x = 0 To Admin!lstProducts.ListCount - 1
    If Admin!lstProducts.Selected(x) Then
        If ConfigCnt Then
            SQLString = SQLString & " OR "
        Else
            ConfigCnt = True
        End If
        TempString = Admin!lstProducts.List(x)
        TempString = Left$(TempString, InStr(1,
TempString, "(") - 1)
        SQLString = SQLString & "CustomerItems.ProductName =
➥'" & TempString & "'"
    End If
Next x
```

Once the query is constructed, it's opened as a snapshot against the `Connection` object. If no records are returned, a message box pops up saying so, and work is done. If there are records, the first record is loaded into the `.To` property of the Mabry mail control. The balance of the customer name/e-mail addresses are placed in the blind carbon copy (`BCC`) property of the Mabry mail control.

Using `BCC` means that each customer gets his or her own e-mail—they don't receive an e-mail with multiple e-mail addresses on it. A comma is placed between each name/e-mail address in the `BCC` property. Once the `BCC` property is fully populated, the `MailActionConnect` constant is passed to the `Action` property of the Mabry mail control, and mail starts to send.

After the sending is done, data objects are closed up and the process is finished:

```
' Run query - first name in To property,
the balance in the BCC property
Set rstEmail = conCustAdmin.OpenRecordset(SQLString,
➥dbOpenSnapshot)
If rstEmail.RecordCount = 0 Then
```

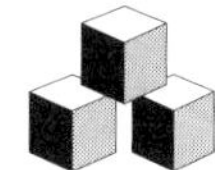


```
    Screen.MousePointer = vbDefault
    MsgBox "There are no customers to email to!",
vbOKOnly + vbCritical, "No Customers"
Else
    ' First record to the To property
    mMail1.To = rstEmail("Name") & " <"
➥& rstEmail("Email") & ">"
    rstEmail.MoveNext
    ' If there are more records, loop
    ' through and build the BCC property
    ConfigCnt = False
    TempString = ""
    Do While Not rstEmail.EOF
        If ConfigCnt Then
            TempString = TempString & ", "
        Else
            ConfigCnt = True
        End If
    TempString = TempString & rstEmail("Name") &
➥" <" & rstEmail("Email") & ">"
        rstEmail.MoveNext
    Loop
    mMail1.BCC = TempString
    State = StateConnecting
    mMail1.Action = MailActionConnect
End If
rstEmail.Close

' Close up
conCustAdmin.Close
wrkAdmin.Close

End Sub
```

Built into the Mabry mail control is extensive debugging data. A `Debug` property on the Mabry mail control is set to one (`1`) to display this information in the Immediate window when the application executes. You can turn this information off by setting the `Debug` property to `0`. However, I'm sure you'll find this information very useful when trying to determine why e-mail isn't being sent.

Host Config Form

The `Host Config` Form is displayed modally when the Host Config button is pressed on the `Email` form. When the `Host Config` form is loaded, the `Form_Load` event is executed. This event opens up a connection to the `CTrack` database and retrieves the data stored in the `Config` table. This e-mail configuration data is loaded into the text boxes on the `Host Config` form.

On the `Host Config` form, there are five text boxes and two buttons (see Figure 15.39). These five boxes conform to the data needed by the Mabry mail control to send e-mail successfully. They are as follows:

- Name—the name of the person sending e-mail.
- Email—the e-mail address of the person sending e-mail (*name@host.com*).
- POP Host—the name of the e-mail server of your ISP (*mail.host.com*).
- User Name—the name you use to log into the e-mail server of your ISP.
- Password—the password you use to log into the e-mail server of your ISP.

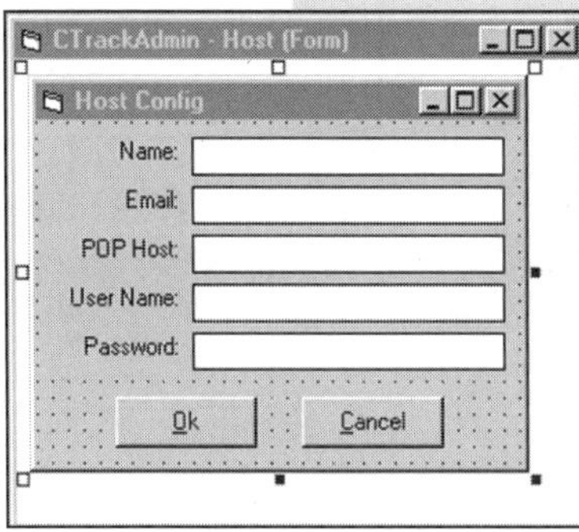

Figure 15.39
The `Host Config` form, showing the five different bits of data needed by the Mabry mail control to send mail. This data is stored in the `Config` table, and retrieved automatically when the `Host Config` form is displayed.

The Cancel button on the `Host Config` form unloads the form—execution returns to the `Email` form.

Clicking the OK button deletes the existing `Config` data for the e-mail parameters, and replaces it with the parameters entered into the `Host Config` form text boxes.

Testing the Administration Utility

Once the Administration Utility is developed, test the Add and Delete product buttons first—the code is simple and straightforward, and it's always nice to start off the testing of a new component with some success.

Testing the e-mail system can drive you crazy—there's a lot that can go wrong. Make sure that the data you use in the `Host Config` form is accurate. Create some dummy records in the `Customers` database that point to your own e-mail address. Then run a test e-mail run (see Figure 15.40).

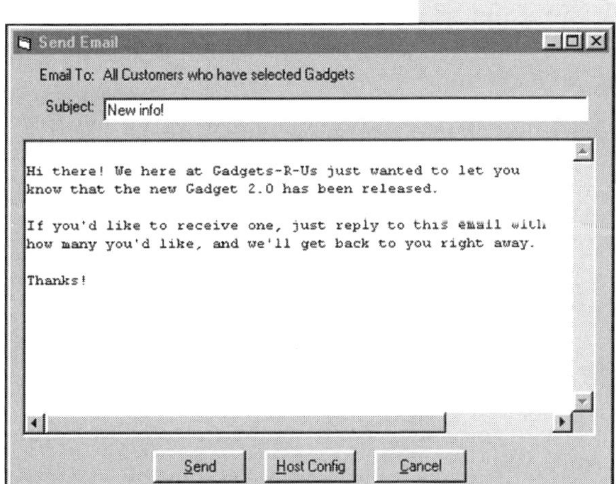

Figure 15.40 Sending an e-mail using the Administration utility.

You'll have to set up your Dial-Up Networking (DUN) connection (or a valid e-mail gateway setup) before you send e-mail—the Mabry mail control doesn't automatically invoke the DUN window when activated. I'd consider that a feature, really—you wouldn't want a prototype e-mail application running rampant all over your modem.

If you DUN connection is active, when you click Send on the `Email` form you'll get a flurry of messages in the Immediate window, from the Mabry mail control `Debug` system. These messages include the details of the e-mail, along with the process of communication with your ISP. If there are any problems, the Immediate window is likely to explain them.

You may need to step through the entire `Send` code block line by line when debugging. See whether the e-mail configuration data actually makes it to the Mabry mail control, whether the customer query returns valid customers, whether the Mabry mail control is properly populated, and whether the `Send Action` actually occurs. It's a lot of steps to get right, all in one chunk of code.

Deploying the CustomerTracker Application

With the Administration utility debugged, the CustomerTracker application is finished. To deploy the application to a production system, you'll need to do the following:

1. Integrate the Web pages with the existing Web site, matching "look and feel."

2. Compile and build a setup version of the Administration utility.
3. Flush out the test data in the `CTrack` database and fill it with valid products.
4. Add any existing customer data you might have.
5. Be sure to put some indication on your Web site home page that there's a new customer information system available.

Summary

The project you have just worked through is a demonstration of the potential of some of the new technologies involving the Internet and Visual Basic. While the CustomerTracker is an advanced project, it should be obvious to you that this is only scratching the surface of the potential of these technologies. The flexibility and performance of Active Server Pages and ActiveX servers is awesome—they're limited only by your creativity.

Project 3 Summary

The third project built upon the techniques used in the previous projects to create a "real-world" application for the Internet. Every commercial Web site needs a way to collect information about its visitors. In this age of junk e-mail, you have to provide facilities to allow potential customers to get off of and onto your lists on demand. To encourage participation, the e-mail notification service offers value back to the visitor.

The real challenge in Internet development is managing scalability. Planning for more sophisticated databases, such as SQL Server, means using convertible data-access techniques such as ODBCDirect. With ODBCDirect, the code you write against your Access MDB is directly portable to SQL Server—you only need to change the connection parameters to make your system function with the new database.

The other facet of scalability comes with object brokering. In a high-demand Web site, the constant requests for ActiveX objects can bury a server. Microsoft Transaction Server manages those requests for you with a minimum of additional work.

Hands On Project 4

The Real Estate Companion

- System prototyping within Visual Basic
- Dynamic HTML development
- ActiveX control development
- Understanding and working with the ActiveX Data Objects model
- Using the Package and Deployment Wizard

Project Overview

The fourth and final project demonstrates using some of the newest and most advanced Internet features of Visual Basic 6.0. In this project, you will combine some of the subjects discussed earlier in the book, including Active Server Pages and HTML. You also will explore some of the newest technologies, including Dynamic HTML, ActiveX Data Objects, and the Visual Studio Package and Deployment Wizard.

You will gather the system requirements for the Real Estate Companion, then generate a prototype of the application. In earlier projects, you used FrontPage to build a prototype. Visual Basic has enough tools, however, to build a prototype without ever leaving the comfort of the VB IDE. Your goal is to build a picture of what your application is going to look like so that users can comment on it and make changes before those changes cost too much.

After building your prototype, you'll set your sights on adding the real code behind the application. You'll learn how to use ActiveX Data Objects (ADO) to write your data to a database file. You'll then learn how to add VB code directly to your Web pages using Dynamic HTML. Next, you'll complete the code for your ActiveX control.

Finally, after building all the components for this system, you'll learn how to package and deploy your application using the Package and Deployment Wizard.

What Is the Real Estate Companion?

In all of the prior projects, you spent your time creating Web-based applications on both the client and the server. This chapter begins the fourth and final project for this book. In this project you build a full set of Web components using both client-side and server-side technology.

Describing the Real Estate Companion

The project you are going to create in this final portion of the book is called the *Real Estate Companion*. The Real Estate Companion demonstrates some of the potential Web components you might build for a real estate company. A real estate example was chosen for a number of reasons. The first reason is the distributed nature of the real estate business—real estate sales comprise one of those businesses where the data entry points and points of data consumption are broadly distributed. The second reason is the rich quality of the data collected by real estate companies. These companies need to track numerous elements for each customer, listing, and sale their office works with. The final reason is that the interfaces for realtors must be intuitive and easy to use. Web interfaces are well-suited to meeting this goal.

The goal of the Real Estate Companion is to create a set of useful Web components that can be used in the operations of a real estate company. The components for this application will be concentrated in two areas—the Web client and the Web server. The Web client will be used to present the interface to the user, while the Web server will be responsible for storing and querying the data for the system.

System Requirements for the Real Estate Companion

The most important stage of the development process is the requirements-gathering stage. This stage is important because it defines the scope of your application. It's crucial to do a good job of accurately gathering the necessary requirements for the system, as the costs of development escalate as the system matures. This results in higher costs of fixing problems with missing features at later stages of the development process. Some studies say that it can cost up to 100 times more to fix a problem in the development stages of a project than in the requirements stage. Missing a crucial requirement can even result in project cancellation.

Now that you understand the need for good requirements, you can begin gathering the requirements for the Real Estate Companion system. This system should do the following:

- **Provide an HTML-based interface for entering and modifying real estate listings.** The HTML interface should validate as much information as possible before sending it to the server. All listings should be stored in some type of database and should be simple to use.
- **Provide customers the ability to request information from the real estate company.** This can be a simple request form. The information should be stored in a database.
- **Provide potential customers the ability to query listings.** The listings returned to the user should be generated from the listing database. Limited information should be returned to the potential customer.
- **Provide potential customers a mortgage calculator form.** This form should let customers key in the amount borrowed, the length of the loan, and the interest rate. It then should show the payment and an amortization table.

- **Use the newest and most appropriate technology for the project.** The company wants to preserve its investment in systems and wants to use the most current techniques.

Goals of the Real Estate Companion

This project is designed to show Visual Basic developers how to build a Web site that involves both client-side and server-side development. This project introduces developers to many new and exciting Web technologies. Some of the topics you learn while developing this project include the following:

- **How to build and deploy ActiveX controls**
  One of the more interesting technologies to be developed for Web pages is the *ActiveX control*. In earlier projects, you learned how to create Active servers, which were simply objects without a visual representation. ActiveX controls are Active servers with a visual representation.
- **How to create Dynamic HTML applications with Visual Basic**
  One of the newest features of Visual Basic is its ability to create *Dynamic HTML* applications. You can create applications that behave like Visual Basic. You also can create applications using only Visual Basic code—this means no scripting code is embedded in your Web pages for the world to see and "borrow."
- **How to use ActiveX Data Objects (ADO) to manage data**
  Microsoft's latest and greatest method of accessing data is a technology known as *ActiveX Data Objects (ADO)*. ADO can be used to query, add, edit, and delete data found in numerous data formats.

Summary

The defining moment for any application is the definition of its requirements. This chapter has described the components and functionality that will be present in the Real Estate Companion. You are creating a system that gives real estate companies the capability to manage their data in an easy-to-use yet highly distributed environment. Now that you understand what needs to be done, you can begin the process of creating the application.

CHAPTER 17

Gathering Information for the Real Estate Companion

Chapter 16 examined the requirements for creating a useful Internet server-based application. This chapter examines the steps necessary for gathering information about this project.

In Chapter 5, "Gathering Information for the VBBrowser," you learned about the different components of creating a requirements document. You learned that when creating an application, you need to find and document the following information:

- **The mission statement.** The purpose of the mission statement is to define at a very high level what the goal of the system is. This mission statement can be one sentence or one page. The goal of the mission statement is to set the focus of the project. A common practice of many system developers is to ask for one page (and only one page) describing the system they're being asked to create.

- **The system users.** For any system to be successful, you need to involve the direct users of the system. Users of a system have the power to make or break whatever developers throw at them. When dealing with users, you should attempt to learn what their job functions are and what impact the system will have on these users.
- **The system managers.** When developing a system, it's important to distinguish between managers and users. The needs of managers are very different from those of users. Users want to do their work and go home; managers are commonly responsible for much higher-level tasks. It's easy to fall into the trap of trying to cater your system to the managers. This is a surefire way to fail.
- **Required features.** This item can be the most difficult to quantify and is the most difficult to rein in. When developing a system, you want to make sure that you prioritize the required features and dedicate your resources to working on those features. The big question is how you derive these features. The easiest method of doing this is to ask a very direct question of the system users: "What are the three most important features to you?" Then force users to pick three and only three (or whatever your number may be), which forces them to prioritize.
- **Out-of-scope features.** When gathering information for a system, this item is commonly overlooked. All user-requested features should be documented. Once the first version of your software is complete, you can return to your out-of-scope features list and go right to work on your next version.
- **Other sources of information.** When you're dealing with Internet applications, you're faced with a sea of information that's available to you. This section should document where you intend to go for your information.

When looking at the information you're attempting to gather, you can break it down into five basic tenets of any project:

- **What.** What are you trying to do?
- **Why.** Why are you trying to do it?
- **Who.** Who is going to use or be affected by the system?
- **Where.** Where can you find the information you need?
- **When.** When is the information needed, or how often will it be accessed?

These items may seem obvious to you, but you'd be surprised how many people forget even the most basic development principles.

Beginning the Gathering Process

Now that you have an understanding of what you need to accomplish in the information-gathering stage of a project, you can begin breaking it down. The first task in the gathering stage is to define the mission statement of the system. The mission statement can be derived from the initial document or Request for Proposal (RFP) sent by the users. Chapter 16 explains that the system should do the following:

- Provide an HTML-based interface for entering and modifying real estate listings.
- Provide customers the ability to request information from the real estate company.
- Provide potential customers the ability to query listings.
- Provide potential customers a mortgage calculator form.
- Use the newest and most appropriate technology for the project.

This list is nice for defining just what the system is supposed to do, but it falls short of defining *why*. This is your job as a system developer—to attempt to figure out why this project needs to do certain things. After analyzing the requirements list, you can derive the following mission statement:

Mission Statement

The purpose of the Real Estate Companion is to facilitate the management of real estate company data. This system will be accessible by customers and employees. The system should be easy to use and flexible to maintain.

The task that immediately follows the mission statement is the process of breaking the requirements document into functional areas. This allows you as a developer to concentrate your time into specific areas. In each area, the information you gather should answer the list of questions defined earlier: what, why, who, where, and when. From this list, you can create a form that will serve as the source of your documentation. Your form can be as simple as the one in Table 17-1.

Table 17-1 Proposed Requirements-Gathering Form

Item	Notes
Project	
Name of Analyst	
Date Created	
Task Description (What)	
Item Purpose (Why)	
Responsible Party or Users (Who)	
Source of Information (Where)	
Access Requirements (When)	
Notes	

Now that you understand what information you need to gather, you can go to work. Using the proposed requirements form shown in Table 17-1, you can begin gathering information for each functional area of your project. The following sections discuss the process of formalizing the requirements for this project.

Provide an HTML-Based Interface for Entering and Modifying Real Estate Listings

Taking the proposed form from Table 17-1, this requirement can be broken down as shown in Table 17-2.

Table 17-2 Listings Interface Requirement

Item	Notes
Project	Real Estate Companion
Name of Analyst	Rod Paddock
Date Created	12/31/98
Task Description (What)	Create an HTML form for entering listing information.
Item Purpose (Why)	The bread and butter of a real estate company is its listings. Numerous agents gather listings and need to be able to key listing information into this system from the Web. Listing information entered should include descriptions of the property, square footage, number of rooms, number of bathrooms, price, and so on.
Responsible Party or Users (Who)	Real estate brokers, realtors, MLS systems
Source of Information (Where)	Customers, realtors, MLS
Access Requirements (When)	Will be frequently accessed by employees and customers.
Notes	

Provide Customers the Ability to Request Information from the Real Estate Company

Table 17-3 shows how this requirement can be broken down.

Table 17-3 Information-Requesting Capability Requirement

Item	Notes
Project	Real Estate Companion
Name of Analyst	Rod Paddock
Date Created	12/31/98
Task Description (What)	Provide customers the ability to request information from the real estate company.
Item Purpose (Why)	Customers that find our company on the Web should be able to request information. This form should include names, addresses, phone numbers, and e-mail addresses from the customers.

Table 17-3 Information-Requesting Capability Requirement *(continued)*

Item	Notes
Responsible Party or Users (Who)	Customers, realtors, office staff
Source of Information (Where)	Customers
Access Requirements (When)	Will be frequently accessed by employees and customers.
Notes	

Provide Potential Customers the Ability to Query Listings

Table 17-4 shows how this requirement can be broken down.

Table 17-4 Listings-Querying Capability Requirement

Item	Notes
Project	Real Estate Companion
Name of Analyst	Rod Paddock
Date Created	12/31/98
Task Description (What)	Provide potential customers the ability to query listings.
Item Purpose (Why)	Customers should be able to query listings from our database. This should be done by allowing customers to query our databases based on criteria such as number of rooms, price, location, and so on. The results should be a table of listings that meet their requirements. The table should contain summary information for the listings and links to more detailed information.
Responsible Party or Users (Who)	Customers, realtors, office staff
Source of Information (Where)	Customers
Access Requirements (When)	Will be frequently accessed by employees and customers.
Notes	

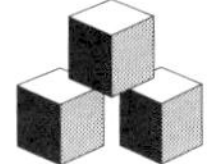

Provide Potential Customers a Mortgage Calculator Form

Table 17-5 shows how this requirement can be broken down.

Table 17-5 Mortgage Calculator Form Requirement

Item	Notes
Project	Real Estate Companion
Name of Analyst	Rod Paddock
Date Created	12/31/98
Task Description (What)	Provide potential customers a mortgage calculator form.
Item Purpose (Why)	People contemplating a real estate transaction always want to know what their costs will be. The system should provide a form for calculating house payments.
Responsible Party or Users (Who)	Customers
Source of Information (Where)	Customers
Access Requirements (When)	Will be frequently accessed by customers.
Notes	

Use the Newest and Most Appropriate Technology for the Project

Table 17-6 shows how this requirement can be broken down.

Table 17-6 Newest and Most Appropriate Technology Requirement

Item	Notes
Project	Real Estate Companion
Name of Analyst	Rod Paddock
Date Created	12/31/98
Task Description (What)	Use the newest and most appropriate technology for the project.

Table 17-6 Newest and Most Appropriate Technology Requirement *(continued)*

Item	Notes
Item Purpose (Why)	During the development process, we will use the most advanced technology available. This will cut down on development costs and time. We will standardize on Internet Explorer and use Visual Basic. Technology to be used includes Dynamic HTML, Web classes, and ADO.
Responsible Party or Users (Who)	Development staff
Source of Information (Where)	Microsoft
Access Requirements (When)	Will be frequently accessed by employees and customers.
Notes	

Summary

You have seen that a lot of critical information can be gathered at this stage of development. If your requirements are lacking any information, that probably will be discovered at this stage, saving large sums of money later in the process. Now you're ready to tackle the next stage of development for the Real Estate Companion—the design stage.

Designing the Real Estate Companion

In Chapter 17, "Gathering Information for the Real Estate Companion," you completed a detailed list of requirements for the system. After gathering a completed set of requirements, you can proceed with the design process. In the design process, you begin putting together a list of detailed technical specifications for your system. These technical specifications will then be used to actually implement your system. This chapter looks at the process of creating the design documents for the Real Estate Companion system.

Designing the Real Estate Companion Using the RAD Method

The Real Estate Companion system will be designed using the RAD method of development (explained in Chapter 6). Taking the requirements documents from Chapters 16 and 17, you can determine that you will be developing a server-based Visual Basic application. This application will be used to produce information about a company's products.

The first item in your documentation will be a list of features to be developed. From the requirements document developed in Chapter 16, you'll find the necessary items:

- Provide an HTML-based interface for entering and modifying real estate listings.
- Provide customers the ability to request information from the real estate company.
- Provide potential customers the ability to query listings.
- Provide potential customers a mortgage calculator form.
- Use the newest and most appropriate technology for the project.

After composing this list, you can go to work identifying the information for each component.

Designing the Listings Entry Page

As you learned in Chapter 6, "Designing the VBBrowser," the primary goal of the RAD method of development is to put as much functionality in front of a user as quickly as possible. This requires that you use a development tool that allows you to create Web pages in a rapid manner. In Chapter 10, "Designing the VBResearcher," you learned how to use Microsoft FrontPage to build Web pages quickly. In this chapter you will use another tool to do this—Visual Basic. Yes, Visual Basic has facilities included to help with development of Web content. These new facilities are called *Dynamic HTML applications* (or *DHTML applications*). DHTML applications utilize Internet Explorer (version 4.0 or later) and Visual Basic to create some very powerful applications.

The first step to beginning your prototype using Visual Basic is to create a Visual Basic DHTML application. Upon running Visual Basic you are prompted with the New Project dialog (see Figure 18.1). Select the DHTML Application option.

After you select DHTML Application and press OK, Visual Basic creates your project and opens it in the VB Project Explorer (see Figure 18.2). You will find this dialog populated with two folders: Modules and Designers. Modules contains the functions and procedures you create for your project. Designers contains your HTML documents. Open the Designers folder and double-click the document contained in that folder. Double-clicking the file causes it to open in the Visual Basic DHTML designer (see Figure 18.3). This designer is a tool you can use to create prototypes of your HTML documents.

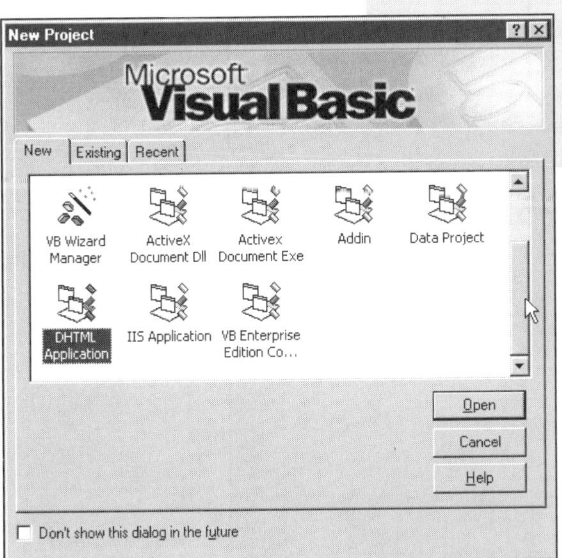

Figure 18.1
This figure shows the Visual Basic New Project dialog with DHTML Application selected.

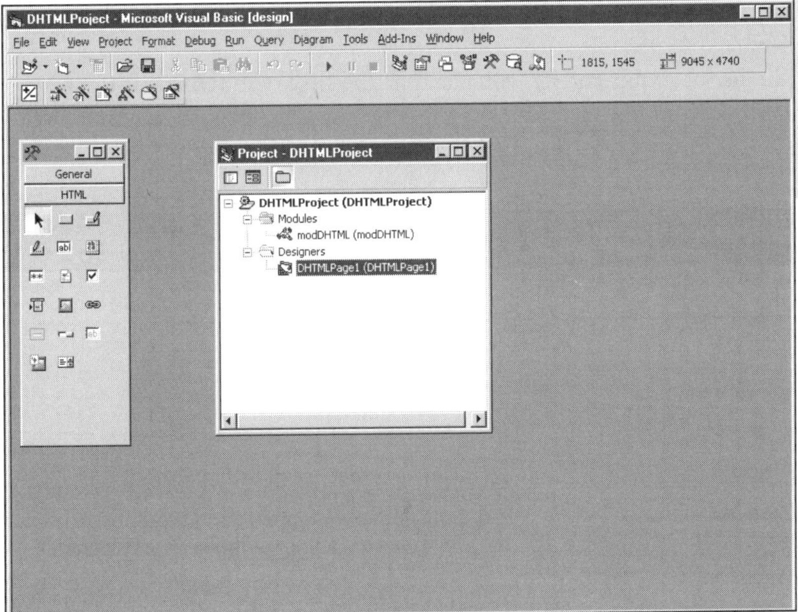

Figure 18.2
The Project Explorer holds the contents of your new DHTML application.

Now that you have created your DHTML project, you can go about the process of creating the prototype Web pages for your application. To find out what the first Web page should be, consult your requirements documentation.

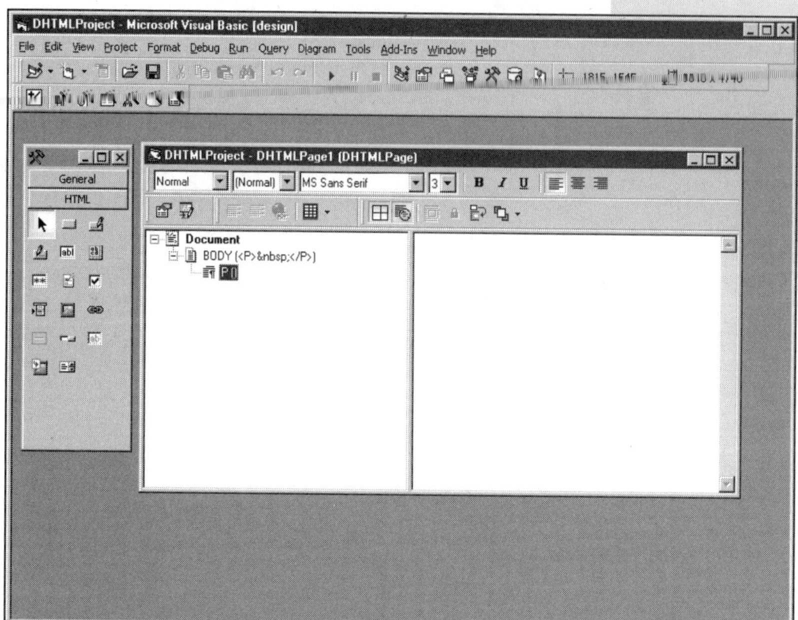

Figure 18.3 The Visual Basic DHTML designer is ready for creating a new HTML Web page.

From the list of requirements, you see that the first requirement is to create a products list from the database. Using the template from Chapter 6, your design specification looks like Table 18-1.

Table 18-1 Real Estate Listings Form

Item	Notes
Project	Real Estate Companion
Name of Analyst	Rod Paddock
Date Created	12/31/98
Task Description	Create a real estate listings page.
Task Inputs	Information about a listing: Description, number of rooms, number of bathrooms, price, address.
Task Outputs	Save information to the listings database.
Source of Information	Listings database and realtors.
Notes	

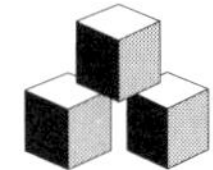

After creating the specification, you can go about the process of creating the actual listings Web page. To create this page, return to the Visual Basic DHTML Designer. Before you begin using the designer, you should understand how it is structured. The designer itself is structured into two basic windows (see Figure 18.4). The left window is the document window, which shows the structure of your document's HTML tags. The right window shows a WYSIWYG representation of your document. You can actually type in this window and the text will be converted into HTML.

You will use two other VB features in conjunction with the DHTML Designer. These are the toolbox and the Properties window. The toolbox contains all the different types of data entry controls you can place on an HTML Web page. The Properties window allows you to manipulate the different parameters of the HTML tags found in your document. Figures 18.5 and 18.6 show these two features.

Now that you have a better understanding of the different tools you will use to prototype your forms, you can begin creating the first form. The first step is to begin adding the different data entry fields to your Web page. As you

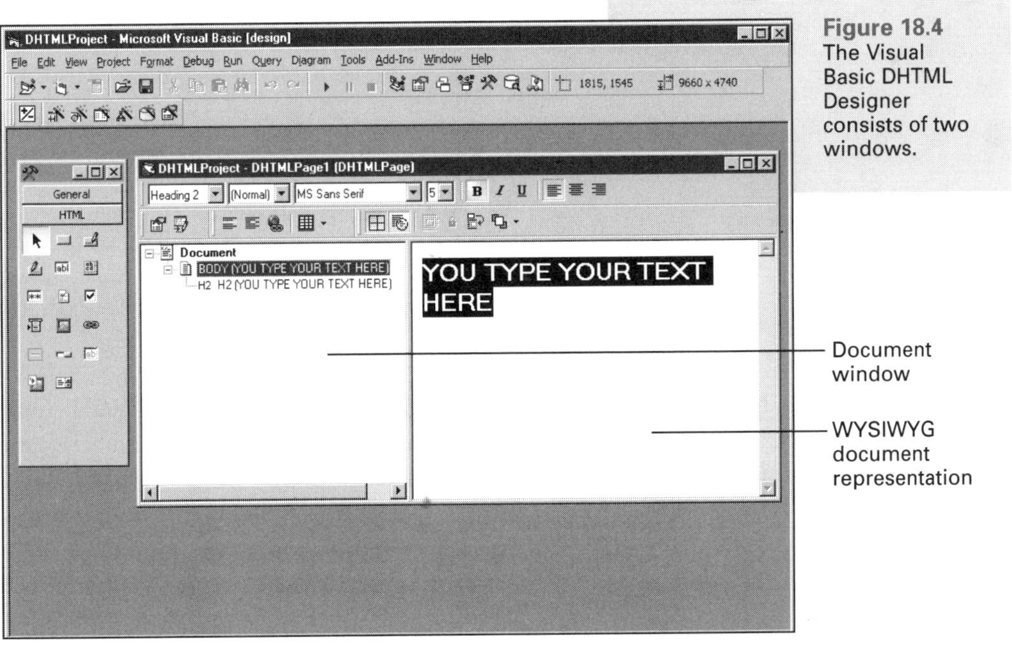

Figure 18.4 The Visual Basic DHTML Designer consists of two windows.

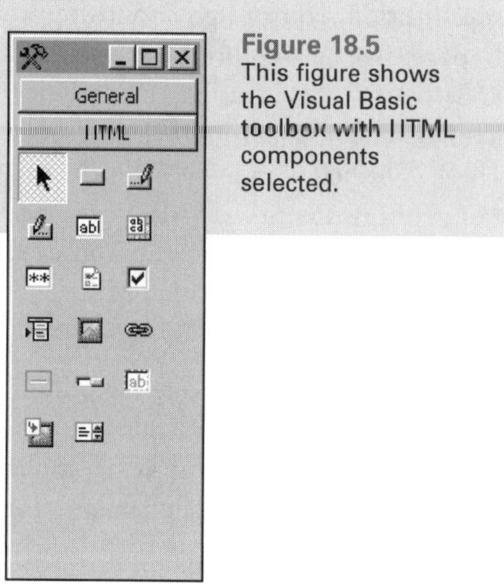

Figure 18.5
This figure shows the Visual Basic toolbox with HTML components selected.

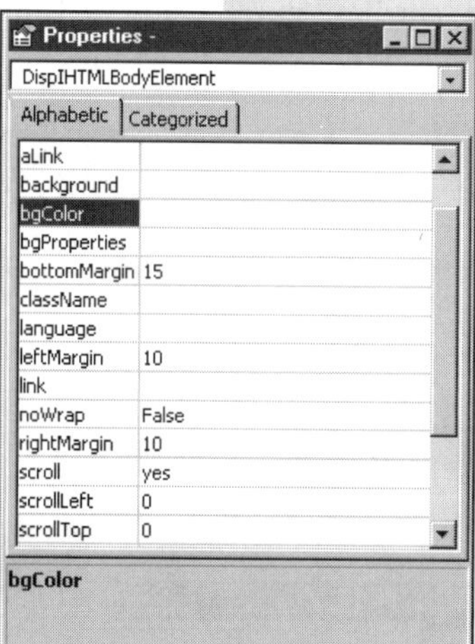

Figure 18.6
This figure shows the Visual Basic Properties window with the parameters of the BODY tag specified.

learned in Chapter 1, a great tool for aligning objects is the HTML table tool. You want your data entry forms to be neat and aesthetically pleasing, so you should use tables to align these controls. To add a table to your HTML page, select the table tool from the Designer toolbar (see Figure 18.7). This drops down a menu that allows you to insert a table into your document. After adding the table, you can change its dimensions by selecting the table in the editor and reselecting the menu. You can insert or remove cells, columns, and rows from this menu. For this form, you should add five rows to your table.

After adding the table, begin adding fields for your listings page. The first step is to add the labels for each of your data entry objects. You do this by moving your cursor to any cell you want to add a label to, and simply typing. Figure 18.8 shows the listings Web page with all of its labels entered.

Now that you've added the labels to your form, begin adding the data entry fields. You add data entry fields to your form by dragging and dropping those elements from the toolbox to the appropriate cells. Figure 18.9 shows the data entry form with all of the appropriate fields entered in their proper places.

Now that you've added all the data entry fields, go back and alter the properties for each data entry field as appropriate. The first necessary change is to clear the `Value` properties for each of the text fields, using these steps:

1. Select the appropriate data entry field.
2. Scroll to the `Value` property in the Properties window and remove the contents of this property setting.

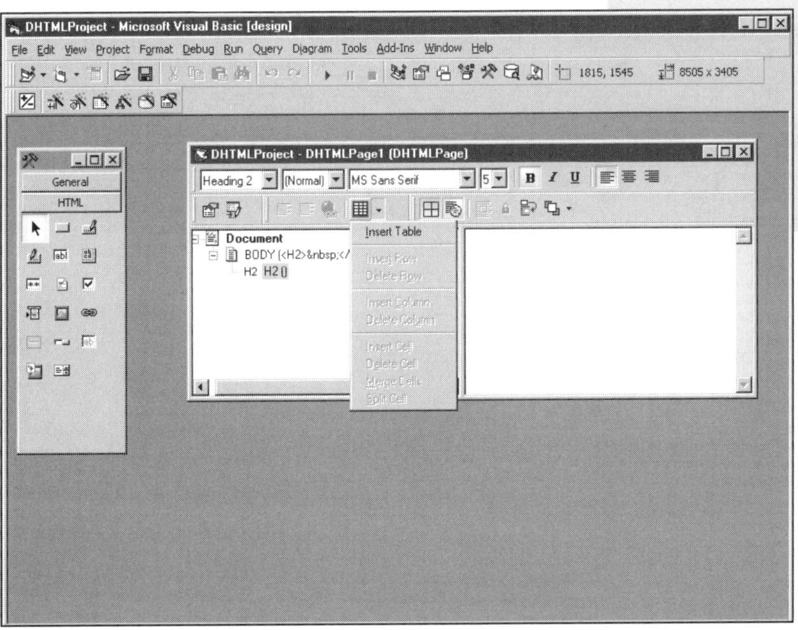

Figure 18.7 This figure shows the DHTML Designer with the table toolbar option selected.

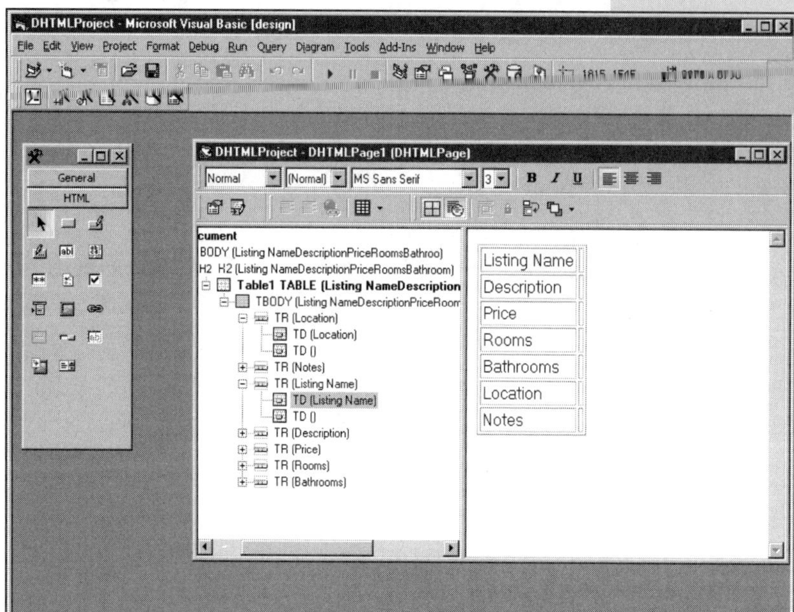

Figure 18.8 The listings page is shown here with its table added and the labels filled in.

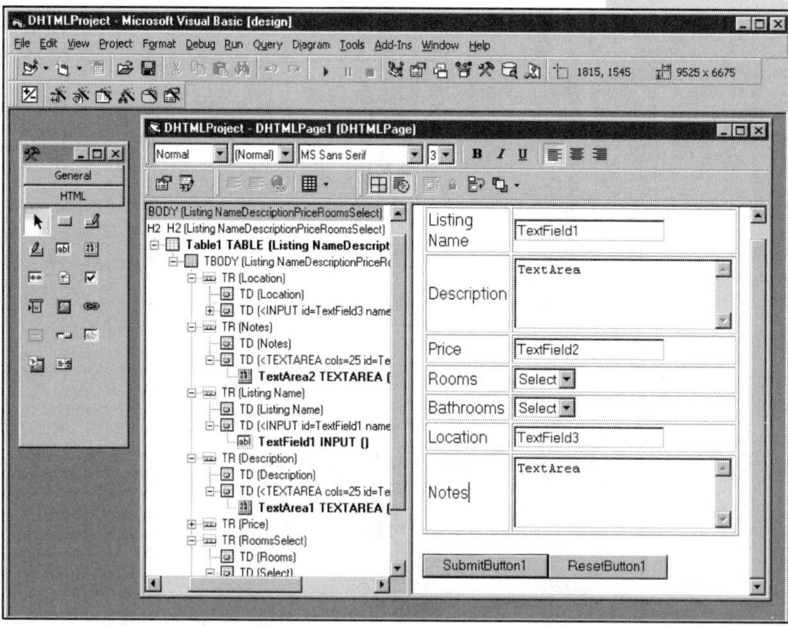

Figure 18.9 This figure shows the listings page with all the necessary data entry fields added.

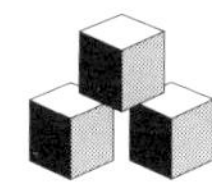

Notice that in the DHTML editor the text field's data is stored in the `Value` property. In normal Visual Basic fields, the data is stored in the `Text` property.

The next items to deal with are the drop-down lists for the Rooms and Bathrooms fields. Follow these steps to alter the properties for these objects:

1. Select the number of rooms list box in the designer and right-click.
2. Select `Properties` from the pop-up menu. This brings up the Property Pages dialog for the selected item (see Figure 18.10).
3. This dialog allows you to add and remove items from the selected list box. Remove the currently entered row and then add rows for the number of rooms. Figure 18.11 shows the dialog with all the necessary options specified.
4. Repeat these steps for the number of bathrooms list box.

After adding all the fields and changing their properties, you're ready to preview your project in the browser. To preview your page, simply select Run, Start from the Visual Basic menu. The first time you do this, Visual Basic prompts you with the Project Properties dialog (see Figure 18.12). This dialog allows you to specify the page to run. Select your Web page and press OK. Visual Basic compiles your application and presents it in your default browser. Figure 18.13 shows the listings page presented in Internet Explorer.

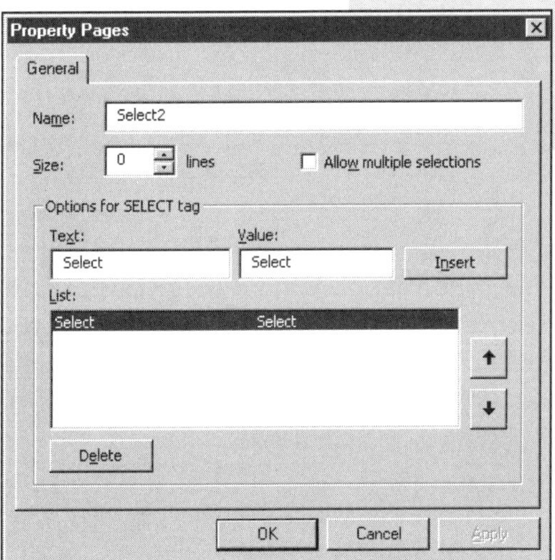

Figure 18.10
This figure shows the Property Pages dialog for a list box item.

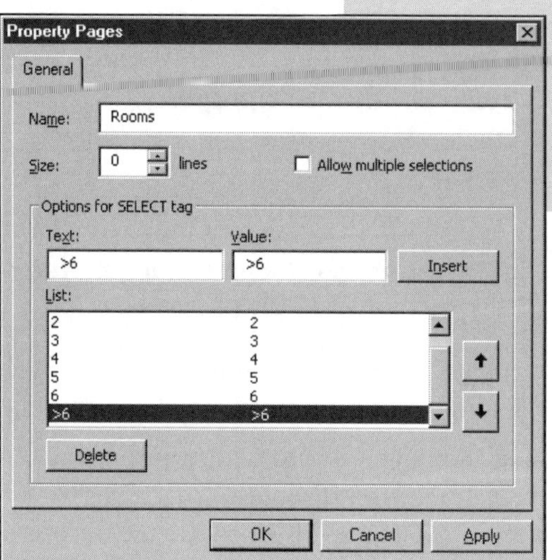

Figure 18.11
This figure shows the completed Property Pages dialog for the number of bedrooms list box.

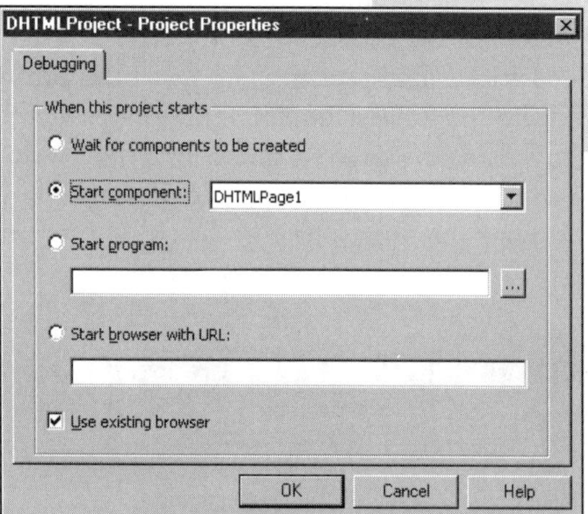

Figure 18.12
This figure shows the VB Project Properties dialog.

After previewing your Web page, it's a good time to save your project. Select File, Save Project from the Visual Basic menu to save your project. Now that you have created the listings page, you can move on to the next item in the set of requirements—the customer information request form. The requirements for this form are shown in Table 18-2.

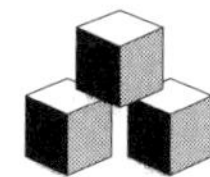

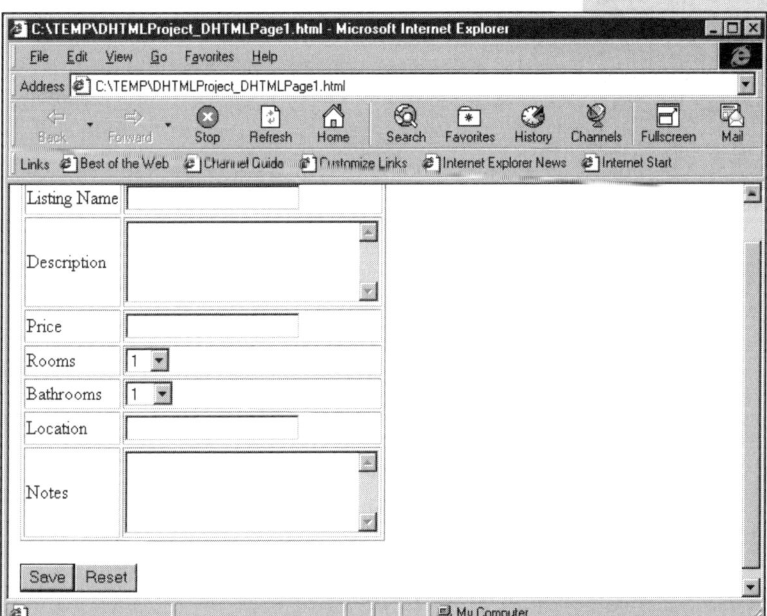

Figure 18.13 The listings prototype form is shown here in Internet Explorer.

Table 18-2 Customer Information Request Form

Item	Notes
Project	Real Estate Companion
Name of Analyst	Rod Paddock
Date Created	12/31/98
Task Description	Customer information request form
Task Inputs	Information about a customer, including name, address, phone number, e-mail address, and which information they've requested.
Task Outputs	Save information to customer request database.
Source of Information	Listings database and realtors.
Notes	

To create this form, you simply need to add another Dynamic HTML page to your project. Do this by selecting Project, Add DHTML Page from the Visual Basic menu. Once you do this, a dialog asks whether you want to add this file as part of the VB project or as an external file. Choosing the external file option allows you to edit the document with external editors like Notepad or Allaire's Homesite. For now, leave the dialog in its default state and press OK. This opens your new DHTML page in the DHTML Designer. Now you simply go through the same steps taken in creating the listings page. Figures 18.14 and 18.15 show the completed customer information request form in the designer and in Internet Explorer, respectively.

Note

To preview your page, you need to go to the dialog accessed by selecting Project, DHTMLProject Properties. Select the Debugging tab and specify your new HTML page component dialog.

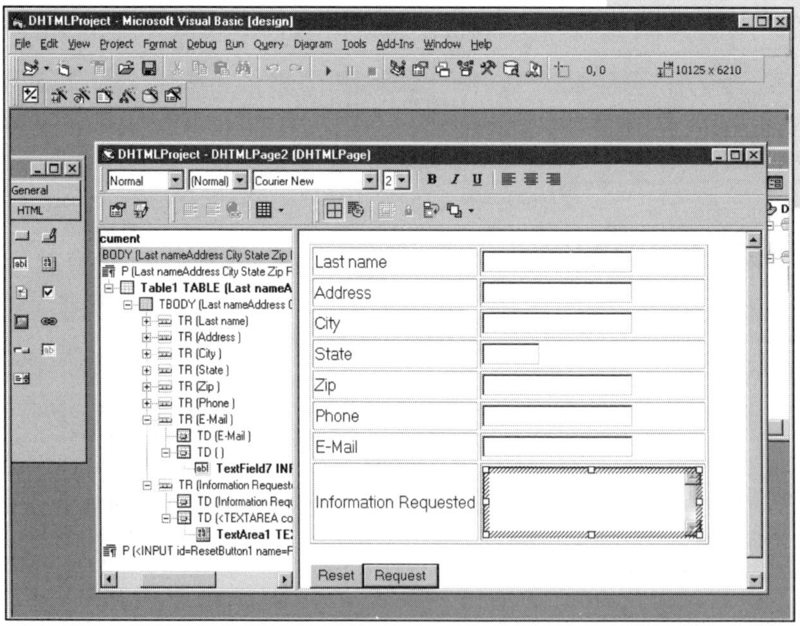

Figure 18.14 This is the customer information request form in the DHTML Designer.

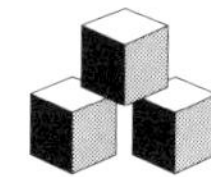

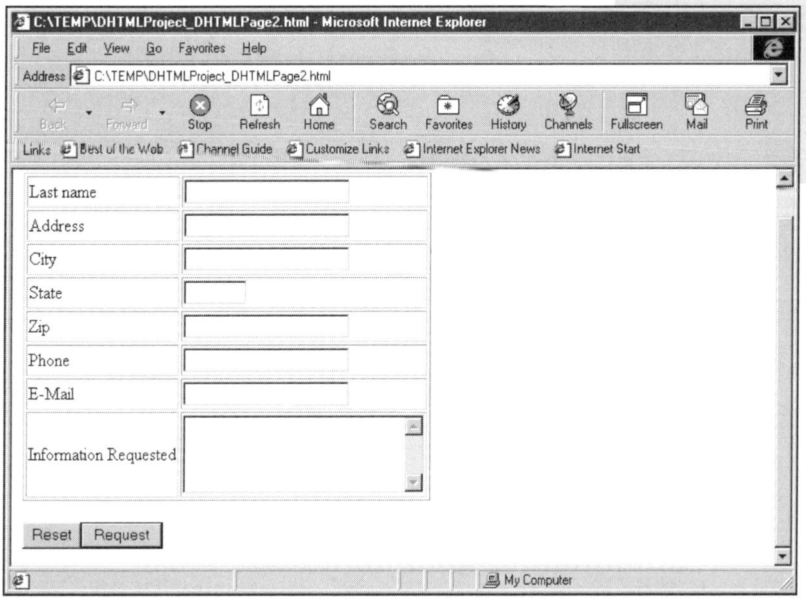

Figure 18.15 This is the same form viewed in Internet Explorer.

To create the query listings page, use the same process as the last two examples. After creating all your Web pages, you can move on to creating the mortgage calculator component. The requirements for the mortgage calculator are shown in Table 18-3.

Table 18-3 Mortgage Calculator Component

Item	Notes
Project	Real Estate Companion
Name of Analyst	Rod Paddock
Date Created	12/31/98
Task Description	Mortgage calculator component
Task Inputs	Amount borrowed, interest rate, period of time for repayment
Task Outputs	Payment amount
Source of Information	Web page users
Notes	This will be an ActiveX control.

To create a Web project calculator, you need to create a new Visual Basic project. Select File, New from the Visual Basic menu. Select ActiveX Control from the New Project dialog and press OK (see Figure 18.16).

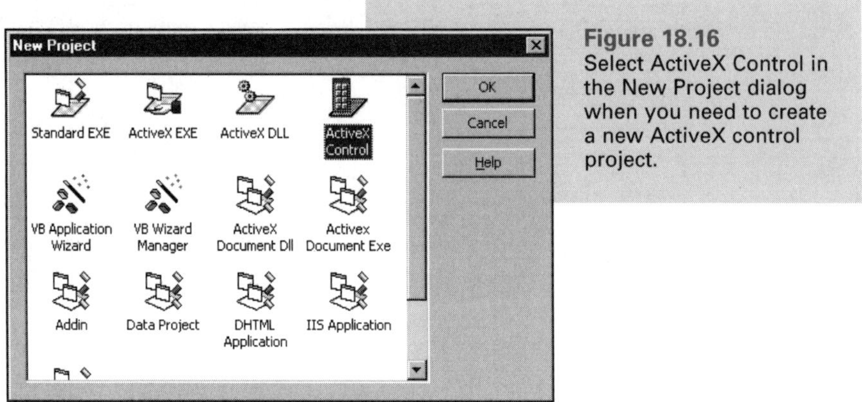

Figure 18.16
Select ActiveX Control in the New Project dialog when you need to create a new ActiveX control project.

Visual Basic opens the project with the control designer active. The first items to add are the fields for the amount to borrow, interest rate, and period of time. Each of these fields consists of a label and a text field object, so add three labels to your form. Change their respective `Caption` properties to **Amount**, **Rate**, and **Periods**. Next, add three text boxes. Change all of their `Text` properties to **0** and change their respective `Name` properties to **txtAmount**, **txtRate**, and **txtPeriods**. Your form now should look like the one shown in Figure 18.17.

The next step is to add buttons for the calculator. Add a command button and change its `Caption` to **1**. Cut and copy this button nine times. When VB asks if you want to create a command array, answer Yes. Align the ten buttons as you would on a calculator or telephone. Change the captions of the new buttons, respectively, to **2**, **3**, **4**, **5**, **6**, **7**, **8**, **9**, and **0**. Your calculator now should look like Figure 18.18.

Now that you've completed your prototype, select Run, Start from the Visual Basic menu. Press OK when VB activates the Project Properties dialog. This opens your control in the default browser specified on your machine. Figure 18.19 shows your new control in a Web page.

You might wonder about the code behind the control. Well, that's what RAD is about—all you should be spending time on is building the visual aspects of your application. Leave the coding until the construction phase.

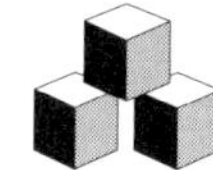

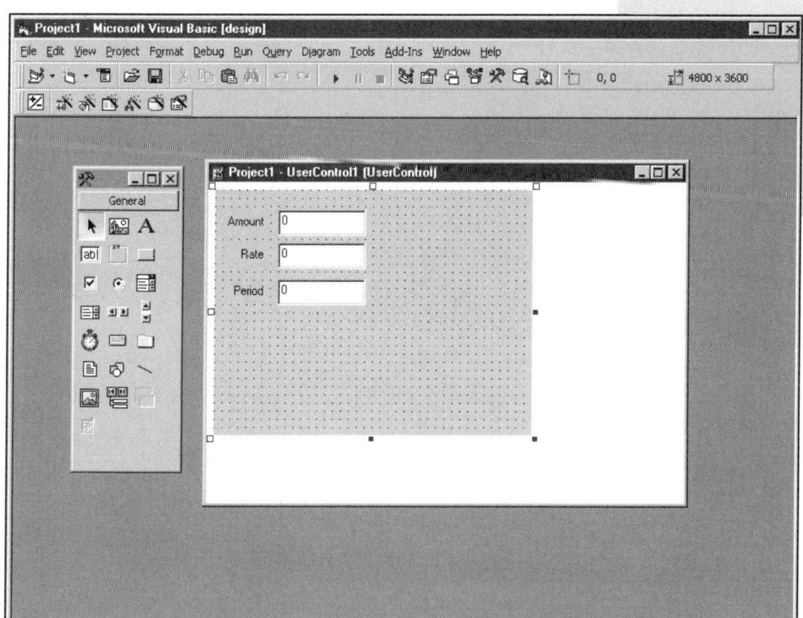

Figure 18.17 This is the preliminary design for the mortgage calculator.

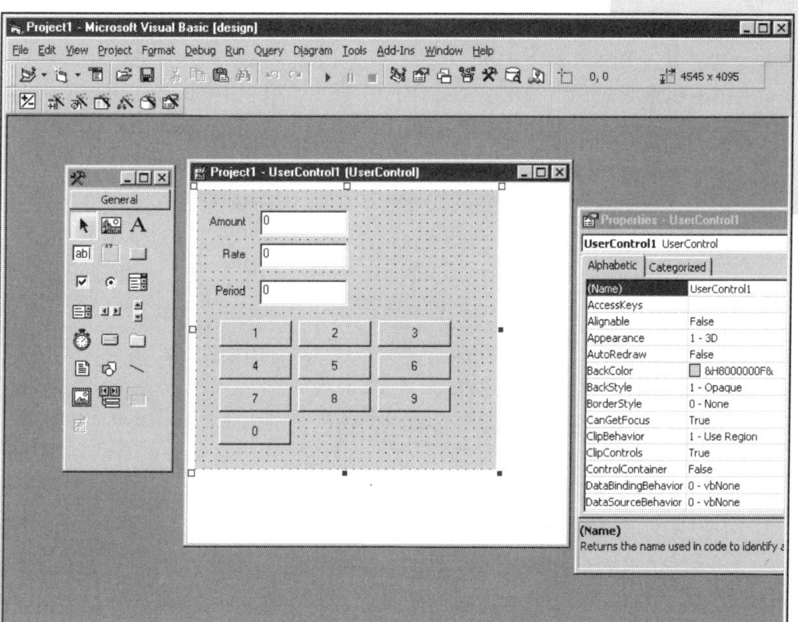

Figure 18.18 This is the next-step preliminary design for the mortgage calculator.

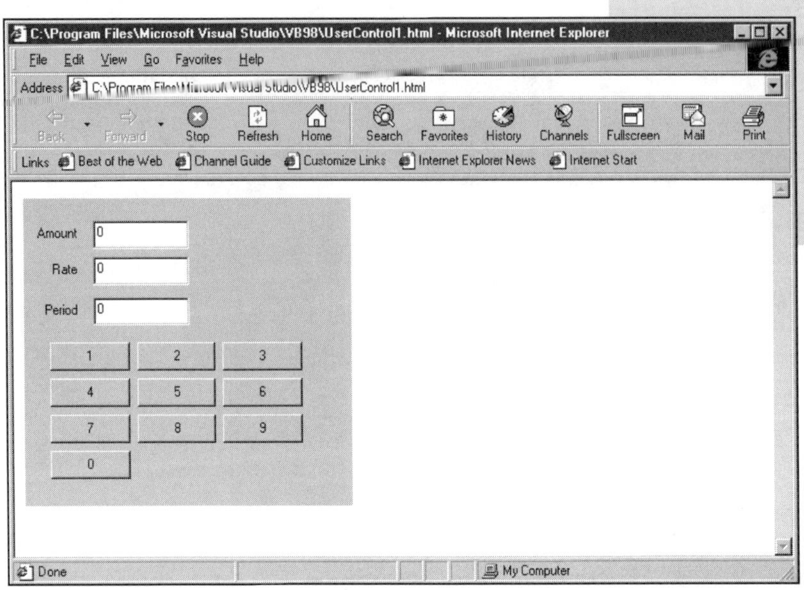

Figure 18.19 This figure shows your new ActiveX mortgage calculator hosted in a browser.

Summary

As this chapter has proven, Visual Basic provides some very nice tools for designing your applications using the RAD method. Once you have constructed all of your pages using this method, you can demonstrate them for your users and make changes to them without incurring too great a cost. Once the design has been approved, you can go to the construction phase, which happens in the next chapter.

Building the Real Estate Companion

In Chapter 18, "Designing the Real Estate Companion," you completed the design for your set of real estate management Web pages and components. In this chapter you will take the prototypes you built, apply the system requirements generated in Chapter 16, and build the remaining components of your application. This chapter shows you the following:

- How to build Dynamic HTML applications
- How to build ActiveX controls
- How to deploy ActiveX controls
- How to use ActiveX Data Objects (ADO) to access databases

Completing the Listings Page

The first item to be completed is the listings page. The listings page will be used to add and edit real estate listings. Figure 19.1 shows the prototype listings page generated in Chapter 18.

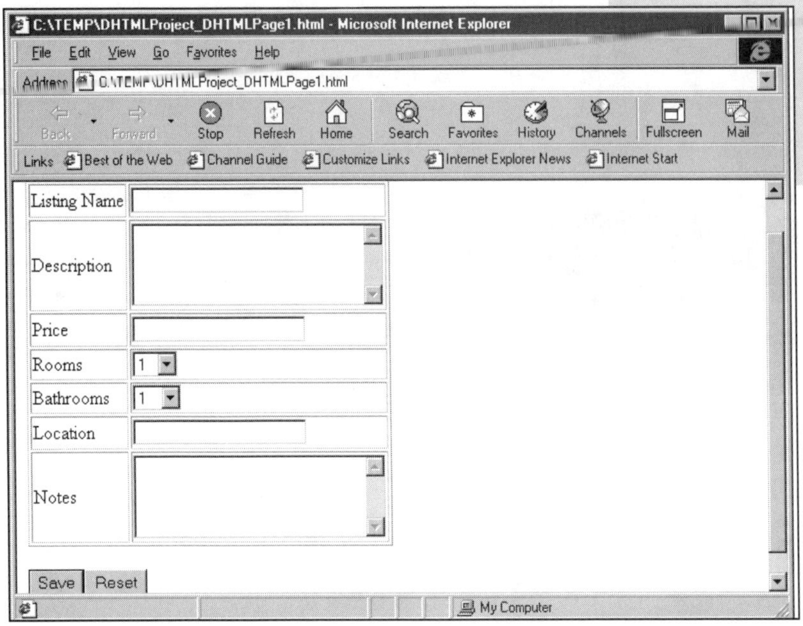

Figure 19.1 This prototype of the listings page was developed in Chapter 18.

At this point, the listings Web page is simply a data entry form that allows users to key in information about a listing. The form actually performs no action. In Chapter 2, "An Introduction to HTML," you learned that the action a data entry form performs can be found in its `<FORM>` tag. Until now no `<FORM>` tag has been specified for the listings form, so your first step is to add this tag to your listings page. Unfortunately there is no immediate way to do this within the Visual Basic IDE—you need to open your Web page in an external editor. To add the necessary tag, perform the following actions:

1. Open the dynamic HTML prototype application you generated in Chapter 18.
2. Press the DHTML Page Designer Properties icon on the Page Designer toolbar (see Figure 19.2).
3. You are presented with the Page Properties dialog. By default, pages are stored as part of your Visual Basic project. Place a check next to the Save HTML in an external file option and type a name for your HTML file (see Figure 19.3).
4. Once you have saved your file as an external HTML file, you're ready to add the `<FORM>` tag. Press the Launch Editor button (next to the Page Designer Properties button) on the HTML Designer toolbar and your default editor opens with your HTML file displayed.

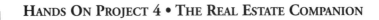

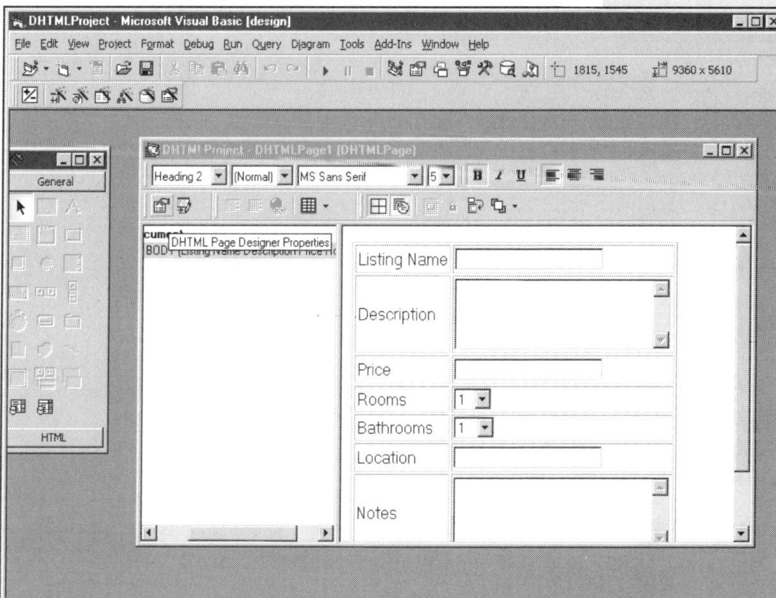

Figure 19.2
This shows the Visual Basic DHTML designer with the Designer Properties toolbar item highlighted.

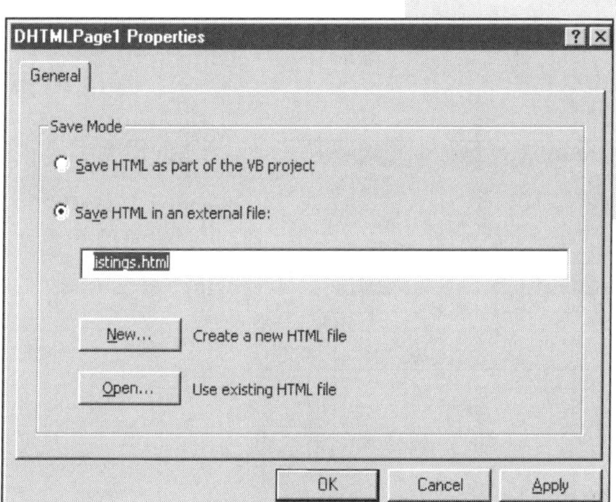

Figure 19.3
This figure shows the Page Properties dialog with options set to save the file as an external HTML file.

5. Add the following line to your code before the <TABLE> tag:

```
<FORM ACTION="SAVELISTING.ASP" METHOD="POST">
```

6. You also need to add a terminating tag. Add the following line immediately after the </TABLE> tag:

```
</FORM>
```

Your code now should look like the following:

```
<HTML>
<BODY>
<H2>
<FORM ACTION="SAVELISTING.ASP" METHOD="POST">
<TABLE border=1 id=Table1 name = Table1>

<!-Code removed to conserve space ->

</TABLE>
</FORM>
</H2>
<H2>
<INPUT id=SubmitButton1 name=SubmitButton1 type=submit value=Save>
<INPUT id=ResetButton1 name=ResetButton1 type=reset value=Reset></H2>
</BODY>
</HTML>
```

7. Save your changes and return to the designer. Notice that the designer now has a `<FORM>` tag in its document tree (see Figure 19.4).

Now that you have added your `<FORM>` tag, you can create the `SAVELISTING.ASP` file. This file will use a combination of Active Server Pages (ASP) and ActiveX Data Objects (ADO) to save your data to a file.

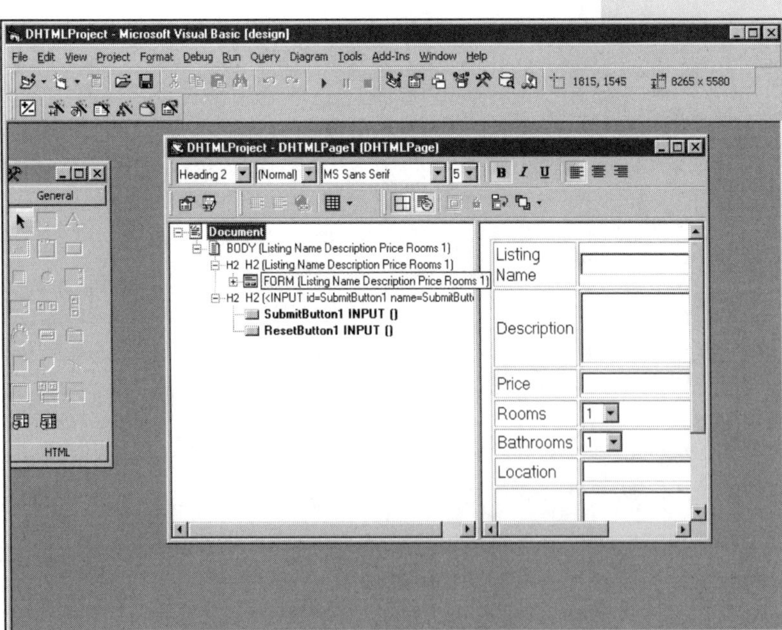

Figure 19.4
This figure shows DHTML designer with the addition of the `<FORM>` tag.

For a discussion of ASP, see Chapter 11, "Building the VBResearcher," or Chapter 15, "Building the CustomerTracker." A discussion of ADO is presented in the next section.

Introduction to ActiveX Data Objects (ADO)

There are numerous methods of querying data using Visual Basic, including DAO, RDO, ODBCDirect, and others. The newest member of this family is ADO. ADO is the newest data access method provided by Microsoft. ActiveX Data Objects is a series of six Active servers that both application and Web developers use to access data in databases. Figure 19.5 shows the object model for ADO.

As you can see, ADO is a collection of objects that you use to access databases. Although Figure 19.5 shows it as a hierarchy, this is misleading. You can create most of the objects on the fly and not through a hierarchy. The objects contained in ADO are:

- **Connection**—Creates connections to databases.
- **Recordset**—An object that represents a table in memory. It can contain the contents of a query or be generated and populated on the fly. The data found in recordsets can be updatable.
- **Fields**—A collection of column information attached to a Recordset object. Recordsets can have zero or more fields.
- **Command**—Used to send commands to a database. Command objects return their results as a Recordset object.
- **Parameters**—Used in conjunction with command objects. Used to hand parameters to stored procedures or parameterized queries.
- **Errors**—Collection of error information. Populated when database errors occur. The Errors collection is attached to a Connection object.

Creating a Connection

The first step in accessing data with ADO is to create a Connection object. Creating a Connection object is a three-step process:

1. Create an ODBC System Data Source using the Microsoft Access driver. This ODBC data source should be named `VB_REAL_ESTATE` and should be connected to your real estate database.

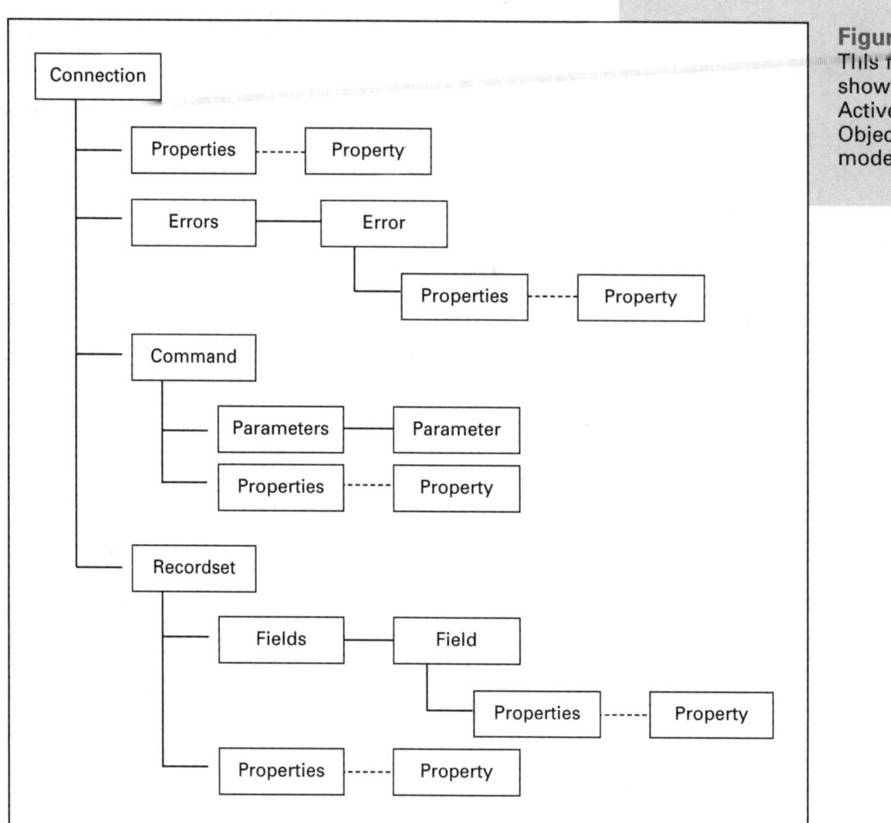

Figure 19.5 This figure shows the ActiveX Data Objects (ADO) model.

2. Instantiate a Connection object with `Server.CreateObject`.
3. Open the connection with the connection object's `Open` method.

The following code demonstrates connecting to the real estate database using the `VB_REAL_ESTATE` data system data source:

```
<%
Set oConn = Server.CreateObject("ADODB.Connection")
oConn.Open "VB_REAL_ESTATE","",""
%>
```

ANALYSIS

This code performs two actions. The first is the creation of an ADO Connection object. The second is opening that connection with the `Open` method, which has three parameters. The first is the `ODBC System DSN` (or, optionally, a connection string) that specifies which database to open. The second and third parameters are a user name and password respectively. These two parameters are used by databases that have security features built into their architecture.

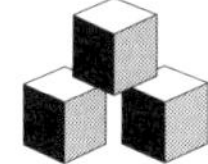

Creating Recordset Objects

After creating a connection, you can begin querying data from the database using a recordset object. Creating a recordset object is a two-step process:

1. Instantiate a recordset with `Server.CreateObject`.
2. Open the recordset with the object's `Open` method.

The following code demonstrates creating and opening a recordset object:

```
<%
Set oConn = Server.CreateObject("ADODB.Connection")
oConn.Open "VB_REAL_ESTATE","",""

Set oList = Server.CreateObject("ADODB.Recordset")
oList.Open "Select * from listings", oConn
%>
```

This code performs two actions. The first is the creation of an ADO recordset object. The second is opening that recordset with the `Open` method, which has the following four parameters:

- A SQL command to be executed on the server (Required)
- A Connection object (Required)
- The type of cursor to generate—by default, cursors are forward-only (Optional)
- Type of locking to use—by default, cursors are opened as read-only (Optional)

As you can see from the defaults specified, the cursors opened are forward-only and read-only. These are the types of cursors that are available:

Value	Constant	Description
0	`AdOpenForwardOnly` (default)	Opens a forward-only, static cursor which means you cannot use `MoveFirst`, `MovePrevious`, or `MoveLast`.
1	`AdOpenKeyset`	Opens a *keyset cursor*, an updatable recordset whose membership is fixed (you don't see rows added by other users, but you do see changes to existing rows).
2	`AdOpenDynamic`	Opens a dynamic cursor (if supported), an updatable recordset whose membership changes (you do see rows added by other users, and you do see changes to existing rows).
3	`AdOpenStatic`	Opens a static cursor, an updatable recordset whose membership is fixed and static (you don't see rows added by other users, and you don't see changes to existing rows).

These are the styles of locking that are available:

Value	Constant	Description
1	AdLockReadOnly (default)	Data is read-only
2	AdLockPessimistic	Pessimistic locking (if supported)
3	AdLockOptimistic	Optimistic locking
4	adLockBatchOptimistic	Optimistic locking with batch updates (if supported)

Using Recordset Data

Once you have created a recordset object, you can begin processing the data returned with that recordset. The following code demonstrates querying the listings table and displaying its contents to the screen in a table format:

```
<HTML>
<BODY>

<%
Set oConn = Server.CreateObject("ADODB.Connection")
oConn.Open "VB_REAL_ESTATE","",""

Set oList = Server.CreateObject("ADODB.Recordset")
oList.Open "Select * from listings", oConn
%>

<TABLE Border="2">
<TR><TH>Description</TH><TH>Price</TH></TR>
<%
Do While not oList.Eof
%>
<TR><TD><%=oList("Listing_description")%></TD><TD><%=oList("price")%></TD></TR>
<%
    oList.MoveNext
Loop
%>

</TABLE>
</BODY>
</HTML>
```

The results of this code are shown in Figure 19.6.

Now that you understand how to connect to a database and query data from a table, you can move on to updating the data.

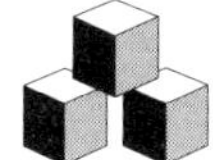

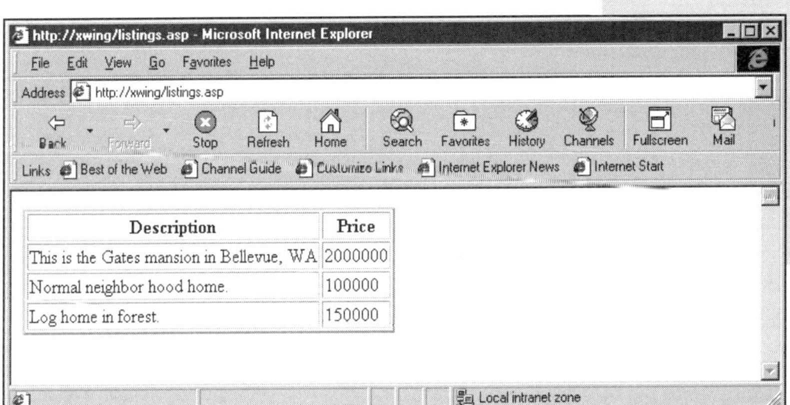

Figure 19.6 This figure shows the results of querying the listings table and displaying the results in an HTML table.

Adding Listing Data

Adding data to a database table begins the same way as a query. You first create a connection, then create a recordset. That's where it becomes different. By default, recordsets are opened in read-only and forward-only status. This prevents you from adding data to the recordset. To open a recordset object in an updatable mode, you simply pass two extra parameters to the recordset object when it is opened. A discussion of these parameters was presented earlier in this chapter. The following code opens a recordset in read/write mode:

```
<%
Set oConn = Server.CreateObject("ADODB.Connection")
oConn.Open "VB_REAL_ESTATE","",""

Set oList = Server.CreateObject("ADODB.Recordset")
oList.Open "Select * from listings", oConn,3,3
%>
```

The recordset in this code is opened with the actual values 3 and 3. For readability, it would be a good idea to use constants (defined in an include file) instead of the literal values.

Now that you understand how to open a recordset in read/write mode, you can begin saving the listing information to the database. To add a record to a recordset object, use the `AddNew` method. This method instructs the recordset object that a new record is about to be added. The next step is to update the field objects for the recordset object with the data from your data entry form. After doing this, you need to call the update method of the recordset object—

this commits the new record to the database. The following code shows how to add data to a database using ADO:

```
<HTML>
<BODY>

<%
Set oConn = Server.CreateObject("ADODB.Connection")
oConn.Open "VB_REAL_ESTATE","",""

Set oList = Server.CreateObject("ADODB.Recordset")
oList.Open "Select * from listings", oConn,3,3

'Add the new record
oList.AddNew

'Update the fields
oList("listing_name") = Request.Form("listing_name")
oList("listing_description") = Request.Form("listing_description")
oList("price") = Request.Form("price")
oList("rooms") = Request.Form("rooms")
oList("bathrooms") = Request.Form("bathrooms")
oList("listing_notes") = Request.Form("listing_notes")

'Insert the record
oList.Update
%>

<H1>Listing Added</H1>

</BODY>
</HTML>
```

Updating Listing Information

After writing the add code, you can set your sights on writing the update code. To perform updates to the listings database, you need to rework a few of the examples you worked on above. To complete an update example, perform the following steps:

1. Modify the `LISTINGS.ASP` page to create hyperlinks to a listing editor form. The listing editor form will query a single record based on a parameter passed in via the hyperlink. This information then will be loaded into the listing editor form. The following code shows the changes:

   ```
   <HTML>
   <BODY>
   ```

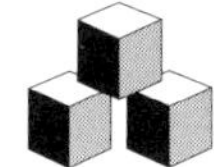


```
<%
Set oConn = Server.CreateObject("ADODB.Connection")
oConn.Open "VB_REAL_ESTATE","",""

Set oList = Server.CreateObject("ADODB.Recordset")
oList.Open "Select * from listings", oConn
%>

<TABLE Border="2">
<TR><TH>Description</TH><TH>Price</TH></TR>
<%
Do While not oList.Eof
%>
<TR><TD>
<A HREF="update_listing.asp?listing_id=<%=oList("listing_id")%>
  <%=oList("Listing_description")%></A>
</TD><TD><%=oList("price")%></TD></TR>
<%
  oList.MoveNext
Loop
%>

</TABLE>

</BODY>
</HTML>
```

2. Copy the `LISTINGS.HTM` file to a file named `UPDATE_LISTING.ASP`. This form will query a record from the listings database and display its contents in each of the respective editing fields. You need to change the `<FORM>` tag's `ACTION` attribute to `record_update_listing.asp`. The following code demonstrates how to create your listing update form:

```
<HTML>
<%
Set oConn = Server.CreateObject("ADODB.Connection")
oConn.Open "VB_REAL_ESTATE","",""

' Select a single record
Set oList = Server.CreateObject("ADODB.Recordset")
oList.Open "Select * from listings where listing_id = "
➥& Request.QueryString("listing_id"), oConn
%>
<BODY>
<H2>
<FORM ACTION="record_update_listing.asp?listing_id=<%=Request.QueryString
➥("listing_id")%>" METHOD="post">
<TABLE border=1 id=Table1 name = Table1>
```

```
    <TR>
        <TD>Listing Name
        <TD>
            <INPUT id=TextField1 name=listing_name Value
➥="<%=oList("listing_name")%>" >
    <TR>
        <TD>Description
        <TD><TEXTAREA cols=25 id=TextArea1 name=listing_description
➥rows=4>
            <%=oList("listing_description")%>
            </TEXTAREA>
    <TR>
        <TD>Price
        <TD>
            <INPUT id=TextField2 name=price
➥Value="<%=oList("price")%>">
    <TR>
        <TD>Rooms
        <TD><SELECT id=Select1 name=Rooms  Value="<%=oList("rooms")%>">
                    <OPTION selected value=1>1
                    <OPTION value=2>2
                    <OPTION value=3>3
                    <OPTION value=4>4
                    <OPTION value=5>5
                    <OPTION value=6>6
                    <OPTION value=&gt;6>&gt;6</SELECT>

    <TR>
        <TD>Bathrooms
        <TD><SELECT id=Select2 name=BathRooms
➥Value="<%=oList("bathrooms")%>">
                    <OPTION selected value=1>1
                    <OPTION value=1.5>1.5
                    <OPTION value=2>2
                    <OPTION value=2.5>2.5
                    <OPTION value=3>3
                    <OPTION value=&gt;3>&gt;3
                    <OPTION value=&gt;6>&gt;6</SELECT>

    <TR>
        <TD>Location</TD>
        <TD>
            <INPUT id=TextField3 name=location
➥Value="<%=oList("location")%>"></TD></TR>
    <TR>
        <TD>Notes</TD>
        <TD><TEXTAREA cols=25 id=TextArea2 name=listing_notes rows=4>
            <%=oList("listing_notes")%>
            </TEXTAREA></TD></TR>
```

```
</TABLE>

</H2>
<H2><INPUT id=SubmitButton1 name=SubmitButton1 type=submit value=Save>
<INPUT id=ResetButton1 name=ResetButton1 type=reset value=Reset></H2>
</FORM>
</BODY>
</HTML>
```

Finally, you need to create a page to perform the update to the database. Using the `SAVELISTING.ASP` file as your starting point, follow these steps:

1. Copy that file into `RECORD_CUSTOMER_UPDATE.ASP`.
2. Copy the ADO connection code from the `LISTING_UPDATE.ASP` file.
3. Add the code to the `oList.Open` line to make the listing updatable.
4. Remove the `oList.AddNew` command.
5. Change the text between the `<H1>` and `</H1>` tags to show the record as being updated.
6. The code for this operation is shown below:

```
<HTML>
<BODY>

<%
Set oConn = Server.CreateObject("ADODB.Connection")
oConn.Open "VB_REAL_ESTATE","",""

' Select a single record
Set oList = Server.CreateObject("ADODB.Recordset")
oList.Open "Select * from listings where listing_id = "
➥& Request.QueryString("listing_id"), oConn,3,3

'Update the fields
oList("listing_name") = Request.Form("listing_name")
oList("listing_description") = Request.Form("listing_description")
oList("price") = Request.Form("price")
oList("rooms") = Request.Form("rooms")
oList("bathrooms") = Request.Form("bathrooms")
oList("listing_notes") = Request.Form("listing_notes")

'Insert the record
oList.Update
%>

<H1>Listing Updated</H1>

</BODY>
</HTML>
```

As you can see, the process of adding and updating data with ADO is not a difficult one. You now can take the techniques you learned here and move them into creating the customer request form and the query form.

Adding Validation to the Listing Form

Now that you've created the basic logic for the listings form, you need to add validation code to that form. The interesting thing about the HTML forms you have been creating is that they are all Dynamic HTML forms. Dynamic HTML forms allow you to add constructs to a form that simply are not available in HTML. With Dynamic HTML, you can alter the contents of screen objects on the fly, validate fields interactively, and also have extensive control of the overall user experience on your Web pages.

The Dynamic HTML forms you are creating with Visual Basic have one other special quality about them. They allow you to use the full power of the VB language to perform your interactive behaviors. This capability does come with a price, though—these pages only work in Internet Explorer. For the purposes of the Real Estate Companion, just assume that the real estate company has standardized on Internet Explorer.

Now begin adding validation code to your forms. The first item you should add is a validation to make sure the price entered for a property is greater than or equal to zero. To add this validation, perform the following steps:

1. Double-click the price field text box to bring up the DHTML designer Code window.
2. Select the `onBlur` event from the Procedure/Event list box (see Figure 19.7).
3. Add the following code to the `TextField2_onBlur` event:

```
Private Sub TextField2_onBlur()
  If CLng(TextField2.Value) < 0 Then
    TextField2.Style.backgroundColor = "Red"
    TextField2.focus
  Else
    TextField2.Style.backgroundColor = "White"
  End If
End Sub
```

4. Run your form by selecting Run, Start from the VB menu.

This code changes the price field to red if an invalid amount is entered. If a valid amount is entered, the field is changed to white.

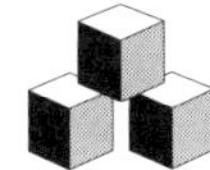

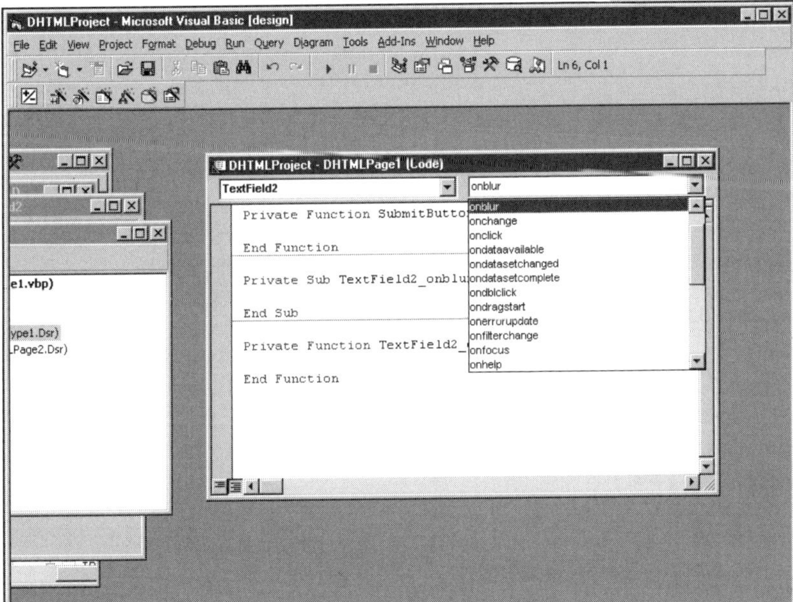

Figure 19.7
The DHTML designer Code window here has the `onBlur` event selected.

The next validation to perform is a form-level validation. This validation will check to make sure the user has keyed in a name and description for the listing being entered. This code goes in the `onClick` event of the submit button. To add this validation, do the following:

1. Double-click the submit button to open the DHTML designer Code window on the `onClick` event of the submit button.
2. Add the following code for this event:

```
Private Function SubmitButton1_onClick() As Boolean
    Dim lError As Boolean
    lError = False

    'Validate the notes field
    If Len(Trim(TextField1.Value)) = 0 Then
        TextField1.Style.backgroundColor = "Red"
        lError = True
    Else
        TextField1.Style.backgroundColor = "White"
    End If

    'Validate the description field
    If Len(Trim(TextArea1.Value)) = 0 Then
        TextArea1.Style.backgroundColor = "Red"
        lError = True
```

```
        Else
            TextArea1.Style.backgroundColor = "White"
        End If

        'Cancel the event
        If lError = True Then
            SubmitButton1_onClick = False
        End If
    End Function
```

3. Run your form by selecting Run, Start from the VB menu.

As you can see from even these simple examples, you can create some very nice interactive Web pages for your users. The best part is that the code can all be written in VB.

Finishing the Mortgage Calculator

In Chapter 18, you created the basic shell for your mortgage calculator. In this section, you will complete the code for the control. The first step to finishing this control is to open the project in Visual Basic. Once you have opened the project, you're ready to add the final code to your form. To complete the control, do the following:

1. Change the `Text` properties of `txtRate`, `txtPeriods`, and `txtAmount` to **10.0**, **30**, and **100000**, respectively. This prevents the `PMT` function from blowing up.
2. Add a text box to your form. Change its `Invisible` property to **False**. Change its `Name` property to **txtStorage**. Change its `Text` property to **txtAmount**.
3. In the `gotFocus` events of the `txtRate`, `txtPeriods`, and `txtAmount` controls, add the following code:

```
Private Sub txtRate_gotFocus()
    txtStorage.Text = "txtRate"
End Sub

Private Sub txtPeriods_gotFocus()
    txtStorage.Text = "txtPeriods"
End Sub

Private Sub txtAmount_GotFocus()
    txtStorage.Text = "txtAmount"
End Sub
```

4. The next step is to add code to tell the ten command buttons which field

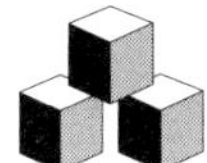

to update and what to add to the field when a button is clicked. Add the following code to the command button control array's `Click` event:

```
Private Sub Command1_Click(Index As Integer)
    Dim strAddValue As String

    'Generate value to add by index of control
    strAddValue = Trim(Str(Index))

    UserControl.Controls(txtStorage.Text).Text =
➥UserControl.Controls(txtStorage.Text).Text & strAddValue

End Sub
```

The above code adds digits to the currently selected text box control. Now you can add code to calculate the actual mortgage values.

5. Add the following code to each of the text box fields' `Change` events:

```
If IsNumeric(txtAmount) And IsNumeric(txtRate) And IsNumeric
➥(txtPeriods) Then
    intPayment = Pmt(CLng(txtRate.Text / 12 / 100), _
        CInt(txtPeriods.Text * 12), CLng(txtAmount.Text)) * -1
    txtPayment.Text = Format(intPayment, "###,###,###.##")
End If
```

6. Select Run, Start from the VB menu. This runs your control in a browser. Figure 19.8 shows the finished calculator.

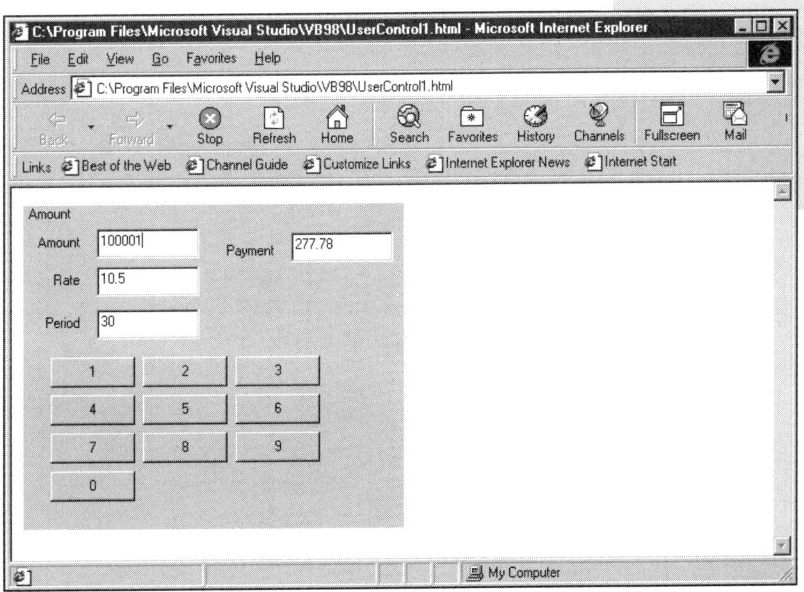

Figure 19.8
This figure shows the new ActiveX control hosted in Internet Explorer.

7. After testing your control, save your changes and select File, Make `Mortgage.OCX` from the VB menu. This creates your distributable ActiveX control.

After completing the code for your ActiveX control, you need to worry about deploying the control to your Web server. The next section discusses deploying your ActiveX controls.

Deploying ActiveX Controls to the Web

The final step to perform in this project is that of deploying your ActiveX controls. Visual Studio 6.0 now includes a tool named the Package and Deployment Wizard. The Package and Deployment Wizard is used to create setup and install programs for your VB and other projects. To distribute your ActiveX control, you need to run this wizard.

To deploy your ActiveX control to the Web, perform the following steps:

1. Run the Package and Deployment Wizard from the Visual Studio Tools menu. You are prompted with a dialog similar to the one shown in Figure 19.9.
2. The next step is to select your Visual Basic project using the Browse button. This brings up a File Open dialog. Locate your VB project with this dialog.

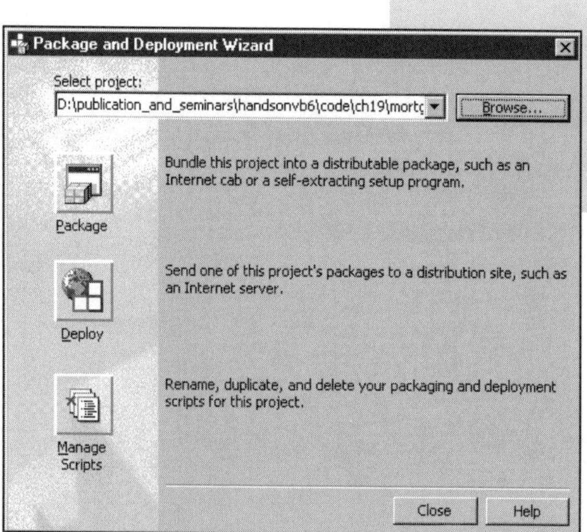

Figure 19.9 This figure shows the main screen of the Package and Deployment Wizard.

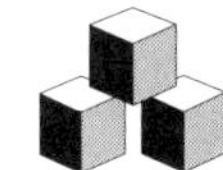

3. Next, you need to package the project. Press the Package button. The wizard instructs you that it needs to find the executable for your mortgage calculator. Select the Compile button to build a fresh copy.
4. After building a fresh copy of your OCX file, the wizard asks you to specify the package type (see Figure 19.10). Select `Internet Package`.

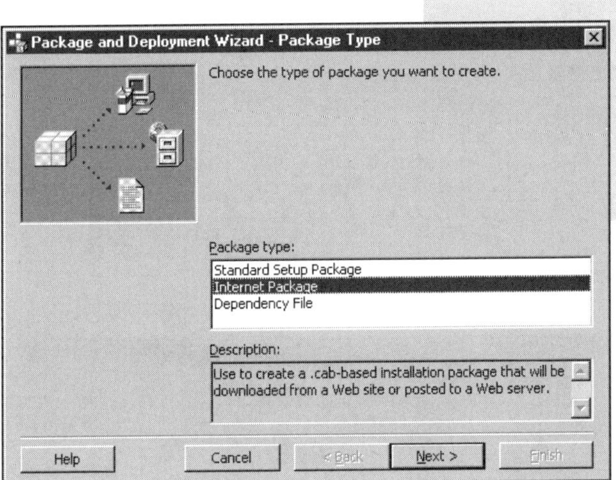

Figure 19.10
This figure shows the Package Type phase of the Package and Deployment Wizard.

5. The wizard then prompts you for a path specifying where you want to put the package. Leave the default value.
6. The next step asks you to specify the files to include. Leave this dialog as is.
7. The next dialog (see Figure 19.11) allows you to specify from where the Web page should retrieve the runtime files. Leave this dialog as is. If you want to distribute the VB runtime files from your site, you can change the settings for that file to address your own Web site.
8. In the next step you are prompted about where the control is safe for scripting. Leave this page as is.
9. You have reached the finish line (see Figure 19.12)! Give your script file a name and press Finish to build your distribution package.
10. The next step is to deploy your control. Press the Deploy button on the wizard screen.
11. The wizard asks you for the script to use. Select the script name you specified in step 9.

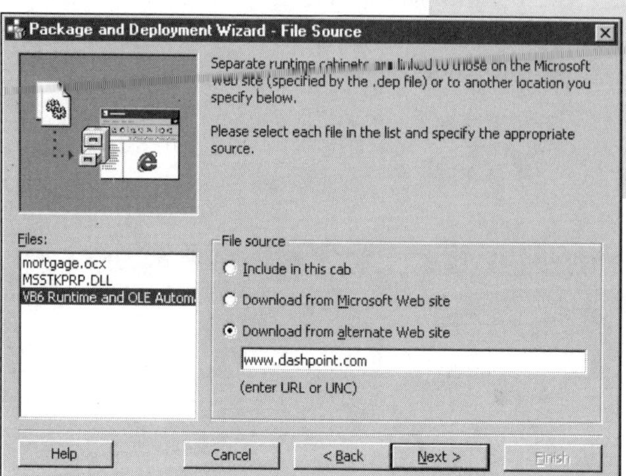

Figure 19.11 This is the File Source step of the Package and Deployment Wizard.

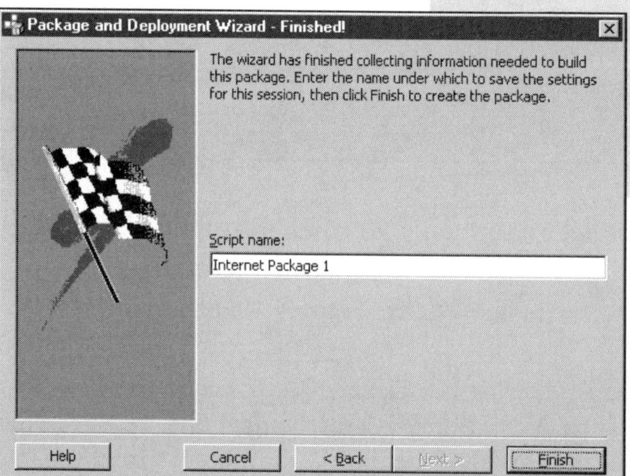

Figure 19.12 This is the Finished screen for the Package and Deployment Wizard.

12. The next step asks whether you want to publish the package to the Web or to a folder. Select the Web option.
13. The next two steps ask you to specify which files to publish. Leave the default options on these screens.
14. After you specify the files to publish, a dialog prompts you for the URL of the Web site you wish to publish to (see Figure 19.13). Enter the name of your Web site in the Destination URL text box.

Note

To publish data to a Web site, you need to install the server-side Visual Studio components. If you do not install these components, the Web deployment wizard will not work. You also need to create a directory with Write privilege turned on. Consult your Web server administrator for help dealing with these issues.

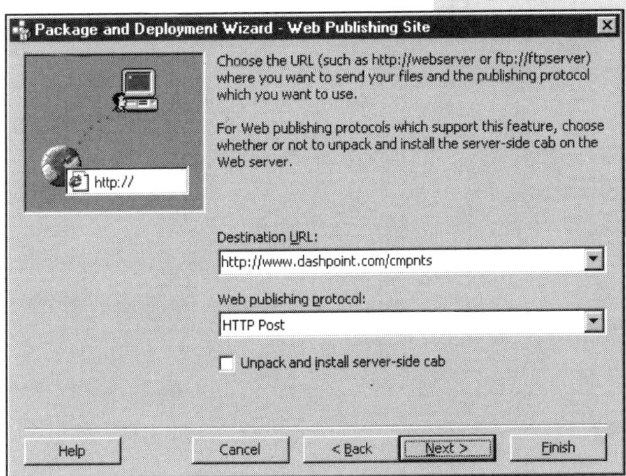

Figure 19.13 This figure shows the Web Publishing Site page of the Package and Deployment Wizard.

15. After you specify the proper Web site address, you are transferred to the Finish line screen. Press Finish and your component is published to the Web. Figure 19.14 shows the progress meter provided by the Package and Deployment Wizard as it completes the job.

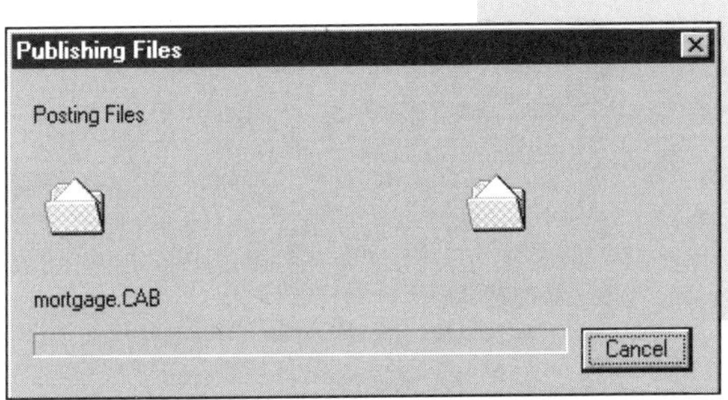

Figure 19.14 This figure shows the progress of publishing a component with the Package and Deployment Wizard.

16. The final step to publishing your components is to test them from a Web connection. Figure 19.15 shows the results of publishing a component to the Web with the deployment wizard.

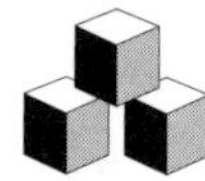

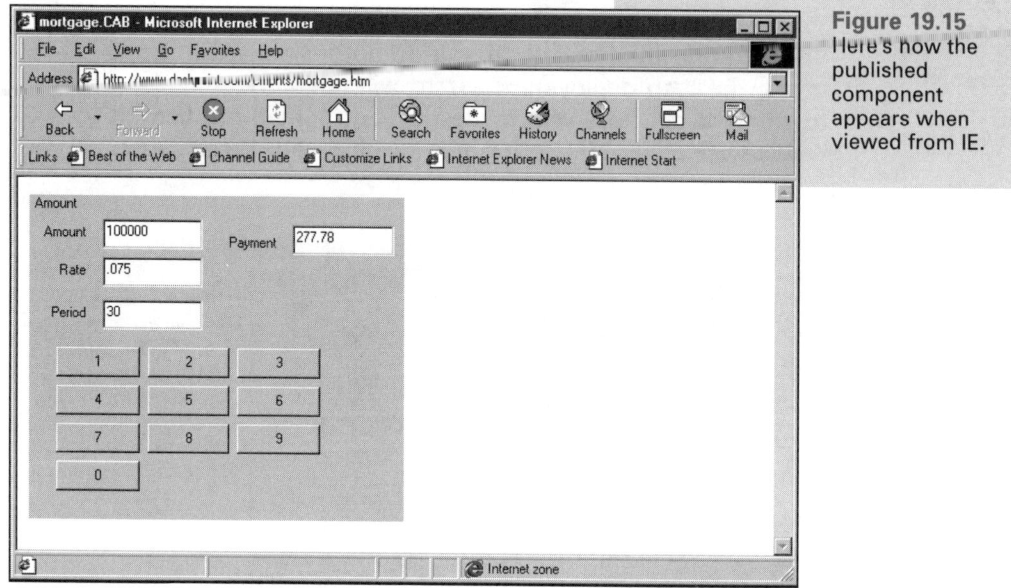

Figure 19.15 Here's how the published component appears when viewed from IE.

Summary

This chapter has demonstrated some of the newest and most powerful Internet features of Visual Basic. You can use Dynamic HTML to create some very nice interactive Web pages, the ActiveX Data Objects model provides the gateway to your data, and the ActiveX components capability of VB allows you to create useful components across your development space. Finally, you can deploy your applications with the Package and Deployment Wizard.

Project 4 Summary

This final project introduced you to the process of building a more complex and robust Web application. You used many of the newest and most advanced features of Visual Basic coupled with ActiveX Data Objects (ADO) and Active Server Pages (ASP).

You began the project by gathering system requirements. After gathering requirements, you built a prototype of your application. Whereas in prior examples you used FrontPage to build a prototype, in this project you built your prototype using Visual Basic only. This prototype facilitated the development of a "picture" of how your application would look and feel.

After creating the prototype, you went about the process of building the actual application. This process included learning about ActiveX Data Objects (ADO) and adding Dynamic HTML to your Web pages. It concluded with building an ActiveX control. After constructing all of these items, you learned how to deploy them to the Web with the help of the Visual Studio Package and Deployment Wizard.

Appendix A

HTML Markup Tags (Alphabetical List)

This appendix contains an alphabetical list of commonly used markup tags. It is difficult to maintain a complete list, as the language is rapidly evolving—new tags are approved by the committees of the World Wide Web standards organization (W3) almost every month. To stay up-to-date on new and revised tags, check with major browser manufacturers such as Netscape or Microsoft, or check directly with W3.

Netscape: `http://www.mcom.com`

Microsoft: `http://www.microsoft.com`

W3: `http://www.w3.org`

Understanding the Tag Syntax

Tags come in single instances and double instances, and may have attributes. A single instance of a tag normally inserts something, such as a character or picture. For example, the tag `<P>` starts a new paragraph. Double instances turn something on and then turn it off again. For example, the tags `<B>...</B>` turn on the bold attribute for all text between them. Some tags take attributes that modify their behavior. An attribute consists of a keyword or a keyword and, optionally, an equal sign (=) and an argument. The argument is either another keyword or some text in quotation marks. For example, look at the following line:

```
<IMG SRC="http://image.com/image1.gif" ALT="A Dog" ALIGN=TOP ISMAP>
```

This line inserts an image in a document. The `ISMAP` attribute is a single keyword, while `SRC`, `ALT`, and `ALIGN` take arguments. `SRC` and `ALT` take an argument as a quoted string, while `ALIGN` takes a keyword.

Most tags, attributes, and keywords can be either uppercase or lowercase, although uppercase is often used to make the tags stand out more in the unformatted text. An exception to this rule is the escape sequences (`&`*`keyword`*`;`) that must be typed exactly as shown.

See Appendix B for a functional listing of all the same tags.

Each description in this appendix starts with the name of the tag, followed by the syntax and a description. Unless specifically mentioned, any attributes listed with a tag are optional. In the syntax statements, *italic* characters are placeholders for literal values, and non-italic characters are typed as is. The source specification to the right of each tag and attribute specifies the original source for the tag, as follows:

Source Specification	Meaning
HTML x.x	The tag was specified in the indicated version of the HTML specification.
IE x.x	The tag originated with the indicated version of Internet Explorer.
Netscape	The tag originated with Netscape's Web browser.

Caution

Keep in mind that the formatting actually performed by the statements is always determined by the browser used to view the pages. The descriptions given throughout this appendix only indicate the most common formatting.

The use of quotation marks around the values of attributes is optional unless the extent of the argument is ambiguous; then they're required. For example, any value that consists of more than one word must be quoted so the browser knows where the value ends. It's a good habit to place all values in quotation marks. If a value itself contains quotation marks, use single quotation marks to surround the value and double quotation marks within the value. Use double quotation marks around the value and pairs of double quotation marks within the value wherever one double quotation mark belongs.

Tag Listing

<!DOCTYPE> Send version information

Syntax:

```
<!DOCTYPE HTML PUBLIC "-//W3C/DTD HTML 3.2//EN">                HTML 3.2
```

Sends the HTML version information to the browser. This must be the first statement in an HTML document and is required for HTML version 3.2 or later.

&#ascii; Insert character

Syntax:

```
&#ascii;
```

Renders the character for the indicated ASCII code. Most characters are stored in computers as ASCII codes. The available codes are listed below. This tag renders the symbol that the code stands for.

Tags for ASCII Codes and Symbols

Code	Symbol	Description
�–		Unused
		Horizontal tab
	Line feed
–		Unused
	Carriage return
–		Unused
		Space
!	!	Exclamation mark

Tags for ASCII Codes and Symbols *(Continued)*

Code	Symbol	Description
"	"	Quotation mark
#	#	Number sign
$	$	Dollar sign
%	%	Percent sign
&	&	Ampersand
'	'	Apostrophe
(	(	Left parenthesis
)	)	Right parenthesis
*	*	Asterisk
+	+	Plus sign
,	,	Comma
-	-	Hyphen
.	.	Period
/	/	Forward slash
0–9	0–9	Digits
:	:	Colon
;	;	Semicolon
<	<	Less-than symbol
=	=	Equal sign
>	>	Greater-than symbol
?	?	Question mark
@	@	At sign
A–Z	A–Z	Capital letters
[	[	Left square bracket
\	\	Backslash
]	]	Right square bracket
^	^	Caret
_	_	Underscore
`	`	Acute accent
a–z	a–z	Lowercase letters
{	{	Left curly brace
		|	Vertical bar
}	}	Right curly brace
~	~	Tilde
		Unused

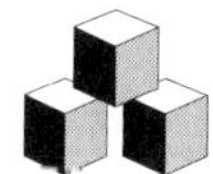

Code	Symbol	Description
		Non-breaking space
¡	¡	Inverted exclamation point
¢	¢	Cent sign
£	£	Pound sterling
¤	¤	General currency sign
¥	¥	Yen sign
¦	¦	Vertical bar
§	§	Section sign
¨	¨	Umlaut
©	©	Copyright
ª	ª	Feminine ordinal
«	«	Left angle quotation mark
¬	¬	Not sign
	-	Soft hyphen
®	®	Registered trademark
¯	¯	Macron accent
°	°	Degree sign
±	±	Plus or minus
²	2	Superscript two
³	3	Superscript three
´	´	Acute accent
µ	µ	Micro sign
¶	¶	Paragraph sign
·	·	Middle dot
¸	ç	Cedilla
¹	1	Superscript one
º	º	Masculine ordinal
»	»	Right angle quotation mark
¼	1/4	Fraction one-fourth
½	1/2	Fraction one-half
¾	3/4	Fraction three-fourths
¿	¿	Inverted question mark
À	À	A, grave accent
Á	Á	A, acute accent
Â	Â	A, circumflex accent
Ã	Ã	A, tilde

Tags for ASCII Codes and Symbols *(Continued)*

Code	Symbol	Description
Ä	Ä	A, umlaut mark
Å	Å	A, ring
Æ	Æ	AE dipthong
Ç	Ç	C, cedilla
È	È	E, grave accent
É	É	E, acute accent
Ê	Ê	E, circumflex accent
Ë	Ë	E, dieresis or umlaut mark
Ì	Ì	I, grave accent
Í	Í	I, acute accent
Î	Î	I, circumflex accent
Ï	Ï	I, umlaut mark
Ð	∂	Eth, Icelandic
Ñ	Ñ	N, tilde
Ò	Ò	O, grave accent
Ó	Ó	O, acute accent
Ô	Ô	O, circumflex accent
Õ	Õ	O, tilde
Ö	Ö	O, umlaut mark
×	x	Multiplication symbol
Ø	Ø	O, slash
Ù	Ù	U, grave accent
Ú	Ú	U, acute accent
Û	Û	U, circumflex accent
Ü	Ü	U, dieresis or umlaut mark
Ý	Ý	Y, acute accent
Þ	þ	THORN, Icelandic
ß	ß	ss, German
à	à	a, grave accent
á	á	a, acute accent
â	â	a, circumflex accent
ã	ã	a, tilde
ä	ä	a, umlaut mark
å	å	a, ring
æ	æ	ae dipthong

Code	Symbol	Description
ç	ç	c, cedilla
è	è	e, grave accent
é	é	e, acute accent
ê	ê	e, circumflex accent
ë	ë	e, dieresis or umlaut mark
ì	ì	i, grave accent
í	í	i, acute accent
î	î	i, circumflex accent
ï	ï	i, umlaut mark
ð	∂	eth, Icelandic
ñ	ñ	n, tilde
ò	ò	o, grave accent
ó	ó	o, acute accent
ô	ô	o, circumflex accent
õ	õ	o, tilde
ö	ö	o, umlaut mark
÷	÷	Division symbol
ø	ø	o, slash
ù	ù	u, grave accent
ú	ú	u, acute accent
û	û	u, circumflex accent
ü	ü	u, dieresis or umlaut mark
ý	ý	y, acute accent
þ	þ	thorn, Icelandic
ÿ	ÿ	y, umlaut mark

`&keyword;` Insert a special character

Syntax:

```
&keyword;
```

Special characters are the symbols normally used to represent tags such as angle brackets (<>) and ampersands (&). To insert these characters in a document and have the browser display them instead of using them as a tag, code them with a special character. Some of the special character codes are listed below. Note that the special character codes are case sensitive. See `&#ascii;` for more special symbols.

Special Character Codes and Their Results

Code	Symbol	Description
<	<	Less than symbol
>	>	Greater than symbol
&	&	Ampersand
"	"	Double quotation marks
ö	ö	o with an umlaut
ñ	ñ	n with a tilde
È	È	E with a grave accent
®	®	Registered trademark
©	©	Copyright
		Non-breaking space

<!- -> Make comment

Syntax:

```
<!-comment text->
```

Any text within the tag is ignored when the page is rendered. Comments are also used to pass code sequences to browsers for execution instead of rendering. See also `<COMMENT>`.

<A> Make hypertext link or anchor

Syntax:

```
<A NAME="anchor">...</A>                                    HTML 2
<A NAME="#anchor">...</A>                                   HTML 2
<A HREF="url">...</A>                                       HTML 2
<A HREF="url#anchor">...</A>                                HTML 2
<A HREF="url?search_-word+search_word">...</A>              HTML 2
REL="relationship"                                          HTML 3.2
REV="revision"                                              HTML 3.2
TARGET="window"                                             Netscape
TITLE="title">                                              HTML 3.2
```

Designates a hypertext link to another document (`url`), to another location in the current document (*anchor*), or marks the location of an anchor. The first

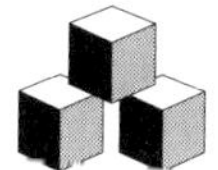

form marks the location of an anchor in a document and names it with the argument of the NAME attribute. The second form creates a hypertext jump to the named anchor in the current document. Text placed between the tags in this and the other forms of the statement is colored, and becomes the button to jump to the anchor location. The third form creates a hypertext jump to the top of another document specified with the *url*. The fourth form creates a jump to an anchor location in another document. The last form initiates a search by a server for one or more search words.

The REL attribute specifies a relative relationship to the anchor. The REV attribute specifies a revision number. The TITLE attribute specifies the title that appears in the status bar when the tag is selected. The TARGET attribute specifies the name of the window that is to receive the page returned by the hypertext link. See <FRAME> for information on creating multiple windows on-screen. A window must be named to be a target, or one of the following four predefined names may be used:

Argument	Description
_blank	Load the link into a new blank window
_parent	Load the link into the parent window to the one containing the anchor tag
_self	Load the link into the same window the anchor tag is in (this is the default)
_top	Load the link into the whole application window

Use the <A> tag to also display full page images by setting the *url* to point to an image file. Images, sounds, and movies can be displayed. Some images are displayed by the browser and others are displayed by helper applications, depending on the capabilities of the browser.

<ADDRESS> Make address

Syntax:

```
<ADDRESS>...</ADDRESS>                                    HTML 2
```

Marks the text between the tags as an address for contacting the author of a document. The text usually is rendered in italic.

<APPLET> Embed a Java applet

Syntax:

```
<APPLET                                   HTML 3.2
ALIGN="position"                          HTML 3.2
ALT="alternateText"                       HTML 3.2
CODE="fileName"                           HTML 3.2
CODEBASE="url"                            HTML 3.2
HEIGHT="pixels"                           HTML 3.2
HSPACE="pixels"                           HTML 3.2
NAME="instanceName"                       HTML 3.2
PARAM NAME="parameterName"                HTML 3.2
VSPACE="pixels"                           HTML 3.2
WIDTH="pixels"></APPLET>                  HTML 3.2
```

Insert a Java applet in an HTML page. The `ALIGN` attribute controls how the applet is aligned with surrounding text. It can take the value `left`, `right`, or `center`. The `ALT` attribute specifies some alternative text to display in text-only browsers or browsers that do not support Java. The `CODE` attribute contains the filename of the applet, and the `CODEBASE` attribute specifies the URL of the applet. The `HEIGHT` and `WIDTH` attributes specify the height and width of the applet window in pixels. The `HSPACE` and `VSPACE` attributes specify the horizontal and vertical space to leave between the edge of the applet window and any surrounding text. The `NAME` attribute specifies a name for this particular instance of the applet. The `PARAM NAME` attribute specifies the name of an applet's parameter so the name can be used to send values to the applet using *`name=value`* syntax.

<AREA> Define hot spot geometry

Syntax:

```
<AREA
COORDS="x1, y1, x2, y2,..."               IE 3.0
HREF="url"                                IE 3.0
NOHREF                                    IE 3.0
SHAPE="shape_name"                        IE 3.0
TARGET="window">                          Netscape
```

Describes the location and shape of a hot spot on an image for a client-side imagemap. Use with the `<MAP>` tag to create an image map for an image declared with the `<IMG>` tag. The `COORDS` attribute defines the coordinates for the hot spot. The coordinates needed depend on the shape. The `HREF` attribute specifies the hypertext link for the hot spot. The `NOHREF` attribute indicates that clicks in this region should cause no action to occur. The `SHAPE` attribute

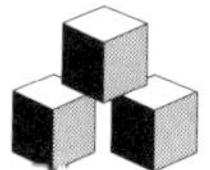

defines the geometric shape of the hot spot. The following list contains the allowed arguments for SHAPE and the coordinates needed. See also <MAP>.

Argument	Coordinates
rectangle	Two x,y coordinate pairs defining two opposed corners or a rectangle
rect	Same as rectangle
circle	x, y coordinates of center and the length of the radius of a circle
circ	Same as circle
polygon	Three or more x, y coordinate pairs defining the corners of the polygon
poly	Same as polygon

The TARGET attribute specifies the name of the window that is to receive the page returned by the hypertext link. See <FRAME> for information on creating multiple windows on-screen. A window must be named to be a target, or you can use one of the following four predefined names:

Argument	Coordinates
_blank	Load the link into a new blank window
_parent	Load the link into the parent window to the one containing the anchor tag
_self	Load the link into the same window the anchor tag is in (this is the default)
_top	Load the link into the whole application window

<B> Make boldface

Syntax:

```
<B>...</B>                                        HTML 2.0
```

Renders any text between the tags in a boldface font.

<BASE> Specify URL

Syntax:

```
<BASE
HREF="url"                                        HTML 2.0
TARGET="window" >                                 Netscape
```

Most pages use incomplete references to specify the specify URLs to other documents on the same server. The `<BASE>` tag is used to set the missing part to combine with a URL to create a complete path to an object. The `TARGET` attribute specifies the name of the window that is to receive the page returned by all the hypertext links on the page. See `<FRAME>` for information on creating multiple windows on-screen. A window must be named to be a target, or you can use one of the following four predefined names:

Argument	Description
_blank	Load the link into a new blank window
_parent	Load the link into the parent window to the one containing the anchor tag
_self	Load the link into the same window the anchor tag is in (this is the default)
_top	Load the link into the whole application window

<BASEFONT> Set font attributes

Syntax:

```
<BASEFONT
SIZE="value"                                    Netscape
COLOR="color"                                   Netscape 2.0
FACE="fontName, fontName,...">                  Netscape 2.0
```

Changes the base font size to the indicated size. The default size is **3**, and the range is 1–7. See also `<FONT>`. The `COLOR` attribute sets the font color. The *`color`* argument is specified either as a name such as `red` or `green`, or as *`#rrggbb`* where *`rrggbb`* represents three hex numbers specifying the red, green, and blue content of the color, respectively. The `FACE` attribute is the name of a font to use as the default font. The value of the attribute is a list of font names, where if the first font is not available on the user's system, the second is used, and so on.

<BGSOUND> Set background sound

Syntax:

```
<BGSOUND
SRC="url"                                       IE 3.0
LOOP=num_repeats >                              IE 3.0
```

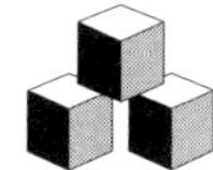

Sets a sound to play while the page is visible. The SRC attribute specifies the URL of the sound file. The LOOP attribute specifies how many times the file plays. If the argument of the LOOP attribute is -1 or infinite, the sound continues indefinitely.

<BIG> Increase text size

Syntax:

```
<BIG>...</BIG>                                              HTML 3.2
```

Text placed between these tags is increased by one size.

<BLOCKQUOTE> Make quote

Syntax:

```
<BLOCKQUOTE>...</BLOCKQUOTE>                                HTML 2.0
```

Quote a block of text within a document by separating it from the rest of the document with white space. The command forces a new paragraph before and after the quoted text and indents the text.

<BODY> Mark document body

Syntax:

```
<BODY
ALINK="color"                                               HTML 2.0
BACKGROUND="url"                                            HTML 3.2
BGCOLOR="color "                                            Netscape
BGPROPERTIES=fixed                                            IE 2.0
LEFTMARGIN="n"                                                IE 2.0
LINK="color"                                                Netscape
TEXT="color"                                                Netscape
TOPMARGIN="n"                                                 IE 2.0
VLINK="color">...</BODY>                                    Netscape
```

Marks the beginning and ending of the body of a document. The ALINK attribute sets the color of a link that is active (selected but not clicked on). The BACKGROUND attribute specifies the URL of an image to use as a background for the page. The BGCOLOR attribute specifies the color for the background of the page. The color is specified either as a name such as red or green, or as *#rrggbb* where *rrggbb* represents three hex numbers specifying the red, green, and blue content of the color. The BGPROPERTIES=fixed attribute specifies that the background does not scroll when the text on the page is scrolled. The LEFTMARGIN and TOPMARGIN attributes set the margins of the body. The margins are measured in pixels. The LINK attribute sets the color of links that have not been visited yet. The TEXT attribute sets the color of the text on the page. The VLINK attribute sets the color of links that have been visited.

 Break line

Syntax:

```
<BR
CLEAR=clear_edge>                                          HTML 3.2
```

In formatted text, causes a line to end and a new line to begin. It does not add another line, as the paragraph <P> tag does. The CLEAR attribute is used with floating images <HREF ALIGN=left> or <HREF ALIGN=right>. The CLEAR attribute can have two arguments: left or right. Each breaks the current line and moves down until the indicated margin is clear. That is, the new line starts below any figure that is attached to the margin. See also <P>.

<CAPTION> Set table caption

Syntax:

```
<CAPTION
ALIGN="alignment"                                          HTML 3.2
VALIGN="valignment">...</CAPTION>                          HTML 3.2
```

The text between the tags becomes the caption for a table. This tag must be used within a table. The ALIGN attribute specifies the horizontal alignment of the caption. The possible arguments are left, center, or right. The VALIGN attribute sets the vertical alignment of the caption and can have the arguments top or bottom. The default is centered text. See also <TABLE>.

<CENTER> Center text

Syntax:

```
<CENTER>...</CENTER>                                       Netscape
```

Center the text between the tags.

<CITE> Make citation

Syntax:

```
<CITE>...</CITE>                                           HTML 2.0
```

Render a citation as in the title of a book. Citations are usually rendered in an italic font.

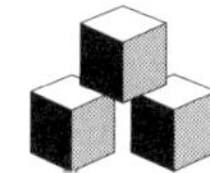

<CODE> Make code

Syntax:

```
<CODE>...</CODE>                                        HTML 2.0
```

Text enclosed by the tags is displayed as a code segment by rendering it in a monospaced font. See also <PRE> and <XMP>.

<COLS> Set column properties

Syntax:

```
<COLS                                                   HTML 3.2
ALIGN="alignment"                                       HTML 3.2
SPAN="numCols">                                         HTML 3.2
```

Sets properties of a column in a table. <COLS> is only valid in a table. The ALIGN attribute sets the alignment of the column. The allowed values are left, center, or right. The SPAN attribute specifies how many columns this tag applies to. Use this with a <COLGROUP> tag to set the properties of individual columns within a group.

<COLGROUP> Set column group properties

Syntax:

```
<COLGROUP                                               HTML 3.2
ALIGN="alignment"                                       HTML 3.2
VALIGN="alignment"                                      HTML 3.2
SPAN="numCols">                                         HTML 3.2
```

Used in the head of a table, this tag combines columns into groups and assigns properties to the group. The <COLS> tag can be used to override any group settings. The ALIGN attribute sets the alignment of the column. The allowed values are left, center, or right. The VALIGN attribute sets the vertical alignment of the column. The allowed values are top, center, or bottom. The SPAN attribute specifies how many columns this tag applies to.

<COMMENT> Make comment (obsolete)

Syntax:

```
<COMMENT>...</COMMENT>                                  HTML 2.0
```

Renders the text enclosed by the tags as a comment, and is ignored unless it contains HTML code. See also <!-.

<DD> Mark definition

Syntax:

```
<DD>                                                    HTML 2.0
```

Renders the text as a definition of a term. Used in a definition table between the <DL> and </DL> tags.

<DFN> Make definition

Syntax:

```
<DFN>...</DFN>                                          HTML 2.0
```

Renders a word or phrase being defined. Any text between the tags is usually rendered in an italic font.

<DIR> Make directory list

Syntax:

```
<DIR>...</DIR>                                          HTML 2.0
```

Creates an interactive directory of items. Use the <LI> tag to mark the items in the directory. Items should be less than 20 characters in length. Items are rendered in multiple columns.

<DIV> Make sections

Syntax:

```
<DIV                                                    HTML 3.2
ALIGN="alignment"></DIV>                                HTML 3.2
```

Break a document into divisions to group related items together. The ALIGN attribute sets the alignment of the column. The allowed values are left, center, or right.

<DL> Make definition list

Syntax:

```
<DL COMPACT>...</DL>                                    HTML 2.0
```

Renders a list of terms and definitions. Terms are marked with the <DT> tags and the definitions are marked with the <DD> tags. The terms are indented and

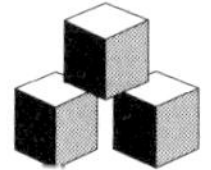

the definitions are doubly indented. Normally, the term is on one line and the definition starts on the next line. The COMPACT argument causes the term and the first line of the definition to be on the same line if there is room.

<DT> Mark defined term

Syntax:

```
<DT>                                                    HTML 2.0
```

Marks a word to be defined. Used in a definition table between the <DL> and </DL> tags.

<EM> Make emphasized

Syntax:

```
<EM>...</EM>                                            HTML 2.0
```

Renders the text enclosed by the tags as emphasized in some way, depending on the browser. It is usually made bold but can be colored so that it stands out. See also <STRONG>.

<EMBED> Embed object

Syntax:

```
<EMBED                                                  HTML 2.0
SRC="inputData"                                         HTML 2.0
WIDTH="pixels"                                          HTML 2.0
HEIGHT="pixels"                                         HTML 2.0
PALETTE="forOrback"                                     HTML 2.0
NAME="name"                                             HTML 2.0
OPTIONAL PARAM="value"...>                              HTML 2.0
```

Embeds an object in a page. Obsolete—use <OBJECT> instead. The SRC attribute is the name of any object supplying data to the object. The HEIGHT and WIDTH attributes specify the height and width of the object window in pixels. The PALETTE attribute sets the object palette to the foreground or background palette. The allowed values are foreground and background with background as the default. The NAME attribute specifies a name for this instance of the object. The OPTIONAL PARAM attribute sets optional values to be passed to the object. There can be multiple instances of OPTIONAL PARAM in a tag.

<FONT> Set font attributes

Syntax:

```
<FONT
SIZE="value"                                  Netscape
COLOR="color"                                 IE 3.0
FACE="name1, name2">                          IE 3.0
```

The `SIZE` attribute sets the size of the font relative to a default size set on the browser. The default value is `3`, the range is `1` to `7`, with `7` the largest. The value can also be relative to the default value by using + or—with the value. That is, a relative value of +2 is the same as an absolute value of 5 (3 + 2). The `COLOR` attribute sets the font color. The color is specified either as a name such as `red` or `green`, or as *#rrggbb* where *rrggbb* represents three hex numbers specifying the red-green-blue content of the color. The `FACE` attribute selects the type face to be used. The argument is a list of font names separated by commas. The first font that matches a font available on the system is used. See also `<BASEFONT>`.

<FORM> Mark form

Syntax:

```
<FORM
ACTION="url"                                  HTML 2.0
METHOD=data_exchange_method                   HTML 2.0
ENCTYPE= encoding_method                      HTML 2.0
TARGET="window">...</FORM>                    Netscape
```

Render the text between these tags as a form to be filled out by the user. The `ACTION` argument specifies the URL that the contents of the form is to be sent to. The `METHOD` argument specifies how the form contents are to be sent to the client URL. There are two options for the data exchange method: `get` or `post`. `get` specifies that the form contents are to be appended to the call to the URL. `post` causes the contents of a form to be inserted into a data body and sent to the URL. `ENCTYPE` specifies the encoding for the form contents. The `ENCTYPE` argument currently has only one possible value:

```
application/x-www-form-urlencoded
```

Insert `<INPUT>`, `<SELECT>`, and `<TEXTAREA>` tags to mark fillable fields in the form.

The `TARGET` attribute specifies the name of the window that is to receive the page returned by all the hypertext links on the page. See `<FRAME>` for information on creating multiple windows on-screen. A window must be named to be a target, or you can use one of the following four predefined names:

Argument	Description
_blank	Load the link into a new blank window
_parent	Load the link into the parent window to the one containing the anchor tag
_self	Load the link into the same window the anchor tag is in (this is the default)
_top	Load the link into the whole application window

<FRAME> Make frame

Syntax:

```
<FRAME
ALIGN="alignment"
FRAMEBORDER="1¦0"                    IE 3.0
MARGINHEIGHT="pixels"                Netscape
MARGINWIDTH="pixels"                 Netscape
NAME="frameName"                     Netscape
NORESIZE                             Netscape
SCROLLING="yes¦no"                   Netscape
SRC="url"                            Netscape
```

Defines a single frame. Use with the `<FRAMESET>` tag to divide the screen into multiple frames, or alone to create a floating frame. See the `<IFRAME>` command for details on creating floating frames. The `ALIGN` attribute sets the alignment of a floating frame with the window. The following values are allowed:

Value	Description
top	Surrounding text is aligned with the top of the frame
middle	Surrounding text is aligned with the middle of the frame
left	The frame is flush left on the page and text flows around it
right	The frame is flush right on the page and text flows around it

The `FRAMEBORDER` attribute controls whether the frame has a border or not. The allowed values are `1` (it has a border) or `0` (it has no border). The `MARGINHEIGHT` and `MARGINWIDTH` attributes set the distance the text starts from the edge of the frame in pixels. The `NAME` attribute sets a name for the frame. The `NORESIZE` attribute locks the size of the frame so the user can not change it. The `SCROLLING` attribute sets if the contents of the frame can be scrolled with scroll bars. The allowed values are `yes` or `no`. The `SRC` attribute sets the source file for the contents of the frame.

<FRAMESET> Align frames

Syntax:

```
<FRAMESET
COLS="colwidth,colwidth..."                          Netscape
FRAMEBORDER="1¦0"                                    IE 3.0
FRAMESPACING="spacing"                               IE 3.0
ROWS="colheight, colheight,...."></FRAMESET>         Netscape
```

This forms a container for <FRAME> tags. The <FRAMESET> tag combines the frames within it into a group that fills the window. The COLS and ROWS attributes set the number and width of columns or rows defined by the tag. The width or height can be set as a percent (%), number of pixels or as relative (*).The FRAMEBORDER attribute controls whether the frame has a border or not. The allowed values are 1 (it has a border) or 0 (it has no border). The FRAMESPACING attribute sets the number of pixels between adjacent frames.

<H#> Make header

Syntax:

```
<H1>...</H1>
<H2>...</H2>
<H3>...</H3>
<H4>...</H4>
<H5>...</H5>
<H6>...</H6>                                         HTML 2
ALIGN="alignment">                                   HTML 3.2
```

Render the text enclosed by the tags as a header for a section of a document. The lower the number, the higher the level of the header. Headers are made prominent by making the text size larger and by making it bold. Level 1 headers are the largest and boldest. The ALIGN attribute sets the alignment of the text. The allowed values are left, center, or right.

<HEAD> Mark document head

Syntax:

```
<HEAD>...</HEAD>
```

Marks the beginning and ending of the head of a document.

<HR> Make horizontal rule

Syntax:

```
<HR                                   HTML 2
WIDTH="pixels¦%"                      Netscape
ALIGN="alignment"                     HTML 3.2
NOSHADE                               Netscape
SIZE="thickness"                      Netscape
COLOR="color"                         IE 3.0>
```

Draw a horizontal line across the page. The `WIDTH` attribute sets the width of the line across the page in either pixels or percent of the width of the page. The `ALIGN` attribute sets the alignment of the line and can have the arguments `left`, `right`, or `center`. The `NOSHADE` attribute makes the fancy shaded line into a solid bar. The `SIZE` attribute sets the thickness of the line in pixels. The `WIDTH` attribute sets the length of the line in pixels or in percent of the width of the page (*n*%).

<HTML> Mark HTML document

Syntax:

```
<HTML>...</HTML>
```

Marks the beginning and end of an HTML document. Optional.

<I> Make italic

Syntax:

```
<I>...</I> HTML 2
```

Renders any text between the tags in an italic font.

<IFRAME> Make floating frame

Syntax:

```
<FRAME
ALIGN="alignment"
FRAMEBORDER="1¦0"                     IE 3.0
MARGINHEIGHT="pixels"                 Netscape
MARGINWIDTH="pixels"                  Netscape
NAME="frameName"                      Netscape
NORESIZE                              Netscape
SCROLLING="yes¦no"                    Netscape
SRC="url"                             Netscape
```

Defines a single floating frame. This is the preferred form for a floating frame. The attributes are identical to those of a <FRAME>. The ALIGN attribute sets the alignment of a floating frame with the window. The allowed values are:

Value	Description
top	Surrounding text is aligned with the top of the frame
middle	Surrounding text is aligned with the middle of the frame
left	The frame is flush left on the page and text flows around it
right	The frame is flush right on the page and text flows around it

The FRAMEBORDER attribute controls whether the frame has a border or not. The allowed valeus are 1 it has a border or 0 it has no border. The MARGIN-HEIGHT and MARGINWIDTH attributes set the distance the text starts from the edge of the frame in pixels. The NAME attribute sets a name for the frame. The NORESIZE attribute locks the size of the frame so the user can not change it. The SCROLLING attribute sets if the contents of the frame can be scrolled with scroll bars. The allowed values are yes or no. The SRC attribute sets the source file for the contents of the frame.

<IMG> Insert inline image

Syntax:

```
<IMG SRC="url"                                  HTML 2
ALT="alternate_text"                            HTML 2
ALIGN=alignment                                 HTML 3.2
WIDTH=img_width                                 HTML 3.2
HEIGHT=img_height                               HTML 3.2
BORDER=border_width                             HTML 3.2
VSPACE=vertical_space                           HTML 3.2
HSPACE=horizontal_space                         HTML 3.2
ISMAP                                           HTML 3.2
CONTROLS                                        IE 3.0
DYNSRC="url"                                    IE 3.0
LOOP=number_of_iterations
START=when                                      IE 3.0
USEMAP "#map">                                  IE 3.0
```

Render a graphic image at the location of the in the text. The image must be in GIF or XBM format. The SRC attribute specifies the location of the image as a URL. The ALT attribute specifies some text to use when the browser is locating the image (or for browsers that do not support images). The ALIGN attribute aligns the inline image with the text in the line. The default is to align the bottom of the image with the bottom of the text. The arguments change the default as follows:

Alignment Arguments for the ALIGN Attribute

Argument	Description
left	Move image to left margin and flow text around it
right	Move image to right margin and flow text around it
top	Align the top of the image with the top of the tallest object in the line
texttop	Align the top of the image with the top of the tallest text in the line
middle	Align the middle of the image with the baseline of the text in the line
absmiddle	Align the middle of the image with the middle of the text in the line
baseline	Align the baseline of the image with the baseline of the text in the line
bottom	Same as baseline
absbottom	Align the bottom of the image with the bottom of the line

The `WIDTH` and `HEIGHT` attributes specify the width and height of the image to speed its display by the browser. The `BORDER` attribute sets the thickness of the border in pixels. The `VSPACE` and `HSPACE` attributes control the space between the edge of a picture and the text that is wrapping around it (`left` and `right` alignment images only). The `ISMAP` attribute specifies that the image has buttons mapped on it, and if it is clicked, the location the user is passed back to the server to determine which button was clicked. The `CONTROLS` attribute displays a set of controls if a video clip is present. The `DYNSRC` attribute specifies the URL of a video clip or VMRL world to be displayed on the page. The `LOOP` attribute specifies how many times a video clip repeats, or `infinite` for continuous play. The `START` attribute specifies when a clip starts to play. It has two possible arguments: `fileopen` to start as soon as the clip is loaded, and `mouseover` to start when the mouse is over the image. The `USEMAP` attribute specifies a local client-side map file to use with an image.

Use the `<A>` tag to display full-screen images.

<INPUT> Make input field

Syntax:

```
<INPUT
TYPE="variable_type"                         HTML 2
NAME="name_of_field"                         HTML 2
VALUE="default_or_label"                     HTML 2
CHECKED=logical                              HTML 2
SIZE="width"                                 HTML 2
MAXLENGTH="max_characters"                   HTML 2
ALIGN=alignment                              HTML 2
SRC="url">                                   HTML 2
```

An input field must be between the `<FORM>` and `</FORM>` tags of a form. The `TYPE` argument specifies what type of data can be typed into the field. The following values are allowed for the `TYPE` argument:

Value	Description
text	Renders a box for typing character data
password	Renders a box for typing character data
checkbox	Renders a check box with a label
radio	Renders a radio button and a label
submit	Renders a button that sends the form to the server
reset	Renders a button that resets the form variables to their default values
hidden	Renders a hidden input field (hidden fields are used to send state data to the server)

The `NAME` argument specifies the name of the field. The `VALUE` argument specifies the default value of an input field or the label on a button. For check boxes and radio buttons, it specifies the value sent to the server if the button is checked. The `CHECKED` argument sets the default value for check boxes and radio buttons. A value of `True` or no argument checks the box or a value of `False` unchecks it. The `SIZE` argument specifies the width in characters of the character fields. The `MAXLENGTH` argument specifies the maximum number of characters in a character field. The `ALIGN` attribute sets the alignment of an image type control with the text in the line. The allowed values are `top`, `middle`, and `bottom`. The `SRC` attribute sets the name of an image to be used for `image` type controls.

<ISINDEX> Mark a searchable database

Syntax:

```
<ISINDEX
PROMPT="prompt_text"                                    HTML 2
ACTION="url">                                           HTML 3.2
```

Marks the current document as a searchable database. To change the prompt shown on-screen, add the PROMPT attribute with the new prompt text as the argument. The ACTION attribute specifies a program to which the string should be passed.

<KBD> Keyboard text

Syntax:

```
<KBD>...</KBD>                                          HTML 2
```

Text enclosed by these tags is rendered as text for the user to type on the keyboard. It usually is rendered in a bold, monospaced font. See also <CODE>.

<LI> Define list item

Syntax:

```
<LI                                                     HTML 2
TYPE=bullet_or_number_type                              Netscape
VALUE=item_number>                                      Netscape
```

Marks items for lists. Used with <OL>, <UL>, <MENU>, and <DIR> lists. The TYPE attribute changes the bullet type for <UL> lists or the numbering style for <OL> lists. The TYPE attribute takes the same arguments as the TYPE attributes in the <UL> or <OL> lists. The VALUE attribute works with the numbered lists <OL> and changes the current value of the number used to number the list for this item and all following items.

<LINK> Static link

Syntax:

```
<LINK                                                   IE 3.0
HREF="url"                                              IE 3.0
REV="relation"                                          IE 3.0
REL="relation">                                         IE 3.0
```

Creates a static link to another document specified with the required HREF attribute. This link is hidden from the user. The REL attribute specifies the relationship with the external document and the REV attribute specifies the reverse relationship of the external document with this document.

<LISTING> Computer listing (obsolete)

Syntax:

```
<LISTING>...</LISTING>                                    HTML 2
```

Renders the enclosed text in a monospaced font just as it was typed. Any tags in the listing are displayed instead of executed. Archaic; see <XMP>.

<MAP> Client image map

Syntax:

```
<MAP
NAME="name">...</MAP>                                     IE 3.0
```

Defines a client image map to use with an image. Use with the <AREA> tags to specify a series of areas on an image, and tie those areas to a command.

<MARQUEE> Make scrolling text

Syntax:

```
<MARQUEE                                                  IE 3.0
ALIGN=alignment                                           IE 3.0
BEHAVIOR=scroll_behavior                                  IE 3.0
BGCOLOR=color                                             IE 3.0
DIRECTION=scroll_direction                                IE 3.0
HEIGHT=height                                             IE 3.0
HSPACE=margins                                            IE 3.0
LOOP=iterations                                           IE 3.0
SCROLLAMOUNT=redraw                                       IE 3.0
SCROLLDELAY=delay                                         IE 3.0
VSPACE=margin                                             IE 3.0
WIDTH=width>...</MARQUEE>                                 IE 3.0
```

Any text between the tags becomes a scrolling marquee. The `ALIGN` attribute specifies how the marquee should align with the surrounding text. It can have the values `top`, `middle`, or `bottom`. The `BEHAVIOR` attribute defines how the marquee should scroll. It can have the values `scroll`, `slide`, or `alternate`. The `BGCOLOR` attribute sets the background color. The `COLOR` attribute sets the font color. The *`color`* argument is specified either as a name such as `red` or `green`, or as *`#rrggbb`* where *`rrggbb`* represents three hex numbers specifying the red-green-blue content of the color. The `DIRECTION` attribute specifies the direction the text scrolls. It takes the arguments `left` or `right`. The `HEIGHT` attribute specifies the height of the marquee in pixels or in percent height of the screen (*`height%`*). The `HSPACE` attribute sets the left and right margins in pixels. The LOOP attribute specifies how many times to scroll the marquee, or -1 or infinite for continuous play. The SCROLLAMOUNT attribute specifies how many pixels the marquee moves before the screen is redrawn. The SCROLLDELAY attribute specifies the time between successive redraws of the scrolling text. The VSPACE attribute specifies the top and bottom margins in pixels. The WIDTH attribute specifies the width of the marquee in pixels or percent of the screen width (*width*%).

<MENU> Make menu

Syntax:

```
<MENU>...</MENU>
```

Creates an interactive list of menu items. Use the <LI> tag to mark the items in the menu.

<META> Set document information

Syntax:

```
<META
HTTP-EQUIV="element"                    Netscape
CONTENT="time;url=url"                  Netscape
NAME="name">...</META>                  HTML 3.2
```

Sends page special information to a browser or other application by associating element names and values. Must be used within the <HEAD> tag. The HTTP-EQUIV attribute specifies the name of the element in an http response header to be set. The header is sent with requests for information about a document. The CONTENT attribute specifies the value of the element. The value depends on the type of element being sent. Some possible values follow:

Element	Content	Description
refresh	time;url=url	Set the page to be refreshed with the indicated url after the indicated time
expires	date	Set a date for the information to expire Must be in a long date format "weekday, dd-mmm-yyyy hh:mm:ss GMT".
Keywords	keywords	Specifies keywords for the page
Reply-to	emailaddr	Specifies the reply to field in the document header—must be an e-mail address

<NOBR> No break

Syntax:

```
<NOBR>...</NOBR>                                    Netscape
```

Do not break the text between the tags.

<NOFRAMES> Define alternative page

Syntax:

```
<NOFRAMES>...</NOFRAMES>                            Netscape
```

Defines a region on a page containing frames for browsers that do not display frames. Browsers that understand frames ignore the <NOFRAMES> region. Browsers that do not understand frames display the <NOFRAMES> region.

<OBJECT> Embed an object

Syntax:

```
<OBJECT
ID="name"
ALIGN="alignment"
BORDER="pixels"
CLASSID="url"
CODEBASE="url;url;..."
CODETYPE="type"
DATA="url"
DECLARE
WIDTH="pixels"
HEIGHT="pixels"
NAME="name"
HSPACE="pixels"
SHAPES
STANDBY="message"
TYPE="type"
USEMAP="url"
VSPACE="pixels">...</OBJECT>
```

This tag embeds an object in a page. The HEIGHT and WIDTH attributes specify the height and width of the object window in pixels. The HSPACE and VSPACE attributes specify the amount of space between the object and any text or objects to the left and right—or above and below—the object. The BORDER attribute sets the width of the object's border. The NAME attribute specifies a name for this instance of the object when it is submitted as part of a form. The ID attribute specifies a name for the object when it is accessed by a script. The

ALIGN attribute sets the alignment of the object with the surrounding text. It takes the following values:

Value	Description
baseline	The text aligns with the bottom of the object
center	The object is centered on the page, text starts below it
left	The object aligns on the left margin and text wraps around it
middle	The text aligns with the middle of the object
right	The object aligns on the right side of the page and text wraps around it
textbottom	The text aligns with the bottom of the object
textmiddle	The object is centered in the page and the text aligns with its center
texttop	The text aligns with the top of the object

The CLASSID identifies the object and is dependent on the type of object. Objects registered in the windows Registry use the CLSID from the registry. The CODEBASE attribute lists one or more URLs where the object may be found if it is not on the user's system. The CODETYPE attribute specifies the Internet media type for the object.

The DATA attribute points to data for the object and is dependent on the object. The DECLARE attribute declares the object without actually inserting it. The SHAPES attribute specifies the object has shaped hyperlinks. The STANDBY attribute specifies a message displayed to the user while the object is loading. The TYPE attribute specifies the Internet media type for the data. The USEMAP attribute specifies an imagemap to use with the object.

Use the <PARAM> tag to set property values.

<OL> Make ordered (numbered) list

Syntax:

```
<OL                                        HTML 2
TYPE=number_type                           Netscape
START=start_number>...</OL>                Netscape
```

Marks the beginning and end of a numbered list. List items are marked with the <LI> tag. List items are indented and marked with consecutive numbers. The TYPE attribute changes the type of characters used to number the list items and can have the values: A (capital letters), a (lowercase letters), I (capital Roman numerals), i (lowercase Roman numerals), or 1 (numbers, the default). The START attribute sets the value of the first number to use when numbering the list.

<OPTION> Define options

Syntax:

```
<OPTION                                  HTML 2
SELECTED                                 HTML 2
VALUE="value">...</OPTION>               HTML 2
```

Define an item to be selected in a select field. The <OPTION> tag is only used between <SELECT> and </SELECT> tags. The SELECTED attribute specifies that the item is selected by default. The VALUE attribute specifies a value to return to a server when a <SELECT> field on a form containing this option is sent to the server.

<P> New paragraph

Syntax:

```
<P                                       HTML 2
ALIGN=center>...</P>                     HTML 3.2
```

Inserts a paragraph mark at the indicated location. Normally, the browser combines all the text it finds into a large paragraph. The <P> tag forces it to start another paragraph and inserts a blank line. The </P> tag is not required. The ALIGN=center attribute centers the paragraph. See also <BR>.

<PARAM> Set object properties

Syntax:

```
<PARAM
NAME="name"
VALUE="value"
VALUETYPE="type"
TYPE="type"
```

This tag sets the values of properties for objects embedded in a page and is only valid within an <OBJECT> tag. The NAME attribute is the name of the property to set. The VALUE attribute is the value of the property to set. The VALUETYPE attribute indicates how to interpret the information in the VALUE attribute. Use the type data for data, ref for a URL, or object for another object on the page. The TYPE attribute sets the Internet media type.

<PLAINTEXT> Render as plain text (obsolete)

Syntax:

```
<PLAINTEXT>...</PLAINTEXT>
```
HTML 2

Renders the rest of the document in a monospaced font just as it was typed. Display tags instead of executing them. Archaic; see <XMP>.

<PRE> Mark preformatted

Syntax:

```
<PRE>...</PRE>
```
HTML 2

Marks the start and end of preformatted text. Text is displayed in a monospaced font exactly as it was typed, with no attempt made to combine text into paragraphs. See also <XMP>.

<S> Strikethrough

Syntax:

```
<S>...</S>
```
HTML 2

Render the text between the tags is in strikethrough type. Same as <STRIKE>...</STRIKE> tags.

<SAMP> Mark status message

Syntax:

```
<SAMP>...</SAMP>
```
HTML 2

Text enclosed by the tags is displayed as a status message by rendering it in a monospaced font. See also <CODE>.

<SCRIPT> Defines a script

Syntax:

```
<SCRIPT                                   HTML 3.2
LANGUAGE="language">...</SCRIPT>          HTML 3.2
```

Defines the text between the tags as a client script. Comment out the script with comment tags (<!- ->) so browsers that do not understand scripts do not try to render it. The LANGUAGE attribute sets the language of the script. The currently allowed values are VBScript or JavaScript.

<SELECT> Make selection list

Syntax:

```
<SELECT                                    HTML 2
NAME="name_of_field"                       HTML 2
SIZE="no_of_items"                         HTML 2
MULTIPLE>...</SELECT>                      HTML 2
```

Renders a list from which the user can select one or more items. The items go between the `<SELECT>` and `</SELECT>` tags, and are marked with `<OPTION>` tags. The `NAME` attribute specifies the name of the field. The `SIZE` attribute specifies the number of items from the list of items to display at one time. If there are more items than specified by `SIZE`, the list scrolls. The `MULTIPLE` attribute allows the user to select more than one line at a time.

<SMALL> Decrease font size

Syntax:

```
<SMALL>...</SMALL>                         HTML 3.2
```

Reduces the current font by one size.

<SPAN> Apply style

Syntax:

```
<SPAN                                      HTML 3.2
STYLE="style">...</SPAN>                   HTML 3.2
```

Applies a style across some block of text. The text between the tags has the style specified in the `STYLE` attribute applied to it.

<STRIKE> Make strikethrough

Syntax:

```
<STRIKE>...</STRIKE>                       HTML 2
```

Renders the text between the tags in strikethrough type. Same as `<S>...</S>` tags.

<STRONG> Make emphasized

Syntax:

```
<STRONG>...</STRONG>                       HTML 2
```

Renders the text between the tags as strongly emphasized. Text is usually made bold and larger to stand out, but can also be colored. <STRONG> is more emphasized than <EM>. See also <EM>.

<SUB> Render text as subscript

Syntax:

```
<SUB>...</SUB>                                              HTML 3.2
```

The text between the tags is rendered in a subscript style.

<SUP> Render text as superscript

Syntax:

```
<SUP>...</SUP>                                              HTML 3.2
```

The text between the tags is rendered in a superscript style.

<TABLE> Mark a table

Syntax:

```
<TABLE
ALIGN=alignment                                             HTML 3.2
BORDER=border_width
WIDTH=width
BGCOLOR=color                                                 IE 3.0
BORDERCOLOR=color                                             IE 3.0
BORDERCOLORLIGHT=color                                        IE 3.0
BORDERCOLORDARK=color                                         IE 3.0
VALIGN=alignment                                              IE 3.0
BACKGROUND="url"                                              IE 3.0
FRAME="frame"                                               HTML 3.2
RULES="rules">...</TABLE>                                   HTML 3.2
```

Marks the beginning and ending of a table. Use with <CAPTION>, <TR>, <TH>, and <TD> tags to create a table. The ALIGN attribute specifies the horizontal alignment of the caption. The possible arguments are left, center, or right. The VALIGN attribute sets the vertical alignment of the caption and can have the arguments top or bottom. The default is centered text. The BORDER attribute sets the width of the border in pixels. The WIDTH attribute sets the width of the table in pixels or in percent of the width of the screen (*width*%). The BGCOLOR attribute sets the background color. The *color* is specified either as a name such as red or green, or as *#rrggbb* where *rrggbb* represents three hex numbers specifying the red-green-blue content of the color. The BORDER-

COLOR attribute sets the border color. The BORDERCOLORLIGHT and BORDERCOLORDARK attributes set the two colors used in creating a 3-D border. The BACKGROUND attribute specifies the URL of an image that is tiled behind the objects in the table. The FRAME attribute specifies which sides of a frame for the table are displayed. The allowed values are as follows:

Value	Description
void	No frame
above	A border along the top of the table
below	A border along the bottom of the table
hsides	A border along the top and sides
lhs	A border on the left side
rhs	A border on the right side
vsides	A border on both sides
box	A border on all sides
border	A border on all sides

The RULES attribute specifies which of the internal borders between table elements are drawn. The allowed values are:

Value	Description
none	No borders
groups	A border is drawn around groups created with the <COLGROUP> tag
rows	A border is drawn between rows
cols	A border is drawn between each column
all	A border is drawn between all rows and all columns

<TBODY> Mark the beginning of a table body

Syntax:

```
<TBODY>                                                HTML 3.2
```

Marks the beginning of a table body. Use with the <THEAD>, <TFOOT>, <COLGROUP>, and <COL> tags to organize a table.

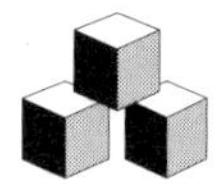

<TD> Table element definition

Syntax:

```
<TD                                         HTML 3.2
ALIGN=alignment                               IE 3.0
BGCOLOR=color                                 IE 3.0
BORDERCOLOR=color                             IE 3.0
BORDERCOLORLIGHT=color                        IE 3.0
BORDERCOLORDARK=color                         IE 3.0
VALIGN=alignment >...</TD>                    IE 3.0
```

Declares the beginning and ending of an element in a table. Use with the `<TABLE>`, `<TH>`, and `<TR>` tags. The `ALIGN` attribute specifies the horizontal alignment of the caption. The possible arguments are `left`, `center`, or `right`. The `VALIGN` attribute sets the vertical alignment of the caption and can have the arguments `top` or `bottom`. The default is centered text. The `BGCOLOR` attribute sets the background color. The *`color`* is specified either as a name such as `red` or `green`, or as *`#rrggbb`* where *`rrggbb`* represents three hex numbers specifying the red-green-blue content of the color. The `BORDERCOLOR` attribute sets the border color. The `BORDERCOLORLIGHT` and `BORDERCOLORDARK` attributes set the two colors used in creating a 3-D border.

<TEXTAREA> Make text field

Syntax:

```
<TEXTAREA
NAME="name_of_field"
ROWS="no_of_rows"
COLS="no_of_columns">...</TEXTAREA>
```

Any text placed between the `<TEXTAREA>` and `</TEXTAREA>` tags becomes the default text in the field. The `NAME` attribute specifies the name of the field. The `ROWS` attribute specifies the height of the field in character heights and the `COLS` attribute specifies the width of the field in character widths.

<TFOOT> Mark the beginning of a table footer

Syntax:

```
<TFOOT>                                     HTML 3.2
```

Marks the beginning of a table footer. Use with the `<THEAD>`, `<TBODY>`, `<COLGROUP>`, and `<COL>` tags to organize a table.

<TH> Table heading

Syntax:

```
<TH
ALIGN=alignment                                HTML 3.2
BGCOLOR=color                                  IE 3.0
BORDERCOLOR=color                              IE 3.0
BORDERCOLORLIGHT=color                         IE 3.0
BORDERCOLORDARK=color                          IE 3.0
VALIGN=alignment >...</TH>                     IE 3.0
```

Declares the beginning and ending of a heading element in a table. Use with the <TABLE>, <TD>, and <TR> tags. The ALIGN attribute specifies the horizontal alignment of the caption. The possible arguments are left, center, or right. The VALIGN attribute sets the vertical alignment of the caption and can have the arguments top or bottom. The default is centered text. The BGCOLOR attribute sets the background color. The *color* is specified either as a name such as red or green, or as *#rrggbb* where *rrggbb* represents three hex numbers specifying the red-green-blue content of the color. The BORDERCOLOR attribute sets the border color. The BORDERCOLORLIGHT and BORDERCOLORDARK attributes set the two colors used in creating a 3-D border.

<THEAD> Mark the beginning of a table header

Syntax:

```
<THEAD>                                        HTML 3.2
```

Marks the beginning of a table header. Use with the <TBODY>, <TFOOT>, <COLGROUP>, and <COL> tags to organize a table.

<TITLE> Specify the title of a document

Syntax:

```
<TITLE>...</TITLE>                             HTML 2
```

The title text is not displayed on the document, but is used to title the window the document is being displayed in.

<TR> Table row

Syntax:

```
<TR
ALIGN=alignment                                              HTML 3.2
BGCOLOR=color                                                  IE 3.0
BORDERCOLOR=color                                              IE 3.0
BORDERCOLORLIGHT=color
BORDERCOLORDARK=color                                          IE 3.0
VALIGN=alignment >...</TR>                                     IE 3.0
```

Declares the beginning and ending of a row in a table. Use with the `<TABLE>`, `<TD>`, and `<TH>` tags. The `ALIGN` attribute specifies the horizontal alignment of the caption. The possible arguments are `left`, `center`, or `right`. The `VALIGN` attribute sets the vertical alignment of the caption and can have the arguments `top` or `bottom`. The default is centered text. The `BGCOLOR` attribute sets the background color. The *`color`* is specified either as a name such as `red` or `green`, or as *`#rrggbb`* where *`rrggbb`* represents three hex numbers specifying the red-green-blue content of the color. The `BORDERCOLOR` attribute sets the border color. The `BORDERCOLORLIGHT` and `BORDERCOLORDARK` attributes set the two colors used in creating a 3-D border.

<TT> Make typewriter text

Syntax:

```
<TT>...</TT>                                                   HTML 2
```

Renders the text between the tags in a fixed-width font similar to that produced by a typewriter.

<U> Make underlined

Syntax:

```
<U>...</U>                                                     HTML 2
```

Renders the text between the tags in an underlined font.

<UL> Unnumbered list

Syntax:

```
<UL                                    HTML 2
TYPE=bullet_type>...</UL>              Netscape
```

Marks the beginning and end of an unnumbered list. List items are marked with the `<LI>` tags. List items are indented with a bullet for each item. The default bullets in multi-level indented lists are disc, then circle, then square. The `TYPE` attribute sets the type of bullet if you want it to be different from the default. The `TYPE` attribute can have the argument `disc`, `circle`, or `square`.

<VAR> Make variable

Syntax:

```
<VAR>...</VAR>                         HTML 2
```

Renders the text between the tags as a placeholder for something the user is to type. Text enclosed by the tags is usually rendered in an italic, monospaced font. See also `<CODE>`.

<WBR> Insert word break

Syntax:

```
<WBR>                                  Netscape
```

Indicates where a no break `<NOBR>` section should break or where a complicated structure may break if needed.

<XMP> Make example (obsolete)

Syntax:

```
<XMP>...</XMP>                         HTML 2
```

Displays the enclosed text in a monospaced font just as it was typed. Embedded tags are displayed instead of executed. See also `<PRE>`.

HTML Markup Tags (Functional List)

This appendix contains a functional list of commonly used markup tags. See Appendix A for syntax and usage information on all these tags. This appendix simply lists each of the tags in functional order, according to the following function areas:

- Page layout formatting
- Character formatting (physical)
- Character formatting (logical)
- Paragraph formatting
- List formatting
- Indented text formatting
- Hypertext links and anchors
- Inserted objects
- Formatting forms
- Formatting tables

Page Layout Formatting

Tag	Description
<HTML>	Marks an HTML document
<TITLE>	Specifies the title of a document
<HEAD>	Marks the head of a document
<BODY>	Marks the body of a document
<ISINDEX>	Marks a searchable database
<BASE>	Specifies the URL to use with incomplete references
<LINK>	Creates a static link
<HR>	Creates a horizontal rule
<!-- -->	Marks a comment
<COMMENT>	Marks a comment (obsolete)
<BGSOUND>	Specifies a background sound
<MARQUEE>	Marks a scrolling marquee
<META>	Force reload
<FRAMESET>	Creates a container for frames
<FRAME>	Defines a frame
<NOFRAMES>	Defines output for a browser that does not handle frames
<IFRAME>	Defines a floating frame
<!DOCTYPE>	Sends HTML version information
<DIV>	Breaks a document into sections

Character Formatting (Physical)

Tag	Description
<B>	Specifies bold font
<I>	Specifies italic font
<U>	Specifies underline font
<S>	Applies strikethrough
<STRIKE>	Applies strikethrough
<FONT>	Sets the font size
<BASEFONT>	Changes the base font size for a page

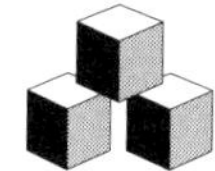

&keyword;	Inserts special characters
&#ascii;	Inserts an ASCII character
<SUB>	Renders text as subscript
<SUP>	Renders text as superscript

Character Formatting (Logical)

Tag	Description
<H#>	Marks header text
<EM>	Specifies emphasized text
<STRONG>	Specifies strongly emphasized text
<KBD>	Marks text for keyboard entry
<VAR>	Specifies variable text
<DFN>	Specifies definition text
<CITE>	Specifies citation text
<TT>	Specifies typewriter text
<CODE>	Specifies code text
<SAMP>	Specifies status message text
<BIG>	Increases the font by one size
<SMALL>	Decreases the font by one size
<SPAN>	Applies a style across some block of text

Paragraph Formatting

Tag	Description
<CENTER>	Centers text
<P>	Starts a new paragraph
<PRE>	Specifies preformatted
<XMP>	Specifies an example (obsolete)
<PLAINTEXT>	Renders the rest of the document in a monospace font (obsolete)
 	Breaks a line
<NOBR>	Specifies no break
<WBR>	Specifies a word break

List Formatting

Tag	Description
<DL>	Marks a definition list
<DT>	Indicates a defined term
<DD>	Indicates a definition
<UL>	Marks an unnumbered list
<LI>	Indicates a list item
<OL>	Marks an ordered (numbered) list
<MENU>	Marks a menu list
<DIR>	Marks a directory list

Indented Text Formatting

Tag	Description
<LISTING>	Specifies a computer listing (obsolete)
<BLOCKQUOTE>	Quotes a block of text within a document
<ADDRESS>	Specifies address text

Hypertext Links and Anchors

Tag	Description
<A>	Specifies a hypertext link to another location
<MAP>	Defines a client image map
<AREA>	Creates a hot spot location for a client image map

Inserted Objects

Tag	Description
<IMG>	Inserts an inline image
<APPLET>	Embeds a Java applet in an HTML document
<EMBED>	Embeds an object in a page

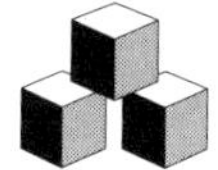

<OBJECT>	Embeds an object in a page
<PARAM>	Sets the value of properties for an object
<SCRIPT>	Defines a client script

Formatting Forms

Tag	Description
<FORM>	Marks a form
<INPUT>	Specifies an input field
<SELECT>	Renders a selection list
<OPTION>	Defines a selection item
<TEXTAREA>	Renders a text field

Formatting Tables

Tag	Description
<TABLE>	Marks a table
<CAPTION>	Specifies a caption for a table
<TD>	Specifies a table element definition
<TH>	Indicates a table heading
<TR>	Indicates a table row
<COL>	Sets properties of a column or group of columns
<COLGROUP>	Sets properties for groups of columns in a table
<TBODY>	Marks a table body
<TFOOT>	Marks a table footer
<THEAD>	Marks a table header

VBScript Language Elements

This appendix contains an alphabetical list of the VBScript language elements and their basic syntax. In these descriptions, *x* and *y* are numbers, *m* and *n* are integers, *string* is a string value, *char* is a single character, and *date* is a serial date (time) number.

Abs() Function — Absolute Value

Syntax: **Abs(*x*)**

Returns the absolute value of *x*.

Addition Operator (+) — Addition

Syntax: *x* + *y*

Returns the sum of *x* and *y*.

`And` Operator — Logical AND

Syntax: *x* **`And`** *y*

Returns the result of a logical And of *x* and *y*.

`Asc()` Function — ASCII Code

Syntax: **`Asc(`***`char`***`)`**

Returns the ASCII code for the character in *`char`*.

`Atn()` Function — Arctangent

Syntax: **`Atn(`***`x`***`)`**

Returns the arctangent of *x* as an angle in radians between $\pi/2$ and $-\pi/2$.

`Call` Statement — Call a procedure

Syntax: **`Call`** *`procedureName`***`(`**[*`arguments`*]**`)`**

or

`procedureName` [*`arguments`*]

Transfers control to the procedure named *`procedureName`* with the indicated *`arguments`*. The `Call` statement is not required to call a procedure—just place the procedure name on a line by itself to call it, and do not place parentheses around the arguments.

`CBool()` Function — Convert to Boolean

Syntax: **`CBool(`***`x`***`)`**

Returns *x* converted to a Boolean value (True or False). Values that are zero convert to False and nonzero values convert to True.

`CByte()` Function — Convert to Byte Value

Syntax: **`CByte(`***`x`***`)`**

Returns the value of *x* converted to a byte (0 to 255 integer).

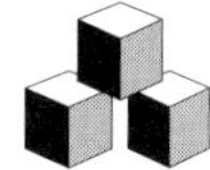

`CDate()` Function — Convert to a Date

Syntax: **`CDate(`*`x`*`)`**

Returns the value of *x* converted to a serial date number.

`CDbl()` Function — Convert to Double

Syntax: **`CDbl(`*`x`*`)`**

Returns the value of *x* converted to a double-precision, floating-point number.

`Chr()` Function — Convert to Character

Syntax: **`Chr(`*`x`*`)`**

Returns the character represented by the ASCII code `x`.

`CInt()` Function — Convert to Integer

Syntax: **`CInt(`*`x`*`)`**

Returns the value of *x* converted to an integer.

`Clear` Method — Clear the Properties of the Err Object

Syntax: **`Err.Clear`**

Applies the `Clear` method to the `Err` object to clear all its properties.

`CLng()` Function — Convert to Long

Syntax: **`CLng(`*`x`*`)`**

Returns the value of *x* converted to a long integer.

Concatenation Operator (&) — String Concatenation

Syntax: *`string1`* **`&`** *`string2`*

Combines *`string1`* and *`string2`* into a single string by concatenating them.

`Cos()` Function — Trigonometric Cosine

Syntax: **`Cos(`***`x`***`)`**

Returns the cosine of *x*.

`CreateObject()` Function — Create an Object

Syntax: **`CreateObject("`***`servername.typename`***`")`**

Returns an object variable that points to another application's objects. Is used to create a link to another application to perform OLE Automation actions on the object. *`servername`* is the name of the OLE server (such as Excel) and *`typename`* is the type of object to create (such as Sheet).

`CSng()` Function — Convert to Single

Syntax: **`CSng(`***`x`***`)`**

Returns the value of *`x`* converted to a single-precision, floating-point value.

`CStr()` Function — Convert to String

Syntax: **`CStr(`***`x`***`)`**

Returns *`x`* converted to a string.

`Date()` Function — Current Date

Syntax: **`Date`**

Returns the current date as a string.

`DateSerial()` Function — Convert Numbers to Date

Syntax: **`DateSerial(`***`year`***`, `***`month`***`, `***`day`***`)`**

Returns a serial date number for the indicated date sent as *`year`*, *`month`*, and *`day`* numbers.

`DateValue()` Function — Convert String to Date

Syntax: **`DateValue(`***`string`***`)`**

Returns a serial date number for the date contained in *`string`*.

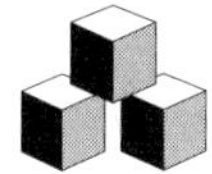

`Day()` Function — Absolute Value

Syntax: **`Day(`***`date`***`)`**

Returns the day of the month from the serial date number *`date`*.

`Description` Property — Error Description

Syntax: **`Err.Description`**

Returns or sets a description for the current error.

`Dim` Statement — Declare Variables

Syntax: **`Dim`**_*`variable`*[**`(`***`dimensions`***`)`**]

Declares a variable and dimensions arrays.

Division Operator (/) — Divide

Syntax: *`x`* / *`y`*

Returns the quotient of *`x`* divided by *`y`*.

`Do-Loop` Statement — Logical Loop

Syntax: **`Do`** [[**`While`**|**`Until`**] *`logicalExpression`*]

`statements`

`Loop` [[**`While`**|**`Until`**] *`logicalExpression`*]

Starts a loop that continuously calculates the statements until the condition is met. The condition can go at the beginning of the loop or at the end, and can watch for a change to False (`While`) or a change to True (`Until`).

`Eqv` Operator — Logical Equivalence

Syntax: *`x`* **`Eqv`** *`y`*

Returns the result of a logical equivalence of *`x`* and *`y`*.

`Erase` Statement — Erase an Array

Syntax: **`Erase`** *`array`*

Reinitializes array. If *`array`* is a fixed-size array, the elements are initialized. If *`array`* is a dynamic array, storage space is deallocated.

`Err` Object — Err Object Link to Runtime Errors

Syntax: **`Err`**

Returns the `Err` object.

`Exit` Statement — Exit Loops Or Procedures

Syntax: **`Exit`**_*`structure`*

Causes a premature exit of *`structure`* where *`structure`* is `Sub`, `Function`, `For`, or `Do`.

`Exp()` Function — Exponential

Syntax: **`Exp`**`(`*`x`*`)`

Returns the exponential of *x*.

Exponentiation Operator (^) — Raise to a Power

Syntax: *`x`*`^`*`y`*

Returns the absolute value of *x* raised to the power *y*.

`Fix()` Function — Truncate to an Integer

Syntax: **`Fix`**`(`*`x`*`)`

Returns the value of *x* truncated to an integer.

`For-Next` Statement — Start a Counted Loop

Syntax: **`For`** *`counter`* `=` *`start`* **`To`** *`end`* [**`Step`** *`step`*]

```
    statements
    Next
```

Starts a counted loop with the variable *`counter`* equal to *`start`* the first iteration, (*`start`* + *`step`*) the second, (*`start`* + (2**`step`*)) the third, and so on, until *`counter`* is greater than *`end`* (unless *`step`* is negative, in which case the loop stops when *`counter`* is less than *`end`*).

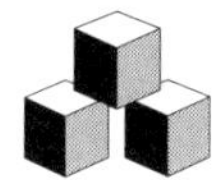

`Function` Statement — Declare a Function

Syntax: **`Function`** *`functionName`*`(`[*`arguments`*]`)`

Declares the start of a function procedure and declares the function's name and arguments.

`HelpContext` Property — Declare a Help Context

Syntax: **`Err.HelpContext`**

Gets or sets a help context for an error. The help context is a pointer into a help file to information about the error.

`HelpFile` Property — Declare a Help File

Syntax: **`Err.HelpFile`**

Gets or sets the name of a help file for use with the `Err` object.

`Hex()` Function — Convert to a Hex String

Syntax: **`Hex(`***`x`***`)`**

Returns the value of *x* as a hexadecimal string.

`Hour()` Function — Convert a Time to an Hour

Syntax: **`Hour(`***`date`***`)`**

Returns the hour of the day from the serial date number *`date`*.

`If-Then-Else` Statement — Block If

Syntax:

```
If logical1 Then
    statements1
    [ElseIf logical2
    statements2]
    [Else
    statements3]
    End If
```

A block If statement. If `logical1` is True, `statements1` are executed. If `logical1` is False, `logical2` is tested and if it is True, `statements2` are executed. There can be any number of `ElseIf` clauses, but only the statements following the first one that tests True are executed. If none of the logicals are True, `statements3` are executed.

`Imp` Operator — Logical Implies

Syntax: *x* **`Imp`** *y*

Returns the result of a logical implies of *x* and *y*.

`InputBox()` Function — Display an Input Box

Syntax: **`InputBox(`***`prompt`*[, *`title`*][, *`default`*][, *`xpos`*][, *`ypos`*][, *`helpfile`*, *`helpcontext`*]**`)`**

Displays an input box with a field for the user to fill in. The value the user types is returned by the function (False is returned if he clicks Cancel). The arguments are: *`prompt`*, a prompt string; *`title`*, the title of the dialog box; *`default`*, a default value for the input field; *`xpos`* and *`ypos`*, the coordinates for the location of the upper-left corner of the dialog box; *`helpfile`*, the filename of the help file; and *`helpcontext`*, the context of the entry in the help file that describes the dialog box.

`InStr()` Function — Locate a Substring

Syntax: **`InStr(`**[*`start`*,]*`searchedstring`*, *`searchforstring`* [, *`compare`*]**`)`**

Searches for the substring *`searchforstring`* in *`searchedstring`* starting at character *`start`*, and returns the first character of the substring. If *`compare`* is 0, a binary (default) comparison is done. If *`compare`* is 1, a case-insensitive text comparison is done.

`Int()` Function — Truncate to an Integer

Syntax: **`Int(`***`x`***`)`**

Returns the value of *x* truncated to an integer.

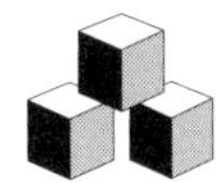

Integer Division Operator (\) — Perform Integer Division

Syntax: `x \ y`

Returns the result of integer division of *x* by *y*.

Is Operator — Compare Objects

Syntax: *object1* **Is** *object2*

Returns True if the two objects are the same object, and False if they are not.

IsArray() Function — Test for an Array

Syntax: **IsArray**(*x*)

Returns True if *x* is an array variable, and False if it is not.

IsDate() Function — Test for a Date

Syntax: **IsDate**(*x*)

Returns True if *x* is a date variable, and False if it is not.

IsEmpty() Function — Test for an Uninitialized Variable

Syntax: **IsEmpty**(*x*)

Returns True if *x* has not been initialized, and False if it has.

IsNull() Function — Test for a Null

Syntax: **IsNull**(*x*)

Returns True if *x* is Null, and False if it is not.

Number Property — Error Number

Syntax: **Err.Number**

Returns or sets an error number.

`IsNumeric()` Function — Test for a Number

Syntax: **`IsNumeric(`***`x`***`)`**

Returns True if *x* is a number, and False if it is not.

`IsObject()` Function — Test for an Object

Syntax: **`IsObject(`***`x`***`)`**

Returns True if *x* contains an object, and False if it does not.

`LBound()` Function — Find the Lower Bound

Syntax: **`LBound(`***`array`*** [, *`dimension`*]**`)`**

Returns the lower bound of the indicated array index.

`LCase()` Function — Convert to Lowercase

Syntax: **`LCase(`***`string`***`)`**

Returns *`string`* with all characters converted to lowercase.

`Left()` Function — Extract a Substring From the Left

Syntax: **`Left(`***`string,n`***`)`**

Returns *n* characters from the left end of *`string`*.

`Len()` Function — Length of a String

Syntax: **`Len(`***`string`***`)`**

Returns the number of characters in *`string`*.

`Log()` Function — Natural Logarithm

Syntax: **`Log(`***`x`***`)`**

Returns the natural logarithm (base **e**) of *x*.

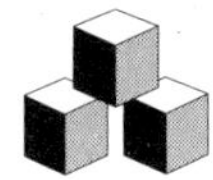

`LTrim()` Function — Trim Blanks from Left

Syntax: **`LTrim(`***`string`***`)`**

Returns *`string`* with all blanks removed from its left end.

`Mid()` Function — Extract a Substring

Syntax: **`Mid(`***`string`*, *`start`*[, *`length`*]**`)`**

Returns a substring from *`string`* starting at character number *`start`* and *`length`* characters long.

`Minute()` Function — Get the Minute

Syntax: **`Minute(`***`date`***`)`**

Returns the minute from the serial date number *`date`*.

`Mod` Operator — Remainder of a Division

Syntax: *`x`* **`Mod`** *`y`*

Returns the modulus of *`x`* divided by *`y`*. (The modulus is the remainder after an integer division.)

`Month()` Function — Get the Month

Syntax: **`Month(`***`date`***`)`**

Returns the month of the year as a number from the serial date number *`date`*.

`MsgBox()` Function — Display a Message Dialog Box

Syntax: **`MsgBox(`***`prompt`*[, *`buttons`*][, *`title`*][, *`helpfile`*, *`helpcontext`*]**`)`**

Displays a message box to the user, returns the button the user clicked (see below). The arguments are: *`prompt`*, a prompt string; *`buttons`*, a code indicating the number and type of button (see below); *`title`*, the title of the dialog box; *`helpfile`*, the filename of the help file; and *`helpcontext`*, the context of the entry in the help file that describes the dialog box.

For the *`buttons`* field, add the appropriate individual codes from the following list to get the correct code:

Code	Button/Icon Displayed
0	OK button
1	OK and Cancel buttons
2	Abort, Retry, and Ignore buttons
3	Yes, No, and Cancel buttons
4	Yes and No buttons
5	Retry and Cancel buttons
16	Critical Message icon
32	Warning Query icon
48	Warning Message icon
64	Information Message icon
0	First button is default
256	Second button is default
512	Third button is default
768	Fourth button is default
0	Application modal
4096	System modal

Returned Code	Button Clicked
1	OK
2	Cancel
3	Abort
4	Retry
5	Ignore
6	Yes
7	No

Muliplication Operator (*) — Multiply

Syntax: *x* * *y*

Returns the product of *x* and *y*.

Negation Operator (-) — Negation

Syntax: *-x*

Returns the negative of *x*.

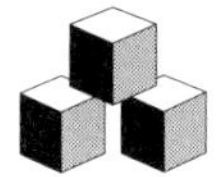

`Not` Operator — Logical Not

Syntax: **`Not`** *`x`*

Returns the result of a Logical Not of *`x`*.

`Now()` Function — Current Date and Time

Syntax: **`Now()`**

Returns the current date and time as a serial date number.

`Oct()` Function — Octal String

Syntax: **`Oct(`***`x`***`)`**

Returns *`x`* as an octal string.

`On Error` Statement — Error Trap

Syntax: **`On Error Resume Next`**

Sets an error trap to skip to the next statement if a runtime error occurs. Tests the `Err` object to see if an error has occured.

`Or` Operator Logical Or

Syntax: *`x`* **`Or`** *`y`*

Returns the result of a logical Or of *`x`* and *`y`*.

`Raise` Method — Generate a Runtime Error

Syntax: **`Err.Raise(`***`number`*, *`source`*, *`description`*, *`helpfile`*, *`helpcontext`*)

Generates a runtime error with the listed error *`number`* and *`description`*. The *`source`* argument is the object that is generating the error. The *`helpfile`* and *`helpcontext`* arguments are the filename of the help file, and the context of the entry in the help file that describes the dialog box.

`Randomize` Statement — Initialize Random Numbers

Syntax: **`Randomize`**

Initializes the random number generator (`Rnd()`).

`ReDim` Statement — Dimension Dynamic Arrays

Syntax: **`ReDim`** *`array`*

Redimensions the indicated dynamically allocated array. Allocate the array using `Dim` but with no dimensions.

`Rem` Statement — Remark Statement

Syntax: **`Rem`** *`statement`*

or

```
'statement
```

Marks the remainder of the line as a remark that does not affect the operation of a program.

`Right()` Function — Extract a Substring From Right

Syntax: **`Right(`**`string,n`**`)`**

Returns *`n`* characters from the right end of *`string`*.

`Rnd()` Function — Random Number

Syntax: **`Rnd()`**

Returns a random real number between 0 and 1. Use `Randomize` to initialize the random number generator.

`RTrim()` Function — Trim Blanks From the Right

Syntax: **`RTrim(`**`string`**`)`**

Returns *`string`* with all blanks removed from the right.

`Second()` Function — Get the Second

Syntax: **`Second(`**`date`**`)`**

Returns the second from the serial date number *`date`*.

Select Case Statement — Logical Selection

Syntax: **Select** *variable*

```
Case value,value,...
    statements
Case value,value,...
    statements
Case Else
    statements
End Select
```

The `Select Case` statement compares *`variable`* to each *`value`* following one or more `Case` statements. When a match is found, the *`statements`* following that `Case` statement are executed. Only the statements following the first matching *`value`* are executed. If there is no match, the *`statements`* following the `Case Else` statement are executed. The values can be explicit values or logical constructs (such as `>3` to match all values greater than 3).

Set Statement — Define an Object

Syntax: **Set** *objVariable* = *AnObject*

Stores the object *`AnObject`* in *`objVariable`*.

Sgn() Function — Sign of a Number

Syntax: **Sgn(***x***)**

Returns 1 with the sign of *x*.

Sin() Function — Trigonometric Sine

Syntax: **Sin(***x***)**

Returns the sine of *x* where *x* is an angle measured in radians.

Source Property — Absolute Value

Syntax: **Err.Source**

Returns the name of the object or application that has caused a runtime error.

`Sqr()` Function — Square Root

Syntax: **`Sqr(`***`x`***`)`**

Returns the square root of *x*.

`Str()` Function — Convert a Number to a String

Syntax: **`Str(`***`x`***`)`**

Returns the number *x* converted to a string.

`StrComp()` Function — String Comparison

Syntax: **`StrComp(`***`string1`*, *`string2`*[, *`compare`*]**`)`**

Compares two strings and returns 0 if they are equal, −1 if *string1* is less than *string2*, or 1 if *string1* is greater than *string2*. The *compare* argument determines the type of comparison. If *compare* is 0 or omitted, then the comparison is binary (case-sensitive). If *compare* is 1, then the comparison is text (case-insensitive).

`String()` Function — Create a String

Syntax: **`String(`***`n`*, *`char`***`)`**

Returns a string containing *n* copies of the character *char*. The argument *char* can be a string or a number (an ASCII code).

`Sub` Statement — Declare a Sub Procedure

Syntax: **`Sub`** *`procedureName`***`(`**[*`arguments`*]**`)`**

Declares a subprocedure and its arguments.

Subtraction Operator (-) — Absolute Value

Syntax: *x* **-** *y*

Returns the difference between *x* and *y*.

`Tan()` Function — Trigonometric Tangent

Syntax: **`Tan(`***`x`***`)`**

Returns the tangent of *x* where *x* is an angle measured in radians.

`Time()` Function — Absolute Value

Syntax: `Time()`

Returns the current time as a serial date number.

`TimeSerial()` Function — Convert Numbers to a TIme

Syntax: `TimeSerial(`*`hour`*, *`minute`*, *`second`*`)`

Returns a serial date number for the time indicated by the numbers in the arguments.

`TimeValue()` Function — Convert a String to a Time

Syntax: `TimeValue(`*`string`*`)`

Returns a serial date number from a string representation of a time.

`Trim()` Function — Remove Blanks

Syntax: `Trim(`*`string`*`)`

Returns *`string`* with all blanks removed from the left and right ends.

`UBound()` Function — Find the Upper Bound

Syntax: `UBound(`*`array`* [, *`dimension`*]`)`

Returns the upper bound of the indicated array dimension.

`UCase()` Function — Convert to Uppercase

Syntax: `UCase(`*`string`*`)`

Returns *`string`* with all characters converted to uppercase.

`Val()` Function — Convert a String to a Number

Syntax: `Val(`*`string`*`)`

Returns a number converted from a string representation of a number.

VarType() Function — Determine the Type of a Value

Syntax: **VarType(*x*)**

Returns a code indicating the type of the value stored in *x*.

Code	Type
0	Empty (uninitialized)
1	Null (initialized but no valid data)
2	Integer
3	Long
4	Single
5	Double
6	Currency
7	Date
8	String
9	OLE object
10	Error
11	Boolean
12	Variant
13	Non-OLE object
17	Byte
8192	Array

Weekday() Function — Get Day of Week

Syntax: **Weekday(*date*,** [*firstdayofweek*]**)**

Returns a number (Sunday is 1) indicating the day of the week for *date*. The *firstdayofweek* value changes the first day of the week (1=Sunday—the default, 2=Monday, and so on).

`While-Wend` Statement — Start a Loop

Syntax:
```
While logicalExpression
        statements
   Wend
```

Starts a `While-Wend` loop. The *`statements`* are repeatedly executed while *`logicalExpression`* remains True.

`Xor` Operator — Logical Exclusive Or

Syntax: *`x`* **`Xor`** *`y`*

Returns the result of a logical Exclusive Or of *`x`* and *`y`*.

`Year()` Function — Get the Year

Syntax: **`Year(`***`date`***`)`**

Returns the year from the serial date number *`date`*.

Appendix D

Glossary

Active servers
Computer programs that contain code and data. They have no user interface.

ActiveX
Components that can be run from Web browsers. Similar to Java applets.

ADO (ActiveX Data Objects)
Microsoft's newest method of accessing data in a database. ADO is a small set of COM components.

Anonymous FTP server
An Internet sites with publicly-accessible material that can be obtained using FTP, by logging in using the account name anonymous.

Applet
A small program that works only inside of another program; for example, a Java program that can be run on a browser.

ASP (Active Server Pages)

A server-based technology that allows Web page developers to process code on their Web servers. Requires Internet Information Server 3.0/4.0, WebSite from O-Reilly, or an add-on from ChiliSoft.

Backbone

A high-speed line or series of connections that forms a major pathway within a network.

Bandwidth

Specifies how much data can be transmitted through a connection. Usually measured in bits per second (bps).

Baud

In common usage, the baud rate of a modem is how many bits it can send or receive per second. Technically, baud is the number of times per second that the carrier signal shifts value—for example, a 1200bps modem actually runs at 300 baud, but it moves 4 bits per baud (4 × 300 = 1200 bits per second).

CGI (common gateway interface)

Technology that allows developers to write programs that will be called from a Web browser.

cgi-bin

The most common name of a directory on a Web server in which CGI programs are stored.

Client

A software program used to contact and obtain data from a server software program on another computer, often across a great distance.

Cookie

A piece of information sent by a Web server to a Web browser, which the browser software is expected to save and send back to the server whenever the browser makes additional requests from the server.

COM (Component Object Model)
A protocol for inter-application communication.

Domain Name
The unique name that identifies an Internet site. Domain names always have two or more parts, separated by dots (periods).

Dynamic HTML

A new model for HTML documents that allows developers to manipulate the contents of a Web page after they have been rendered in a browser.

E-mail (electronic mail)
Messages, usually text, sent from one person to another via computer.

Fiber distributed data interface (FDDI)
A standard for transmitting data on optical fiber cables at a rate of around 100,000,000 bps.

FTP (file transfer protocol)
Protocol used to facilitate the transfer of files.

Finger
An Internet software tool for locating people on other Internet sites.

Firewall
A combination of hardware and software that separates a LAN into two or more parts for security purposes. One common application of a firewall is to protect a LAN from access via the Internet.

GIF (graphical interchange format)
Graphics file format commonly used to display images in Web pages.

Gopher
A widely successful method of making menus of material available over the Internet.

Home page
The home page is the main page of a Web site. When a Web site is accessed, the home page is the first page displayed.

Host
Any computer on a network that is a repository for services available to other computers on the network.

HTML (hypertext markup language)
A method of marking up text files for interpretation by a Web browser. HTML uses formatting tags that can be inserted into text files and used by browsers to display text or graphics in a formatted manner.

HTTP (hypertext transfer protocol) or (hypertext transport protocol)
Protocol used to facilitate the transfer of documents across the Internet.

Hypertext
Technology that allows documents to be linked together by creating hyperlinks from one document to another.

Integrated services digital network (ISDN)
Basically a way to move more data over existing regular phone lines, at speeds of up to 128,000 bps.

Internet
Global network that links computers together. The Internet is based on the TCP/IP networking protocol.

Internet Explorer
Commonly used Web browser, developed by Microsoft Corporation.

Internet relay chat (IRC)
A huge multiuser live-chat facility, running on IRC servers around the world that are linked to each other.

Internet server
Programs that run on host machines. These programs respond to requests using the HTTP.

Internet service provider (ISP)
The organization through which an individual or a business will establish a dial-up networking connection to gain access to the Internet. ISPs usually provide e-mail services as well as Internet access services.

Intranet
A private network inside a company or organization—intranets provide the same kinds of software that you would find on the public Internet, but for internal use only.

IP Address
A unique number consisting of four parts. An example of an IP address is 120.110.201.1. Every machine on the Internet has its own IP address.

Java
Object-oriented programming language that allows developers to develop applications to be run on a client's Web browser. These programs are known as applets.

JPEG (Joint Photographic Experts Group)
Graphics file format commonly used to display images in Web pages. Known for its good compression.

Listserv
The most common kind of mail list.

Mail list
A (usually automated) system that allows people to send e-mail to one address, whereupon their message is copied and sent to all of the other subscribers to the mail list.

Moving Pictures Expert Group (MPEG)
A multimedia file format deployed across the Internet.

Multipurpose internet mail extensions (MIME)
The standard for attaching non-text files to standard Internet mail messages.

Netscape Navigator
Commonly used Web browser, developed by Netscape Corporation.

Network news transport protocol (NNTP)
The protocol used by many newsgroups on the Internet.

Newsgroup
Discussion groups on Usenet.

PING
A method of checking to see whether a particular system is online.

Point-to-point protocol (PPP)
The protocol that allows a computer to use a regular telephone line and a modem to make TCP/IP connections and thus gain access to the Internet.

Post office protocol (POP)
The POP server receives and stores e-mail text files. When checking e-mail for new messages received, the e-mail client (the e-mail program) logs onto the POP server and asks to see the messages in a mailbox.

Protocol
A standard that permits two computers to exchange data.

Router
A special-purpose computer (or software package) that handles the connection between two or more networks.

Secure sockets layer (SSL)
A protocol designed by Netscape Communications to enable encrypted, authenticated communications across the Internet.

Security certificate
A chunk of information (often stored as a text file) used by the SSL protocol to establish a secure connection.

Serial line Internet protocol (SLIP)
A standard for using a regular telephone line (a serial line) and a modem to connect a computer as a real Internet site.

Server
A computer or software package that provides a specific kind of service to client software running on other computers.

Simple Mail Transport Protocol (SMTP)
The SMTP server sends e-mail text files. When sending e-mail, the e-mail client (the e-mail program) contacts the SMTP server. The SMTP server moves the e-mail to a POP server for storage.

T1
A leased line connection capable of carrying data at 1,544,000 bits per second.

T3
A leased-line connection capable of carrying data at 44,736,000 bits per second.

TCP/IP (Transmission control protocol/Internet protocol)
Packet-based networking protocol.

URL (uniform resource locator)
Notation used to access Web sites and Web pages; the standard way to give the address of any resource on the Internet that's part of the World Wide Web (WWW). An example URL is `www.microsoft.com/vbasic`.

Usenet
A worldwide system of discussion groups, with submissions by members of the group passed among hundreds of thousands of machines.

Web browser
Computer program that allows users to view HTML documents.

Web page
An HTML document that can be viewed by users with Web browsers.

Web site
A page or collection of pages on the World Wide Web, accessible to anyone with Internet access and Web browser software.

World Wide Web (WWW)

The collection of resources that can be accessed using Gopher, FTP, HTTP, Telnet, Usenet, WAIS, and some other tools. Also, the universe of hypertext servers (HTTP servers) that allow text, graphics, sound files, and so on to be mixed together.

XML (Extensible Markup Language)

XML is a new standard that gives developers the ability to develop and process custom HTML tags in a Web page.

Appendix E

What's on the CD?

The CD that accompanies this book contains example projects and code from the book, as well as some handy utilities to assist you in your Visual Basic Web-related development efforts.

Running the CD

To make the CD more user-friendly and take up less of your disk space, no installation is required. This means that the only files that will be transferred to your hard disk are the ones you choose to copy or install.

Caution

This CD has been designed to run under Windows 95/98 and Windows NT 4. Please be advised that, while it will run under Windows 3.1, you may encounter unexpected problems. In addition, some of the programs included are 32-bit programs and will not run at all under Windows 3.1.

Getting Going under Windows 95/98/NT4

Running the CD under Windows 95/98/NT is a breeze, especially if you have `autorun` enabled. Simply insert the CD in your CD-ROM drive, close the tray, and wait for the CD to load.

If you have disabled `autorun`, place the CD in the CD-ROM drive and then follow these steps:

1. From the Start menu, select Run.
2. Type **D:\prima.exe** (where **D:** is the CD-ROM drive).
3. Click OK.

The Prima User Interface

Prima's user interface is designed to make viewing and using the CD contents quick and easy. The opening screen contains four category buttons, and a command bar with three navigational buttons. Click a category button to jump to the associated page containing the available software titles or book examples.

Category/Title Buttons

These are the category buttons:

- **Book Examples.** Example files and source code from *Hands On VB6 for Web Development.*
- **Chili!ASP.** This application, which is the exact functional and syntactical equivalent of Microsoft's Active Server portion of IIS, enables developers to build powerful ASP applications that run on nearly every Web server across Solaris and NT.
- **WinZip.** One of the most popular file compression utilities around.
- **WS_FTP.** A leading Windows-based file transfer client application.

Notice: Any shareware distributed on this disk is for evaluation purposes only and should be registered with the shareware vendor if used beyond the trial period.

Command Bar Buttons

These are the buttons on the command bar:

- **Exit**. When you're finished using the CD, shut it down with this button.
- **Explore**. Use this button to view the contents of the CD using the Windows Explorer.
- **Navigate**. Click this button to display a pop-up menu containing links to the various category pages.
- **Next and Previous**. The arrows located at either end of the command bar are Previous (at the left) and Next (at the right) buttons that will move you to the page before or after the current page.

Action Options

These are the available action options:

- **Install.** If the selected title contains an install routine, choosing this option begins the installation process.
- **Explore.** Choosing this option allows you to view the folder containing the program files, using Windows Explorer.
- **[View] Information.** Choose this menu item to open the `Readme` file associated with the selected title. If no `Readme` file is present, the help file will be opened.
- **Visit Web Site**. If you're running Windows 95/98/NT4 *and* a recent version of Internet Explorer or Netscape Navigator, and you have an established Internet connection, choosing this option will launch your browser and take you to the associated Web site.

Index

A

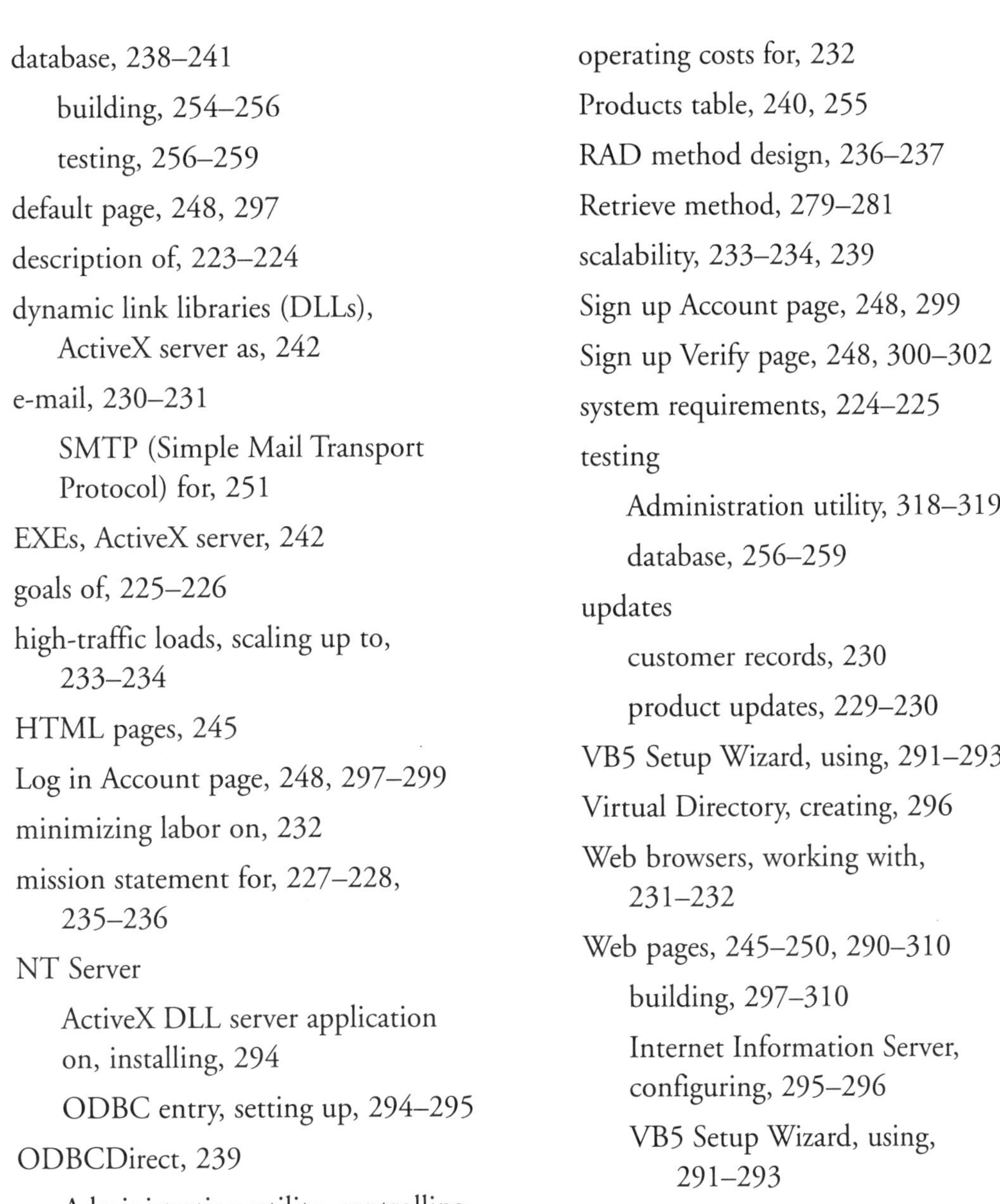

D

L

M

W

Send Us YOUR COMMENTS

Dear Reader:

Thank you for buying this book. In order to offer you more quality books on the topics ***you*** would like to see, we need your input. At Prima Publishing, we pride ourselves on timely responsiveness to our readers needs. If you'll complete and return this brief questionnaire, ***we will listen!***

Name: (first) ____________ (M.I.) ____________ (last) ____________

Company: ____________ Type of business: ____________

Address: ____________ City: ____________ State: ____________ Zip: ____________

Phone: ____________ Fax: ____________ E-mail address: ____________

May we contact you for research purposes? ❑ Yes ❑ No

(If you participate in a research project, we will supply you with your choice of a book from Prima Tech)

❶ How would you rate this book, overall?

- ❑ Excellent
- ❑ Very Good
- ❑ Good
- ❑ Fair
- ❑ Below Average
- ❑ Poor

❷ Why did you buy this book?

- ❑ Price of book
- ❑ Content
- ❑ Author's reputation
- ❑ Prima's reputation
- ❑ CD-ROM/disk included with book
- ❑ Information highlighted on cover
- ❑ Other (Please specify): ____________

❸ How did you discover this book?

- ❑ Found it on bookstore shelf
- ❑ Saw it in Prima Publishing catalog
- ❑ Recommended by store personnel
- ❑ Recommended by friend or colleague
- ❑ Saw an advertisement in: ____________
- ❑ Read book review in: ____________
- ❑ Saw it on Web site: ____________
- ❑ Other (Please specify): ____________

❹ Where did you buy this book?

- ❑ Bookstore (name) ____________
- ❑ Computer Store (name) ____________
- ❑ Electronics Store (name) ____________
- ❑ Wholesale Club (name) ____________
- ❑ Mail Order (name) ____________
- ❑ Direct from Prima Publishing
- ❑ Other (please specify): ____________

❺ Which computer periodicals do you read regularly? ____________

____

____

____

❻ Would you like to see your name in print?

May we use your name and quote you in future Prima Publishing books or promotional materials?

❑ Yes ❑ No

PRIMA TECH

❼ Comments & Suggestions: ____________

____

____

PRIMA PUBLISHING
Prima Tech Division
3875 Atherton Road
Rocklin, CA 95765

PLEASE PLACE STAMP HERE

8 Where do you use your computer?

Work	☐ 100%	☐ 75%	☐ 50%	☐ 25%
Home	☐ 100%	☐ 75%	☐ 50%	☐ 25%
School	☐ 100%	☐ 75%	☐ 50%	☐ 25%

Other ____________________

9 How do you rate your level of computer skills?

- ☐ Beginner
- ☐ Advanced
- ☐ Intermediate

10 What is your age?

- ☐ Under 18
- ☐ 18-24
- ☐ 25-29
- ☐ 30-39
- ☐ 40-49
- ☐ 50-59
- ☐ 60-over

11 I would be interested in computer books on these topics

- ☐ Word Processing
- ☐ Networking
- ☐ Desktop Publishing
- ☐ Database:
- ☐ Spreadsheets
- ☐ Web site design

Other ____________________

SAVE A STAMP

Visit our Web Site at **www.prima-tech.com/comments**
and simply fill in one of our online Response Forms

OTHER BOOKS FROM PRIMA TECH

ISBN	Title	Price
0-7615-1363-9	Access 97 Fast & Easy	$16.99
0-7615-1412-0	ACT! 4.0 Fast & Easy	$16.99
0-7615-1348-5	Create FrontPage 98 Web Pages In a Weekend	$24.99
0-7615-1294-2	Create PowerPoint Presentations In a Weekend	$19.99
0-7615-1388-4	Create Your First Web Page In a Weekend, Revised Edition	$24.99
0-7615-0428-1	The Essential Excel 97 Book	$27.99
0-7615-0733-7	The Essential Netscape Communicator Book	$24.99
0-7615-0969-0	The Essential Office 97 Book	$27.99
0-7615-1396-5	The Essential Photoshop 5 Book	$34.99
0-7615-1182-2	The Essential PowerPoint 97 Book	$24.99
0-7615-1136-9	The Essential Publisher 97 Book	$24.99
0-7615-0967-4	The Essential Windows 98 Book	$24.99
0-7615-0752-3	The Essential Windows NT 4 Book	$27.99
0-7615-0427-3	The Essential Word 97 Book	$27.99
0-7615-0425-7	The Essential WordPerfect 8 Book	$24.99
0-7615-1008-7	Excel 97 Fast & Easy	$16.99
0-7615-1534-8	FrontPage 98 Fast & Easy	$16.99
0-7615-1194-6	Increase Your Web Traffic In a Weekend	$19.99
0-7615-1191-1	Internet Explorer 4.0 Fast & Easy	$19.99
0-7615-1137-7	Jazz Up Your Web Site In a Weekend	$24.99
0-7615-1379-5	Learn Access 97 In a Weekend	$19.99
0-7615-1293-4	Learn HTML In a Weekend	$24.99

ISBN	Title	Price
0-7615-1295-0	Learn the Internet In a Weekend	$19.99
0-7615-1217-9	Learn Publisher 97 In a Weekend	$19.99
0-7615-1384-1	Learn QuickBooks 6 In a Weekend	$19.99
0-7615-1251-9	Learn Word 97 In a Weekend	$19.99
0-7615-1296-9	Learn Windows 98 In a Weekend	$19.99
0-7615-1193-8	Lotus 1-2-3 97 Fast & Easy	$16.99
0-7615-1420-1	Managing with Microsoft Project 98	$29.99
0-7615-1382-5	Netscape Navigator 4.0 Fast & Easy	$16.99
0-7615-1162-8	Office 97 Fast & Easy	$16.99
0-7615-1786-3	Organize Your Finances with Quicken Deluxe 99 In a Weekend	$19.99
0-7615-1405-8	Outlook 98 Fast & Easy	$16.99
0-7615-1677-8	Prima's Official Companion to Family Tree Maker 5	$24.99
0-7615-1513-5	Publisher 98 Fast & Easy	$19.99
0-7615-1699-9	SmartSuite Millennium Fast & Easy	$16.99
0-7615-1138-5	Upgrade Your PC In a Weekend	$19.99
0-7615-1328-0	Web Advertising and Marketing, 2nd Edition	$34.95
1-55958-738-5	Windows 95 Fast & Easy	$19.95
0-7615-1006-0	Windows 98 Fast & Easy	$16.99
0-7615-1007-9	Word 97 Fast & Easy	$16.99
0-7615-1316-7	Word 97 for Law Firms	$29.99
0-7615-1083-4	WordPerfect 8 Fast & Easy	$16.99
0-7615-1188-1	WordPerfect Suite 8 Fast & Easy	$16.99

TO ORDER BOOKS

Please send me the following items:

Quantity	Title	Unit Price	Total
________	______________________________	$________	$________
________	______________________________	$________	$________
________	______________________________	$________	$________
________	______________________________	$________	$________
________	______________________________	$________	$________

Subtotal	$________
Deduct 10% when ordering 3–5 books	$________
7.25% Sales Tax (CA only)	$________
8.25% Sales Tax (TN only)	$________
5.0% Sales Tax (MD and IN only)	$________
Shipping and Handling*	$________
TOTAL ORDER	$________

*Shipping and Handling depend on Subtotal.

Subtotal	Shipping/Handling
$0.00–$14.99	$3.00
$15.00–29.99	$4.00
$30.00–49.99	$6.00
$50.00–99.99	$10.00
$100.00–199.99	$13.00
$200.00+	call for quote

Foreign and all Priority Request orders: Call Order Entry department for price quote at 1-916-632-4400

This chart represents the total retail price of books only (before applicable discounts are taken).

By telephone: With Visa, Mastercard, or American Express, call 800-632-8676 or 916-632-4400. Mon.–Fri. 8:30–4:00 PST.

www.primapublishing.com

By E-mail: sales@primapub.com

By mail: Just fill out the information below and send with your remittance to:

PRIMA PUBLISHING
P.O. Box 1260BK
Rocklin, CA 95677-1260

Name______________________________ Daytime Telephone________________

Address ____

City ______________________________ State ________ Zip ______________

Visa /MC# ______________________________Exp. ______________

Check/Money Order enclosed for $______________________ Payable to Prima Publishing

Signature ____

License Agreement/Notice of Limited Warranty

By opening the sealed disk container in this book, you agree to the following terms and conditions. If, upon reading the following license agreement and notice of limited warranty, you cannot agree to the terms and conditions set forth, return the unused book with unopened disk to the place where you purchased it for a refund.

License:
The enclosed software is copyrighted by the copyright holder(s) indicated on the software disk. You are licensed to copy the software onto a single computer for use by a single concurrent user and to a backup disk. You may not reproduce, make copies, or distribute copies or rent or lease the software in whole or in part, except with written permission of the copyright holder(s). You may transfer the enclosed disk only together with this license, and only if you destroy all other copies of the software and the transferee agrees to the terms of the license. You may not decompile, reverse assemble, or reverse engineer the software.

Notice of Limited Warranty:
The enclosed disk is warranted by Prima Publishing to be free of physical defects in materials and workmanship for a period of sixty (60) days from end user's purchase of the book/disk combination. During the sixty-day term of the limited warranty, Prima will provide a replacement disk upon the return of a defective disk.

Limited Liability:
THE SOLE REMEDY FOR BREACH OF THIS LIMITED WARRANTY SHALL CONSIST ENTIRELY OF REPLACEMENT OF THE DEFECTIVE DISK. IN NO EVENT SHALL PRIMA OR THE AUTHORS BE LIABLE FOR ANY OTHER DAMAGES, INCLUDING LOSS OR CORRUPTION OF DATA, CHANGES IN THE FUNCTIONAL CHARACTERISTICS OF THE HARDWARE OR OPERATING SYSTEM, DELETERIOUS INTERACTION WITH OTHER SOFTWARE, OR ANY OTHER SPECIAL, INCIDENTAL, OR CONSEQUENTIAL DAMAGES THAT MAY ARISE, EVEN IF PRIMA AND/OR THE AUTHOR HAVE PREVIOUSLY BEEN NOTIFIED THAT THE POSSIBILITY OF SUCH DAMAGES EXISTS.

Disclaimer of Warranties:
PRIMA AND THE AUTHORS SPECIFICALLY DISCLAIM ANY AND ALL OTHER WARRANTIES, EITHER EXPRESS OR IMPLIED, INCLUDING WARRANTIES OF MERCHANTABILITY, SUITABILITY TO A PARTICULAR TASK OR PURPOSE, OR FREEDOM FROM ERRORS. SOME STATES DO NOT ALLOW FOR EXCLUSION OF IMPLIED WARRANTIES OR LIMITATION OF INCIDENTAL OR CONSEQUENTIAL DAMAGES, SO THESE LIMITATIONS MAY NOT APPLY TO YOU.

Other:
This Agreement is governed by the laws of the State of California without regard to choice of law principles. The United Convention of Contracts for the International Sale of Goods is specifically disclaimed. This Agreement constitutes the entire agreement between you and Prima Publishing regarding use of the software.